BHARATA NATYAM

From Temple to Theatre

BHARATA NATYAM

From Temple to Theatre

ANNE-MARIE GASTON

MANOHAR
2005

ISBN 81-7304-146-6

First published 1996
Reprinted 2005

Published by
Ajay Kumar Jain for
Manohar Publishers & Distributors
4753/23 Ansari Road, Daryaganj
New Delhi - 110002

Typeset by
AJ Software Publishing Co. Pvt. Ltd.
New Delhi - 110005

Printed at
Lordson Publishers Pvt. Ltd.
Delhi - 110007

Contents

Acknowledgements

This book and the research which made it possible could only have resulted from the cooperation and full support extended to me by many Bharata Natyam dancers, dance teachers, critics and musicians, among whom Usha Srinivasan deserves particular mention. The debt I owe to all of them can never be repaid.

My knowledge of Indian dance and music began with practical training in the oral tradition. It was the care and dedication extended to me by my dance masters that prompted me to engage in research that resulted in a D.Phil. from Oxford University from which some of this material has been taken. My dance teachers were for Bharata Natyam: the late K. Ellappa Pillai, the late Swarna Saraswati, Kalanidhi Narayan, the late V.S. Muthuswamy, K.N. Dakshinamurthy, Adyar Lakshmanan, Jayalakshmi Eshwar, the late K. J. Govindarajan, Uma Dandayudapani, Usha Srinivasan, Gayatri Venkataraman, Padma Subrahmanyam, and Sudha Chandrashekar; for Odissi: Kelucharan Mahapatra, Hari Krishna Behra, and Mayadhar Raut, for Kuchipudi, the late Prahalad Sharma, Raja Reddy, Narasimhachari and Vasantalakshmi, for Kathakali, Delhi International Centre Sadanan, P.V. Balakrishnan, and Kalamandalam Balasubramaniam, for Mohini Attam, Bharati Shivaji, for Baripada Chhau Krishna Chandra Naik, and for Seraikela Chhau: Shri Acharya and his son Shashadhar.

This whole venture would not have been possible without the trust and enthusiasm extended to me over many years by Professor Richard Gombrich (Boden Professor of Sanskrit, Oxford University). It was he who first suggested that as a dancer trained in Indian classical dance, I embark on an M.Litt. thesis at Oxford University. This resulted in a study of the relationship between Dance, Myth and Iconography that was published by Oxford University Press as *Siva in Dance, Myth,and Iconography* (now in its third edition). Several years elapsed during which I performed and lectured extensively throughout Canada, USA, UK, India, Holland and France. I continued to return to India to study the dance and engage in"participant observation" research. In 1984 I was invited to give a lecture at Queen Elizabeth House, Oxford University on "The Effect of Social Change on Indian Classical Dance". This resulted in the suggestion by Professor Gombrich that I begin a much larger systematic collection of material on the dancers and dance teachers who have made Bharata Natyam into what it is today.

I wish to express my gratitude to my thesis supervisor, Bryan Wilson (Reader in the Sociology of Religion, All Souls College Oxford), for his assistance, invaluable insight, and encouragement extended to me throughout the period that much of this work was prepared. Others who have read my work and offered useful comments are: T.S. Parthasarathy, V. Subramaniam, Subbudu, V.A.K. Ranga Rao, N. Pattabhi Raman, K.S. Srinivasan, B.M. Sundaram, Mohan Khokar, Julia Leslie, Tapan Raychaudhuri and Sanjukta Gupta. I would like to thank Dr Kapila Vatsyayan for her constant inspiration. There are many others who offered oral suggestions and they are listed in Appendix A. I thank them all and beg forgiveness if I have unknowingly omitted anyone.

Both Saskia Kersenboom and Amrit Srinivasan, whose work is important for this study spent many hours with me sharing their expertise. I also wish to thank them for the enthusiastic and lively discussions we shared.

For some financial assistance I am grateful to the Social Science and Humanities Research Council (SSHRC), Max Mueller Fund, Spalding Trust, and Wolfson College. Other financial assistance has been generated by persons who have presented my dance recitals and lectures, or written letters of recommendation. Without this support I could not have continued my work.

Norma Shastri, of the Theosophical Society, Adyar, Madras very kindly assisted me in gaining permission to use their library.

Georges Mailhot and Stan and Nancy Gooch and Patwant Singh were very generous in providing hospitality for me in Delhi which allowed me to oversee the publication.

The greatest encouragement came from my husband, Tony Gaston, an environmentalist with particular interest in Indian birds and wildlife. He shares with me a respect and appreciation for artists trying to survive in the modern changing world. Both of us view artists and eco-systems as endangered species worthy of preservation. Much of our life together has revolved around participating in, and sharing Indian dance, music and other artistic traditions. It is his ability to share my complete involvement with the dance, music and art of India that has sustained me.

Wolfson College, Oxford   Anne-Marie Gaston
May 1995

Introduction

Practically all Indian performing arts trace their origin to religion, or have close ties with it. Some are specifically devoted to presentation in religious contexts and are usually the preserve of hereditary practitioners, many of whom are still supported by Hindu temples.[1]

In south India the dancers, dance teachers and musicians of the *isai vellala* community constitute a distinctive group of hereditary performing artists. For those who worked in temples, this group was further divided into the *periya melam* and *cinna melam*. The distinction centred on the type of instruments they played and whether they accompanied dance. The *periya melam* (literally large band), included the *nagasvaram* (reed instrument) and *tavil* (drum) and the *cinna melam* (small band, included the instruments used to accompany dance: *mridangam* (drum), *tutti* (drone), cymbals, etc. The dancers were women known as *devadasis*. The dancers also belonged to the *isai vellala* community. Although the *devadasis* undertook many functions, the accomplishment for which they are universally known is their dance. For that reason the expression *devadasi* and hereditary or traditional female dancer are often considered synonymous. The *devadasi* and her dance were important adjuncts to both religious and secular occasions.

Until 1920, dancing in south India was the almost exclusive preserve of *devadasis*. In the late nineteenth century a public campaign[2] to abolish the institution of *devadasi* began, which ended in 1947 with the passing of the *Devadasi* Bill. The bill banned dancing in the then Madras state as a part of temple ritual.[3] Much of the agitation centred around the dancer's role within secular society, where she was perceived as either a courtesan or a prostitute.

Simultaneous with the campaign to abolish dance in the temples, a significant interest in the dance appeared among families not traditionally associated with it. In 1932-33 the new version of the dance became known as Bharata Natyam (Raghavan 1967, Khokar 1987, *Sruti* 27/28). Two parallel dance traditions existed at that time —the sacred, ritual dance performed in temples or as part of religious festivals, and the secular which was performed elsewhere. The latter was the concert form and was known as *sadir* or *dasi-attam*. Dance was important and served several functions. It was an essential part of ritual in south Indian temples and was also a regular part of life-cycle celebrations such as weddings and was frequently presented as entertainment in royal courts. It was from this secular version of the dance that Bharata Natyam developed. A conscious effort was made to dissociate it from both the ritual dance in temples as well as the practices and validation ceremonies for *devadasis*. The new name was part of the process of divorce.

This book describes the evolution of Bharata Natyam from an esoteric temple ritual to an artistic presentation performed in theatres. Formerly the dance was associated with the Hindu temple complexes and courts of south India, especially the Kaveri river delta area of Tamil Nadu State and part of Karnataka. The cultural life and patronage which once centred around the temples and major festivals of most south Indian towns has shifted during the twentieth century to metropolitan centres. The transition from the great temple towns to the cosmopolitan city of Madras, the capital of Tamil Nadu; and from regional to national, and now international art forums, gained momentum after India's independence in 1947. In only sixty years Bharata Natyam has become an internationally respected classical art, accommodating itself to new venues and the demands of the modern media. It is there, in a completely new context, that the dance flourishes today.

Classical Indian dance and music are frequently performed abroad. The position of Bharata Natyam is similar to that described for Indian music by Neuman: "The music culture of India is the only major system outside the West that has succeeded in maintaining its traditions largely unmarked by the West ... and that has also

journeyed away from its cultural home to be welcomed elsewhere".
(Neuman 1980: 17).

The popularity of Indian dance by 1977 is confirmed by the dance
critic Shanta Serbjeet Singh:

Now no international festival of performing arts anywhere is complete
unless it represents one, if not two, of India's major classical and folk
forms. Three things have combined to bring this happy state of affairs
about. Dancers ambition and their tireless zeal for conquering pastures
new, their increasing awareness of the theoretical aspects of their art, and
the need to explain them in a simple, succinct form for the benefit of the
uninitiated, and last but not least, the role of the Indian Council For
Cultural Relations and the Department of Culture, reflecting national
policy at the highest level. (*India Today* Sept. 16-30, 1977: 50-5).

In the second half of this century, Bharata Natyam dancers began
to seek change. Little by little new themes, new techniques, and new
methods of staging were introduced.

As I have studied and performed Bharata Natyam for nearly
thirty years I am very aware of these changes. My main concern in
this book is with the perceptions of these changes by dancers,
teachers, critics, and *rasikas* (knowledgeable enthusiasts). I describe
how changes in the social background of dancers and teachers, and
the general loosening of hereditary restrictions, have affected the
studying, interpretation and performance of Bharata Natyam. I
discuss the context in which Bharata Natyam was, and is presented,
and the conditions under which Bharata Natyam is now created and
valued.

I believe that the sociology of art is an especially fertile area for
investigation in India, where there remains a strong repository of
indigenous classical art. In addition, although Indian artistic
expressions are very diverse, they share certain fundamental
characteristics: hereditary transmission, oral rather than written
instructions, and tight bonds between students and teachers. These
allow for generalizations and comparisons. Consequently, I believe
that my conclusions apply not only to south India, but in differing
ways to many parts of India.

The practice of most arts in India is hereditary. Many were, until
recently, inward-looking and somewhat secretive, jealously

preserving their historical roots as a source of authenticity. Divine worship, incorporating devotion (*bhakti*), service (*seva*) and the presentation of royal honours to the deity are central to most artistic traditions, which, in traditional India, served both religious and secular needs.

In studying the many facets of what makes up modern Bharata Natyam, I enjoyed special privileges by virtue of my background as a student and performer of this classical dance style. It also gave me an entrée into other Indian performing arts. Over the years I have studied with both hereditary masters from families with a long association with temple service in the arts and with modern teachers, men and women who were not born into the profession but took it up by choice. Instruction took place in the homes of teachers and in more modern settings such as dance schools. I have visited the temple towns where the dance was once important; but by and large most of my association with the dance has been where it now flourishes, in the large metropolitan cities.

A significant interest in developing the 'temple dance' of Tamil Nadu as a classical art form began in the early twentieth century. It was led by families not traditionally associated with the dance. The term 'revival' has been applied by many writers to describe the widespread interest in indigenous dance that blossomed especially after 1930, when persons from outside the hereditary tradition ('revivalists') began studying and performing. Once members of non-hereditary families began to study and perform the dance, they gave it the sanction and respectability which enabled it to become a sought-after accomplishment. Although the term 'revival' is commonly applied, I concluded that there was less a revival than a conscious movement to discourage those who might otherwise have taken up dance as a hereditary profession from doing so. The fact that the social background of the dancers has changed much more than the visual spectacle of the dance itself, suggests that the acceptability of Bharata Natyam has depended more on the dancer than on the dance.

The initial need for non-hereditary dancers to distance themselves from the earlier *devadasi* traditions and validation ceremonies accounts for many changes introduced by the revivalists. The reasons for the revival were discussed in detail by. A. Srinivasan (1984) and therefore do not form an important part of this book. With the fading of public antipathy towards *devadasis*, there has been a return to earlier practices, and one of the current trends has been towards placing greater emphasis on the religious roots of the dance. Bharata Natyam today appears to be pursued largely as a means of affirming Indian (Hindu) identity. The role of religion in the dance is, however, a matter of continuing debate.

The new Indian middle class, made up largely of literate Hindu upper castes, reacted against many western social values in its struggle to adjust to western challenges in politics, administration and missionary work. V. Subramaniam (1985) discussed the revivalism of the arts as a phenomenon based in, and engendered by, the middle class. The mood of radical revivalism was the background against which the whole phenomenon of the revival of music and dance took place (Mitter 1977, 1983; V. Subramaniam 1983; A. Srinivasan 1984).

There has been a tendency, among both Indian and non-Indian writers, to emphasize the unchanging nature of Indian arts. This is especially true of the rather voluminous popular literature on Indian classical dance, a great deal of which is descriptive and somewhat uncritical. Certainly there is strong continuity within Bharata Natyam, but there have been changes. While some of them may be a little obscure, artistically these changes cannot be regarded as trivial. It is typical for teachers and performers alike to recall the ancient pedigree of the dance, implying that it has remained unchanged for centuries. This emphasis on antiquity has tended to obscure the changes that have taken place and continue to do so. Not that such change is entirely unrecognized by current dancers. A commonplace criticism I heard was that such and such a dancer had changed (corrupted, diluted, popularized) their version of the dance. Until recently, change was nearly always something popularized by others. While western dancers rush to claim innovation, the majority of classical Indian dancers, until the late 1980s denied it even as they were part of the process.

In the last few years, innovation within Indian dance has become respectable. Conferences on the subject are held in India and abroad. Financial assistance is given to dancers to create new work and the impact of Indian trained dancers living abroad on the evolution of the form is enormous. Nevertheless most of these innovators still draw heavily on traditional forms. To trace and record all of these developments would be a major feat. I leave this task to others.

Given the general neglect of performing arts in scholarly research, the only recourse for the researcher who seeks an understanding of cultural phenomena of this kind is to investigate the life circumstances and life histories of the people actually instrumental in making or consuming such an art. This appears to be a consequence of the general neglect of artistic and cultural issues by sociological investigators. The performing artist constitutes a vital element of cultural achievement and powerfully characterizes motifs and preoccupations that typify the social psychology and *mentalité* of a people. Yet, whereas for all kinds of issues in the economic, political, and educational areas, there is a body of systematic evidence and research that is institutionalized as a matter of public policy, the performing arts have not generally been considered serious subjects for social enquiry. Music and dance evolve into distinctive traditions within different cultures; but the very diffuseness of their manifestation, and the absence of conscious, articulated, systematic coordination of such activities has caused them largely to escape sustained research enquiry. For this reason, research into Indian dance is best conducted at a very personal level, and requires that the researcher have firsthand knowledge of the art as it is practised. Indian dance in particular engages a number of essentially autonomous individuals, constantly forming and re-forming for single recitals, both in India and abroad. The elusiveness of the subject matter compounds the general neglect and makes research of this nature labour-intensive.

Understanding the sociology of both hereditary and non-hereditary Bharata Natyam dancers and teachers requires knowledge of their historical contexts. The whole socio-economic structure maintaining

Bharata Natyam has altered radically in this century, transforming it from a hereditary profession with rights, obligations and a means of obtaining a livelihood, into a stage entertainment. Most dancers today are non-hereditary and the majority of them do not depend entirely on their art for a living. For Bharata Natyam, as with many artistic endeavours, data on the economics of the dance are hard to come by; hence I have not emphasized this aspect of the dance.

I have not dealt at length with the political implications of the changes that have taken place in Bharata Natyam, or with a detailed examination of the temple tradition from which it sprang. These issues have been well covered by previous authors (A. Srinivasan 1984; Kersenboom 1987).

Some other issues have been omitted. I have not addressed the role of the cinema in helping to sustain the dance. Before the second World War, many teachers of Bharata Natyam, and some dancers, found employment with the cinema industry (Bhaskaran 1981). The film medium provided an important financial and artistic outlet for dancers and teachers. In particular it was instrumental in the economic survival of many of the hereditary exponents. Classical music and dance were important components of early films. Investigating this connection would have taken me far beyond the range of my sources, and I chose to leave this aspect for others.

As an example of the role of cultural institutions in propagating Bharata Natyam, I have discussed performances presented at the Madras Music Academy, a body devoted to preserving the classical traditions of music and dance. I have not, however, investigated the role of the *Tamil Isai Sangam* and other cultural organizations (*sabhas*) that have presented Bharata Natyam. Likewise, I have not explored the role of government patronage in the arts (Erdman 1984; *India Today* June 15, 1985: 54-7). These omissions are just some of the exciting possibilities for further research in the field of Bharata Natyam.

One of my primary goals in writing this book has been to make my material accessible to an audience with diverse backgrounds and needs. With this in view I have tried to explain important technical terms. My guiding principle throughout has been a comment made by my friend and mentor, Professor Richard Gombrich. After the completion of a seminar, largely devoted to theoretical speculation, he commented to the speaker at the Oriental Institute, Oxford: "Yes, that is all very well, but what really happened?" Anyone who has been an eye witness to an important event can attest, however, that "what really happened" is harder to discover than one might at first think. Because accounts, recollections and perceptions vary, I have included the accounts from as wide a variety of people as possible.

My approach has enabled me to explore the development of contemporary Bharata Natyam through the experiences and opinions of those who have practised, taught and criticised the art. I have tried to juxtapose their comments with my own observations of how the dance is disseminated and performed, and to place them against a wider background of social currents flowing through present day south Indian society. The book itself is a very personal search to place the dance and the makers of this art into a realistic setting. I also hope it will sow the seeds for further studies. The expertise and insight of practitioners who are directly involved in the day-to-day transmission and presentation of the performing arts is too frequently dismissed. If I can do a little to illuminate the contribution of those involved in the art especially those whose achievements do not yield them headlines in the press I shall be satisfied.

LITERATURE, SOURCES AND METHODS

Two scholarly works particularly pertinent to my study preceded it: Saskia C. Kersenboom 1984 (doctoral thesis for the University of Utrecht); and its published version, 1987: *Nityasumangali, Towards the Semiosis of the Devadasis Tradition of South India*, and Amrit Srinivasan, 1984 (doctoral thesis for Cambridge University), *Temple Prostitution and Community Reform, An Explanation of the Ethnographic, Historical and Textual Context of the Devadasis of Tamil Nadu, South India*. Both dealt with the *devadasis* of Tamil Nadu at the period of their decline and both examined the existing literature on the dance. Kersenboom reviewed the Tamil and Sanskrit texts which describe the early history of the dance and its place in temple ritual which is the focus of her study. A. Srinivasan's inquiry began at the beginning of the nineteenth century. The concern of both of them was with the person of the *devadasi*, her dance as ritual and entertainment and her enigmatic place in both the religious and cultural fabric of south India. Neither chose informants who were actively involved in the dance at present, presumably because their prime concern was to describe the duties and function of *devadasis* and place them in historical perspective. My interviews with members of the *isai vellala* community and with others who remember the *devadasis* have allowed me to offer some comparisons between current practice in Bharata Natyam and the original tradition from which it sprang.

I have also made much use of S. Sarada's book, *Kalakshetra—Rukmini Devi* (1985), an excellent source of information on the life of Rukmini Devi, one of the most influential non-hereditary dancers and teachers. Rukmini Devi founded the important dance school, Kalakshetra. Her comments, both in S. Sarada's book, and in conversation with me, were invaluable. They shed light on perceptions of the dance, persons involved in creating the dance repertoire, the teachers, dancers, and general activities associated with the dance when it ceased to be restricted to hereditary families.

Although many involved in the dance continue to feel that things were better in the past, the amount of activity surrounding the dance in the 1980s, the number of active teachers, the frequency of recitals, and the size of classes, all suggest that gloomy predictions have not been fulfilled. About the quality, we may argue, but about the quantity, the enthusiasm and the financial investment, there can be no doubt.

My own material comes from interviews conducted between 1981 and 89, combined with participant observation since 1964 while studying and performing dance in India with many well-known masters. My main sample was chosen on the basis of their involvement in the dance either as dancer, teacher, performer or dance critic. Most of those whom I interviewed were based in Delhi or Madras, and even there my inquiries were not exhaustive. I also conducted interviews in Bombay, Bangalore, Ahmedabad, Baroda, Kumbakonam, Pandanallur, Tiruvidaimarudur, Tanjore and Pudukottai. I made every attempt to include as wide a sample as possible.

The names of those who generously gave their time to talk to me about their experiences with the dance are given in Appendix A. I interviewed one hundred and forty-five Bharata Natyam dancers (ninety-seven of whom also taught dance), forty-two dance teachers and twenty-seven others, including scholars and critics. I also interviewed the family members of most of my sample. Where dance teachers did not teach at home, I visited at least one of each of their teaching centres. These centres varied from students' homes to a central place ("school") where the students gathered. I have also included material on thirteen deceased dance teachers, on whom I obtained information from students and relatives.

I recorded responses to an open-ended questionnaire, with a standard set of questions. The material was so diverse, and the experience so varied, particularly in the case of the dancers, that the most effective way of discovering what had occurred was to let people tell me their recollections in their own way rather than to have a rigid battery of questions into which I would thrust answers. I used some set questions, but the main purpose was to create a situation in which I elicited free responses and life histories. I found it invaluable to spend time in the informants' households. Many musicians or their relatives would also call socially, thus adding to the total picture of the professional teacher or dancer. In most instances the wives of male dance masters had grown up in households devoted to music and dance. They often knew a great deal about the family lineage, traditional teaching methods and the various students and apprentice teachers. The gap of several months or years between sessions also allowed me to update material. In some cases the increasing popularity of the dance had meant that children from hereditary dance families had become more involved in teaching or accompanying Bharata Natyam, at times abandoning secure jobs to pursue a full-time artistic career.

This transformation occurred in the late 1980s.

Using the testimony of those who contributed to and continue to be involved in the making of Bharata Natyam, I have attempted to provide historical depth and clarity to the perception of this important artistic tradition. Bharata Natyam is changing rapidly. My observations and conclusions should be valid up until the late 1980s and I ask my readers to view them in that light.

NOTES

1. The terms hereditary and traditional are used interchangeably to describe those who belonged by birth to families connected to dance and music.
2. The campaign was known as 'anti-*nautch*'. *Nautch* is a corruption of the north Indian, Hindi/Urdu word for dance.
3. Its ultimate demise has been attributed to public pressure, largely instigated by Dr Muthulakshmi Reddy (1886-1968). As well as being a member of the Madras Legislature Dr Reddy was also a medical doctor. According to A. Srinivasan (1984) the mother of Muthulakshmi Reddy was a *devadasi* and her father a brahmin. Narasimhan (1986: 13), however, states that both Dr Reddy's parents were brahmins. For a more detailed look at Dr Reddy's achievements see Basu 1986.

1 The Devadasis and the Origins of Bharata Natyam

SOME GLIMPSES OF EARLY HISTORY

Dance in traditional Indian culture permeated all facets of life. Its outstanding function was to give symbolic expression to abstract religious concepts. The close relationship between dance and religion, particularly as a philosophical metaphor, began very early in Hindu thought. There are numerous references to dance which include descriptions of its performance in both religious and secular contexts. As traditional Indian society has never clearly demarcated secular from religious activity, it is difficult to ascertain in which milieu dance may have originated. For this and other reasons, there continues to be ambiguity surrounding the secular and religious components of the dance tradition.

The earliest references to dance and dancers in the *Rg Veda* and early legal texts such as the *Laws of Manu* and the *Arthasastra*, stress its secular function. The metaphor in the *Rg Veda*, of dawn as a dancing girl putting on her ornaments (*Rg Veda* I. 92) is devoid of any link between dance and religious activity. The Laws of Manu provide for rules to curb dancers in a secular setting and make no mention of a possible religious association. The king is advised: "Gamblers, dancers and singers—let him instantly banish them from his town" (Manu IX. 222). The advice seems to have been largely ignored. Dancers were often given a respected place in society on account of their accomplishments. Ambapali, a courtesan during the time of the Buddha, was, for example, considered one of the treasures of the city of Vaisali (Horner 1930: 89-90). Some of these early attitudes to dancers seem to have been different from those towards *devadasis* in the early twentieth century.

Another source of information are theatrical plays written during the classical period. Many of them include a dancer as one of the main characters and provide further information about the social position of dancers in both temples and courts.

Kalidasa (fifth century AD), who lived in Ujjain, describes the dancers in the Mahakala temple during the evening worship of Siva: "The temple girls' cinctures tinkling with the dance steps, their hands weary with the yak-tail fans" (Kalidasa, *Meghaduta,* trans. Egerton 1.35).

In his play *Mallavikagnimitra*, Kalidasa describes the dance of the courtesan Mallavika in the royal court. We may therefore surmise that as early as the fifth century dance took place in both temples and courts.

Three writers in the eleventh century refer to dancers in temples: Somadeva from Kashmir, Jinavallabha from Rajasthan, and Al-Beruni, a foreign traveller who made observations on life in northern India. All gave some indication of how widespread dance was, and made it clear that dance, at that time, had a secular as well as a ritual function.

Somadeva, in the *Kathasaritsagara*, tells the story of Isvaravarman, who went to the Hindu temple at Kanchanapura (not to be confused with Kanchipuram in south India) and saw Sundari, a *devadasi*, dancing there. At the end of the dance he sent a friend there to solicit her, and she bowed and said: "I am highly favoured". The Jain reformer, Jinavallabha, in his *Sanghapattaka* was concerned about the large number of dancing girls distracting monks in the Jain temples of Rajasthan (Sharma 1959: 225). The explorer, Al-Beruni, observed that in the temples in north India: "The kings made them an attraction for their cities. ... By the revenue they derive from the business both as fines and taxes, they want to recover the expenses which the treasury has spent on the army" (Sachau 1987 Vol I: ix; Vol II: 157).

Six hundred years later, Tavernier writing in the seventeenth century observed that in the Deccani kingdom of Golconda, the ruler also encouraged dance for financial reasons; he benefited from the tax on alcoholic drinks and dancers promoted heavy consumption (Tavernier, trans. Ball 1925: I,127-8).

The dual role of dance is also described in the religious chronicles (*puranas*), several of which recommend dedicating girls to temples (Altekar 1962: 183). The *Vamana Purana* takes a humorous look at the hazards of trying to remain pious while on pilgrimage in the holy city of Banaras: "Where the Vedic accents of great Brahmans, mingled with the sounds of the girdles of sportive women, are transformed into the sounds of great sanctity" (*Vamana Purana* 3.36.31).

Dance was not restricted to Hindu temples. There are references to its being performed in places of worship of both Buddhists and Jains, the two other indigenous faiths of the subcontinent. An inscription dated AD 1270 at Gaya records dance in a Buddhist shrine: "Worship is here (offered) three times a day by means of instrumental music in the highest key (*panchama gata*, which is said to be erotic) and Rambha-like (a celestial dancer) *Bhavanis* (dancing girls attached to temples) dancing round wonderfully" (Sircar 1963: 197).

ROYAL COURTS

Dancers were important adornments to a royal court, where the king assumed godlike powers. Certain ceremonial activities were performed by dancers, such as holding the royal umbrella and fanning the royal couple with yak-tail fans. They were also present at state occasions such as royal consecrations (Kautilya, trans. Shamasastry 1967: 139). The same ceremony was accorded to a king as to the god in the temple. In fact temple ritual was modelled on court ritual. The religious power vested in the king empowered him to transfer *devadasis* to religious duties or to call *devadasis* for secular activities. It is recorded of King Jalauka of Kashmir that: "A hundred out of his seraglio, who had risen to dance (in honour of the god) at the time fixed for dancing and singing, he gave out of joy to Jyestharudra (Siva)" (Kalhana Vol I.1 151: 28).

This practice was not restricted to Hindu rulers: a twelfth century inscription records the transfer of a dancing girl from one of the Buddhist "temples" (*stupa* or cave) at Salonapura to the harem of a local king (Sircar 1963: 97).

Dancers enhanced the king's prestige. This was why, in the eleventh century, the ruler of Tanjore, King Rajendra I, ordered four hundred temple dancers to be brought from nearby temples to be attached to the Brihadisvara temple in Tanjore, which was the main temple in his kingdom. The inscription recording the event names all the temples, both Saivite and Vaishnavite, that had dancers attached to them (South Indian Inscriptions 1985: II.II: 259-60). The centralizing of the dance tradition around the city of Tanjore made it a focus of culture in South India. Many musicians and dancers received generous patronage over many generations from the Tanjore court, as well as the Brihadisvara and other temples in the town of Tanjore. By the beginning of the nineteenth century the climate was ripe for the Tanjore court to support the four poet-musicians, now known as the Tanjore Quartet. They came from a hereditary family of musicians and dance teachers and it is their musical and dance compositions that have had the greatest effect upon the Bharata Natyam repertoire as we see it today.

Without patronage, either by rulers or temples, the professional dancers (*devadasis*), dance teachers and musicians could not have developed the art to the high standard that it achieved. The influence of the Tanjore rulers for several centuries was extensive. For example, in the eleventh century the Chola king Vira Rajendra (1063-70): "ordered some land at Tiruvorriyur to be reclaimed and the produce used for services in the temples including ... mainte-nance ... of dancing masters and girls" (Ayyar 1920: 128 of 1912).

CONTEXT OF THE DANCE

When the dance was a hereditary profession, the *devadasis* had a well-defined and important role in society. The most important validation ceremony for the *devadasi* who danced as part of temple ritual was to be formally married and dedicated to the temple deity or to a ritual object (*kalyanam*). This usually took place before puberty and allowed her to dance as part of temple ceremonies and celebrations. For the *devadasi* who danced in temples her marriage and dedication to a deity ranked as a more important qualification than her dancing ability.

There were six prescribed ceremonies of dedication before *devadasis* could take part in temple ritual: marriage (*kalyanam*); dedication (*muttirai*); ritual first dance lesson;[1] the presentation of ankle bells (*gejjaipuja*); the debut recital (*arangetram*) after the completion of dance training; and the selection of a patron (Kersenboom 1984: 333; A. Srinivasan 1984: 177, 231). All six ceremonies were supposed to be completed, at the latest, just after the first menstrual cycle. There were, however, exceptions in practice.

The Madras legislative debates of 1922 on the abolition of the *devadasi* system describe the qualification for the marriage ceremony: "Above the age of sixteen the religious tenets prohibit their enrolment. A girl to be dedicated according to the rules observed from time immemorial must be a virgin ... no temple authority would think of dedicating a girl above fourteen".

But in the same debate it was also pointed out that there was no scriptural basis for this tradition (Legislative Assembly debates February 27, 1922: 2600).

The pathos of child dedication underlies the comments made by Carmichael, who shared the views held by many that the ritual marriage limited a girl to a profession that she had not freely chosen. Some of the attitudes were derived from Christian missionaries, and liberal Indian thinkers who viewed the practice of dedicating young girls with horror. "But by far the most sorrow laden hour was spent in the village from which the little child was taken to the temple near our home ... they chained her fair young body to the cold and cruel stone ... married her to the god" (Carmichael 1907).

In the 1920s, interim legislation was passed forbidding the dedication of minors. This meant that if a girl were to be dedicated before puberty some other type of ceremony had to be devised. The need for dedication before puberty was a very real concern for the *isai vellala* community who introduced a practice known euphemistically as "the Rose Garland Ceremony" (*rojapumallai*). This consisted of a rose garland, with the symbol of marriage, the *pottu*, hidden in it, being placed around the neck of the young girl to be dedicated. Dedication continued, usually in secret from the authorities, but with the knowledge of the temple authorities and the local townsfolk and villagers (A. Srinivasan 1984).

The rose garland ceremony was not universal and girls were still being openly dedicated. The age of dedication also varied.

I encountered several women who had been dedicated in the normal way, even in the 1920s and 30s. One of them, T. Rajalakshmi, remembered her dedication to the deity in the Mahalingesvara temple in 1928-29 in the village of Tiruvidaimarudur, when she was eleven or twelve years of age: "Yes, yes, that is the tradition. I was dedicated to the god. It was called *pottukattu*."[2]

Because the Lord was her husband, the *devadasi* was always auspicious (*nityasumangali*). Hence, one of her important duties was to perform the *arati* ceremony.

A lamp made of kneaded rice-flour is placed on a metal dish or plate. It is then filled with oil or liquified butter and lighted. The women each take hold of the plate in turn and raise it to the level of the person's head for whom this ceremony is being performed, describing a specified number of circles with it (Dubois 1897: 149).

Arati was intended: "to counteract the influence of the evil eye, and any ill effects which, according to Hindu belief may arise from the jealous and spiteful looks of an ill-intentioned person" (ibid: 149).

The *arati* ceremony was important as part of religious ritual in the temples: "After the dancing-girls have finished all their other duties in the temple, they never fail to perform this ceremony twice daily over the images of the gods to whom their services are dedicated" (ibid.). It was also performed outside the temples. "It is performed with even more solemnity when these idols have been carried in procession through the streets, so as to turn aside malignant influences, to which the gods are as susceptible as any ordinary mortal" (ibid.).

This ceremony was widespread and was performed both publicly and privately:

It is performed daily, and often several times a day, over persons of high rank such as rajahs, governors of provinces, generals and other distinguished members of society. Whenever people in these positions have been obliged to show themselves in public or speak to strangers, they invariably call for the courtesans or dancing girls from the temples to perform this ceremony over them, and so avert any baleful glances to which they have been exposed (ibid.).

The importance of *arati* in the secular world cannot be underestimated: "Kings and princes often have dancing girls in their employ who do nothing else but perform this ceremony" (ibid.). Only married women, whose husbands were still alive, and *devadasis* were permitted to perform this ceremony. A 'pot' could take the place of the lamp. "Instead of using a lighted lamp they sometimes content themselves with filling a vessel with water coloured with saffron, vermilion and other ingredients" (ibid.). As the embodiment of auspiciousness, the presence of a *devadasi* was important at marriages.

As a *Dasi* she can never become a widow. The beads in her *tali* (marriage symbol) are considered to bring good luck to women who wear them ... some people send the *tali* required for marriage to a *Dasi* who prepares the string for it, and attaches to it black beads from her own *tali*. A *Dasi* is also deputed to walk at the head of Hindu marriage processions ... it is believed that *Dasis*, to whom widowhood is unknown, possess the power of warding off the effects of inauspicious omens (Thurston 1909).

Another description of *devadasis* accompanying marriage processions describes their dance. "At intervals, a halt was made to give the dancing girls an opportunity of exhibiting. Their motions were slow, their attitudes generally not ungraceful, but occasionally too expressive for the meridian of chastity" (Anon 1821).

The account of a dance teacher from a hereditary family confirms the erotic nature of the *devadasis'* activities during wedding celebrations in the 1920s and 30s: "Being a *dasi* was not something to be proud of as a little licence was taken with them. For example during the marriage celebrations she was called upon to put sandal paste on the bridegroom. This was made compulsory and no-one liked to do this."

Dance as part of the ritual in divine worship was listed as fifteenth in the sixteen acts of honour and homage paid to deities (Loganayaky 1969: 59; Kane 1941: 704-40; Appadurai 1981: 22).

An inscription dating to the reign of Kulottunga III (1205-18) (Sastri 1958: 211) establishes that there was a time-table for the presentation of dance and the dancers took turns: "the assignment of a fixed period in the day for every dancing girl to perform her services by turn in the temple" (*State Inscriptions of Pudukkottai* 1929: 20, no. 169).

The number of times dance took place however, varied. Abbe Dubois in the nineteenth century told of singing and dancing twice a day in temples of importance (Dubois 1972: 585).

There are very few descriptions of dance in the twentieth century as part of ritual; this one, in the temple in Ramesvaram, was recorded with some accuracy:

At 4.30 or 5 a.m. (the *puja* begins) the dancing girls (*muraikari*) officiating for the day, with *rudraksha* beads in place of jewels, dressed up as a Brahmani and her hair uncombed ... open up all the doors to the *mahamandapa*. Later the god is taken in procession preceded by musicians and attendant dancing girl ... the dancing girl repeats a *tevara ujal* or verse in honour of Siva (Ayyar 1920: 193).

The dress described here appears to be very simple and suggests that of a renouncer (*rudraksha* beads, hair untied), rather than of the bride of god.

Some who have seen the dance in temples are still around. Pandanallur Srinivasan is one. He is a *mridangam* player (drummer) from a hereditary family who gives solo recitals and accompanies dance. He remembered a more elaborate dress worn by the *devadasis*: "She [the *devadasi*, Saradambal] wore only a white sari and white choli. That was the custom in those days ... no make-up, no *talaisaman* (head jewellery), but only flowers and the usual jewellery".

He describes the activities in the temple when he played for *devadasis*:

Yes, I played for *devadasis*. They were the ones married to the god. I played in the Brihadisvara temple in Tanjore for the dancer, (Karaikkal) Saradambal. It did not look like a formal programme. In the Lord's procession outside the temple the *devadasis* did the work of the priests, such as putting flowers at the idol's feet and offering *puja* in the nine directions (*navasandhi*). This was around 1946. I was about fifteen. As the deity was carried from the *garbha griha (sanctum sanctorum)* to the *raja gopuram* (gateway) for each *sandhi* or direction they performed a different *tala*. The *devadasis* walked in front of the procession. When the procession was over they placed the god at the entrance of the temple and the *devadasis* performed a *puja*. The dancer, *nattuvanar, mridangist, tavil, nagasvaram* and *ottu* players circled the deity three times. Saradambal, must have been about fifty then. Minakshisundaram was not her guru. I forget who it was.

Subbadra, wife of a Bharata Natyam dance teacher, the late K.N. Dandayudapani, had many opportunities to see the dance. In 1985 she related to me what she could remember from the 1920s, when she was nine or ten years of age. She describes the dancers in the temple of Murugan in Velrampattu near Vadalur, Tamil Nadu. They were more richly adorned than those described above in Ramesvaram and they were not young: "[They] ... dressed up at home. They wore neither make-up nor the *talaisaman* that some dancers wear today. They did wear ear-rings, armlets and bangles of real gold. The ones I saw had grey hair so they must have been forty."

Because she was intimately associated with the dancers and their families she could not be specific about the exact time for what seemed like a natural event.

I knew the dance was going to be performed because I was staying at their house. All the *devadasis* wore the *sari* like the brahmin ladies [the sari would have been nine yards long, the lower half tied like a *dhoti*]. When the brahmin priest did the *puja* the *dasis* performed the same actions using hand gestures to show the bell, the light, the fly whisk, etc. They did not wear ankle bells. When they danced in the temple it was in the evening, during *kudamrai*. However, during festivals they danced both in the morning and in the evening.

She also remembered seeing dance concerts as part of a family's celebration of life-cycle events such as the onset of menstruation: When girls from rich families attained puberty, people would celebrate by having a dance performance.

Weddings have always been a time for dance recitals. Kalidasa, in his play *Kumarasambhava*, described the god Siva and his new bride Parvati being entertained with dance at their wedding (Griffin 1853: 90). Dance as part of festivities at Hindu weddings continued to be popular during the British rule and was portrayed in woodcuts and paintings.

V. Subramaniam (1993) records that the increase in the number of wealthy brahmin landowners in the late nineteenth and early twentieth century provided a new source of patronage for *devadasis*. The newly affluent invited *devadasis* to dance at weddings. This financial support was crucial in helping the dance of the *devadasi* to survive.

The changing situation of hereditary dancers may be seen in the case of a couple from a *devadasi* lineage who married in 1957. The groom, who was both a dance teacher and drummer (*mridangist*), was marrying a woman who had studied and performed dance as late as 1957. This demonstrated that although she was from a traditional family her dance training had no apparent effect on her marriage potential. One of the groom's brahmin dance students gave a recital as part of the festivities; it was an interesting reversal of roles, where a brahmin dances at an *isai vellala* wedding. Apparently the *devadasi* tradition of dancing at weddings was, by that time, acceptable for anyone, demonstrating how fluid the dance profession had become.

There were also early examples of the bride and groom, both brahmins, dancing at their own wedding. Chandrabhaga Devi and U.S. Krishna Rao remembered: "Our wedding in 1940 was a grand affair and several ministers and VIPs attended. After the reception, both of us performed two dances in Bharata Natyam (*alarippu* and *jatisvaram*) and some dances in the Kathakali style."

This contrasts with the traditional situation in which dancers had been forbidden to marry.

Dance is now an important event at weddings, but dancers do not depend upon it as a source of income, nor are they required or permitted to perform those rituals which only *devadasis* were empowered to perform.

At my own wedding in 1970 in New Delhi, my friend Usha Srinivasan (brahmin), now a Bharata Natyam teacher in Madras, danced and our Bharata Natyam dance teacher at that time, K.N. Dakshinamurthy (*isai vellala*), conducted the recital. I myself have danced at various weddings. In India, in Mathura, the preparations were lavish and I was one of many dancers, singers and instrumentalists who were engaged over a ten-day period to dance at the wedding of the son of the hereditary head of the Vallabha *sampraday*, the Tilkayat Shri Shri Govardhanlalji, who presides over the Shri Nathji *haveli* in Nathdvara Rajasthan. As well, I have been invited to perform at Hindu weddings in Canada.

There are some examples of *devadasis*, both dedicated[3] and undedicated who married and gave up their dance careers. A dance teacher from the village of Pandanallur recounted: "Even after the *devadasi* had undergone the *trisul* (ritual) marriage, her brother, who was educated, decided to get her married to a film producer in Madras."

There are also examples of *devadasis* becoming the second or third wife to someone already married. Pandanallur Jayalakshmi was one example. The Raja of Ramnad used to invite her to dance in his palace during the Dussehra festival held every year. Later, the two married; she was his fifth wife. P.S. Swaminathan, a hereditary dance teacher, recalled one of her three performances at Ramnad where he accompanied her as a musician:

In 1945 when I was about eighteen I saw the Raja of Ramnad give her a *gajalakshmi* (a type of necklace) studed with diamonds and a diamond ring. He gave all of us musicians a *dhoti* each. Jayalakshmi's brother played the *mridangam*. Rajayee her mother, and her sister Jivayee, sang the songs for her descriptive dances. Jivayee was also a *devadasi*. She did not marry.

Some *devadasis* married widowers. After marriage, *devadasis* seldom danced for the public.

SOCIAL STIGMA

The son of a *devadasi* remembered how his mother reminisced with him about how she had suffered. The suffering was social, not financial, as they had their own house and lands.

In those days, many believed that by merely watching these women participate in the rituals, men became sexually excited. Why is it that when brahmins began to perform the dance, the dancers were given respect and my mother wasn't. The brahmins have taken over the dance.

As a child he was told that his father had been a wealthy Mudaliar. He himself had an arranged marriage. He described his wife as "a Pillai of another variety", by which he meant that she belonged to his caste (*isai vellala*) but had not danced or been associated with it. He recalled that in 1986, in "a moment of weakness" he had allowed his daughter to take dance classes but he "stopped her dancing after a month". At that point he proudly showed me her wedding photographs.

Learning the dance could lead to humiliation later. Several women from *isai vellala* families reported being taunted by their in-laws on this account. One hereditary *nattuvanar* remarked: "If a girl studied dance it could be held against her. During family arguments her in-laws bring up her former connection with the dance to humiliate her, even though she had never danced publicly."

Association with the dance was thus seen as a taint on one's character. Implicitly it was seen as equal to being a *devadasi*. A hereditary dance teacher said: "Even if they were *devadasis* we do address them as such, it is not proper."

Would parents allow a daughter to learn dance in the hope that she would become famous, even if it might affect her marriage prospects? Some parents said they might chance it. But most said: "I can not afford to take the risk on the presumption that she will become famous".

For some families, however, attitudes were changing. These changes were reflected in the artistic options they gave to their daughters, particularly the youngest. A woman from a hereditary family commented: "I had five children. We only encouraged my youngest daughter to study dance and now she wants to be a dancer. This is because until recently (before 1980) it was not proper for members of our community to encourage our daughters."

FESTIVALS

In addition to dancers being used in both temple and court, they were also an important part of festival celebrations, which were ostensibly religious, but also secular in function. There are many references to dance at festivals from all over India and for many centuries. King Jogaladeva of Nadol in Rajasthan was insistent that all festivals be celebrated with dance. In 1147 he decreed: "When a festival of any god commences, the courtesans attached to the temples of other gods must also put on their ornaments and best garments ... to celebrate it by [playing] instrumental music, dancing and singing and so forth" (Bhandarkar E.I. 1911-12: 27).

Jogaladeva forbad anyone to abolish dance at festivals. He also called a curse upon any prince who does not maintain this practice (ibid.). Such was the importance of this event.

According to European travellers, dance remained popular at festivals. Fray Sebastein Manrique in the seventeenth century wrote of the car festival in Bengal during Durga *puja*:

This strumpet [Durga] is carried along in a highly ornamental triumphal car with a large band of dancing girls, who besides dancing, gain a livelihood by prostitution. These dancers go in front, dancing and playing various musical instruments and singing festal songs (Travels of Fray S. Manrique, trans. Eckford-Lourard 1927, Vol 1: 71).

Abbe Dubois in the nineteenth century saw dance during the car festival at Tirupati in southern India (Andhra Pradesh) and recorded that the presiding deity of the temple, Lord Venkatesvara, through his servants, the brahmins, selected new dancing girls to serve him from the crowd that came to celebrate his festival.

While the image of Venkatesvara is borne through the streets on a magnificent car, the brahmins, who preside at the ceremony, go about among the crowd and select the most beautiful women they can find, demanding them of their husbands or parents in the name of Venkatesvara, for whose service, it is asserted, they are destined ... it is thus that the seraglio of Tirupati is recruited (Dubois 1897: 601).

Abbé Dubois also recorded seeing dance on the last day of the harvest festival of south India, Pongal.

The idols are afterwards taken from the temples and carried in procession, to the sound of music, to the place where the cattle have again been collected. The temple dancing-girls who are to be found at all feasts and public ceremonies ... march at the head of the concourse of people, and from time to time pause to delight the spectators with their lascivious dances and obscene songs (ibid.: 574).

As late as 1910 *devadasis* were displayed in the floating festival at Dohnavaur, Tiruneveli district: "On the dais of the barge, in place of honour nearest the image, stood three women and a child" (Carmichael 1910: 338).

Comments from several former *devadasis* indicate that, up to 1947 they took part in temple festivals and many of the dance teachers still actively teaching in the 1980s can remember providing the musical accompaniment for them.

DANCE IN TEMPLES AS PART OF RECENT FESTIVALS

Dance was not allowed to be re-instated as a regular part of ritual because many believed that brahmins in the temples would once again exploit dancers. Today, more than forty years later, Bharata Natyam is once again being performed in temples, as part of specific festivals, by non-hereditary dancers. Many of these dancers are relatives of those same women who, until the 1940s and 50s were forbidden to see it. R. Nagaswamy (brahmin), who organizes the annual dance festival in the Nataraja temple in Chidambaram commented on the *devadasi* way of life:

The *devadasi* way of life was an entire way of life.... They danced for the deity as an artistic extension of the elaborate worship by the priests.... They danced for god inside the temple and outside too, and again for him when he went outside in procession and at festivals (R. Nagaswamy 1985).

Nagaswamy provides the rationale for erotic love (*sringara*) which is the essence of the dance repertoire.

The esoteric psychology of *sringara* 'union with the lord' wedded the *devadasi* to a single state owing allegiance to no man except *Natya Seva* (dance service). If they accepted a mortal as a patron they could discard him also at will, their preoccupation was with god and their *Natya Seva* (dance service) was to him ... as a result of their dedication their art acquired profound depth and *bhava*. It was wholly natural (ibid.).

This description is surely an idealized picture, but it illustrates the value placed on that elusive quality "*bhava*". Nagaswamy went on to suggest that modern Bharata Natyam had lost that quality. Reporting the reaction of the former *devadasi*, Kamalambal when she watched non-traditional dancers performing in the Nataraja temple, he commented:

The absence of this superior level of expressiveness (*bhava*) in contemporary classical Bharata Natyam was felt by Kamalambal of Tanjore, now in her seventies. She commented with the extreme caution of the old, that it is all very good but.... Her reluctant remark clearly implied that progress and skill in technique had been achieved, sacrificing the emotive quality of a weighty dance culture (ibid.).

DEVADASIS AND PATRONS

Besides the ritual marriage (*kalyanam*), which marked the dancer as a ritual specialist there was another validation ceremony which had implications for her secular role as a courtesan. This was the formal celebration of the debut recital (*arangetram*) after the completion of dance training. This occasion celebrated not only the end of her dance training, but acknowledged publicly that she was ready for the selection-of-a-patron ceremony. The custom was that after the *arangetram* a patron would be selected by a senior female member of the girl's family and a formal relationship established.

For a man, married or single, association with a *devadasi* enhanced his prestige and publicly confirmed his status and wealth. "Both bachelors and married men have intercourse with them promiscuously. A married man is in no way ashamed of such lustful proceedings, but rather thinks it an honourable act. This conduct is even approved by his wife and family" (Dubois 1897).

A dance teacher recalls the time when he was growing up in his village of Pandanallur during the 1920s and 30s.

There were a lot of *zamindars* (landowners) who were rich and the *devadasis* would stay with them, usually permanently with one. I used to see one particular landlord who was rich and powerful. A servant held a lamp, and when he came people would move aside. The houses of the *devadasis* were always on the north side beside the temple. The old landlord would leave the *devadasi's* house at about five o'clock in the morning.

The status of a *devadasi's* patron was very important. The *devadasis* were encouraged to select patrons who had both social and economic weight. This was important for the whole community to maintain status. Hence, if a *devadasi* had "any dealings with men of the lowest castes", she would be "tried by a *panchayat* (council) of the caste, and visited with excommunication" (Thurston 1909).

Some accounts limited patrons to brahmins. "All handsome girls are trained to dance and sing and are keeps of brahmins" (Buchanan 1870).

Other more numerous accounts stress only that the patron's caste should not be inferior to that of the dancer.

They [the dancers] do not marry; but are permitted to prostitute their person to any individual of an equal or superior caste to themselves or to live in professional concubinage; such practice in no way degrades them from the right to caste privileges, provided they do not form intimacies or cohabit, with outcastes (Shortt 1870 Vol III).

There were penalties, sometimes a fine, if they consorted: "with a Mohammadan, a blacksmith, a goldsmith or a *chetti*, a *nokkam* or any man of low caste" (Hemingway 1906).

Money could overcome some of the taboos. Muslim officers paid "lavishly for their entertainment" (Buchanan 1870). Buchanan also noted that in the early nineteenth century the brahmins, rather than paying for the *devadasis* favours exerted "their authority over the women". The son of a *devadasi* recalled his mother's vulnerability:

It was the custom in those days to offer a girl to a big landlord or a rich person once she had been given the *pottu'* symbolising her ritual maybe to the deity. The girl was then "kept" by these people in the name of god. My father being a relative of one of the trustees of a temple enjoyed this privelege. It was a social evil which continued until the government put an end to it.

The brahmin-*devadasi* liaisons extended beyond the confines of the temple. At the beginning of the nineteenth century, many brahmins were working in secular jobs in the East India Company, rather than in their traditional role as ritual specialists in the temple. These men were important sources of patronage for the *devadasi* and her art (Buchanan 1870).

It was necessary to be careful where one performed. There is an account of a *devadasi* losing her right to perform in a temple because she had performed in the home of someone deemed to be of low social status. The priests of the temple gave her the option of purifying herself by drinking *panchagavyam* (five products of the cow) but she refused and was therefore expelled from the temple (Lawsuit 1883 in Thurston 1909).

A *devadasi's* patron entered into a relationship with her for a specific period, sometimes it was for life. His wife might not take kindly to it and this resulted in tension. This is reflected in the dance repertoire. A good example is the wife's complaint in the Tamil song (*padam*) *Arrevenne Ayya,* enacted by the courtesan. Its caustic humour would not have been lost on the originally all-male audience. The lyrics would have been enacted by a dancer-courtesan taking the role of the wife.

I know all your secrets, I understand your devious ways, you and I are married but that woman has stolen your heart. Why is a strong man like you running after her? You respect and worship that courtesan, but with me, you use foul language. With her, money is no problem, but with me, you inspect the accounts. Don't think I don't know what you are up to? (translated from the Tamil).

Sarcasm and hurt feelings underlie the emotions portrayed. We also get a glimpse of the power of the legitimate wife, confident in her status as a married woman and, in this instance, able to challenge her husband.

Chandrabhaga Devi (brahmin) remembered that in the 1940s she and her husband studied *javalis*, considered the most secular and erotic compositions in the Bharata Natyam repertoire: "In those days we showed jealousy. I think it was an important emotion for *devadasis* because a rich man could have relations with different women, and even though he had a wife."

While *devadasis* dedicated to the deity did not have a regular marriage, in most instances a career as an undedicated dancer also precluded a regular marriage. Like dedicated temple dancers, the undedicated ones too had patrons chosen for them and pursued careers as courtesans. Dance was one of their accomplishments. Hence, all female dancers from the *isai vellala* community were called *devadasis*, whether or not they married the deity.

The comments of a high caste male dancer and teacher show that he was unable to reconcile the ritual and sacred function of *devadasis* with their secular, sexual role.

If I see one of the old *devadasis* now, I have a sort of respect for her. I can never think of them as having many patrons. The *devadasis* must have experienced an internal conflict between their two roles. They were obliged to perform services in addition to those for the god.

He was very aware of artistic differences created by the fact that their dance had another purpose: "Because they had to attract patrons, their dance was somewhat different from the dance we were taught in the 1940s and 50s at Kalakshetra. We avoided many gestures. I was aware of this. We were told not to use mouth and lips. Gauri [a *devadasi*] used her mouth."

Literature is full of slurs on the character of *devadasis*. It was said, for example, that a *devadasis's* loyalty was not to be trusted and they needed to be watched carefully: "Indeed almost every girl who is tolerable is kept for the special use of a particular officer and is seldom permitted to go to the temple except in his presence" (Buchanan 1870). A hereditary dance teacher contradicts this perception: "*Dasis* were trained by my grandfather. They never did any wrong, never cheated."

The *devadasis'* charm, beauty and knowledge of fine arts are well known.

The daughters of the caste who are brought up to follow the caste profession, are carefully taught dancing, singing, the art of dressing well, and the *ars amores*, and the success in keeping up with their clientele is largely due to the contrast which they present to the ordinary Hindu housewife, whose ideas are bounded by the day's dinner and babies (Thurston 1909).

Obviously it was the intellect and culture of the *devadasis* which was important, "The women of the brahmans are beautiful but the insipidity of their conduct makes native husbands seek the dancing women" (Buchanan 1870). Perhaps these comments are unfair if we consider that wives would have been bearing children soon after their first menstrual cycle and were usually not taught how to read, or write, and discouraged from intellectual pursuits. One of the impediments to introducing universal education in India was that initially only *devadasis* were permitted to read and write: "Courtesans, whose business in life is to dance in the temples and at public ceremonies, and prostitutes are the only women who are allowed to learn to read, sing or dance. It would be thought a disgrace to a respectable woman to learn to read; and even if she had learned she would be ashamed to own it" (Dubois 1897: 337).

THE QUALIFICATIONS OF A PATRON

Devadasi families looked for patrons with both intellectual and artistic excellence so that this genetic combination would be reflected in their offspring. The beauty, talent, and artistic skill of *devadasis* when combined with a patron who possessed sophistication, and academic and artistic learning increased the chances of producing superior children (A. Srinivasan 1984). The most sought-after patron was a brahmin who combined both wealth and learning. Men from castes such as *vellala* or *chettiar* were accepted, if they were rich (ibid.). One former *devadasi*, Radha Annamalai, said that her late husband, a *chettiar* who died in 1972, owned a lot of land in Burma but lost it all in 1942 during the Second World War. She was married in 1940 at sixteen. The lavish wedding took place in Mambalam, a suburb of Madras and lasted for five days. He had seen her perform at a wedding and expressed an interest in marrying her. He had another wife, a *chettiar* like him. He divorced her and married me but after ten years he took to vice.

Her husband did not like or know anything about music or dance.

It is my fate. All I knew before my marriage was that he was rich and my grandmother arranged it. When my husband was away I would sing and dance which he did not mind. My dance teacher, Kandappa, would come to our home to train me. I did this until I was twenty-three or twenty-four. The servants did not tell my husband. Even after my marriage, I was able to give dance programmes.

She confirms the hereditary nature of her profession: "Only when my mother, sang for my recitals did I dance well".

Many men in traditional marriage situations were attracted to the artistic accomplishments of *devadasis*. Some of them were knowledgeable critics and connoisseurs and kept the artistic standards high. Others were musicians, singers and composers and added to the repertoire. The fact that both brahmin males and *devadasis* studied and performed music encouraged many liaisons. One such example is Dharmapuri Subbarayar, whose attachment to the *vina* player, Dhannamal, was the inspiration for many of his *javalis* which he composed and premiered in her music salon in Madras. This rich interchange helped music and dance to flourish as it was a highly regarded pursuit for high caste men. The effect of this intense interest in the arts has meant that even today there are a group of knowledgeable persons who encourage excellence.

Money could be lavished upon dancers but it had to be from a patron with social status.

When their services are required outside the temple, large sums of money have to be paid for them, the charge being increased by the renown and position of the girl, as some few of them take a very high position in this matter, and will not give their services, however highly paid, to any one of small importance, unless a Raja, or some such big person. Some travel to other districts when their services are needed by petty Rajas or *zamindars* and they are contracted for as many days as they have to perform (Shortt 1870 Vol II).

The combination of beauty, charm and artistic expertise could enhance the earnings of a *devadasi*. "In addition to being well paid, should they please the master of ceremonies, they frequently receive valuable presents in money, shawls, gold bangles, or rings, which are bestowed on them during a performance" (ibid.).

PATRONS AND THE REPERTOIRE

The tradition of temple dance was part of a highly developed system whereby the god of the temple was treated with royal honours. One of these honours was to entertain the deity with dance. The same dancers also performed in palaces and it would appear that sometimes the repertoire overlapped. The records of the Tanjore court are explicit to whom songs can be addressed. The songs for the court should be dedicated to the deity or the Maharaja. No other songs eulogizing human beings should be composed or performed (Tanjore Palace Records Bundle 201C: 987-1000).

As many of the rulers had the same names as deities there was often ambiguity. Naturally this was a useful device that could serve to flatter the king without offending religious sentiments. Other patrons were generally large landowners. It was an accepted practice for dancers and musicians to be rewarded for flattering patrons with their songs. Performing dances with lyrics which praised secular patrons (*nara-stuti*) was severally criticized by some non-traditional exponents.

NUMBERS

It is difficult to ascertain the exact number of dancers. In the seventeenth century Tavernier observed that there were 20,000 dancers in the Deccani region, then known as Golconda, but their function appears to have been purely as courtesans (Ball 1925: 127-8). Those attached to temples were often listed in temple records; the Suchindram temple in Kerala recorded seventy-one in 1919 (Pillay 1952: 285). Certainly temple dancers were very much in evidence in south India in the nineteenth century. Abbé Dubois stated that every temple of importance had eight to twelve *devadasis* attached to it (Dubois 1897: 585), while Buchanan observed that the two large temples of Kanchipuram had about one hundred dancing girls attached to them (Buchanan 1870: 12-13). The local government reports of 1912 stated that temple dancers were in Assam, Madras and the Jagannath temple in Orissa, but not in Bengal, Sind, United Provinces or Gujarat (Legislative Debates 1922: 2610). Even in 1932, by which time it had become apparent that dancing in temples would be declared unlawful, P.G. Sundaresa reported in the Annual Conference of the Madras Music Academy: "We all know that today, even in Pandaripur, daily worship is being done in the temple accompanied by *natyam* (dance) similarly in Srirangam, during the ten days preceding the Mukkotai *Ekadasi* day, worship is generally accompanied by *natyam*" (*Journal of the Madras Music Academy* 1932: 122).

Historical accounts of the dance and personal interviews with older dancers and teachers reveal that some dancers danced predominantly in the temples, and in the streets when the images were carried in procession; some danced on secular occasions and some combined all these activities. Kersenboom (1987: 172) records that the former *devadasi* T. Ranganayaki was emphatic that the dancers in the Tiruttani tradition never danced "on the roads". However, the *devadasi* Gauri and her mother M. Doraikannu danced in the streets of Mylapore when the deity was taken out in procession. Those who saw them commented on the beauty of these women, particularly when dressed as *Bhiksatana*, or Siva as a wandering mendicant.

Undedicated *devadasis* mainly performed on secular occasions, providing entertainment at marriages and private parties. Some of them, however, reported dancing at temple festivals and celebrations, often along with *devadasis* who had been dedicated.[4]

SELECTION OF *DEVADASIS*

It was important that a girl chosen to be a *devadasi* be good looking. Amy Carmichael, a missionary makes it clear that such girls were often carefully selected.

The ideal temple child is refined in manner; that passes too often as the years pass, but the child at first is an attractive little thing. No other is of use. She is usually "fair" as the word goes here, anything from olive to hazel-nut colour. She has a certain manner and way of her own, and she is responsive to influence, keen-brained, bright (Carmichael 1907: 255-256).

The wife of a traditional *nattuvanar* gives a different description of *devadasis*, especially their skin colour. The standards for comparison, however, may differ. Many present-day dancers are brahmins and very fair. Seen from that perspective hereditary dancers may be seen as much darker: "The dancers of my time were very dark and danced without jewels. The present lot of fancers are fair and wear lots of jewels and people look at their figure."

Today studying the dance is open to all who can pay the fees. But when the dance was a hereditary profession dancers were selected mainly from the *isai vellala* community. There were also other ways of joining the profession such as by adoption, or being sold or donated by parents for religious motives. It was not unknown for parents without children to promise to dedicate their first daughter to a temple (Dubois 1897). As most couples desired a son, this was not the hardship it might at first appear.

... their ranks are recruited by the purchase of female children of any caste, and also by members of certain Hindu castes vowing to present daughters to the temples on recovering from illness, or relief from other misfortune. The female children of the dancing women are always brought up to the mother's profession, and so are the children purchased by them or assigned to temple service by the free will of the parents (Cornish 1871).

There were certain procedures before a girl could be dedicated. New applicants to the temple authorities were mainly the daughters of *devadasis* but their dedication had to be agreed upon by the temple authorities. Heredity alone was not sufficient. If there was suspicion about a girl's character she could be denied dedication and the rights and privileges that went with it.

One of the main misconceptions regarding *devadasis* was that they were a separate caste: At the present day they form a regular caste, having its own laws of inheritance, its own customs and rules of etiquette, and its own *panchayats* (councils), to see that all these are followed, and thus hold a position which is perhaps without a parallel in any country" (Thurston 1909: 127).

In fact *devadasis* were governed by the rules of the larger *isai vellala* community which also included men, their wives and children.

Thurston describes various artistic occupations for the sons of *devadasis*.

Some of the sons remain in the caste, and live by playing music for the women to dance to, and accompaniments to their songs, or by teaching singing and dancing to the younger girls and music to the boys. These are called *nattuvans* (ibid.).

In actual fact these activities were open to all men in the *isai vellala* community. Thurston comments on the women of the *isai vellala* community who married musicians and *nattuvanars*: "Others marry some girl of the caste who is too plain to be likely to be a success in the profession, and drift out of the community" (Thurston 1909).

In addition to daughters of *devadasis*, the daughters of married *isai vellala* couples could also become *devadasis* if their parents so wished. One example is the hereditary dance teacher Kattumunnar Muthukumar. His parents were married. His father was an accountant and not involved in the arts. Muthukumar became a dance teacher and his sister, Kannamba was dedicated as a *devadasi* in the Siva temple in the village of Kattumunnar (Khokar 1993: 16). Although rare, it was not unknown for wealthy sons of *devadasis* to be allowed to marry girls of respectable parentage from other castes. This continues to be rare although there are a few examples of teachers marrying their high caste students.

Recruitment into the *devadasi* community was also by adoption. "... *devadasis* are the only class of women who are, under Hindu law, as administered by the British courts, allowed to adopt girls to themselves" (Thurston 1909). The comments of some observers indicate that *devadasis* had few children, so if the profession were to continue *devadasis* had to adopt: "As a rule, it is seldom that these women have children of their own, unless, perhaps, they had lived in continual concubinage with some single individual" (Shortt 1867). I found that in many instances most of the adoption was from other members of their family. This could be for a variety of reasons: desire to bring up a child, someone to inherit one's wealth, or to look after one in old age. One woman told me that she had been adopted by her aunt, Kamalambal,[5] a *devadasi*, and studied dance with her. In 1947, at the age of seven, she presented a debut recital (*arangetram*) in Tanjore in the ancestral home of Kamalambal's teacher. She remarked: "I can't remember much ... my teacher Kamalambal sang some of the songs. My future husband was not invited, even though he was a distant relation of both my teacher and myself." At fourteen she danced in the Tanjore Palace. Later she married and continued to teach dance. Other women from hereditary families performing at that time such as T.A. Rajalakshmi and K. Bhanumati also reported dancing in various palaces such as the one in Travancore. Many of them recalled very active dance careers up to 1952. T. A. Rajalakshmi remembered: "Between 1947 and 1952 I was living in Tiruvidaimarudur. I gave many programs and I would not be home for even ten days. I performed in Chetinad, Tanjore etc. In Chetinad they preferred 'double dance', two of us dancing together." K. Bhanumati later married and gave up any association with the dance. T.A. Rajalakshmi continued to teach until 1993. My data as well as most family trees suggest that the majority of *devadasis* had small families: up to three children, though there were exceptions. Married *isai vellala* couples from the same period were more likely to have larger families.

In the families of all *devadasis*, sons and daughters did not always inherit equally as Thurston (1909) suggests:[6] "Among the *dasis* sons and daughters inherit equally, contrary to ordinary Hindu usage [custom]." It was notable that inheritance in *devadasi* families passed through the female line.

Among dancing girls property descends in the female line first, and then to males as in other castes. In the failure of issue [children] the property of a dancing girl goes to the *pagoda* [temple] to which she belongs—a simple recognition on the part of the dancing girl, of a child as her daughter, in the presence of one or more individuals is sufficient to constitute her claim to adoption ... they are always anxious to adopt girls, not only to become their successors in the temple, but that they may inherit their property like-wise, which is no easy matter to effect nowadays (Shortt 1871).

A lawsuit (in 1876) involved a girl who claimed to be the adopted daughter of a *devadasi*. Her adoptive mother had died before she was dedicated. The temple authorities denied the daughter's application to be dedicated to the deity. Consequently she lost all the hereditary rights of her mother. The reasons given were that:

... the plaintiff could not enter on the office until a *bottu-tali*[7] had been tied on her in the temple, and that the trustees did not permit this to be done. The prayer of the plaintiff was that the defendants be compelled to allow the *tali* to be tied in the temple in view to the girl performing the dancing service and enjoying the honours and endowments attached thereto (Thurston 1909).

The case, however, was more complicated than that. In particular the girl was seventeen, too old for dedication which was supposed to occur before the first menstrual cycle. Perhaps for that reason the judge dismissed the suit "as being in effect a claim by the plaintiff to be enlisted as a public prostitute" (Lawsuit of 1896 in Thurston 1909).

REMUNERATION AND ECONOMIC STATUS

Unlike most married women who did not have any economic control, or even own their own children, *devadasis* were economically independent. They managed their own finances. The head of a *devadasis* family was the oldest female member known as the *Taikkizhavi* (Thurston 1909). Sons of *devadasis* being dependent upon their mothers rather than their fathers were generally regarded as inferior to daughters. Women made all the major decisions regarding the household, which included controlling the finances (A. Srinivasan 1984). In a joint family the earnings of all of its members were shared. Because family wealth lay in artistic knowledge as well as the beauty and attractiveness of their women, men were often required to give artistic support to the female members of their family. This usually meant being part of the musical accompaniment for their dance. The sons of *devadasis* became dance teachers or musicians. Many of the men in the *devadasi* community could not marry, either because of the shortage of women within the community (because well over half became dedicated *devadasis*) or because they lacked the financial security to do so. A significant number of these men had to postpone their marriage until they were established as dance teachers or musicians. Some of them became independent enough to move out of the female-dominated joint family and establish a separate residence. It was rare to find a *devadasi* family with a married son still living with them. This was in contrast to the male-dominated households of the *nattuvanar* families where sons often brought their wives to live in their ancestral home. These women were then obliged to help with the housework and contribute to the common good of the family with home-making skills rather than artistic ones. Here too financially secure males preferred to move out of the joint family and establish separate households.

A recent trend has been for members of the same family to establish schools in various cities around India rather than compete for students in the same localities. This has helped to maximize the earning power of their family members. Competition within the family would not benefit the whole group, whereas an artistic network in different centres ensured that it would create a teaching empire in which students, whose families were posted to different cities in India, could continue to train in the same tradition.

The *Taikkizhavi* also exerted her control over the artistic training of members of the family. Satyajit Ray's film on the life of T. Balasaraswati gives us some insight into the women's decisions in this important family.

It was Dhanamal who insisted that her granddaughter Bala should train to become a singer ... but Bala at the age of two had already seen the greatest temple dancer of her time [no name] and her ambition was to surpass her.... In those days, dancing as a profession meant dancing in temples and temple dancers were frowned upon in polite society ... it was Bala's mother Jayammal, herself a fine singer, who decided to brave the social risk and fixed up Kandappa to teach her daughter [dance] (Text from film, *Balasaraswati*, made in 1977 by Satyajit Ray).

Many *devadasis* became wealthy in their own right. It was not unusual for them to own houses and lands. Several comments support the fact that some of the hereditary dancers in this century were wealthy. One woman from a hereditary family, reminisced: "Dancers then [before 1947] were all very rich. They owned groundnut fields." The son of a former *devadasi*, to whom I spoke also said that his own mother was well off.

The fact that for many centuries dancers contributed generously to religious institutions confirms that many must have been well off. This practice was in accordance with the *Kamasutra* which described dancers as courtesans but whose money was worthy of being used on religious institutions such as to construct temples, water tanks and gardens (Vatsyayan, trans. Upadhyaya 1961: 214, v.25).

A Telugu inscription dated AD 1053 mentions Kasadi Suramadevi, a concubine of the Kota chief, Ketaraja, giving some money to keep a lamp burning in the temple of Ramesvara of Velpunuru (*SII* 1948: no.249). Not all *devadasis*, however, were wealthy. Several non-hereditary dancers painted a pathetic picture of one of the most important *devadasis* of the revival period, M.D. Gauri, who taught them *abhinaya*. They all remember that Gauri, out of necessity, was forced to live in the home of many of her students. In return for room and board and possibly some pocket money she taught her art. Rukmini Devi told me that she arranged and paid for Gauri's funeral.

In return for a substantial donation to a temple, *devadasis* were often given privileges. In the reign of Rajaraja III (1298-1322) a dancer constructed high walls inside the temple of Vellaimurti Alvar. In return she and her descendants received the privilege of waving yak-tail fans before the deity in processions and a daily gift of rice (*SIE* 1923: 106 No. 172 of 1923). The duty of waving yak-tail fans must have been a coveted one because the granting of this honour to *devadasis* is recorded in several inscriptions. As early as the fifth century, Kalidasa's *Meghaduta* describes the performance of this ritual in the Mahakala temple in Ujjain. A dancing girl holding a yak-tail fan is a common sculptural motif throughout India.

For their ritual performances, *devadasis* were given some remuneration in cash, or kind, such as rights to a house or produce from temple lands.

When these girls are attached to *pagodas* (temples), they receive certain sums as wages, the amount of which is dependent on the worth, sanctity, and popularity of the particular temple which they have joined. The money salary they receive is nominal—seldom exceeding a few *annas*, and sometimes a *rupee* or two a month. The chief object in being paid this salary is to indicate that they are servants of the temple (Dubois 1897).

Dubois' comments indicate that this practice extended to all temple servants. A hereditary dance teacher, K.N. Dakshinamurthy, recalled his own obligations and rewards as a young musician attached to a temple, "We got rice and money for this service. The temple would pay according to the number of children one had. During the three or four big *pujas* we would accompany the *nagasvaram* by palying on cymbals, and *tavil* [drum]."

One of the early brahmin girls to study the dance remembers accompanying one of her teachers, a former *devadasi*, to the temple once a month to collect coconuts and other small tokens of payment that were part of her hereditary salary. A hereditary dance teacher from Bangalore remembered the situation of one of his relatives: "One of my relations danced in the Parthasarathy temple in Nelamangalam. For her services she was given a lot of land. After the *devadasi* tradition was forbidden, her lands were taken away. Gundappa (her son) fought in the courts to get them back but he did not succeed. The government took it all back."

There was an established code for remuneration for secular concerts. One hereditary dancer remembers that the payment was always given to her teacher to distribute: "Master was always fair and generous. If the payment was five hundred rupees, he would give seventy-five rupees to the dancer, fifty rupees to each orchestra member [flute or violin, *mridangam* (drum), and vocal] and the balance of about two hundred and seventy-five rupees went to him."

When the tradition changed to include non-hereditary dancers, so too did the conventions for payment. The question of money was also a source of tension between the traditional *nattuvanars* and the non-hereditary dancers. The late V. Ramaiya explained why he refused to conduct recitals for some of his students: "It is not that I do not want to do *nattuvangam* for them. The reason is money. When they received one thousand rupees for a recital they gave me five hundred rupees. When they received several times that, they wouldn't give me half of it any longer" (*Sruti* 27/28). While the teacher saw the performances as joint undertakings, the dancers apparently saw the teacher merely as a hired musician with a set rate. Traditionally, it had been the teacher's role to hire the dancer.

RETIREMENT AND FUNERAL RITES

It was important for a *devadasi* to have a daughter to look after her in old age. A retirement ceremony is mentioned in the records of the Suchindram temple for *devadasis* who had reached an advanced age or had become chronically ill. Facing the assembly of priests (as at her enrolment), the *devadasi* unhooked her ear-rings and presented a gift of money. The ear-rings were returned to her, but she no longer wore them (Pillay 1953). Thurston (1909) also records the removal of jewellery on retirement and a reduction of salary.

All aspects of the *devadasi's* life were provided for, including her funeral: "When a *dasi* dies her body is covered with a new cloth removed from the idol, and flowers are supplied from the temple, to which she belonged. No *puja* (worship) is performed in the temple till the corpse is disposed of, as the idol, being her husband, has to observe pollution" (Hemingway 1907). Even the fire for her pyre was from the temple: "The funeral pyre of every girl of the dancing girl caste dying in the village should be lit with fire brought from the temple. The same practice is found in the Srirangam temple near Trichinopoly" (ibid. 1907).

NAMING CONVENTIONS AMONG
THE *ISAI VELLALA*

The term *isai* (*icai*) appears in classical Tamil literature and refers to special music played in the court of kings. In association with *vellala*, a respected term for dominant Tamil, non-brahmins, it has become the name of the community for hereditary musicians and dancers. This title was adopted by the caste association, the *Isai Vellala Sangam*, at a conference in Kumbakonam in 1948. Srinivasan (1985: 1876) discusses this in detail.

Most *devadasis* and their offspring have one name which is preceded by one, and sometimes two initials. There appears to be no fixed rule whether to include one or two initials. The first initial indicates the ancestral village. The second initial indicates the mother's name. In those instances where there is only one initial it is usually reserved for the village of one's ancestry.[8] For example T. Balasaraswati, and her relatives such as her male cousin T. Sankaran, the T. stands for Tanjore, both of them being offspring of *devadasis*, with hereditary associations with the city of Tanjore. This family has chosen not to include their mother's initial. In the case of the *nattuvanar*, the late V.S. Muthuswamy, whose mother was a *devadasi*, the V. stands for his native village Vaidisvarankovil, and S. for the name of his mother, the *devadasi* Sethuramu. V.S. Muthuswamy's family now lives in Kutralam but he chose to link himself with his ancestral village, Vaidisvaran-kovil. Many *nattuvanars* and dancers have similarly chosen to associate themselves with a town with which their family has been historically associated, even though they may no longer own land in it, or have anything, other than a sentimental attachment to it.

V.S. Muthuswamy also added Pillai to his name, which is the most common surname for male dance teachers and musicians from the *isai vellala* community. It is usually only used by men. Recently however, the tendency has been to drop Pillai,[9] largely because it indicates their particular community. Males from the *isai vellala* community whose mothers were not *devadasis*, in addition to a personal name, are usually referred to by the name of their ancestral village, followed by their father's name. Thus the naming conventions adopted by the *isai vellala* community indicated the marital status of one's mother, and the professional involvement of their women.

URBANIZATION

The naming conventions provide documentation of the villages and towns from which the artistic heritage of Bharata Natyam derived.[10] The banning of dance in temples and the profession of *devadasi* was followed by a shift of the art from smaller towns to the larger urban centres, in particular Madras. Some of the *devadasis* who were resident in Madras from the 1940s—M.D. Gauri, Swarna Saraswati, and Saradambal—are remembered by today's dancers more as teachers. T. Balasaraswati's dance however continues to be regarded as the ultimate in the expression of the "traditional" Bharata Natyam technique. There were other *devadasis* who taught: in Calcutta, T.A. Rajalakshmi, and in smaller towns such as Tanjore—Kamalambal and Lakshmi Kantham, but it has been the Madras-based *devadasis* who have had the greatest impact upon the new generation.

DISCUSSION

Despite the fact that by the turn of the century it had become clear that dance as part of temple ritual would soon be abolished, many hereditary families continued to train their daughters. There was still an active interest in including dance at weddings and wealthy patrons considered dance important. Later the cinema industry needed dancers trained in the classical tradition as well as dance teachers who could coach film stars. Though present-day dance in films bears little resemblance to classical dance, in the initial stages of the industry, the support that dancers and teachers received from work in films allowed many of them to continue their traditional profession.

After the dedication of *devadasis* was abolished in 1947 the system disappeared in Tamil Nadu. Those women who were already dedicated, either found work as dance teachers, married (an option made possible by the new liberal attitudes), or found other employment. Only a few taught dance, either in provincial centres such as Pudukkottai, Tanjore and Kumbakonam or in Madras. T. Balasaraswati, who later achieved international fame for her dance and music developed her own school, with considerable assistance from Dr. V. Raghavan and the Madras Music Academy. The two traditions—the *devadasi* and the revivalist—persisted side by side for some decades (1930-50) and then the *devadasi* style faded rapidly away.

In 1972, I watched an old *devadasi*, P. Muthulakshmi, teaching some young girls in Pudukkottai, a small princely state in Tamil Nadu. I was struck by the similarity between what she taught and what I was familiar with on the concert stage in Madras. I asked her whether she was teaching what she had learnt as a young girl. She laughed and told me that what she taught was adapted from her son (Kalyanasundaram), who worked in the film industry in Madras. She did not feel that her students would be interested to learn the art as she had been taught. Afterwards, she showed me some of her original descriptive songs—simple, direct and, to me, wonderfully moving, but essentially a lost art.

Was anything lost in the transition? Here I can speak as a dancer. The lack of contact between the majority of the last generation of *devadasi* dancers and the early non-hereditary performers led to changes in some aspects of the dance, especially the facial expression and gesture. There is no doubt that modern venues, such as large concert halls, are less suitable for the presentation of expression (*abhinaya*) than the intimate settings of courts and salons of great houses, with the result that the importance of *abhinaya* in the dance has been reduced. Moreover, the changing social climate made the type of courtesanship espoused by the *devadasi* system no longer acceptable, making some of their repertoire irrelevant. That something has been lost is not in doubt. Whether it could ever have survived into the world of the late twentieth century is also doubtful. Today's Bharata Natyam provides a different function for a different group of dancers and audiences. We are left only with the faint flavour of the *devadasi* style of dance.

NOTES

1. Dance classes usually commenced before the age of seven. Many accounts describe the dance teacher lifting the girl's ankle and helping her to strike her foot on pounded rice paddy (Thurston 1909: 138; Khokar 1964; *Marg* 1979 and Kersenboom 1987: 201). This particular custom is not followed today but the offering of fruits, flowers, incense and some cash, all arranged on a large round plate, continues in most circumstances.
2. She reported that she had taken off the *pottukattu* about ten years ago because she was "fed up".
3. Kersenboom 1987 suggests that some were frightened to marry a dedicated *devadasi* because of her special religious status.
4. For the various categories of dancers, see Thurston 1909: 125,128,141; Chatterjea 1945; Iyer 1935; Kersenboom 1987.
5. Kamalambal had two daughters (Rajeshwari and Ranjitam). She did not teach dance to either of them. Ranjitam married the son of a *devadasi*, J.(Jayalakshmi) Natarajan. He had studied dance with Kamalambal, taught dance in her school in Tanjore and performed with her.
6. Srinivasan (1984: 193) states that if the father of the children were a brahmin the children would not inherit from him but if he were from another caste the children could expect some inheritance from him.
7. *Bottu-tali* can also be spelt *pottu-tali*.
8. L'Armand 1978: 117 discusses this with reference to musicians in Madras.
9. See Thurston 1909. It is very rare in the 1980s amongst the younger generation of *isai vellala* males to use Pillai as their last name. Woman, married or single, from this community do not usually use Pillai as part of their name.
10. L'Armand (1978: 122) lists the royal courts and temple towns that were important musical centres.

Plate 1.1: The Tradition of the Devadasi
B.(Balammal) Lakshmikantham (c. 1925-1958)

This is a poster for the dance recital of B. Lakshmikantham (*devadasi*) whose career spanned the "revival" period. Her mother, Balammal, and grandmother were also dancers in the Brihadisvara temple, Tanjore shown behind. Lakshmikanthan studied with Picchaiya Pillai (died 1943) and gave her *arangetram* at age eleven (1936). She taught her younger sister B. Revati (Dorai, born 1930) and they used to dance together. (There is a parallel here with Kamala Lakshman one of the brahmin revivalists who taught her younger sisters and used to perform with them.) B. Lakshmikanthan founded her school, *Picchaya Natya Kaluri* in 1946, in Tanjore.

She wears the nose ring known as the *bullock* in her nose. For many years this piece of jewellery was not worn by upper caste dancers as it was the symbol of the *devadasi*. Today it is worn by many non-hereditary dancers.

2   Present State of Bharata Natyam

DEVELOPMENT OF BHARATA NATYAM

In its modern manifestation, Bharata Natyam appears to occupy the same niche in Indian society that ballet occupies in the West. Both are considered the pinnacle of classical dance within their respective cultures and regarded as suitable accomplishments for the daughters of the educated middle classes (Gaston 1991). Bharata Natyam and ballet are classical arts. In contrast to folk forms, both can be judged by recognized standards. Some knowledge of the technique is necessary for them to be fully appreciated. Both are patronized by the elite, and are performed on the concert stage. There is usually a fee for entry into the concerts. Dancers are usually paid professionals and perform only after several, usually many, years of training.[1]

Because Bharata Natyam developed from dancing that had an important role in temple ritual it has a dimension entirely lacking in western ballet. Bharata Natyam is identified as an expression of the Great Tradition (Singer 1972: 167). It is one of seven classical Indian dance styles[2] that are frequently performed, within India and abroad, on both stage and television. As Bharata Natyam boasts more students and more performances than any other, it can claim to be the most popular style today. Outside India, it is synonymous with traditional Indian culture and is a skill much sought-after among expatriate Indian communities.

More important, Bharata Natyam is recognizably the same dance that previously formed part of both religious and secular celebrations in south India. The transition of a dance style that was an important component of both temple ritual and secular celebrations to the dance style now called Bharata Natyam is marked by several changes. In particular the hereditary system that determined how dancers and teachers were recruited is no longer applicable. Anyone can study, perform and teach Bharata Natyam as long as they can pay for their classes, sponsor their own performances, and attract students. This profession, which was once defined by community association, is now based on economics. There is no central professional body which confers on an individual the right to perform or teach dance. Standards were, and continue to be, fluid.

Today, while the majority of those associated with Bharata Natyam in the capacity of dancer, teacher and critic are aware of the origins and previous function of the dance, most of the top performers and many teachers never actually saw the dance in its original setting. Although many changes have taken place within the lifetimes of people still alive, there is disagreement about which religious elements in the dance were once part of the temple legacy—hence hallowed by tradition—and which are modern accretions. Some rituals, symbols, practices and repertoire now associated with the dance can be traced to earlier practices, while others have been created recently. An analysis of what modern exponents have chosen to emphasize, and what they have reduced or eliminated, gives a strong indication of the present social significance of the dance. Despite the claim that the older form was "purer" and "better", the majority of dancers who formed part of the hereditary tradition are rarely consulted or emulated. A great deal of filtering and selecting has taken place. Despite the lip service paid to the antiquity of the form, what is being created is a dance style that is acceptable for performance in its new context by people from a different social class.

When dance was performed by *devadasis* it was a profession and everyone associated with dance was a professional. It was a full-time occupation and participants earned their livelihood from it. Today there are few professional, self-supporting dancers. Most of those who perform in public make little financial profit out of their public recitals. This is true even though Bharata Natyam is one of the most popular Indian classical dance forms and regular performances take place in all the major and many of the minor urban centres of India. In contrast to the growing number of dancers who do not rely on the dance as their sole source of income, all the teachers and the musicians associated with the dance are fully professional. Teaching the dance continues to be an expanding profession and the sudden and escalating popularity of the dance has increased the demand for teachers and musicians.

For the majority of students, the reasons for studying Bharata Natyam in the 1980s were very much the same as in the mid-1950s. Most families of the younger students were interested, not in having their daughters become professional dancers, but in having them learn a social accomplishment. Their study was "art for arts sake" (Singer 1959; 1972: 176), and a "manifestation of their nostalgic turning back to a traditional way of life" (Redfield 1956:193). This phenomenon has continued to gain momentum and has been a major force behind the frequent public recitals throughout India and abroad.

Singer's widely known study, "The Great Tradition in a Metropolitan Centre, Madras" (1959), provides some useful comments about Bharata Natyam in Madras during the 1950s. Unfortunately, he made no attempt to survey the entire dance community, which he mentions as including about twenty-five hereditary families (Singer 1959: 168). Singer gives the impression that there was little dance teaching going on at the time, while Bowers, who was writing during the same period (the 1950s), noted that there was a lot of activity. My research agrees with Bowers' conclusions that the dance was not in danger of disappearing (Bowers 1953). Bhushan, writing even earlier (1939), noted: "Go to a metropolitan town and you will not fail to perceive the enthusiasm for dance vibrating in the air" (Bhushan 1939: 11). Many were, however, pessimistic about its survival as a classical art form: "Bharata Natyam is being mutilated beyond recognition by the degenerated nattuvanars (dance teachers and orchestra conductors)

who migrate to cities for a living ... [to teach even]... worse pupils"
(Venkatachalam 1946: 8). One of Singer's main informants, a
dance critic and scholar, commented: "The renaissance of Indian
culture which started with great hopes in the 1920s and 30s ... has,
in its contemporary sequel, proved a failure. The development of
modern dance and music schools has merely increased the scope for
fraud" (Singer 1959: 162).

This view was shared by A.P. Chokkalingam, a dance teacher
from a hereditary family and T. Balasaraswati, a hereditary dancer
teaching at that time. Both of them were convinced that the old
teaching methods could not continue to be followed, or the same
type of dancers produced (Singer 1959: 168).

Although many of those involved in the dance continue to feel
that things were better in the past, the amount of activity surrounding
the dance in the 1980s, the number of active teachers, the frequency
of recitals, and the size of classes, all suggest that the gloomy
predictions have not been fulfilled. About the quality we may
argue, but about the quantity, the enthusiasm and the financial
investment there is no doubt.

During the course of my research I discovered a large number of
women (both brahmin and *isai vellala*) who had either been studying,
performing or teaching during the period when the controversy
around the abolition of the *devadasi* tradition was at its height
(1920-47). I was interested by the fact that girls from the *isai vellala*
community were still being trained during the 1930s and 1940s, a
time when it was already clear that dancing in temples would soon
be banned. At the same time, other girls from non-hereditary
communities were also being trained. The inspiration for the non-
hereditary group was, at least partly, a way of demonstrating their
families' nationalism, and adherence to "Indian" culture and values.

The desire of both the "revivalists", who were mainly from the
brahmin community, and the hereditary *isai vellala*, to encourage
their daughters to study the dance, amidst the movement to ban it,
seems remarkable. This is particularly so, considering that the
agitation was aimed primarily against the person of the *devadasi*.
By virtue of her profession she was barred from a regular marriage

but was free to form liaisons with one or more men. The result was the close association of dance and prostitution in the eye of the public. Such extraordinary adherence to the dance emphasizes how deep rooted the tradition of dancing was among the *isai vellala*.

In 1947, when the dance was banned, at least one *devadasi* founded a school of Bharata Natyam in Tanjore. Even after 1947, there are examples of girls from the *isai vellala* community performing on the stage as professionals. An important reason for the sustained interest in the art by these dancers and their families was a continuing demand for dance performances outside the temple.

The full extent of dance activity before 1947, among both *isai vellala* and other communities, is hard to judge. According to Singer (1972: 172) "between 1915-1919 there were at least five-hundred professional dancing teachers in Madras and many *devadasis*". It is impossible to gain an exact picture because most of the teaching of dance took place in unofficial institutions such as the private homes of students or teachers, and only a few recitals were announced in the newspapers. Even today, the activity generated by dance is much greater than would appear at first and publicity continues to be minimal. There are probably several unpublicized recitals for each one that obtains a mention in the press. Considering this, we have to conclude that the dance activity before 1947 was considerable, at least in certain pockets.

For many Indian girls, the dance is regarded as an important vehicle for becoming familiar with Hindu myths and traditional Hindu social values. Bharata Natyam has become an educational tool. Its function today transcends the artistic, providing instead the medium for acquiring cultural identity and projecting examples of female role models. It has become an integral part of the education of the upper and middle classes in most cities and towns in India. This is highlighted by the fact that themes in the Bharata Natyam repertoire are drawn largely from Hindu mythology.

In 1987, a former *devadasi*, K. Bhanumati, commented on the modern way of learning the dance: "Now everyone wants to learn dance. Some do it as a hobby and others for exercise. Today academic education is important and for many dance is just another qualification."

However, she felt the dance had definitely been improved and attributed it to Rukmini Devi the founder of Kalakshetra: "Rukmini Devi wanted to improve the status of the dance so she studied it and gave performances. She taught dance and her pupils gave public performances. For the first time the accompanying dance musicians sat on the stage. She also improved the dance costume. She was a brave women and broke the tradition." K. Bhanumati not only endorsed the reforms but told me in 1987 that she had sent her own grand-daughter to study the dance with a brahmin woman (Padma Subrahmanyam), rather than teach her herself or send her to a teacher from a hereditary family. Her action indicates that she fully endorsed the artistic vision of the non-hereditary dancers and teachers.

Although Bharata Natyam is often referred to as a 'temple dance' what is regarded today as traditional Bharata Natyam reflects the secular version *sadir*. The ritual function of dance in temples has disappeared. The most striking indication of this change of function is the fact that, amongst the educated middle class, dance training has, for girls, become the social accomplishment par excellence. No amount of money or time is spared in preparing daughters to appear on stage. A great deal of money is lavished on the first public recital (*arangetram*). The importance of this recital in attracting a suitable husband is but one important issue for the social role of Bharata Natyam.

Perceptions of what the dance was rely on texts which describe it, literary references, and accounts of early travellers and government officials. It would be naive to think that previous accounts provide anything more than either restricted views of specific cases, or descriptions of ideal states which may never have been achieved in practice. Not surprisingly this has led to differences of opinion concerning what the 'proper' manner for presenting Bharata Natyam should be. Changes in the social background of dancers have affected the style and content of performance, but most modern practitioners claim authenticity by virtue of antiquity for their particular tradition. Hence, it might be concluded that the art has been extremely conservative. Exponents of the art have consciously attempted to conserve its character in adapting the dance to modern circumstances. An examination of modern Bharata Natyam shows, however, that not all that is claimed as traditional is necessarily based on precedents in the *devadasi* tradition.

To understand the present dynamics of the dance it is necessary to know not so much what *is* authentic or traditional in the dance, but what is *believed to be* original and traditional. Hence people's opinions about who the *devadasis* were, and how they studied and performed, become just as important as what actually took place in the south Indian temples and courts in what is now held to have been a golden age. Because Bharata Natyam as we see it today owes much of its content to the dance of the *devadasi*, it cannot be studied completely outside its historical context.

THE EARLY NON-HEREDITARY DANCERS

To distance themselves from the *devadasi* profession and practices, the early non-hereditary dancers stressed that they were amateurs and that they did not have to rely on dance for a living. They performed for charity and would not accept money for recitals. Kalanidhi Narayanan, a prominent brahmin teacher, related her experience in the 1930s:

I can't remember my first programme. If I were a *devadasi* girl my first recital would have been called an *arangetram* with all its rituals, but I broke the tradition. My parents liked dance. For my family dancing was not to earn a livelihood but to learn an artform. The programmes were always free in aid of something.

The financial support came from their family. Payment for dancing had another connotation and most early non-hereditary dancers reported that they did not receive remuneration.

Just as the new non-hereditary dancers performed only for worthy causes in prestigious venues and for important people the *devadasis* were also selective. The dance was always for the elite.

Today there are levels of acceptability where performances can take place. It is considered very 'low' to perform in a restaurant or hotel when the audience is eating and drinking, particularly if alcohol is served. Several of the early non-hereditary dancers mentioned that they had played a key role in elevating the dance to its present stature. Kamala Lakshman a non-hereditary dancer commented:

The *devadasis* were not just married to the gods. They were exploited by the kings and the wealthy landlords to satisfy their desires. They were used as prostitutes. Today, however, dancers have better status. People are better educated and they are able to accept the fact that an unmarried girl can give a dance performance in public and still get married. Dance is now considered respectable. It is because of people like us that it acquired this new status.

Despite changing attitudes towards the dance itself, doubts lingered about the *devadasis*. A member of one of the most important hereditary families, T. Sankaran told me that there was an ambivalent attitude towards his late cousin, T. Balasaraswati:

Even in 1949-50 people said that Bala was a *devadasi*. This is a double-edged weapon. It may be a compliment or damning with faint praise. They say even today that *devadasis* were pure. Fifty years ago only *devadasis* danced and did music and no brahmin woman would even attend the recitals.

DEVADASIS AND BHARATA NATYAM

Before the new dance could be created, the basic technique had to be acquired from hereditary masters. T. Sankaran again commented on the continuing dependence of non-hereditary dancers upon hereditary families for artistic knowledge:

... ladies from all classes of society were only too willing to (put) on the jingling anklet and they had to turn for assistance, as they still do, to the fountain head, viz. the Tanjore Quartet (a hereditary family associated with dance and music) for initiation in the art (T. Sankaran 1981 in A. Srinivasan 1984: 145).

Several *devadasis* became prominent stage performers between 1930 and 1950. Some of the most famous were P. Kalyani, P.K. Jivaratnam, P.K. Rajalakshmi, M.D. Gauri, K. Varalakshmi, K. Saranayaki, P.N. Sabharanjitam, K. Bhanumati, T. Balasaraswati, T. Mathuratambal, K. Nagaratnam, Swarna Saraswati and P. Jayalakshmi (see chapter 8). Most of them continued to perform the pre-existing repertoire of *sadir*, in the traditional style. During the same period, the non-hereditary dancer, Rukmini Devi, developed her vision of a more austere, less sensual dance. Later, graduates from her school, Kalakshetra, usually well educated, and articulate, began to dominate the institutional teaching of Bharata Natyam. At the same time the preferences of audiences began to encourage pure dance (*nritta*) at the expense of expression (*natya/abhinaya*), the *devadasis* trademark.

Some *devadasis* taught, especially Swarna Saraswati (initially in Madras, and later in Delhi) and Gauri Ammal (in Madras). Even then there was selection in the repertoire and style which they passed on. The comments of a non-hereditary male brahmin dancer/teacher reflected the changing status of the *devadasi* tradition in 1989: "The *devadasi's* dance was full of erotic intent. When I studied with Gauri (a *devadasi*) I did not use the mouth gestures. Now I use them a bit, but only to show sarcasm. NEVER BEFORE." Even in the 1940s, when he was studying dance, the *devadasis* themselves knew that their dance had to be edited and adapted for high caste practitioners.

She [Gauri] herself would say: "Do not show these things to children." Only the senior teachers and older students attended her classes. Even for them special permission was necessary. We knew that there were two traditions, the Kalakshetra and the *devadasi*. We were told that we must present the dance so that it would be acceptable to all. The dance had to be changed a little to be acceptable. In those days (1950s-60s) it was a small brahminical audience.

Another non-hereditary female dancer/teacher lamented the current state of affairs: "But now in the 1980s all the girls enact the erotic gestures in the dance, probably more so than the *devadasis*." The non-hereditary dancers who are now India's cultural ambassadors have been granted the freedom to present the dance as they wish, with the result that many critics are calling for restraint.

Most teaching was performed by male *nattuvanars*. The *nattuvanars* adapted the dance for their non-hereditary students. Chandrabhaga Devi, a brahmin, recalled her teacher's comments in the 1940s: "Minakshisundaram cut out the eroticism. He said, You are a respectable couple coming from a cultured family and the *sahitya* [lyrics] for this dance is meant only for *devadasis*. I won't teach them to you."

A recurring theme is that hereditary dancers, regardless of age, could be taught the erotic repertoire because they had an innate affinity to it. The perception that persons from the *isai vellala* community who trained in dance are somehow different still exists. These comments about a dance performance in Madras, in 1986 by Indra Rajan (an *isai vellala*) confirm that for some people the dance of the hereditary practitioners was not to be emulated:

Conference convenor Lakshmi Vishwanathan [brahmin] noted that Indra Rajan's rendering (of a *javali*) disclosed her links to an earlier generation of dancers and her training in the *gurukula* system. This was a euphemistic way of saying that Indra Rajan reflected the artistic elements of the *devadasi* tradition ... Lakshmi Viswanathan did not say this explicitly, but another implication of her remarks that 'we' should not seek to emulate Indra Rajan and others who are from her "environment" is that girls from respectable families, brought up in cloistered environments and affected by all kinds of middle class inhibitions wouldn't be able to handle the explicitly romantic elements of *javalis* as Indra Rajan can, and does (from a review in *Sruti* No. 21, 1986: 31).

It would appear that the rendering of the dance depends on the person of the dancer. In this respect little seems to have changed since 1946:

Because of its sensuous character it has within it unsuspected levels of emotional experience and equally unsuspected level of sexual degradation. Therefore the wise men of the past codified it and had it taught to women of certain birth and breeding and certain attainments (Venkatachalam 1946).

Women of the *isai vellala* community who did not enter the

dancing profession were not termed *devadasis* and usually took great pains to distance themselves from any association with dance or music. This was to avoid the opprobrium which resulted from *devadasis*, unable to contract a regular marriage, living with one or several men. A great deal has been written about their association with prostitution (Dubois 1897; Thurston 1909; Carmichael 1904, 1910; Srinivasan 1984, 1985). In fact it was this perceived connection that eventually led to dance being banned from temples by the *Devadasi Act* of 1947. The stigma connected with dance still affects the perception of it and the extent to which it is regarded as an acceptable pursuit by women from the *isai vellala* community. In particular it affected a girl's marriage prospects. Bowers' comments, written in 1953, reveal the status of the *devadasi* and the taint of being associated with her art.

To take the dance out of the hands of the artists, even if they are prostitutes as well, in whose blood, families and profession it has resided for generations, is obviously a dangerous experiment. Their removal has not, however, removed the stigma on the art, which is apparent from the fact that many fathers of reputable families even today forbid their daughters to dance, and a good many conservative men would hesitate to marry a girl who has ever danced in public (Bowers 1953: 19).

Attitudes within the *isai vellala* community towards the participation of female members in the dance contrast sharply with those from outside that group. This has been an important factor in changing the role and position of the *isai vellala* among dancers and teachers of Bharata Natyam.

MARRIAGE AND THE DANCE

The acceptability of professional association with Bharata Natyam vis-a-vis a girl's marriage prospects has gone through several phases. Originally it carried social stigma and had the potential to be an impediment in a dancer's ability to attract a suitable husband. In the next phase girls from hereditary families were not taught the dance while girls from non-hereditary families were allowed to study with the tacit agreement that they would abandon it after marriage. This loosened so that some women were allowed to teach and occasionally perform for family and friends. By the 1980s, association with the dance had become fully accepted and indeed a sought-after commodity by some husbands who wished to be associated with what they perceive to be a glamorous way of life.

Just as important, knowledge of the dance allows dancers to augment the family income. Most teaching is done in the family home, allowing the wife to contribute to the family income while still being at home to ensure that her husband's comforts are taken care of. The mothers of several non-hereditary dancers remembered that for them studying music was acceptable, whereas for their grandmothers it had still been largely the preserve of the hereditary families. Their daughters chose dance and consider themselves fortunate that they were allowed to continue their dance after marriage.

Karunambal, from a hereditary family was aware of the changing perception of the dance and dancers and saw a career in dance as improving a girl's marriage potential through affirming her adherence to Indian culture.

Before, there was a social taboo so people were hesitant to study the dance. Things are better now. A man will marry a dancer because she will probably know the customs, traditions and language. It also makes her a candidate for sophisticated society. Before, when *devadasis* did it, people had no respect for dancers; they treated it as cheap. People would look lustfully at the dancer, not at the dance as art. Now people are cultured and they go for art.

Continuing a dance career after marriage was not always a straightforward decision. A dancer I interviewed said that she decided against dance after marriage. Although her husband did not object, there would have been important repercussions for the whole family if she had continued. In particular, it was not deemed socially acceptable in the 1930s for a married woman to display herself in public. Besides there was her step-daughter's marriage potential to consider:

It was a second marriage for him, he was a widower of forty-four and I was sixteen. He married me after having seen two or three of my programmes and because I was a good dancer.He wanted me to continue danceing but I myself stopped. His daughter was the same age as me and my own stepdaughter looked more mature than me. In those days, it would not have been proper for both the mother and daughter to be dancing. My stepdaughter was of marriageable age and it would have hurt her marriage chances if I danced in public.

There are also accounts of *devadasis*, after a varied career dancing in the temple, during marriage celebrations and in the films, stopping and getting married.

Thus dancing before marriage was acceptable but not afterwards. Dancers had various strategies to change this. One high caste dancer told me that before her marriage was arranged there had been no discussion about her continuing to dance. When I asked what would have happened if her husband had forbidden her to dance she replied: "I would have discussed this with him and tried to make him understand that dancing was important to me. For me dancing has been something different; I never thought I would get married and settle down."

She saw it as her duty to get married in order to facilitate the marriage of her brothers and sisters: "I did not want to get married. It was only to clear the way for my brothers and sisters that I agreed."

It appears she was fortunate. Another high caste dancer remembered her dancing as being the cause of continuing tension with her husband's family. She recalled her father's words at the first meeting with her prospective husband's family: "My father said, "I have ensured that my children were given good instructions in dance and music and I would like them to continue to dance and lecture about dance".

Before the wedding her prospective in-laws had made it very clear that they did not want her to dance. Her father, however, had insisted on it and the marriage took place.

We [my father and I] thought there would be some give and take. I realized that my in-laws and husband did not like my performing at all. However, if there was a good offer for a program I did it. My husband allowed me, but not wholeheartedly; there is always some tension. The whole feeling was that it was not liked.

Her tenacity paid off: "I was doing it because my father had taken so much trouble to encourage my training. This art does not come to everyone. Even if girls are talented they do not get good teachers. I had one. I love this art."

Another high caste woman remembered her brief encounter with dance growing up in a joint family, in the 1950s, where the wishes of the grandparents had to be followed. It also reflects the perceived shame that could have fallen on the family if she had continued: "We were all dancing for the school celebration. My grandmother, seeing me perform for the first time, rushed on the stage and announced that I will not appear on the stage again and dragged me into the audience. That was the end of my dance career."

The comments of Leela Ramanathan [brahmin] regarding her dance lessons in the late 1930s in Bangalore credit her mother with foresight and hint at the pressure put on her to stop her daughter from taking classes.

My mother was a brave woman. She said to our relatives and friends, "She is a good dancer. Let her learn." So Puttappa came to our house and gave me lessons. I later performed in public and Ram Gopal saw me and invited me to be his student. He was recruiting girls from good families to form his dance troupe.

For another non-hereditary dancer in 1949 the reaction varied among family members. She was allowed to take dance classes but they were not mentioned at home where the women of the household were against it.

My father was interested but his mother did not allow it. My grandmother was afraid I would join the films. Father was a music scholar and he was broad minded. The teacher lived in old Mambalam and my father took me and I went regularly. My mother was not in favour but she never objected.

Clearly families were often divided on the issue and the outcome was determined by who wielded the most influence.

For many girls, dance before marriage was part of their education but after marriage it usually could only be sustained in conjunction with having one or more children, particularly a male child, and balancing home duties with their career.

A brahmin dancer, based in Madras, who married in 1965 recalled:

When I was first married my family did not want me to dance. I did not stop, except for nine months for the birth of each of my sons. My in-laws knew that I was a dancer when I got married and in the beginning they did not like me to give many recitals. Now they don't mind because my sons are grown up.

Another of those with whom I spoke met her future husband when he came to watch his sister's classes. The marriage was arranged on the basis of "no dance after marriage". But she kept up her practice and after her two sons were born she proved that she could manage the house and not upset her husband's life so that she was able to pursue an active career as a teacher and performer.

Her experience contrasts with that of the well-known dancer and teacher, Mrinalini Sarabhai, who had the wholehearted support of her husband:

I met my husband when he was studying and he was deeply interested in dance ... I came to Ahmedabad in about 1948. We registered the dance school but for many years I didn't have any students. In those days nobody danced in Ahmedabad and in North India people had hardly heard of Bharata Natyam. I started a small school and for 3-4 years there was only the teacher and myself. Muthukumar taught me and I gave recitals all over.

Gradually she achieved some success. The most important ingredient was the fact that she was married, and from a respected family, yet another example of the need to make the dance respectable: "I gave them the right atmosphere. The fact that I was married into a very good family, and after marriage I was dancing, helped a great deal." By 1984, the enrolment in her school had grown to five hundred and it was one of many in Ahmedabad.

The debate over arranged marriages, which are the norm over self-arranged, or "love" marriages, featured for many of the girls. Because dancers were in contact with a greater variety of males than if they were not dancers, this provided opportunities for them to be attracted to, and get to know a potential husband. When love blossomed there were mixed reactions. One example is that of the brahmin dancer and teacher, the late Lalita Shastri. Her husband was a professional *vina* player and they met after he saw her perform. It was their decision to get married. She explained that as they were both from the same caste (brahmin) their families did not object. Her comment shows that her family recognized the need for art in her life: "My father was happy because at least I would marry an artist."

Her husband also recognized that she should maintain a link with the dance: "My husband gave me permission to teach. He likes the art. From the beginning there have never been any restrictions."

Caste is a major consideration in marriage. For one couple, even though they were of the same caste, there were difficulties. Their comments confirm that self-selecting one's partner was not normally sanctioned and the individual's wishes had to be subservient to the betterment of the family and the whole community. The husband of the dancer and teacher, Malati Srinivasan recalled:

I knew her family very well as I was living next door. We decided to arrange our marriage ourselves but there was some objection from the family because this type of thing was just not done. We finally got married in 1961. Brahmins are very conservative. In fact we are both brahmin. She is a Saivite Iyengar and I am a Vaishnavite Iyer.

Once again what mattered was the effect on the marriage prospects of the other siblings.

Both our families objected to our marriage, but mine more than hers. As I was the oldest in the family, all my younger sisters' marriages could have been hampered. It was only after I managed to get my younger sisters and brother married off that I could go ahead with my own marriage and that meant waiting for 15 years. Malati's brother and sister got married after us and there wasn't any problem.

The effect of marriage on the whole family was mentioned often. Another example was the non-hereditary dancer, Kamala Lakshman, a brahmin who danced in the 1930s on both the stage and in the films, beginning at the age of four. As the eldest daughter she was very aware of her responsibility to marry even if it also meant that she had to give up her dance career which had been a part of her life since she was about four years of age: "My mother said that I should give up the dance because I had two sisters who were to be married.

In south India it is like that. If the first daughter is not married the other daughters will suffer. No one will come with proposals for them." Kamala also experienced a shift in attitude: "Things are changing now. Now the boys want girls who are well versed in dance and music, and the in-laws say, Yes, it is good that she is a dancer. Before, it was a taboo." Earlier this was not the case:

It counted against me that I was a dancer when my first marriage was arranged. My husband was also an artist and the same caste as me, a brahmin, so my mother arranged it and thought it would work out. It didn't.

In 1964 she married again and commented that her second husband was willing to make concessions.

Naturally his family wanted me to give up dance; everyone did in those days. My in-laws said, "You must give up dance." I did and for two years, 1964-66, I did not perform. After that my husband said, "Yes, you can now dance. You have been dancing since you were four, so why give it up." Even though his parents told me to stop he sided with me. But when they learnt that he was on my side they encouraged me.

Her love of the dance, which was her profession, is evident, "It was discussed and agreed before both marriages that I give up my dance. The first time I gave up films and performances. I felt very sad that I had to give up the dance. I prayed to god, why can't I just do what I enjoy? After all it is not a sin to dance."

In 1986 the late V. Ramaiya, an important dance teacher and *nattuvanar* summed up attitudes regarding life for women after marriage: "Brahmin husbands have a broader outlook than *isai vellala* husbands."

Many traditional families now regret that they discouraged their daughters and wives from dancing. A hereditary teacher related:

I did not allow my wife to continue with her dance after we were married. Later, after I changed my mind, I could have taught her at home, but as we were living on the second floor and the dance is very noisy, it was impossible. I did not have a proper place to teach, so I went to my student's homes. I now feel it was a mistake not to have encouraged my wife.

Many dancers were aware of the special tensions that marriage and a performing career brings, in particular in India where social expectations are stringent on women. A high caste dancer commented on her marriage to another dancer which had ended in divorce: "Yes I suppose it was a love marriage. There were problems as we both travelled a lot, and worked in a highly competitive situation. It is very difficult to combine marriage, as it works in our society, with a career." There were many comments regarding social pressures:

In India they don't date as they do in the West so when they are growing up they have to concentrate on other activities such as dance or other arts. Some men like dance and it is according to your luck if you can continue dancing after marriage. Some men say they will allow it and then change their mind. Some Indian men don't like others praising their wife.

Some parents believe that there is a time for marriage and it is important to know when to cut off a daughter's career and move on to marriage and a family, even if it means abandoning a successful dance career. One mother, who had also been a dancer, was happy that she had been able to get her daughter married. The daughter's wishes to remain single were no longer considered when she reached her mid-thirties.

I did not want my daughter to be a professional dancer. I wanted her to be a housewife. How long can a dancer continue to give programmes. After a certain age one must see what is a family, what are children, what is a husband, what is the work of a woman. Besides, what is the use of dancing today? The dance is such that you have to pay the organizers for a programme. I do not want to have her pay. A friend of the groom met my daughter and then rang up and the whole marriage was arranged in four days. It is better that way.

Those who have encouraged their wives to continue with the dance are usually more satisfied if they teach, as this brings in a stable income. The teaching can be done at home where they can combine it with household duties. In fact dance is so popular that classes taught in the home can considerably augment a family's income.

Some dancers have been allowed to remain single. All of them, from both hereditary and non-hereditary families, reported that their families respected that it was their choice, and they were happier unmarried.

COUPLES PERFORM THE DANCE
OF THE *DEVADASI*

In the 1940s a few non-hereditary men and women began to perform. These dances differed from the earlier *devadasi* duos ('double dance') in that the dancers did not necessarily perform the same movements which was usually the case when two girls danced together. Instead, they performed as a male and female with all the interaction that this presents. They could be married couples, but not always. Pattakudi Ramaswamy, a brahmin, remembered that in the 1940s there were many dance programmes in conjunction with marriage celebrations. In 1948, he danced at a wedding along with a brahmin girl. He was dressed as a man, unlike some other men such as K. Muthukumar who dressed as girl. At this time it was an innovation: high caste men and women dancing together, each with their own sexual identity.

Prominent among the brahmin dancer couples in the 1940s were U.S. Krishna Rao and his wife Chandrabhaga Devi. Their performances together extended the possibility of combining marriage and a dance career. As a married woman, Chandrabhaga Devi was open to a great deal of criticism, as was her husband for allowing her to dance. On July 7, 1941, Krishna Rao received a fourteen-page anonymous letter attacking him. The author touched on several taboos which recurred during this transitional period: dancing in public, receiving payment for dance, encouraging one's wife to dance and the low status of dancers. These were characteristic of attitudes among many high-caste persons at the time.

You are not content to dance for amusement but you also aspire to become a public dancer. ... You want fame through dancing. Infamy be on such aspirants. I am however writing these words of caution just to prevent you from becoming a public dancer or professional dancer. Even your benefit performances are no less wrong.

The fact that Krishna Rao, a college graduate, would not only teach dance and give recitals, but accept payment for this was shocking. To be an amateur, and not accept payment filtered the perception of one as a "professional"

It [dancing] is not the mode by which an educated fellow should acquire money. If you have any knowledge of our old scriptures you will know that the dignity of a dancer is no higher than that of a beggar. Whoever earns his money by singing, dancing, playing on an instrument, on the stage ... shall be classified as *sudra* (person without caste).

The author made one concession: he allowed dancing in private for god, but even that had risks. His suggestion that Krishna Rao forced his wife to dance in public suggests that he was using her for immoral purposes and underlies the point that dancing in public was not acceptable for a respectable, high caste married woman and she was being forced to dance against her will. He also pointed out rightly, that the actions of an individual can adversely affect the whole extended family.

If you think you will cultivate god by dancing these dances by yourself, do it in a lonely place, but not a public performance. It may be by some, that dancing is recognized as a high art. Dance encourages impurity of person and degenerates the character of the person. To have made your wife dance in public is irreparable and unpardonable. This much I hope will suffice to convince you that the dance is nothing great for which you must sacrifice your nobility and purity as well as that of your family.

Their status as brahmins did not protect the Krishna Raos from the general contempt for dance.

THE ABOLITION AND THE REVIVAL

During the latter part of the nineteenth century a public campaign to abolish the institution of *devadasi* began.[3] With the passing of the *Devadasi* Bill, in 1947, dancing in the temples of Tamil Nadu was no longer permitted as a part of temple ritual. Its ultimate demise has been attributed to public pressure, largely instigated by Dr S. Muthulakshmi Reddy (1886-1968). As well as being a member of the Madras Legislature Dr Reddy was also a medical doctor. According to A. Srinivasan (1984) Muthulakshmi Reddy's mother was a *devadasi* and her father a brahmin.[4]

The penalty imposed if a girl was dedicated after November 26,

1947 was stipulated as follows: either six months imprisonment or a fine of five hundred rupees, or both for any person of the age of sixteen or more who dances in contravention of the provision.

Dr S. Muthulakshmi Reddy's comments verify that, although she, like many at that time, was very much in favour of banning the dance in temples, she was also in favour of encouraging the dance, but as an art form.

Encouragement of fine arts must not be at the expense of good morals and health of the race... The arts must be restored to their original purity and grandeur so that respectable, good and virtuous women may come forward to learn and practise them so as to inspire and elevate society to a higher plane of thought and action (The *Hindu*, December 2, 1932: 5).

Muthulakshmi Reddy's call for a 'revival' was followed by the non-hereditary dancer/teacher Rukmini Devi founding a dance school, Kalakshetra (1936) where she "improved" the dance (Sarada 1985).

The overlap that occurred between the traditional and modern phases of the dance is illustrated by the fact that in 1925, T. Balasaraswati, presented her debut recital (*arangetram*) which formalized her entry into the *devadasi* profession. A year before, Uday Shankar performed Indian dance with the ballet dancer Anna Pavlova in London. Clearly the *devadasis*, for whom dance was their hereditary profession, were still being trained and showed a confidence that they would pursue it as a career, at the same time as the dance was being adapted and presented in a non-traditional context. The transition period when both hereditary and non-hereditary dancers were dancing was full of contradictions. While agitation against the dance in its traditional setting continued, Uday Shankar and his dance troupe were based in Europe[5] performing and touring, as was Ram Gopal[6] a little later. Abroad these dancers were meeting many famous and established dancers and were generally accepted on an equal footing with the greatest western artists. This is less often the case today.

We have few records of the extent of the activity before 1947. What little evidence there is, suggests that much more dance activity was going on than has generally been recognized. Testimonies from members of the *devadasi* community whose relatives were performing, and the number of them who began their training either just before, or after 1947, when temple dancing was officially banned, both seem to indicate a confidence in the survival of the art, or at least a desire to fulfil their hereditary obligations and maintain their rights and status. The comments in *Sruti* Dec 1986/ January 1987 that "no one could claim to have revived Bharata Natyam, as it was quite alive and well", are all too true. I found it significant that Ram Gopal did his last all-India tour in 1947 and left to be based in England (Gopal 1957).

Possibly, outside of Madras, the dance was better thought of than the present literature suggests. Because dance was a perfectly normal event little was recorded. Consequently, we must rely on recollections.

Descriptions of contact with the dance before 1930[7] give contrasting impressions regarding its status and the status of the audience. Rukmini Devi's biographer, S. Sarada, commented on the first occasion that she saw Rukmini Devi perform in Madras in 1935: "I had never witnessed a dance performance before, as women from good families did not go out to witness them, either in the temples, or elsewhere."

Greatly impressed by Rukmini Devi's dance and vision of it, S. Sarada was later to become an important teacher and dance notator at Rukmini's dance school, Kalakshetra.

Not all high caste women were so sheltered. Rajam Iyer, a brahmin lady living in Mayavaram, a town in south India, prior to 1934, remembered a different attitude to the presence of women at dance recitals. She commented about her youth: "Whenever a dancer performed anywhere in Mayavaram I was sure to be there, in weddings and temple festivals" (*Sruti* No 45/46).

In 1934, her daughter, Kamala (Lakshman), was born and five years later, in 1939, danced on the concert stage, and in films. She immediately charmed south Indians, and become the darling of Madras. Another event in the mid-1930s that helped to prepare for the acceptance of Bharata Natyam was a performance by T. Balasaraswati, in 1934, at the All India Music Concert in Banaras. The universal appeal of the dance was emphasized by the fact that persons of non-Indian origin such as the American dancer, Ragini

Devi, also performed Bharata Natyam at the same music concert. Ragini Devi's daughter, Indrani Rehman, informed me that both her mother and T. Balasaraswati danced the same descriptive piece, *"yahi madhava"*, an *ashtapadi* from the *Gita Govinda*. Presenting Bharata Natyam at the Banaras Conference helped to give it recognition in north India.[8] The Nobel Prize winner, Rabindranath Tagore, presided over the conference which helped to enhance the respectability and prestige of the dance. A noted educator, Rabindranath Tagore had already introduced dance as part of the curriculum in his school by 1917 (Massey 1967: 61).

It was the exception to find parents who would support their child's aspiration to become a dancer. The influential writer Kalki is an example of someone who first took a vow not to see the dance. Later, he not only became sympathetic to the art, but enrolled his daughter Anandi in dance classes and encouraged her to perform on stage. Likewise the reactions in the 1930s of the internationally recognized male Bharata Natyam dancer, Ram Gopal's parents when he announced his intentions were not enthusiastic:

She [his mother] never dampened my spirit, or my desire to dance. But father! I was up against a stone wall. His son take to dancing? That ignoble and vile art that had so fallen from its original pedestal and purity, which only temple prostitutes danced and offered other services with their body (Gopal 1957:21).

This makes quite a contrast to his own description of the dance of two *devadasis* in the 1930s: "In Kumbhakonam[9] I saw Varalakshmi and Bhanumati ... it [their dance] was as delicate as the finest brush strokes of a Mogul court painter, as refined and languid as the temple frescos of Ajanta. They made an unforgettable impression on me" (Gopal 1957: 38).

MAKING THE DANCE RESPECTABLE

In the early days of the British rule in India, dance was often included at state functions. In 1791 the Governor of Madras entertained the Nabob of the Karnatic after dinner with 'dancing wenches' (Thurston 1909: 131). But official patronage was soon to be withdrawn, as this circular from a European official writing at the beginning of the twentieth century illustrates:

During my *Jamabandy* (land revenue settlement) tour people have sometimes been kind enough to arrange singing or dancing parties, and, as it would have been discourteous to decline to attend what had cost money to arrange, I have accepted the compliment in the spirit in which it was offered. I should, however, be glad if you would let it be generally known that I am entirely in accord with what is known as the anti-*nautch* movement in regard to such performances (Thurston 1909: 132-3).

The importance of this letter for his career becomes clear when we learn of the unanimous decision taken in 1905 by the executive committee planning the reception for the Prince and Princess of Wales visit to Madras that "there should be no performances by *nautch* girls at the entertainment to be given to their royal highnesses" (Thurston 1909: 133).

In the 1930s E. Krishna Iyer (1897-1968), a lawyer, took it upon himself to encourage "respectable" audiences in Madras to support Bharata Natyam. He had seen a lot of dance in Kallidai Kuruchi, the village in Tamil Nadu where he grew up. His comments support the view that there was a lot of dance at the village level. In 1926, when already a trained lawyer, he decided to study the dance and present it in traditional *devadasi* dress[10] before respectable audiences (Chatterjee 1979: 5-6; *Sruti* No. 30,40). Although it might seem outrageous for a man to dress in female attire, there were precedents for brahmin males to perform like this in the Bhagavata Mela/ Kuchipudi dance style.

Certainly there were early references to royal women studying dance particularly at the Vijayanagar court (Saletore 1934, II: 409-10). There was, however, no recent historical precedent for high caste women, from socially prominent families, to become dancers, perform on the concert stage and keep their status as high caste, respectable, married or marriageable women. Consequently their association with the dance was generally looked down upon.

The "revivalist" E. Krishna Iyer endeavoured to change this as he was aware that it was absolutely essential to involve this social group if the status of the art was to be lifted. He began by presenting the dance in a socially acceptable venue. As a result of his efforts, the first dance recital presented by the Madras Music Academy was by two *devadasis* (P.K. Jivaratnam and P.K. Rajalakshmi) on 15 March, 1931. Many more recitals at the Madras Music Academy followed (chapter 8). The repercussions to all this activity were enormous. One of the most important was that Rukmini Devi (brahmin), after seeing the dance recitals of P.K. Jivaratnam and another *devadasi* M.D. Gauri at the Music Academy "resolved to revive it" (*Sruti* Dec., Jan. 1986-87: 30; Sarada 1985: 43). Soon after, Rukmini Devi, a married[11] woman from a "respectable" family, gave her first public dance recital. In the same decade, Kamala Lakshman,[12] another brahmin, barely five years old, gave hers. From this point on, the brahmin community had two models, the one a married woman, the other a child. The dance was no longer a hereditary profession, nor were there restrictions on marital status or age for the debut recital.

NOTES

1. Dance concerts in India are increasingly not charging admission. Many dancers are not being paid; some are actually paying to perform.
2. The seven Indian classical dance styles are: Bharata Natyam, Kathakali, Kathak, Kuchipudi, Odissi, Manipuri and Mohini Attam.
3. Other reforms dealing with the status of women were the abolition of *sati*. See A. Srinivasan 1984.
4. Narasimhan (1986: 13) states that both Dr Reddy's parents were brahmins. For a more detailed look at Dr Reddy's achievements see Basu 1986.
5. Bowers (1953: 1) predicted that tourists would help in the dance revival. This is confirmed in *Sruti* (May 15, 1985, 16.S, 1984: 3) where the Khajuraho Festival is described.
6. Bowers (1953: 20) "Ram Gopal was the first male dancer to revert to the ancient tradition depicted on temple sculptures and perform Bharata Natyam both in India and abroad. See Ambrose (1950: plate xiv) which shows Ram Gopal in 1948 with Nijinsky, and in Paris, and Stockholm.
7. Further evidence is provided in the documented activity in George Town, a section of Madras City during that period (*Sruti* 1984: 14-15).
8. Bharata Natyam was not as insular as it would appear. In particular, *devadasis* from Tanjore had been attached to the court of Baroda from the

mid-nineteenth century.

9. Kumbhakonam is usually spelt Kumbakonam.

10. E. Krishna Iyer studied the dance with Madurantikam Jagadambal a disciple of Samu *Nattuvanar*, who is the maternal grandfather of the late V. Ramaiya whose son Samraj teaches dance in Madras.

11. Rukmini Devi married an Englishman, Arundale. This, she said, caused a far greater stir amongst the brahmin community than her dance, although it too was suspect. She and Arundale were forced to leave the country and live in Australia immediately after their wedding. It was during their exile that Rukmini Devi first became interested in the dance (pers. comm. 1986).

12. Kamala Lakshman first danced Kathak, another classical Indian dance style. Later she studied Bharata Natyam and this was to be the style for which she was, and continues to be, famous.

3 The Sacred and Profane in Bharata Natyam

SRINGARA/BHAKTI

Bhakti or devotion is the dominant mood in all Hindu classical performing arts and many would argue that it is their *raison d'etre* (Subramaniam 1980). The manifestation of *bhakti* is usually couched in the language of romance (*sringara*). Its ultimate goal is realized through ecstatic union with god: "The supreme Bhagavan (God) took on the form of a lover so that the devotee could gain access to the sacred, the infinite, and eternal through expression rather than suppression of earthly desires" (Siegel 1978: 22). In many instances the poetic metaphor and analogy used is of the soul in search of god. "Human love, physical passion, became the perfect analogy for divine love, the spiritual passion. As secular language was used to describe religious love, so too was religious language used to describe secular love" (Siegel 1978: 6).

These concepts permeate the lyrics of the songs to which Bharata Natyam dances are set. Among practitioners of Bharata Natyam there is controversy around how devotion is expressed. Some dancers and critics feel that *bhakti* should be expressed through an erotic interpretation of *sringara*, while others support an interpretation which suggests surrender to the deity—something less physical and more distant. The nature of *bhakti*, the appropriate metaphor for it and the symbolic language (*abhinaya*) used to express it, have been the subject of vigorous debate within the south Indian dance community for over fifty years.

CONVENTIONS FOR PERFORMING *SRINGARA*

Sringara is one of nine sentiments (*rasas*) that may be portrayed in the expressive portions of Bharata Natyam.[1] Understanding the erotic component (*sringara*) of Bharata Natyam and its role in the dance requires familiarity with both the function of the dance prior to the revival, and the social changes that have taken place among practitioners. The attitudes and perceptions which arise from the dual role of the *devadasi* as both ritual specialist and courtesan, are essential to understanding and interpreting *sringara* inherent within the expression of *bhakti*.

In the repertoire of *sadir*, before the 'revival', the expression of *bhakti* appears to have been largely through *sringara*. Central to the expression of *sringara* is the expression of the experience of different psychological states. These are the result of the presence or absence of one's beloved. In the dance repertoire the beloved is usually a very personal deity, or patron, such as a ruler or landlord. The songs are addressed to him and the dancer enacts their intimate relationship. This theme is still considered by many to be the most appropriate for the majority of descriptive dances in Bharata Natyam. There is, however, a growing resistance to these themes, which have been described as "degrading to the modern woman and irrelevant".

The situations and emotions that are portrayed use the convention of the eight idealized heroes and heroines (*nayaka-nayika*). Of the eight *nayikas*,[2] only one is experiencing a state of joyous love brought on by being united with her beloved. All the other *nayikas* describe anxiety at being separated from him.[3] The classification of the eight *nayikas* are as follows: *vasakasajjika*, the one who arranges everything for receiving her beloved; *virahotkanthita*, the one who longs and pines for him; *proshitapatika*, a more extreme state of the latter who waits for her beloved who is abroad; *vipralabdha*, the maiden who is upset as her lover has not been true to his word; *khandita*, the angry mistress; *kalahantarita,* the one who is estranged because of jealousy; *abhisarika*, the one who ventures forth because she cannot wait for her beloved to arrive; and the last, *svadhinapatika*, joyous after their union (Raghavan 1963; K.S. Srinivasan 1985).

The erotic sentiment is believed to be heightened during separation and aroused by expectations of future fulfilment. Hence *sringara* is dominated by love in separation (*viraha*).[4] Love in separation, is an analogy for the soul in search of the divine and is the most popular theme in all Indian art: painting, music and dance. It dominates the themes of the traditional Bharata Natyam repertoire (K. Vatsyayan 1968).

HISTORICAL PERSPECTIVE, EVOLUTION OF *SRINGARA*

The absorption of *sringara rasa* into the existing Bharata Natyam repertoire originated with the *bhakti* tradition which "equated the deity in the temple with a munificent king" (Subramaniam 1985: 31).[5] Later texts (*agamas*) legitimized this concept of a god-king and also established dance and music as one of the prescribed ways to worship in a temple (*upacharas*). As many temple dancers also performed in the courts, the groundwork was laid for the dance repertoire to include the expression of erotic desires equally towards god and king. Here began the ambiguity about interpreting *sringara* in Bharata Natyam; more so if the king was named after a deity. The traditional repertoire includes lyrics which describe an intensely personal relationship between the dancer, who takes a female role, and a male god or patron.

Sringara can be portrayed in a variety of ways. The form appropriate to Bharata Natyam has been open to debate. Both sides believe that *sringara* is the expression of a poetic metaphor for union with god, but differ about its appropriate expression. The debate has centred around two important personalities in the dance. One was a hereditary dancer, T. Balasaraswati (1918-84), who, during her lifetime, came to epitomize the hereditary/traditional style. The other, Rukmini Devi (1904-86), founded Kalakshetra, one of the most important and influential dance schools in Madras. Because Kalakshetra has produced many important dancers, Rukmini Devi may be regarded as one of the most influential of the "revivalists" in shaping modern Bharata Natyam. These women were from opposite ends of the social spectrum, the former a *devadasi*, the latter a brahmin. Both were performing during the revival period 1930-50; T. Balasaraswati by virtue of her birth, and Rukmini Devi out of personal choice. Both had active performing careers. T. Balasaraswati gave her first recital at the age of seven in 1925. She continued to perform until her death in 1984 at the age of sixty-six. Rukmini Devi's first recital was in 1935 when she was thirty-one years of age. One of her last performances was in 1950 in New Delhi at the age of forty-six (Sarada 1985).

By virtue of their very high profiles, the *sringara/bhakti* debate became practically synonymous with the views of T. Balasaraswati and Rukmini Devi. Both were asked frequently to comment upon their understanding of the depiction of *sringara* in dance. Confusion arises from the fact that they expressed seemingly similar views: both stressed the importance of *bhakti*. Their statements must, however, be interpreted in the light of the different meaning that they attached to specific terms. When Rukmini Devi spoke of *bhakti* she intended formal devotional gestures of supplication offered to a deity; if T. Balasaraswati used the same term, it included *sringara* as a form of *bhakti*.

Songs in praise of secular patrons (*nara-stuti*) were continually attacked by some non-hereditary dancers. Rukmini Devi challenged the accepted practice of showing equal deference when addressing a deity or patron. She limited the expression of *bhakti* in the dance to hymns addressed to an explicitly named deity expressed in non-sexual metaphors. It was partly her omission of songs that included sexual metaphors, or her interpretation of them, using hand signs and facial gestures devoid of eroticism, that created and defined the Kalakshetra style of dance.

Hindu thought abounds in sexual metaphors. Hence their explicit rejection brought Rukmini Devi's artistic vision into conflict with many hereditary practitioners:

The dance was much patronized by Kings, zamindars (land- owners), and other rich men ... *Varnams* (dance compositions) and songs that were used for the dance were often in praise of patrons ... I found the king described as if he were God. I had definitely decided that the dance was essentially spiritual and I could not accept that which had gone away from the true spirit of Bharata Natyam (Rukmini Devi 1985: 18).

In other words an essentially spiritual art could not be erotic. The reference to the "true spirit" of Bharata Natyam also suggests that, for Rukmini Devi, the dance possessed a devotional core, around which eroticism was a degenerate accretion. This attitude was fundamentally at odds with much of Hindu religious art. Rukmini Devi insists, however, that she was faithful to the core of tradition:

I learnt fully in the traditional way and with great love for the pure and traditional Bharata Natyam. I must say that I could not accept all I found. We are very anxious to follow the traditional way, but within the tradition there are elements that are of permanent beauty, as well as those that have to be discarded. Even in the days when today's modernism was absent, there was much in the dance that had to be eschewed (Rukmini Devi 1985).

She therefore took a conscious decision to create a dance that was acceptable to her vision of it: "I found a great deal to be reformed and I could understand why the dance was considered improper ... with the enthusiastic guidance of Shri Meenakshisundaram[6] Pillai (her dance teacher) I entered into the creative spirit" (Rukmini Devi 1985: 18).

Rukmini Devi believed that *sringara* in Bharata Natyam was best expressed when sublimated to the expression of her perception of *bhakti*. Because of this, the poetry of Kshetrayya, an important composer in the traditional Bharata Natyam repertoire, posed problems (Sarada 1985: 46; Seetha 1981). Eventually her repertoire was stripped of those pieces involving explicit eroticism and others were carefully edited: "Rukmini Devi's dance repertoire was unique and varied ... She expressed the *Sringara-Rasa*—the emotion of love fully, but in its most refined form, without any trace of vulgarity" (S. Sarada 1985: 45).

Rukmini Devi's decisions concerning the suitability of a particular piece of music for dance appear to have been governed by consideration to whom the dance was addressed.

What might her response have been to a dance composition extolling her own virtues, that was composed and performed after her death in 1984. It is ironic that even before her death a dance composition was performed in which she was eulogized. The portrayal of Rukmini Devi as a great patron surely was in opposition to her own vision: "A new *varnam* (dance composition) on (addressed to) Rukmini Devi, who was throughout her life against *nara-stuti* or praising man, is an interesting turn of events" (*Sruti* 25 Oct. 1986: 7).

Considering the attitudes towards *devadasis* and their dance, it is easy to see why the hereditary dancer, T. Balasaraswati was usually on the defensive about her approach to the expression of *sringara*. In her address to the *Tamil Isai Sangam* in 1975, she described *sringara* as the "ruling mood of *abhinaya*". For her, "lover-beloved" songs[7] had always been an expression of *sringara*, but *sringara* that was "never carnal; ... never, never". She added: "I emphasize this because some seek to purify Bharata Natyam by replacing the traditional lyrics which express *sringara* with devotional songs [i.e. those where the imagery does not involve sexuality]" (T. Balasaraswati 1980: 100).

T. Balasaraswati has written very little and fewer visual records of her work are available: thus, much of the impact that she has had on Bharata Natyam must be judged from the reminiscences of others. In a paper[8] given at the Congress for Research on Dance (CORD) Conference in 1978 in Hawaii, she gave some insight into the gravity of the attack on sensuality in Bharata Natyam and her concern to justify the traditional approach. In her view, neither the pure dance movements (*nritta*), nor the expressive portions (*abhinaya, natya, nritya*) were to be performed in a suggestive manner:

The *nritta* part (abstract dance) is utterly bereft of sensual movements. It is a world of art all its own ... With god as the centre, all these [erotic] emotions and feelings are also divinized (sic) and elevated from the level of the sensual to that of the spiritual ... there is only pure spirit with nothing of the sensual (T. Balasaraswati 1982: 4).

I would suggest that she felt the erotic, in the context of the dance, to be without connotations of sexual arousal, but merely to be a vehicle by which extreme emotion could be projected. This is at the heart of *bhakti*.

T. Balasaraswati explains why, for her, *sringara* is the essence of Bharata Natyam:

Sringara stands supreme in the range of emotions. No other emotion is better capable of reflecting the mystic union of the human with the divine, I say this with deep personal experience of dancing to many great devotional songs which have had no element of *sringara* in them. Devotional songs are of course necessary. However *sringara* is the cardinal emotion (Balasaraswati in *Sruti* 1984, March).

Here, 'devotional songs' mean those not employing erotic imagery.

This difference in interpretation of *sringara* between T. Balasaraswati and Rukmini Devi has done much to affect the recent Bharata Natyam repertoire. In defending the use of explicitly erotic descriptive songs (*padams*), to portray *sringara*, T. Balasaraswati was explaining the aesthetic basic to the concept of *bhakti* or personal surrender to god. In doing so she was justifying not only the traditional presentation of the dance, but also the whole way of life, of which she had formed a part. This was a reaction to those who felt that, though the art itself was admirable, it was in the wrong hands when dominated by a community tainted by the associations that surrounded the hereditary professionals.

The acceptable expression of *bhakti* in the context of the dance appears to be determined by the sacredness or profaneness of the dancer who expresses that devotion. The altered impression created by Bharata Natyam in the hands of non-traditional dancers was described by E. Krishna Iyer, in a review written in 1944, of a performance by the non-hereditary (brahmin) dancer couple U.S. Krishna Rao and his wife Chandrabhaga Devi:

For once in his life he [P.S. Minakshisundaram] has been fortunate in entrusting his art in the hands of a proper and intelligent couple. Their charm, chasteness and dignity remind us of the spiritual associations.

Rukmini Devi's remarks confirmed his observations:

The *devadasi* system which had been helpful in the past to preserve the best classical traditions in dance, deteriorated. Temple ritual dances became a lifeless formality. Patronage from discerning royal courts declined and shifted to a few rich marriage parties ... the life of the *devadasi* was none too respectable (*Marg* 1963: 8).

Notwithstanding the above remarks, Rukmini Devi studied with the traditional, hereditary dance master, P.S. Minakshisundaram, who was also training *devadasis* at the same time. Presumably she would not have described his art as a 'lifeless formality'. The fact that a strong array of hereditary teachers was available to teach the dance and conduct the orchestra as soon as demand was created by the revivalists, demonstrated that the original tradition was by no means moribund. The true reason why she felt obliged to 'recreate' the dance was revealed in her final statement, that the contemporary practitioners were, "none too respectable".

Not all non-hereditary dancers wished to suppress the erotic content of the dance, or believed that the original temple dance had been free of sexual metaphor. Ram Gopal, a male non-hereditary dancer of international repute, derived a different interpretation from temple art:

Rukmini ... has bleached Bharata Natyam ... we worship the *linga* (male sex organ) and the *yoni* (female sex organ). That is sex. How can we deny sex between a man and a woman? How can you not feel that erotic drive? It is a charge between human beings.

He looked to the sculptures and bronzes associated with temple worship to assist him in creating his dance costumes.

I am going to follow the bronzes in the temple. I have a beautiful figure. Rukmini Devi used to say, "where do you get the ideas of dancing naked?" and I would say, "where did you get the idea of going inside the temple with your eyes closed? Look at those bronzes, Siva is almost naked.

Certainly some of the costumes of the early non-hereditary dancers were more revealing than the costumes of the present-day dancers. This is in contrast to the costume worn by the *devadasis* immediately before the 'revival' which revealed very little of their bodies and did not resemble the earlier depictions of dancers in sculptures (Gopal 1957; Bhavnani 1965: plates between 26-7; Khokar 1964; Ragini Devi 1989).

In *Sruti*, March 1984, when the dance and the dance public had become more relaxed and accepting of a variety of interpretations of *sringara* Balasaraswati confidently used the term 'sanitized' to describe *sringara* which has been shorn of eroticism.

INTERPRETING THE PERFORMANCE
OF *SRINGARA*

Although the idea that the dance had degenerated in the hands of *devadasis* was repeated in most historical accounts, a description of T. Balasaraswati's dance[9] sometime in the 1940s suggested dignity and artistry rather than overt eroticism: "The hymn sung and played by the musicians had the traditional theme of Divine love, and this superb artist directed all her charms at us, and we sat spellbound whilst she played with our feelings in the way which marks out the stage genius in any land" (Ambrose 1950: 36).

Ambrose felt that the rendition of the *devadasis*, forming part of a genuine cultural tradition, was at least meaningful. She found eroticism in the hands of non-traditional performers less acceptable: "For the genuine *devadasi*, even if they transgressed the laws of contemporary society, they at least made seduction into a fine art, whereas the charlatans of the present day have resorted to lewd looks ... In other words Bharata Natyam is in danger again" (Ambrose 1950: 40).

It is generally accepted that the underlying aesthetic of the concert repertoire of the *devadasis* dance was to generate *sringara*. It was not always thought appropriate to teach the same repertoire to non-hereditary dancers. Once again the high caste non-hereditary dancer, U.S. Krishna Rao, commented on the attitude taken by his hereditary dance teacher, P.S. Minakshisundaram:

He decided that we should study the *varnam* (a dance composition), *Sami Ni Ramanave*, which is full of sensual things. He refused to teach us the poetry that accompanies the last section of the music. He said, You are too decent, you are a husband and wife ... these things were not meant for you.

Times have changed. In 1986, U.S. Krishna Rao taught his mature students that same poetry, but not the younger ones. He explained: "You see, it was all right for the *devadasis*, but the custom was that they would be offered to someone who could look after them. This occurred when they were about fourteen or fifteen.[10] They knew about life and love."

P.S. Minakshisundaram seems to have considered not only the suitability of certain lyrics for his students, but also the possible

effect when carried outside India, prefiguring the role of Bharata
Natyam as a flagship of Indian culture abroad. U.S. Krishna Rao
recorded in his diary P.S. Minakshisundaram's parting words to
him in the 1940s:

'People like you must work for this art and propagate it. That is why I have
taught you with such interest. I have taught you not only to perform but to
teach. I *have not taught to you what I teach to the devadasis*. This Bharata
Natyam must spread all over the world and bring glory to our motherland'.
Then he blessed us and sent us away with moist eyes.

One of Rukmini Devi's earliest students described the dance of
M.D. Gauri, a *devadasi*, who was teaching *abhinaya* at Kalakshetra.
Her comments make it clear that some dancers, at least, were aware
of the adaptations being made:

Rukmini took us to see the *dasi* style of dance. The expressions were not
very refined so they had to be modified, refined and reformed which
Rukmini did. Certain types of *sringara*, which they made a big issue about,
had to be eliminated because they were quite crude. Rukmini did that
beautifully. Gauri did not do that.

Initially the aspiring dancers at Kalakshetra were taught the
dances of the traditional repertoire, but as Kalakshetra developed its
own repertoire, they were replaced. For example, a particular
varnam, *Dhanike*,[11] was taught at Kalakshetra by A.Γ.
Chokkalingam, to Sarada Hoffman. Nevertheless, "We dropped
that because the *sringara* was too sensual and Rukmini Devi
thought I was too young to get into that".

Both Sarada Hoffman and U.S. Krishna Rao (non-hereditary
dancers) commented on the extreme *sringara* in *Payadar*, one of
Kshetrayya's compositions (Seetha 1981). They felt that it should
be omitted from the dance repertoire. Another non-hereditary
dancer, Yamini Krishnamurthy, stated however that it was one of
her favourite performance pieces, having studied it with M.D.
Gauri. A description of Yamini's *abhinaya* suggests that she
projected an acceptable level of eroticism: "In *abhinaya*, Yamini's
treatment of *shringar* is highly enticing. The uninhibited display of
passion within the traditional framework has been full-blooded and
enchanting" (*Marg* 1982: 167).

A non-hereditary dancer summarized the approach taken by Rukmini Devi, and her philosophy behind the purpose of the dance: "Rukmini did not want the dance to be very sexy, as the others did; she eliminated this from the dance. She wanted the dance to be sublime. ... It is a pity that some of the very highly cultured and knowledgeable people now dance these pieces, I don't know why."

The modifications made to the traditional repertoire by some of the early non-hereditary dancers were a product of the times. Today, for some they can seem dated and prudish. Most dancers now regard themselves as progressive, and are not put off by erotic lyrics. Hence, composers such as Kshetrayya are performed just as much today as earlier, although they may not be taught to the youngest students.

While the debate between Rukmini Devi and T. Balasaraswati regarding the correct depiction and interpretation of *sringara* was well documented, the majority of hereditary teachers continued to teach the traditional repertoire of *sadir*. Naturally, if the traditional repertoire was taught, then *sringara* had to be interpreted. Minakshi Sabhanayagam (non-hereditary) explained her first encounter with the depiction of *sringara* when she was nine years old:

My mother would say to my teacher (P.C. Subbarayan), "Please tell her the meaning so that she will have some expression (*abhinaya*) on her face." My teacher replied, "No need. I have told her to look at her hands, and keep a small smile on her face. She will reach an age when she herself will know and that is when the *abhinaya* will come out."

Maran (the nearest English equivalent is Cupid) is featured in many of the dance lyrics. Minakshi was confused and approached her teacher for clarification:

For two years I have been learning this dance and I still don't know who *Maran* is. At that time our Chief Minister's[12] nephew was called Mr Maran, so I inquired if he was being invoked. My teacher replied "When you yourself know who *Maran* is you will understand. Now just do what I teach you."

Today she can see the humour of the situation.

Bharata Natyam expresses certain traditional themes, and these are expressed in well established metaphors. The dance had its own conventions and traditions. But the dance repertoire that was acceptable for the young *devadasi* girl began to be questioned when the dance ceased to be a hereditary profession.

Minakshi commented on the choreography:

I can remember I had to walk to one side and sit down and look to one corner and sigh. I had no idea why I was sighing, why I was looking up there, and why those arrows were piercing my heart. ... When I look back on it I find it quite absurd.

In another dance I had to depict a girl telling a man that his beloved, was anxious waiting by her bed, for him to embrace, kiss, and make love to her. I made the actions for the bed, a kiss, and being one with him (sexual union). I just did it. I didn't feel shy.

The innocence of young girls' interpretation of the erotic component was important. If girls were to perform in public it was important that their innocence lent charm to it; an inhibited teenager could make it awkward.

Minakshi believes that is why many teachers encourage their students to present their debut recital before age ten: "At that age she will do just what she has been taught. Basically she is natural and free of inhibitions. He [her teacher] always said, that that age is a lovely age, you should not miss it."

But for the very same reason, other teachers object to teaching *sringara* to children. They contend that it is difficult, if not impossible, to teach them the nuances of highly erotic lyrics. One dance teacher from a hereditary family, Uma Dandayudapani, voiced the predicament faced by many teachers:

As you know, the themes are always the same in the *varnam* and Kama or Maran [the god of love][13] is usually depicted shooting his flower arrows and causing pain which is accompanied by the fever of desire. ... Well, many of my students think that they have been shot ... yes, and they are dying.

For girls below the age of sixteen, the imagery and the symbolism of such excessive pangs of desire are often quite outside their own experience. Some teachers also report that the young students of the 1980s have started to ask questions, whereas before they imitated

their teachers unquestioningly. Questions regarding the content of
the dance are not easy to answer. A major objection to *sringara* is
the perception by the audience that it is inappropriate for young girls
to mime erotic stories irrespective of whether or not they are aware
of their content or of the religious allegory.

SRINGARA IN THE 1980S

The debate used to be about *sringara* and how much eroticism
should be permitted in its interpretation. Subsequently however, the
suitability of retaining *sringara* as the dominant emotion in Bharata
Natyam was being questioned. Several dancers believed that the
content of the dance, the mode of expression, and many of the
traditions connected to the dance were condescending to women.
They pointed to the milieu in which the dance is studied, where male
teachers often exercise complete control, and the student is
subservient. They also object to much of the traditional repertoire
which depicts a dependent woman, unable to function in her state
of *viraha*, brought on by the absence of a man. For these dancers,
enacting *sringara* was degrading and out of place in a modern
society.[14] Chandraleka was perhaps the most prominent advocate of
this latter opinion. Her aim was to 'demystify' the dance and rid it
of its dependence on nostalgic sentiments. For this group, Bharata
Natyam in its present form is no longer relevant to modern Indian
society. They advocate a complete break with the traditional
repertoire.

MEN PERFORM THE DANCE
OF THE *DEVADASI*

The historical evidence of the ritual and artistic purposes of *sadir/
dasi attam* indicates that it was a dance style intended to express
sringara and to be performed by women. While several of both the
early, and present-day, male hereditary and non-hereditary male
teachers did perform, most of them confined their activities to

teaching. There are historical reasons for the objections to male Bharata Natyam dancers. According to the ritual function of the dance, Bharata Natyam could be performed only by women, although it was possible for men to do the dance if its purpose was artistic, or for entertainment. For many critics and connoisseurs, because Bharata Natyam emphasizes *sringara*, it is suitable only for women dancers. G. Venkatachalam (1946: 10) wrote: "Male dancers of this art are likened as widows, as harbingers of evil." This is in contrast to the otherwise auspicious role of the dance.

Yet it is clear that from the beginning of the revival the hereditary teachers had no objection to teaching high caste men whose intention it was to perform solo Bharata Natyam (*sadir*). I stress "to perform", because for generations men had been associated with the dance as teachers, orchestra conductors (*nattuvanars*) and musical accompanists but none from the hereditary families had taken an extended career as a dancer (chapter 5). Most *nattuvanars* would agree with P.C. Subbarayan's comment that although *nattuvanars* might have danced in class, the intention of their training was not to be performers: "I danced the *adavus* [basic steps] and progressed up to *alarippu* and *jatisvaram* (two dances); after that I sat down. We are teachers and conduct recitals and do not give dance recitals."

One of the main objections to males performing Bharata Natyam centres around the expression of *sringara*. The poetic conventions are not always considered appropriate for men and certain audiences may find it difficult to relate to a man expressing passion by using intensely feminine gestures and imagery. For some it is impossible to transcend the person of the dancer, even though the passion is directed primarily towards god and there are explicit philosophical precedents in the philosophy of *bhakti* where all mortals are considered to be female and god alone is male.[15]

Once again there are contradictions as there are examples of men teaching the expressive component of the dance (*abhinaya*) which is dominated by *sringara*.

The cross-sexual nature of the dance has always been present. In particular, Kuchipudi, a style originally performed only by men dressed as women and assuming female roles, has cross-fertilizationed the teaching of *abhinaya*. To my knowledge the transfer has largely been one way: Kuchipudi to Bharata Natyam. Even in the teaching of the most delicate and suggestive expressions there are examples of male Kuchipudi hereditary practitioners teaching women the erotic nuances of the songs.

In particular, Chinnaiya Naidu taught *abhinaya* to many of the early female dancers from both brahmin (Kalanidhi) and *devadasi* communities (T. Balasaraswati, M.D. Gauri). He also taught men (for example Ram Gopal and U.S. Krishna Rao). Ram Gopal remembered that he selected other aspects of the repertoire for them: "He taught me all the masculine roles. You see you can look like an emasculated eunuch if you are a male dancer."

Rukmini Devi however did train men to be dancers and some of her male students went on to present their debut recital (*arangetram*).[16]

Because Bharata Natyam has always been entertainment there are accounts of some men from hereditary families performing it. In about 1884, at the age of ten, K. Muthukumar, a dance teacher and *nattuvanar* danced, dressed as a girl, and performed with his *devadasi* sister, Kannamba. He continued this until he was twenty-seven. They performed "double dance" which mimicked the practice of two *devadasis* dancing synchronously. It was seen mainly at weddings where dance was an important event (pers. comm. Nala Najan, and Khokar, *Sruti* 1993 No. 108).

In the late 1930s, not only women, but men from non-hereditary families started to study the dance with a view to perform it. The trend of men preparing to be performers rather than just teachers added a new dimension to the already changing focus of the dance. Objections to men performing the dance are numerous. T. Sankaran, a cousin of T. Balasaraswati, was totally against men performing Bharata Natyam:

In the West male dancers have their own costume. However, the Bharata Natyam costume which has been designed for the female figure is also worn by male dancers. A Bharata Natyam dancer must have round beautiful breasts. That is one of the qualifications. A man dances, bare chested with perspiration flowing down his body. I find this offensive and indecent. The dance should also be a pleasure for the eyes.

The repertoire is full of erotic imagery, so some non-hereditary female teachers such as Kalanidhi Narayan have made a point not to teach men particular descriptive songs, "... it is difficult for a woman to explain the meaning of a *sringara padam* (song) in detail to a man" (Ranga Rao 1991: 41).

Ram Gopal's comments to me in 1984 which are given above, also indicate the need to adapt the dance repertoire to suit the male form.

Recent remarks by Jivan Pani (former Director of the dance school, the Kathak Kendra) support male dancers. He believes that the male body when it plays a female role acquires: "an identity which does not arouse physical responses in the spectator the same way as a female dancer does. The natural grace of the female is apt to draw attention to her natural endowments" (*Sruti*, 1994, 116: 8). His remarks confirm the reflections of the son of former *devadasis* when asked why the dance had to be banned:

My mother used to talk to me about these things a lot. She was married to the God. She performed rituals in the temple. Pious people said that the rituals of the dancing girls gave an evil effect. Learned people said that when lower class people saw the girls they might feel sexually excited. When brahmins took over the dance, dancers got respect.

The historical evidence of the ritual and artistic purposes of *sadir/dasi attam* indicates that it was a dance style intended to express *sringara*, erotic love, and to be performed by women; "The appearance of these women draws all eyes on them, to the utter distraction of everything else for the time being" (Dubois 1879).

One of the first non-hereditary male dancers to study with the same *nattuvanars* who trained *devadasis* was Ram Gopal. He also performed their solo repertoire. Just as parents of girls from non-hereditary families objected to them studying dance, so too did the families of male aspirants.

Ram Gopal chose to adapt and edit the traditional repertoire, very much like the female non-traditional dancers who were studying at that time. This shows how flexible and adaptable the dance teachers were. Although Ram Gopal did include items from the traditional repertoire he expanded the repertoire and had dances composed for him which reflected the *tandava* or masculine element of Bharata Natyam. Soon both men and women were performing these dances but Ram Gopal in 1984 thought such repertoire was suitable only for men. One of these dances was *Natanam Adinar*.

Natanam Adinar was composed specially for me by Minakshisundaram. I was the first to perform it. Now they don't do it properly. It should be danced by a man.[17]

It is safe to say that even today men are not accepted unreservedly by all as capable of dancing the true essence of Bharata Natyam. One of the main objections is that a man's person does not reflect the intensely erotic aspect of the dance, which for many is its true essence. The nature of this eroticism and the correct way to portray it have been discussed elsewhere but much of it centres around to whom the dance is addressed: a patron or god (chapter 9).

DISCUSSION

The interpretation of *bhakti* in Bharata Natyam is open to both erotic and non-erotic interpretations. For a small, but influential group of dancers, who reject the traditional themes of the dance, *bhakti* itself has become irrelevant. These dancers are committed to art in the Western sense, emphasizing creativity and social relevance, rather than tradition. Some dancers have questioned the suitability of retaining *sringara* as the dominant emotion for Bharata Natyam. For this group, the dance and its milieu are no longer relevant to modern Indian society. While maintaining much of the classical technique, they advocate a break with the traditional repertoire. Previously the dance had cohesion and unity of purpose, now its artistic direction is more fluid. *Bhakti*, in either its erotic or non-erotic form, is no longer its *raison d'être*. Increasingly the former associations of the dance are losing their meaning.

One step taken to make the dance acceptable included staging performances in socially prominent venues. P.K. Jivaratnam was the first *devadasi* to perform in 1931, for the prestigious and socially respectable Madras Music Academy. Several other *devadasis* also performed there making it obvious that some traditional performers maintained a classical artistic rendition into the "revival" period (chapter 8).

In the early revival period, the stereotype of the *devadasi* as a lascivious performer predominated. This view was so universal that the existence of a degenerate and sexually explicit version of *sadir* cannot be doubted. But it is also clear that there was a refined component within the hereditary tradition as personified by T. Balasaraswati and many others. With the passage of time, it was the *devadasi* attitude to *sringara*, sanctioned by tradition, that became increasingly accepted as "correct", particularly as the search for authenticity intensified. Some of the more recent non-hereditary dancers and their families still affirm that they come from a "good" family but that is more to establish their social status than the need to identify their dance as somehow different from that of the *devadasis*. Like the early revivalists, the new dancers state that their dance is purer in technique. This, however, is less to rehabilitate their art than to project the superiority of their own personal technique.

The many factors affecting attitudes towards Bharata Natyam and its presentation during the period of the "revival" are hard to evaluate now. To some, the performance of the *devadasis* was crude and overly sensual, to others it was simple and moving. Everyone studied with the same traditional hereditary dance teachers, from the *isai vellala* community. Some teachers adjusted the traditional repertoire according to the social background of their students: others encouraged their students to reproduce the traditional dances, which they believed should not be altered. The expression of certain things in the artistic sphere which could not be expressed in the social sphere was legitimized by defining it as religious. To legitimize and make *sringara* sacred the dance had to maintain a religious connection. To be in love with god could not be carnal.

The search for authenticity has led to the introduction of several quasi-religious elements in the dance. These are discussed in chapter 9. These were not necessarily part of the pre-existing tradition, but are thought of now as "traditional" in the sense that they re-affirm the religious roots of the dance.

T. Balasaraswati, who never compromised in her presentation of the *devadasi* style, was universally honoured, but rarely emulated. This is not because her *devadasi* style was not appreciated, but rather, as she trained few students, the impact of her style of Bharata Natyam has been small. In contrast, the momentum provided by Rukmini Devi in establishing Kalakshetra, where many professionals were trained, gave her interpretation of Bharata Natyam a higher profile.

As the dancers and the dance move further from the original spirit and context of the art, there is an increasing need to re-affirm authenticity. Erotic *padams* in the modern repertoire, despite their omission from the dances taught at Kalakshetra, may have more to do with the need to maintain continuity with the past than with the interests of today's dancers and audiences.

In the 1980s, with a search for greater "authenticity" in the dance, and perhaps an increase in liberal opinion, the use of *sringara* increased. With the passage of time, it is the *devadasi* attitude to *sringara*, sanctioned by tradition, that becomes increasingly accepted as "correct" leading to a revival of the original *devadasi* repertoire of erotic themes; in effect a counter revolution.

The dancers will determine if *sringara* will remain central to the dance tradition and the form that it will take. Freed of the prejudice that was once synonymous with the person of the dancer, today's dancers have the artistic licence to choose the songs that will be interpreted and the degree of eroticism they wish to portray without the same risk of public censure. The demands of audiences and the new patrons in the form of government departments of culture will also direct and shape the relevance of *sringara* to modern Bharata Natyam.

NOTES

1. There is some dispute over the number of *rasas*. Some texts such as the *Natya Sastra* list eight; others nine.
2. The classification of the *ashtanayikas* is dated to around the eighth-ninth centuries, which is later than the *Natya Sastra*.

3. See Raghavan 1963, where he gives examples of dance pieces from the repertoire of Kshetrayya for several *nayikas*.

4. Siegel remarks on the importance of love in separation. "Actual union is avoided because if the beloved and the lover become one, there is no longer any active love" (Siegel 1978: 25). Also see Hardy 1983.

5. V. Subramaniam discusses the absorption of a pre-existing secular erotic literature (*aham*), and another genre which dealt with heroism and war (*puram*), into religious *bhakti* poetry. This *bhakti* poetry was written by both the Vaishnavite poets, the Alwars, and the Saivite poets the Nayanars. See Hardy 1983, Kersenboom 1987.

6. This is an alternative spelling for Minakshisundaram.

7. She mentions the songs composed by Jayadeva and Kshetrayya.

8. Her article, published in V. Subramaniam (1980) appears to be trying to justify her art, a reaction that would scarcely have been necessary had she belonged to a higher caste.

9. Ambrose would have seen T. Balasaraswati's dance in the 1940s which indicates that Bala was in her early thirties. "I blinked to see this rather heavy, tired, hot woman, that could change herself at will" (Ambrose 1950: 36).

10. In actual fact the girls were often younger than fourteen or fifteen. See Carmichael 1904, 1910.

11. *Dhanike* was T. Balasaraswati's favourite *varnam*. She studied it with T.N. Kandappa. He had probably studied it with his teacher P.S. Minakshi-sundaram, who had almost certainly also taught A.P. Chokkalingam. For that reason some of the choreography could have been similar. Unlike Kalakshetra, T. Balasaraswati kept it in her repertoire.

12. This dancer's family was involved in politics and Mr Maran would have been a family friend.

13. Kama (Sanskrit), and Maran (Tamil) can be translated by the nearest English equivalent Cupid.

14. The confusion over the manner in which *sringara* is to be depicted is expressed by Venkataswami Naidu in his presidential address to the Madras Music Academy in 1941 (*Journal of the Madras Music Academy* 1941).

15. For several years now Keluchuran Mahapatra has been performing Odissi, a style of dance that is intensely erotic. His pièce de resistance is one of the *ashtapadis* by Jayadeva, "*Kuru Yadunandana*". A dancer/teacher (U.S. Krishna Rao) commented that this poem had no place in the Bharata Natyam repertoire because of the explicit sexual imagery in it. Keluchuran and many of the Odissi teachers did perform the dance, when they were young, as *Gotipuas*. It is from this tradition that his style of Odissi dance has been created. Although such a tradition is unknown for Bharata Natyam teachers, a parallel tradition can be found in the Bhagavata Mela dance drama tradition which has a historical link to Bharata Natyam.

16. Although today, some dance teachers such as Adyar Lakshman, do not see

any contradiction in men performing the dance, as he himself did while at Kalakshetra, his own performing career was in dance dramas in which he assumed the role of a particular male character. It has also been a tradition at Kalakshetra for men to dance male roles. In dance dramas, women also perform male roles but not *vice versa*.

17. I studied *Natanam Adinar* with K. Ellappa in 1964, and later with K.N. Dakshinamurthy, Swarna Saraswati and K.J. Govindarajan. Many women were performing it and many teachers were teaching it. See chapters 6 and 8.

4 Training of Bharata Natyam Teachers

RECRUITMENT OF DANCE TEACHERS

Until the 1920s Bharata Natyam was almost exclusively the domain of the *isai vellala* community. Most non-hereditary aspirants had to learn dance from them. The total involvement of the *isai vellala* families with dance and music until the 1940s is exemplified by the account of Naga, the wife of K.N. Dakshinamurthy, a *nattuvanar* and dance teacher. Her lineage is interspersed with dancers, teachers and musicians. Her recollections are important because they form part of an unrecorded history: "As my relative Amaniammal was a *dasi* it will not be recorded who her husband was, but she had five children. Her two daughters: one Kalyani became a dancer and another, Gunavati became a singer. All her three sons became musicians: Kandasami played the clarinet, Vaithyalingam, the *mridangam* (drum) and Pasupati, the *tavil* (drum)." Dance and music continued in the next generation:

Kalyani had four children. Her two sons were both associated with dance and music: T. Swaminathan was a dance teacher and *nattuvanar*; he received the Central Sangeet Natak Award. Krishnamurthy played the violin. Her two daughters: Rajalakshmi, and the other, whose name I cannot remember, were good dancers. Rajalakshmi's two daughters, Jivaratnammalla and Kasturi, were also good dancers.

The list is endless until the 1940s and 50s, when many hereditary families stopped training their children in both dance and music. From the early 1950s to the late 1970s, few girls from *isai vellala* families studied or performed the dance. Most dancers were from higher castes, usually academically well-educated, and often from wealthy and influential families. Teaching continued to be dominated by men of the *isai vellala* community. They were perceived as the true repositories of authenticity because their families had been associated with music and dance for generations. The education of these hereditary dance teachers was usually confined to the artistic and their families usually were neither wealthy nor influential. Socially the teachers and dancers were far apart. Thus a fairly clear division could, at one time, be discerned between the higher caste dancers and the traditional *isai vellala* teachers.

To highlight changes that have taken place in the past years, I have divided the teachers, some of whom were also dancers before becoming teachers, into two categories. The "older" category is for those born before 1942, and "younger", for those born after 1942.

Since the 1930s, and particularly in the past decade, the distinction between teachers and dancers has become increasingly blurred. Now dancers from the *isai vellala* community, as well as the more numerous examples from other castes, both teach and conduct recitals.

NATTUVANARS

The person who conducts a dance recital is known as a *nattuvanar*. Because *nattuvanars* have been central to the transmission of the dance, their background requires some explanation. Traditionally, the Bharata Natyam orchestra was led by a male *nattuvanar*, who knew the dance choreography and music intimately. He was also a senior musician and in most instances, a dance teacher. *Nattuvanars* who taught the dance and organized the music for *devadasis'* performances were also the main medium by which, from the 1930s onwards, the dance was transmitted to non-hereditary dancers.

A *nattuvanar* performs *nattuvangam*. This involves several duties: striking cymbals, one of which is approximately three, and the other two inches across, and held in either hand; uttering rhythmic syllables (*jatis*);[1] singing in the classical style of Karnatic music; controlling the tempo (*laya*) of the dance; and conducting the dance orchestra. As each of these is an art in itself, it takes many years to become a *nattuvanar*. Skill in *nattuvangam* is important for a dance teacher. Its technique is often a closely guarded professional secret. No recital of Bharata Natyam is considered authentic unless conducted by a *nattuvanar*. A recent innovation which has occurred in the last ten years is to dispense with the *nattuvanar*. This dance music usually lacks the tension and excitement that the percussive beating of the *nattuvanar's* cymbals brings.

Until the 1930s, the profession of *nattuvanar* encompassed both teaching dance and conducting dance recitals. Many still combine both activities, but there is also a tendency towards the bifurcation of roles. Today the skills to perform *nattuvangam* and conduct dance recitals have been acquired by many musicians (vocalists, percussionists and others). Because many of these new *nattuvanars* do not teach dance, the word *nattuvanar* may now be used for a specialist who only conducts Bharata Natyam recitals. At the same time, the ability to perform *nattuvangam* is an extremely important additional professional qualification for a dance teacher. With it, they are able to present public performances of their students and thus attract more students. It gives teachers full artistic and financial control over the performing situation of their students which they would not have if they had to hire a *nattuvanar*. If they lack skill in *nattuvangam*, a teacher's only alternative is to train a *nattuvanar*, in their repertoire, otherwise their students will not be able to perform. Likewise dancers need a *nattuvanar* who is familiar with their repertoire if they wish to perform.

BECOMING A *NATTUVANAR*

Knowledge of rhythm and music is basic to *nattuvangam*. Singing is an important skill. If the *nattuvanar's* voice is not very good, he/she must still have the necessary musical knowledge to direct the rest of the orchestra and be able to provide vocal accompaniment during practice and rehearsals. Many vocalists have their first professional exposure to Bharata Natyam as accompanists. While working with dancers they gradually develop other skills required to be a *nattuvanar*. Another route to becoming a *nattuvanar* is as an instrumental accompanist. Several *nattuvanars* have been violinists. By being exposed to the dance, accompanists learn the dance repertoire and may later become teachers. Because vocal training normally precedes the study of any form of Indian music, many instrumentalists also have the skills to sing for dance recitals.

Older *nattuvanars* reported that it used to be customary to have two *nattuvanars* in an orchestra—the senior and an apprentice. Both would beat the cymbals (*talam*) and sing. The apprentice usually took the dominant role in the first three pieces (*alarippu*, *jatisvaram* and *sabdam*), while the senior *nattuvanar* spoke the complex rhythmic passages in the central piece, *varnam*. Even though the student conducted the recitals he/she would very often hand over the payment to the master. Gradually the apprentice took over the master's work and the master then retired, generally leaving the big city and returning to his native village.

Nattuvanars were jealous about imparting the skills of their profession to others, at first, only a few from outside the community chose to learn. Several musicians for Bharata Natyam reported that they were not taught *nattuvangam* but "just did it". There did not seem to be any organized way for teaching the beating of the cymbals. One *nattuvanar* explained: "In the beginning I taught all my master's junior classes and gradually worked my way up. Even now I encourage my senior students to conduct my junior classes so that they will learn how to beat the cymbals as they go along." Another was completely self-taught: "I used to watch my father but he never taught me exactly how to do it. By the time I decided that I wanted to make teaching my career he had died so I just picked up the cymbals. It is not that difficult when you have grown up with it." The teaching of *nattuvangam* became institutionalized after 1944, when it began to be taught at dance schools such as Kalakshetra. At Kalakshetra it was taught along with dance, music, Sanskrit and academic subjects. The graduates of this institution, both male and female, emerged fully equipped to teach all aspects of Bharata Natyam, the practical as well as the theoretical. Because the medium of instruction was English, it was possible for them to find employment all over India and abroad. The demand for these graduates led to a trend towards acquiring a diploma to teach dance.

From the very beginning of the dance revival, higher caste women and men began to perform and teach dance, and to conduct their students' recitals. Today, persons from a wide variety of backgrounds are active as *nattuvanars*, thus eroding the prerogative of traditional practitioners. Whereas most of the early hereditary male dance teachers added the word *nattuvanar* to their name, as it identified their profession, this practice has recently gone out of vogue. Now the title of *nattuvanar* is attached only to older male members of the *isai vellala*. The late V.S. Muthuswamy *Nattuvanar* identified himself as such all his life, both in conversation and in the sign on the door of his home and studio. "Modern" dance teachers either add the prefix *vadiyar* (teacher), the Tamil equivalent for *ustad* (Neuman 1980; Kippen 1988), or guru, which has connotations of a spiritual guide. Another title is the Sanskrit term *natyacharya* (senior dance teacher), clearly a form of sanskritization. While the function of *nattuvanar* is performed by persons from various communities, those from the higher castes usually describe themselves as *natyacharya* or *guru* but not as *nattuvanar*.

SKILLS REQUIRED TO TEACH BHARATA NATYAM

To become a full-fledged Bharata Natyam dance teacher, able both to teach and to conduct recitals, takes many years. Of all the skills required, the ability to dance ranks lowest, though some teachers are, or were, dancers. Among the teachers I interviewed, only half the older generation of teachers from traditional families had undergone intensive training in the basic steps, and not all of these had proceeded as far as dancing the first two dances of the concert repertoire (*alarippu, jatisvaram*). This, however, constitutes no problem since Bharata Natyam teachers do not usually demonstrate the dance by dancing alongside their students. This is primarily because the teacher provides the rhythmic accompaniment for the class by beating a stick held in one hand on a block of wood (*tattu-kal*) while seated cross-legged on the floor. In addition, the highly codified and symmetrical nature of the dance makes it possible to demonstrate the movements with one or both hands while remaining seated. Thus a convention has grown up whereby the role of the teacher involves providing rhythmic accompaniment and a watchful eye, but does not usually include demonstrating the dance. This is despite the fact that many teachers today are, or were, dancers. The teaching methods used in the 1930s and 1940s were similar to those in evidence today. For example as Shanta Rao, one of the best-known non-hereditary dancers of the early period of the revival explained:

In his teaching of this tradition [P.S.] Minakshisundaram would never demonstrate a movement or gesture for imitation by his pupils. He sat in the corner of the room beating the *thata kulli* [*tattu-kal*, block of wood and stick] ... sometimes his face would express joy, sorrow or love, according to the mood of the song ... he might make the slightest gesture of the body or hands, giving one just a hint. It used to surprise me how much I could learn without following any actual movements demonstrated by the teacher (Ashok Chatterjee 1979: 47).

Minakshisundaram would however, often have one of his senior students demonstrate. Rukmini Devi reported that two of his *devadasi* students (P. Jayalakshmi and P.K. Jivaratnam) would demonstrate the dance for her benefit.

Although it is rare for a teacher to stand and demonstrate, there are examples of those who did so in the past (e.g. K. Muthukumar, Khokar 1964:20; Parvati Kumar), or continue to do so. In my own experience, K. Ellappa occasionally demonstrated the intricacies of a movement, while V.S. Muthuswamy regularly stood to demonstrate and make suggestions about alternative ways of arranging the steps. Muthuswamy had an active dancing career as a young boy, dressed as a girl as did his teacher K. Muthukumar. (Khokar 1963; pers. comm. Nala Najan).

ACQUIRING TEACHING SKILLS:
RHYTHMIC COMPONENT

A Bharata Natyam dance class begins with the beating of the feet. The first and most important skill to be acquired is mastery over the rhythmic component. In a dance class a wooden stick strikes a block of wood (*tattu-kal*); whereas during dance recitals cymbals (*talam*) are used. Unlike the cymbals which engage both hands, the *tattu-kal* leaves one hand free to demonstrate the arm and hand positions (*hastas/mudras*) while the other continues to beat the rhythm. This is essential during a dance class. For concerts, however, cymbals are more suitable on account of their musical quality. Both the cymbals and the *tattu-kal* are often referred to collectively as the *talam*. Both serve the same purpose, to guide the rhythmic beating of the dancer's feet. During recitals, and occasionally during a dance class, the *mridangam* (south Indian drum) is also played. When the dance is being taught, the teacher beats the *tattu-kal*, and recites syllables (*solkattus*) that accompany the dance steps (*adavus*). Once the basic steps are mastered, dance compositions, including both abstract and descriptive dances, are taught. Most of the older generation of dance teachers had received some instruction in the music of the dance repertoire while serving their apprenticeship with a senior dance teacher. Others worked as accompanists for dance recitals, before becoming *nattuvanars* and sometimes dance teachers. Knowledge of the dance, combined with musicianship, is still the hallmark of the most successful dance teachers.

VENUE OF APPRENTICESHIP

Training in dance and music for the older generation took place in an apprenticeship situation in the household of their teacher or with a member of their own family. Families with a long tradition of teaching dance usually taught all the skills required to be a *nattuvanar*. In most families in which a tradition of teaching dance had been maintained over several generations, the sons studied exclusively

with their fathers, or with a blood relation. They taught them the
basic dance steps and the vocal accompaniment. Training in
nattuvangam was given by allowing the apprentices to conduct
classes for the junior dance students of the master. Dance instruction
to potential teachers was nearly always given by immediate family
members. Hence, dance traditions may be regarded as close to
family traditions; new musical knowledge is, however, sometimes
introduced.

A greater proportion of the older generation than of the younger
generation obtained an all-round training in dance, leading directly
to working as a *nattuvanar*. This was probably linked to their
training while living in dance households. The influence of receiving
training in the teacher's household was reflected among the younger
generation teachers as well. In my experience, all the younger
generation teachers who had received an all-round training studied
with teachers who ran an institution in their own home. It gave a
greater opportunity to practice teaching dance and the allied skills
needed to enter the profession. Initially, many struggling teachers
travelled to the home of their students to teach. While this was
convenient for the student it was also their loss. Dance, when taught
in the student's home, isolates the student from the total environment
of the dance and the training is compartmentalized rather than
embracing the various aspects of the dance. Travelling to the
various student's homes was also very tiring and time-consuming
for the teacher. Subsequently some teachers, as they became more
successful, established their own institutions, within or adjacent to
their homes. The teachers with institutions belong to three different
communities: *isai vellala*, brahmin and non-brahmin. This
development re-established the situation that must have existed in
the traditional context, where the children of teacher's families
grew up in a home where dance and music was taught. P.S.
Swaminathan trained in the home of his grandfather, P.S.
Minakshisundaram, in Pandanallur. Later he lived in modest quarters
in Delhi for most of his adult life. He makes it quite clear that he was
very aware of the importance of teaching in one's own home so that
the younger generation are constantly exposed to dance and music:

"My children were never exposed to dance or music at home. I have always had to travel around Delhi giving tuitions. Now that my son is older and lives in Delhi, he has a government job, and it would be hard for him to accompany me." He lamented the shift of dance teaching from the temple towns to cities and the present policy of granting scholarships rather than the traditional *gurukulavasa* system in which the student lived with the teacher and performed *seva* for knowledge.

In the 1970s and 80s, there weren't any active artists in my village of Pandanallur. They had either given up their art, died or migrated to the big cities. I belong to a family of traditional artists (Tanjore Quartet). Now if I asked the government for a scholarship to teach my son our hereditary occupation, I would feel bad.

THE LEARNING SITUATION FOR
THE OLDER GENERATION, *GURUKULAVASA*

Musical training for the older generation of the *isai vellala* community began before the age of ten and usually involved living with their teacher (*gurukulavasa*). The student visited his/her parental home about once a month. In many cases, their own fathers had students training in the family home in the same manner. Often there were several students, at different levels of expertise, studying different skills from the same teacher (vocal, violin, dance, etc). Those students who lived in the same village as their teacher, became day scholars and spent varying amounts of time in their teacher's home. For some, there were definite hours for classes, but for others, the learning situation was less structured. T.A. Rajalakshmi remembers her early training with T.P. Kuppaiya in Tiruvidaimarudur: "He would send for us when he had free time, as we lived in the opposite house."

The musical traditions associated with Bharata Natyam were mainly passed on through the *isai vellala* and brahmin communities. Amongst the older generation there are examples of high caste persons providing vocal accompaniment for Bharata Natyam but very few examples of brahmins who conducted dance recitals before 1950. The low status accorded to the dance also degraded the *nattuvanar* profession. T.V. Venkataraman, a brahmin dance teacher said that his father T. Vitthal Iyer[2] gave him *mridangam* training but did not approve of him performing *nattuvangam*: "It is very rare to find a brahmin *nattuvanar*. My father thought that it would not be proper for me to take up *nattuvangam*. He wanted me to play the *mridangam* and be a musician, but not a *nattuvanar*."

During the revival all of the non-hereditary dancers had to study the dance from the *isai vellalas* who had a lower social status. To overcome the impurity implications of contact with them several strategies were adopted. U.S. Krishna Rao and his wife, Chandrabhaga Devi lived with P.S. Minakshisundaram, but had their food prepared by their own cook. The implications of the different communities' status are evident in Krishna Rao's remarks:

We are brahmins and he belongs to the Pillai class (*isai vellala*). In the dance class he was the boss, but after the class he would ask us to sit and he would sit below, because we are brahmins. He had to respect us. This is the greatness of the man. Only while teaching he was god.

TRAINING AND EDUCATION OF
THE YOUNGER GENERATION

Most dance teachers of the older generation had no professional qualifications other than their artistic credentials.[3] Uma Dandayudapani from a hereditary family was a university graduate. She commented on her relatives: "Long ago in our family nobody studied or did anything else outside of the tradition, just music and dance. I don't think they could read or write. From the moment they were five they were taught music or dance."

Women teachers from both hereditary and non-hereditary families are becoming more numerous as dance teachers, especially in training beginners. Some are displacing male dance teachers. Some of the reasons for this have to do with education and adapting to the new modes of teaching. Until recently, many male *nattuvanars*, from hereditary families, spoke only Tamil, which restricted their horizons. As dance is taught all over India, English, as well as regional languages other than Tamil are important. In addition many of the traditional masters had only a limited education outside of the dance. A dance teacher summed up the situation: "Now women have started teaching: they are given more importance because of language and education. These girls can speak several languages (English, Hindi, Gujarati, etc). Most *nattuvanars* know only Tamil."

As the dance becomes more academically oriented educated teachers do not feel threatened by inquiries from their students. One high caste male dance teacher was aware of his own shortcomings, "Some women have already studied dance theory before they come to a dance master, to learn the practical aspects. These women then become masters themselves. And because they ae able to explain things better, they attract more students."

The lack of appreciation for their traditional expertise was particularly upsetting for teachers who had devoted their lives to dance and music, "Many students who come to you want to learn dance but they do not know the guru's background. They do not know who we are."

These traditional masters could recognize that teaching methods were changing so that verbal communication was replacing the traditional methods. As one teacher explained: "The girls who can express themselves can impress people."

The new non-hereditary female teachers have usually trained with several traditional masters. They are also able to go beyond the traditional ways of teaching, which is mainly by rote. One non-hereditary female teacher contrasted the background and teaching methods of the older with the more recent dance teachers. She believed: "The new group of teachers are smarter, more educated, more scientific minded. I could not question my teacher. He would just look and say, carry on with your dance. All my students, however, ask me questions. I like it and I answer them."

Non-hereditary dancers/teachers who were educated extolled the importance of a well-rounded education.

They [traditional teachers] were very narrow minded. They are afraid that if they give you too much knowledge there will be nothing left for them to teach. It is like a miser hoarding his money. They are frightened. All professional musicians are like that. If you ask something they scoff and say: "You think you know a lot? You can't sing a note and you ask me questions!" They feel threatened because they have only that art. They had no other interests in life. That art brought them money, fame and land, so why should they share their knowledge?

The intimate teaching situation is an important consideration for preferring women teachers. Unmarried dance teachers may be viewed as potentially hazardous. One male teacher explained: "The students come and sit and talk to the teacher and they get to know each other. Sometimes they even discuss their troubles. Purposely for this dance field I married, otherwise how would high class people allow their daughters to study with me?"

Many of the younger generation had employment skills besides their dance, having received a more extensive formal education than their parents. More than half the males and females of the younger generation had acquired a university degree. Some teachers hoped that their children would find jobs outside dance, and most sought to ensure that their children had alternative means of earning a living. This safety net was important until the late 1970s. By the mid-1970s, the current boom in Bharata Natyam had begun; soon teaching Bharata Natyam would became a viable occupation. Members of traditional families were particularly in demand because association with them conferred an assurance of authenticity.

Kalyani, the niece of K.N. Dandayudapani, remembers growing up in his home where he taught dance: "I used to cry every day. I said, I only want to dance but my uncle, Dandayudapani, sent me to college. I was not interested in studies. I joined his group classes, and he saw my interest develop he started teaching me. My mother [who was his sister] and I lived in his house." She remembered her interaction with K.N. Dandayudapani's daughter, Uma:

Uma, was in school and was not interested in dance. I used to force her and say we must learn this art. After your father we have to do all this; it is our tradition. Her father wanted her to have a regular job. She did her B.A. in Fine Arts and then started to work in the National Textile Corporation working as an assistant manager, or something. In 1978 she started a small dance class. Now she has a large school of over three hundred students and I have a big school in Delhi.

Both women were from hereditary families which no doubt accounts for some of K.N. Dandayudapani's reluctance to teach them. Neither of these women had given a debut recital, but had studied music which is essential to teach and conduct dance recitals. They also continued to improve their musical skills after they had started to teach. I studied and performed with Uma in 1979 and was aware of the initial difficulties she encountered in establishing herself. Both these women became successful dance teachers in the 1970s. It would have been difficult earlier because of the lower demand. In the 1980s Bharata Natyam received a further boost with a veritable explosion in student numbers.

In the 1980s, with the renewed interest in the art of the traditional families, the trend has been for fathers to actively encourage at least one of their offspring. Sons were usually encouraged to take up a more steady profession. Nevertheless those who were able to maintain both careers: a regular job and that of a dance teacher— have recently been able to support themselves by teaching dance and conducting recitals full-time.

Until the late 1980s, most children of dance teachers received some training in music and/or dance, but relatively few took it up as a full-time profession. Most teachers preferred their sons to take up other professions and did not encourage them to teach dance full-time. There was sometimes tension between the "realistic" older generation, who had struggled to survive before the recent dance boom, and the younger generation who wanted to abandon their secure jobs and be involved in the dance full-time. The confidence and flexibility afforded by their academic education was not readily available to their parents, whose main education was artistic. The latter had no choice about their source of livelihood. Even amongst the older generation, those few who had obtained additional educational qualifications did not depend on teaching dance alone for their livelihood. Because they could earn a steady income with their modern occupation, they taught dance as an extra source of income in their spare time. Younger teachers mainly described their motives for making a career in dance in terms of job satisfaction. At present, teaching dance may also be more lucrative than other job opportunities.

Over the past twenty years, the number of people wishing to learn the dance has increased. Dance teachers with an academic education, and therefore other options, reported that since about 1975 they have been able to earn a living by teaching dance. Though some are still in the transition stage and combine regular employment with teaching dance, many are choosing to teach it full-time. Their reasons are that they regard teaching dance as more satisfying, although more precarious, than an office job. This trend, which involved only a small proportion of the older generation, is almost the rule for the younger generation. Education is the key to diversification.

PAYMENT

The majority of the *isai vellala* students reported paying for their training by working for their teacher. They described this barter system as performing service (*seva*) for their master. The actual tasks and duties were not fixed but included such things as: shopping in the market for vegetables and other daily requirements, running errands, escorting the teacher's children to school, washing clothes, chopping vegetables and other tasks associated with preparing food, sweeping, looking after the cows and massaging the teacher. If the student's family owned land his/her parents might give a sack of unmilled rice (paddy) to the teacher, at least once a year. Usually the teacher fed, clothed and taught the students for several years before presenting them to the public in the debut performance (*arangetram*). On that occasion the teacher would be honoured with a present (*dakshina*), which might be substantial or just a token gesture. The older generation of non-*isai vellala* generally paid cash for their dance or music training. Others rendered *seva* (service) in return for their initial training. A combination of two kinds of *seva* in return for exposure to the dance was common for musicians who had completed their musical training: doing menial chores and playing in the teacher's dance orchestra.

The majority of the younger generation from all communities paid fees for both music and dance training, when they studied with non-relatives. Generally a cash payment conferred a higher status on the student than payment with *seva*. Usually the period of training, the number of dances to be mastered and the amount to be paid, were agreed beforehand. It was the practice to pay in advance. The contract was, in most cases, honoured. The *seva* method of payment, however, was often open to abuse. C. Radhakrishna remarked: "The *seva* was much, the teaching was limited to—about fifteen to twenty minutes a day. Whatever my teacher needed I had to bring from the bazaar."

There are, however, also positive examples of *seva* being an effective method of payment. By itself, the concept of *seva* is important. Whereas previously students performed menial household tasks, today dancers from influential families are able to help their teachers in other ways such as securing railway reservations, or other favours reserved for the wealthy and influential. While *seva* can be viewed as an impediment to the professionalization of the art, it is a formalized way for the student to reciprocate for the personal attention given by the teacher.

Many dancers and teachers were quick to differentiate the circumstances of their training. For example, P.S. Swaminathan was in Pandanallur at the same time that the non-hereditary dancer Shanta Rao was undergoing training with his uncle, P.S. Minakshisundaram, and he described her as a "paying guest". Swaminathan was also specific when he confirmed that while high-caste dancers had lived in their family home, no *devadasis* would have been allowed to live there. His family, descended from the Tanjore Quartet, were distinct from other dance families, in that until approximately 1987 there is no record of their women being allowed to dance or have any professional association with it.

While the Tanjore Quartet family was adamant that no *devadasi* live in their home, T.K. Ganeshan, also a descendant of the Tanjore

Quartet, lived at the home of the hereditary dancer, T. Balasaraswati. Her family is a leading hereditary music and dance family. Balasaraswati's grandmother, Dhanammal was a *vina* player, and her mother, Jayammal, was a vocalist. Balasaraswati had two brothers who studied music: Ranganathan became a *mridangist* and Vishwanathan a flautist and singer. T.K. Ganeshan learned much of his late father's (T.N. Kandappa) dance and music repertoire from Balasaraswati and her family. He had no choice; his father died when he was eighteen and the family heritage was continued by her as his father's most illustrious student.

Among families descended from the P.S. Minakshisundaram branch of the Tanjore Quartet, none of the present teachers taught their own children until the late 1980s. On November 19, 1989, K.P. Kittappa's granddaughter, gave her debut recital (*arangetram*) in Tiruneveli and he conducted the recital. Hence an earlier prediction that the hereditary tradition would be broken in this family after the present generation may not come true. Similarly, until 1950 K.P. Kittappa earned his living as a vocalist. His father, T. Ponnaiya, had forbidden him to perform *nattuvangam* because of the stigma attached to the dance. But in the 1950s he began performing *nattuvangam*. Both these events mark a gradual elevation of the status of dance, and a decline in the stigma attached to it by traditional families. Also, the temple has been reinstated as a venue for the *arangetram* for girls from all communities, including that of the *isai vellala*.

GENDER ROLES: PERFORMING/TEACHING

Attitudes within the *isai vellala* community towards the participation of their female members in the dance contrast sharply with those of practitioners who have come from outside the community. This has been an important factor in changing the role and position of traditional families among dancers and teachers of Bharata Natyam. Initially, dance orchestras were usually composed entirely of male musicians. Before the microphone was introduced, it was thought that male voices were more suitable, being stronger, and therefore better able to project. Although several early dancers noted that women had, on occasion, sung for them, this was unusual and generally limited to the latter part of the programme, which was dominated by the descriptive genre of songs.

Before 1940, it was uncommon for a woman to perform *nattuvangam*; I know of no examples from that period where a performing artist was also a *nattuvanar*. The first documented occasion on which three women conducted a dance recital was in 1943 at Kalakshetra. A traditional *nattuvanar*, A.P. Chokkalingam, withdrew his services for an important Bharata Natyam recital, and three women, Rukmini Devi, Radha Bernier (both dancers), and S. Sarada (musician and Sanskrit scholar) took the plunge into this hitherto male domain. Their qualifications for the task were obtained after a very short period of intensive training from a percussionist (*mridangist*) who specialized in accompanying Bharata Natyam. Sarada recounts how necessity became the mother of invention and forced the women to break with tradition and study and perform *nattuvangam*.

Chokkalingam Pillai (a hereditary teacher) left Madras in 1943 because of monetary considerations ... The *arangetram* of A. Sarada and Rukmini's performance at the Madras Music Academy were to take place ... Nagasvaram Vidwan Veeruswami Pillai ... sent the *thalam* on metal cymbals by post ... Bhairavan Pillai, who used to play the *mridangam* at Rukmini Devi's dance recitals, and was an expert in this art, came to our rescue and taught Radha and me to do *nattuvangam* with cymbals. Rukmini Devi with her great capacity to learn quickly, mastered this art soon (Sarada 1985: 50).

For high-caste women to perform a function that was traditionally allotted to men was a revolutionary innovation. More specifically these men were from another community, at that time regarded as socially inferior to their own. S. Sarada quotes Rukmini Devi:

One great new thing that has come as a result of these difficulties is the complete separation of our work from the traditional dance teachers. It is well known that they are a small clan of people who have never believed it possible for anybody to conduct a dance performance. I have always had a determination that this must go (Sarada 1985: 50).

Rukmini Devi took up the challenge to democratize the performing of Bharata Natyam, "They used to think that, except the usual class of people, no one else would be able to dance. Now there are so many girls from good families who are excellent dancers. The second aspect is to train nattuvanars from good families" (Sarada 1985: 50). Other dancers, including isai vellala women soon followed their example. Today women from a wide variety of backgrounds perform nattuvangam and there is an increase in the number of actively performing dancers who now run schools and conduct recitals.

The trauma of being beholden to the whims of the male nattuvanars from the isai vellala community, together with the newly attained confidence that they too could perform this function, meant that from 1943 onwards, Kalakshetra, one of the major dance institutions where Bharata Natyam is taught, never again employed a nattuvanar from the isai vellala community. Between 1943 and 1980 only one isai vellala student (the late T.R. Devanathan) was trained to become a nattuvanar at Kalakshetra. The 1943 incident and subsequent decisions, whether conscious or unconscious, were regarded by many as the first major step in loosening the hold that hereditary male nattuvanars exercised over female dancers. No longer would non-hereditary dancers be dependent on a professional community of nattuvanars. Within the traditional community, however, little changed. Hereditary dancers who continued to perform after the revival continued to depend on nattuvanars from their community.

ATTITUDES TOWARDS FEMALE INVOLVEMENT IN THE DANCE

Among the younger generation, most of those coming into teaching from a predominantly dance background were females. By contrast, males of the younger generation in hereditary families came to teaching from a predominantly musical background, although some also performed dance on stage.

Among the older generation, the female teachers were equally divided into brahmin and *isai vellala*. Only one, from the *isai vellala* community, did not marry. Four female dancers (two brahmins and two *isai vellala*) were married to dance teachers and both taught and conducted dance recitals.

Among the *isai vellala* families, whom I interviewed, there were more daughters than sons working as *nattuvanars*. Three important *isai vellala* families, those of T.R. Devanathan, S.K. Rajaratnam, and K.N. Dandayudapani, have daughters rather than sons engaged in teaching dance, while two *isai vellala* families, those of V. Ramaiya and T.P. Kuppaiya, have both sons and daughters and grandchildren teaching and conducting dance. However, in 1985 the sons tended to be more active. Some examples among brahmins who have daughters who teach dance are S.K. Kamesvaran and T.V. Venkataraman. V. Sadasivan, a brahmin, has a son who does so.

WOMEN FROM *ISAI VELLALA* FAMILIES:
WOMEN AS DANCE TEACHERS

Among the *isai vellala*, attitudes towards allowing daughters to study and perform dance were ambiguous. Most families refused to train their daughters, perhaps because they believed it would be detrimental to their marriage prospects. Others allowed their daughters to study dance, but did not encourage professional careers as dancers, although some performed *nattuvangam*. Recently several families have even allowed their daughters to give an *arangetram*, despite its strong association with the *devadasi* tradition. Not only did they call this first recital an *arangetram*, but these girls then actively pursued a performing career. In 1989, most of these girls were under the age of twenty, and were very often the youngest of several children.

With the democratization of education, those daughters who had been allowed to dance were in many ways socially equal to their brahmin counterparts; often educated in an English-medium school and exposed to a cosmopolitan life-style. In many instances, the opportunity to dance had been denied to their elder sisters. It seems that, until recently, attitudes towards daughters were constrained by the need for the community to overcome the social opprobrium attached to the institution of *devadasis*.

Another important force amongst hereditary families is that in those cases where all the children were discouraged from taking up a career in dance or music, very often it was the daughters who were present while their father taught at home. Without formal training, many of them picked up the dance by watching. Sometimes they were allowed to perform along with the other students in the annual day of their father's school. The initiative to study dance has sometimes come from the girls themselves as the male members of the family usually had other plans for them. In the 1950s and 60s their fathers were anxious that they attend college, for several reasons: first the dance for hereditary families was still not totally acceptable, second, having had a limited academic education themselves they saw higher education as offering other employment options.

THE EFFECT OF URBANIZATION[4]

When interest in the dance revived, many teachers moved from their villages, mainly in the Tanjore District of Tamil Nadu, to large urban centres. K. Muthukumar was one of the first to go to Madras to seek employment. Members of P. S. Minakshisundaram's family (A.P. Chokkalingam, P.C. Subbarayan), as well as V. Ramaiya, T. Swaminathan, K. Ganeshan, M. Durairaj, S. Manikkam, V.S. Muthuswamy followed soon after. To most of them the film industry was the greatest attraction in Madras. I shall not discuss the role of the cinema here, but it is worth noting that when dance was first featured in films it was classical. The popular style that is current in modern movies developed only later.

Other cities also attracted teachers in the 1950s and 60s: members of the P.S. Minakshisundaram family went to Delhi (P.S. Swaminathan) and Bangalore (P.M. Muthaiya, K.P. Kittappa), while members of the T.P. Kuppaiya family went to Bombay. This generation left their villages because they could no longer sustain the artistic traditions in which they were trained in their original setting. Teachers to whom I spoke include representatives from the following towns and villages: Pandanallur, Tanjore, Vaidisvarankoil, Tiruvaluputtur, Tiruvidaimarudur, Kutralam, Kiranur, Seyyer, Chidambaram, Swamimalai, Pudukkottai, Tiruchendur, Tiruvarur, Mannargudi, Kanchipuram, Vazhuvur, Tirumuruganpuni, Kattumunarkoil, Mellattur, and Karaikkal.

Not all the early *nattuvanars* retained their connection with their native place. By and large the older teachers returned to their villages, sending their younger relatives to the urban centres to continue the work they had begun. In order to study with these teachers, in particular P.S. Minakshisundaram, many dancers during the 1930s and 40s lived in the temple towns where the dance had once flourished. The notable exception was Rukmini Devi who brought *nattuvanars*, teachers and singers to Madras, housing them in her institution, Kalakshetra.

The paths taken by two important hereditary dance families, those of T.P. Kuppaiya and of the Tanjore Quartet, provide an interesting contrast. The Tanjore Quartet family, headed by P.S. Minakshisundaram, remained closely attached to the village of Pandanallur. Minakshisundaram himself went to Madras briefly in the 1930s, but soon returned to Pandanallur. Others of the same family, who shifted permanently to Madras, chose to live in lodgings, leaving their families in the village. This form of movement to the large urban centres was presented to me as a major factor in preventing the children of the Tanjore Quartet *nattuvanars* from taking up dance as a profession: they could not train their sons (born in the 1940s and 50s), who remained behind. When A.P. Chokkalingam, P.C. Subbarayan's father, first left home, Subbarayan's grandfather, P.S. Minakshisundaram was still teaching dance in the village of Pandanallur. It was in this way that Subbarayan was exposed to the dance. Minakshisundaram's death in 1954 resulted in a lost generation from this particular family. Subbarayan's son, now (1989) in his late thirties, is one example of this "lost generation". He regretted not studying with his father, but he was also very clear that it was only recently that teaching dance came to be regarded as a worthwhile occupation.

In contrast to P.S. Minakshisundaram's family, that of T.P. Kuppaiya moved *en masse* to Bombay in the 1940s. They therefore maintained a much looser association with their native village, Tiruvidaimarudur. This may have been because the patriarch and custodian of the artistic knowledge, T.P. Kuppaiya moved as well. Once in Bombay, the older *nattuvanars* taught and were involved in the dance full-time. The youngest member, T.K. Kalyanasundaram studied *mridangam*, but also qualified as an accountant. For many years he accompanied Bharata Natyam, but did not rely on this as his sole income. In the 1960s, when the demand for *nattuvanars* increased, Kalyanasundaram stepped into the "family firm". At first he worked with the overflow of dance students being trained by his elder brother, T.K. Mahalingam and brother-in-law, A.T. Govindarajan. He later trained his own students.

The V. Ramaiya and K.N. Dandayudapani families shifted to Madras. The V. Ramaiya family remains rooted in Madras, while the K.N. Dandayudapani family has dispersed to various urban centres. Dandayudapani's younger brothers first went to Hyderbad before returning to Madras (K.N. Pakkiriswami) and Delhi (K.N. Dakshinamurthy). All three brothers trained many dancers and dance teachers.

From the early 1940s, V. Ramaiya taught many famous dancers, in particular Kamala Lakshman, and many aspiring *nattuvanars* and dancers have lived and studied in his home. Some came as trained singers (S.K. Rajaratnam, S.K. Kamesvaran); others trained as dancers before acquiring training as accompanists on the spot (K.J. Sarasa). All of them are now successful *nattuvanars* with their own schools.

A major attraction of the dance for the younger generation was the opportunity to travel and perform abroad. These opportunities have become common recently for the younger generation, particularly for those who are single and able to stay away for long periods. The younger generation are quite capable of looking after themselves outside India. They usually speak some English, are more cosmopolitan and more flexible in dealing with unfamiliar situations than the older generation.

DISCUSSION

Whereas previously Bharata Natyam and other allied arts flourished in the great temple towns of the south, it now exists outside its original context, divorced from the artistic stimuli, festivals, crafts and traditional way of life of which the dance was one component. The younger generation of teachers, whether they migrated to the urban centres, or stayed in temple towns, have not experienced this "wholeness". This has had repercussions for the dance. As well, the paucity of information about exactly how *sadir* was presented makes it difficult to assess the magnitude of the changes brought about.

The lack of a strong hereditary association between the present older generation of teachers and the likely next generation makes it probable that the current trend towards a sharing of the various interpretations of Bharata Natyam will continue. The artistic vision of Bharata Natyam dance masters has always been diverse and will continue, as all art forms adapt and change. While it would be naive to suggest that this cross-fertilization is a new development, unique to modern times, it is evident that it is proceeding more rapidly than at any other time in history. The fact that the younger generation spends less time than the older did in studying music and dance in their formative years, suggests that standards may suffer.

On the other hand, although the children of the older *nattuvanars* began their artistic training later than their parents did, they may have studied with a greater sense of purpose and in a more systematic manner, more as a matter of choice and less as a hereditary imperative. Armed, as many of them were, with a B.A. or B.Com. degree, they had many other options open to them. Because of their educational qualifications, the social difference between the younger generation of *nattuvanars* and their dance students was not as wide as it was at the beginning of the dance revival, in the 1930s. This has had an influence on the *nattuvanar*/dancer relationship, the dynamics of which are constantly in flux.

Clearly, Bharata Natyam is being modernized, and teachers are not being trained in the same way as before, yet Bharata Natyam has never been more popular. Interest and enthusiasm in the dance continues to increase, with the result that many more members of traditional families may be encouraged to return to the profession.

Although the dance has attracted many from outside the *isai vellala* community, there continues to be a reverence for the artistic knowledge of traditional families. It is significant that in the end Rukmini Devi conceded: "Traditional dance teachers have something in them that the others do not have. They have complete dedication. I cannot define this quality. Tradition has its own atmosphere which you cannot describe."

NOTES

1. *Jatis* are rhythmic syllables uttered in a fixed sequence. They have both a rhythmic and sonorous quality.
2. See Sarada (1985: 32) for more details about T.V. Vitthal Iyer.
3. Some of the notable exceptions are V.P. Dhananjayan, U.S. Krishna Rao, H.R. Keshavamurthy and C. Radhakrishnan, as well as some others.
4. Neuman (1980: 26) remarks on the effect of urbanization on the Muslim musicians in New Delhi.

*Plate 4.1: Pandanallur: The Dance Hall in the
Ancestral Home of P.S. Minakshisundaram*

The dance hall in the ancestral home of P.S. Minakshisundaram. T.P. Kittappa's
father married two of P.S. Minakshisundaram's daughters. K.P. Kittappa's son,
K. Picchaiya, is on the left with another relative, Mahadevan, a violinist. They are
standing beside the family *puja* area which includes a large Tanjore painting of the
infant Krishna.

Plate 4.2: Kamalambal's Dance School, Tanjore 1947

Kamalambal, a *devadasi* founded a dance school the *Ponnaiya Natya Kaluri* in 1947. Kamalambal's teacher had been T. M. Kannuswamy, a descendant of Sivananda, one of the original Tanjore Quartet. T. M. Kannuswamy had also trained Jayalakshmi (*devadasi*), the mother of J. Natarajan, Kamalambal's dance partner, seen seated on the left. Punitavadi, Kamalambal's granddaughter (in a dance costume) is on the left. Also shown is Mythili Kalyanasundaram, who was related to Kamalambal and later married T.K. Kalyanasundaram, whose father T.P. Kuppaiya is the founder of a Bharata Natyam *bani*. Mythili studied dance, with Kamalambal, performed an *arangetram* and now teaches dance in Bombay with her husband. All of their five children have had exposure to dance and music but none of their daughters performed an *arangetram*.

Another girl from the *isai vellala* community, Indrani, related to K. Ganeshan is also in this photograph.

Plate 4.3: Teaching Dance: R. Samraj

R. Samraj (*isai vellala*) teaching in his dance studio in Madras (December 1985). The room, built as an annex in the compound of their home in Madras, is long and narrow. Several girls are dancing at the same time while he beats the *tattu-kal*. His school does not have a dance uniform. Some of the girls have come straight from school and are wearing their convent uniform. Their mothers are seated to one side. On the left is a large photograph of V. Ramaiya, Samraj's father, and the founder of the V. Ramaiya *bani*. Along the same wall are photographs of various gods and goddesses including Siva as *Gajasurasamharamurti* (Gaston 1982: 152-61), the deity worshipped in Vazhuvur, the ancestral village of the V. Ramaiya family. Behind Samraj is a life-size photograph of one of his wealthy students who is a frequent performer. On the right wall is a photograph of Nataraja with a lamp beneath it.

Plate 4.4: Demonstrating Dance: T.K. Kalyanasundaram

T.K. Kalyanasundaram (*isai vellala*), the son of T.P. Kuppaiya, is demonstrating a step to one of his senior students in his dance studio in Bombay (February 1985). On the wall is a photograph of his late brother-in-law A.T. Govindarajan, a dance teacher and *nattuvanar* who trained with T.P. Kuppaiya and then married his teacher's daughter, Karunambal. His photograph is garlanded (with sandalwood garland), which is a mark of respect. Also on the wall is a photograph of Nataraja. The clock on the wall shows 12.40 (p.m.) which indicates that this dancer has completed her education (in this instance college), and is studying Bharata Natyam full-time. T.K. Kalyanasundaram and his family have several studios all over Bombay. This one is an apartment below the residence of the late A.T. Govindarajan.

Plate 4.5: Nattuvanar in Performance:
Family Provides Accompaniment

The late K. J. Govindarajan (*isai vellala*), *nattuvanar*, and his three sons accompany a Bharata Natyam recital. His eldest son, Vasudevan, plays the *mridangam*, his second son, Illangovind, assists his father as a singer; his youngest son, G. Raghuraman, plays flute. His daughter Kalaivani (not seen here) performs and teaches Bharata Natyam.

Plate 4.6: Teaching Nattuvangam: Tamil Nadu College of Karnatic Music, Adyar, Madras 1985

Nadanam Sigamani (*isai vellala*), seated far left, holds the wooden stick and four women copy his actions. Behind them are various images of gods and goddesses, a photograph of one of the relatives of one of the musicians who works in the college and a drawing of the Hindu deity Nataraja and the goddess Parvati. The apprentices are watching dancers so that they can practice directing the rhythmic beating of their feet. Note the use of mirrors while teaching dance, a modern innovation.

Plate 4.7: Teaching Dance: Usha Srinivasan

Usha Srinivasan (brahmin), dancer and teacher teaching in Madras in her school *Hasta*. Like most dance teachers she teaches in her own home. Here classes are conducted on the terrace where a roof has since been constructed. She is one of the leading disciples of the K.N. Dandayudapani *bani*.

Plate 4.8: Teaching Dance: T.M. Vasudevan

The late T.M. Vasudevan (*isai vellala*) teaching in P.C. Subbarayan's dance school, The Lalita Subramanyam Bharata Natyam Academy. He was one of P.C. Subbarayan's assistant's. During his classes a *mridingam* provided rhythmic accompaniment. This was not the usual practice in most of the dance schools. The *mridangam* player is also training to accompany Bharata Natyam and would also be studying the various rhythmic combinations. Here the girls are dancing *alarippu*, the first dance in the traditional concert repertoire. Note the auspicious drawings or *kollams* on the floor.

5 *Banis* of Bharata Natyam

Bharata Natyam is a generic term used to describe the classical dances that conform to certain conventions of movement, symbolic gesture, posture and choreography. While these features distinguish Bharata Natyam from other classical styles, within the limits of such conventions, Bharata Natyam is open to a wide variety of interpretations.

There are several ways to look at the diffusion of style in art: one is to trace affinities and shared characteristics; another is to look at who studied with whom. In trying to trace the origins of recent Bharata Natyam, and how current exponents and teachers acquired their particular version, I have chosen to rely mainly on the evidence of who studied with whom. The importance placed on historical pedigree makes Bharata Natyam easier to trace through teacher-student relationships than most art forms. The method of passing on an oral artistic legacy from teacher to student is known as *guru-shishya parampara*. The relationship between teacher and student not only ensures the passing on of artistic knowledge but places a mark of identity on it. To describe a particular branch of the Bharata Natyam tree that can be traced to a teacher, group of teachers or institution I use the word, *bani*, which can be roughly equated to style. I realize that *bani* usually implies antiquity here it does not have the same implications as in north India where, to qualify as a *bani* or *gharana* it is generally accepted that the teaching of the founder of the *bani/gharana* must have endured for at least four generations (Neuman 1980). Some of the *banis* I include have their origin within this generation. The word "school" is used here to refer to actual institutions. Critics and connoisseurs do distinguish certain *banis* within Bharata Natyam on the basis of the dancer's teacher(s). For instance, two versions of Bharata Natyam that are frequently mentioned are the Tanjore Quartet/Pandanallur *bani* and the Kalakshetra (after the well-known dance school).

Some dancers and teachers have developed strikingly original interpretations, deviating markedly from those in which they were trained. In some instances they have created something not recognizable as stemming from either that which was taught to them by their teacher, or from other pre-existing *banis*. These people have their own individual *bani*. By shifting the emphasis of certain movements, rhythmic sequences or modes of expression, they show how their particular *bani* is different from others. In judging what constitutes a break with an earlier *bani*, and hence the foundation of a new one, I have relied on my own artistic judgement as well as informed and perceptive comments by knowledgeable persons and general consensus. For instance, the dancer Padma Subrahmanyam studied originally with several teachers, one of whom was V. Ramaiya. Subsequently, she developed and incorporated movements not usually seen in Bharata Natyam in the 1960s. There was little difficulty in assigning her interpretation of Bharata Natyam (recent dance) to a new *bani*. She herself acknowledges that she has created one.

I do not claim to be exhaustive in my treatment of Bharata Natyam *banis*. Nevertheless, those dealt with here include the majority of teachers in Delhi, Madras and Bangalore, and several important ones in Bombay, Ahmedabad and Tanjore.

HEREDITARY/NON-HEREDITARY

Banis have been described as hereditary where they were maintained within a given family up to 1980s. I include relationships by marriage as hereditary connections, because marriage within the traditional dance families usually involves a distant relative. A non-

hereditary tradition is one in which none of those teaching it in
1980s were members of the founder's family.

FOUNDERS OF *BANIS*

Those teachers who developed a recognizable technique, or
repertoire, which has been perpetuated by their students, I consider
to have founded a *bani*. Under this criterion several teachers have
founded their own *bani*, by virtue of the fact that they have created
a distinct interpretation of Bharata Natyam.

Banis of Bharata Natyam are not static and probably never have
been, They continue to evolve. Neither do they emerge from a
vacuum. The making of a *bani* relies on many artistic components.

In addition to skills in dance, choreography, music and
nattuvangam, another important ingredient is the ability to train
dancers or attract good (well-trained) dancers who also have a high
profile. This is essential for teachers and *nattuvanars* to exhibit their
work and become known because, however good they are, they are
likely to remain unknown without them. Another important
ingredient is the receptivity of the public. Bharata Natyam is
performed all over the world but the same kind of Bharata Natyam
does not receive the same level of acceptance and appreciation
everywhere.

Because I actively sought out a broad range of teachers, I became
familiar with a greater range of *banis* than is evident from the
everyday concert offerings. The literature which records the era
1930 to 1960 indicates that this period was dominated by dancers
who trained with P.S. Minakshisundaram or his relatives or students.
This *bani* is called either the Pandanallur, after the village of
Pandanallur where Minakshisundaram lived, or the Tanjore Quartet
bani, after the Tanjore court which offered patronage to its four
founding members.

Creating an artistic profile of Bharata Natyam teachers is very
difficult. Some teachers were formerly dance musicians. They

trained in several *banis* of Bharata Natyam, usually while serving as accompanist (vocalist, instrumentalist, or percussionist before launching into a career as both teacher and *nattuvanar*. Dancers who became teachers also studied with several teachers some of whom belonged to the Tanjore Quartet lineage. Rukmini Devi, the founder of Kalakshetra, studied with several hereditary teachers, one of whom was from the Tanjore Quartet *bani*. Subsequently she developed the distinctive interpretation now known as the Kalakshetra *bani*.

Bharata Natyam is taught in hundreds of centres, but up to 1990, most successful concert artists had the distinctive background of having studied with the same small circle of teachers. Both these dancers as well as their teachers have the greatest influence in determining the direction of the dance, in terms of technique, repertoire and choreography. Most successful concert artistes studied and performed with several *nattuvanars* over their careers. Some were more influential than others in moulding their dance style. The dancers themselves usually had firm views about which teachers were responsible for the artistic direction of their dance. Their claims, however, may also have been influenced by considerations such as a teacher's seniority, reputation and public profile.

Some *banis* have been in families for several generations; others have been founded by the present generation. I describe eighteen different *banis* existing within Bharata Natyam in the 1980s, classifying them into four main divisions. Three of these divisions comprise principally *isai vellala banis*. The first division includes only the Tanjore Quartet *bani*, which until recently did not marry into families with *devadasis* in their lineage. The second division comprises those *banis* which historically have had *devadasis* in their lineage. The third division comprises *banis* originating with important influential *devadasis* of the present era. The fourth division consists of recent innovative *banis* or those that have revived earlier "lost" techniques.

For the most part, I have named the *banis* after their seniormost teacher. Previously only *isai vellala* families developed hereditary *banis*. Nowadays the children of all communities are being trained by their parents, which opens up the possibility for other hereditary *banis* to develop.

This chapter provides a brief account of some of the *banis* that have made an impact on the development of Bharata Natyam. For most *banis* I have identified the seniormost teacher, and his/her ancestral village. This information gives some indication of the former centres of dance activity.

The attitude of each *bani* towards the involvement of women whether as dancers, teachers or *nattuvanars*, varies with each family. The number of children in each *bani* and their involvement in the dance gives some indication of whether the *bani* will be carried forward by hereditary exponents.

The amount of information provided on each *bani* does not reflect its artistic importance. I selected material which was both interesting and historically important. I have tried to record comments which reflect universalities in the transmission of all *banis*. Most of them can be regarded as general statements on the creation of Bharata Natyam.

Some teachers have been largely forgotten, probably because no important dancers emerged from their *bani*. I included some of these teachers to illustrate that the roots of present day Bharata Natyam may be more diverse than is currently recognized.

I regard this chapter as a catalyst and hope that my information can contribute to a more exhaustive investigation. The material presented here is intended to evoke an empathy for the many who spent their whole lives in the transmission, creation and performance of dance, and for whom that way of life was commonplace and natural.[1] I have concentrated on those teachers born before 1941. There are one hundred and thirty-nine in this sample. I refer only to some of the younger generation—those born after 1941. The number of *banis* is by no means exhaustive and their definition is quite arbitrary.

DIVISION I: DANCE TEACHERS WITH NO *DEVADASIS* IN THEIR LINEAGE[2]

1. THE TANJORE QUARTET *BANI*: P.S. MINAKSHISUNDARAM BRANCH

1A: HEREDITARY

P. (PANDANALLUR) S. (SURYAMURTHY) MINAKSHISUNDARAM (1869-1954)

The Tanjore Quartet were four brothers: Chinnaiya, Ponnaiya, Sivanandam and Vadivelu who were court musicians under Raja Sarfoji II of Tanjore (1798-1832). The quartet had an enormous influence on Bharata Natyam. Many of their compositions are performed regularly today. Some have been published (K.P. Sivanandam 1961) and are therefore easily accessible. They form the basis of the Bharata Natyam repertoire that evolved from *sadir*. The hereditary component of this *bani* consists of those teachers descended from, or married into, the family of the Tanjore Quartet. The non-hereditary component includes their students.

As previously mentioned, the Tanjore Quartet *bani* is unique within the *isai vellala* community, in that, until recently it has not had any hereditary dancers (*devadasis*) in their family tree, nor has the family allowed its women to have professional artistic accomplishments. It is the male members of this group who are associated with music, and teaching dance. Present day Bharata Natyam reflects the influence of two branches of this *bani*: that of P.S. Minakshisundaram which is presently both hereditary and non-hereditary, and that of T.N. Picchaiya which has become non-hereditary. The latter branch is currently maintained by non-hereditary teachers who trained with T.N. Picchaiya,[3] or one of his students.

During the revival, the most famous and influential teacher in the

Tanjore Quartet *bani* was P.S. Minakshisundaram (1869-1954).
Minakshisundaram was trained by Kumaraswamy *nattuvanar* in
Pandanallur. Later he went to Tanjore to study with Mahadevan,
son of T.S. Sivanandam, one of the founders of the quartet.
Minakshisundaram later married Mahadevan's daughter (*Marg*
1982: 126). He, in turn, trained many of his wife's relatives as well
as his own son, P.M. Muthaiya.

Some examples of teachers from the P.S. Minakshisundaram
branch of the Tanjore Quartet *bani* are: K.P. Kittappa (born 1913),
P.C. Subbarayan (born 1917), P.S. Swaminathan (born 1927), and
the late A.P. Chokkalingam (1896-1968), and M. Muthaiya (1902-
1978),[4] all of whom studied with their relative, Minakshisundaram.

Training was not limited to their male family members but
extended to other *isai vellalas* of both sexes.

T.(Tiruvalaputur) Swaminathan (1883-1972) was among the
important *nattuvanars* from outside the family trained by
Minakshisundaram. Swaminathan's mother and sisters, all *devadasis*
were also trained in this *bani*. Swaminathan later trained V.
Sadasivan, a brahmin. Both these men are discussed under the non-
hereditary members of the *bani*.

Artistic Involvement of Women

It is only recently that women from this family have been taught
music (the daughters of K.P. Sivanandam) or dance (granddaughter
of K.P. Kittappa). Sarada, a brahmin, married K.P. Sivanandam,
K.P. Kittappa's younger half-brother in 1948. Both she and her
husband teach and perform on the *vina*. It is their daughters who
have been allowed to study music, otherwise a rarity for this family.
In 1987 Sarada said that she would allow her daughters to study
dance, but her husband and his elder brother K.P. Kittappa would
not hear of it: they said that such activity was inappropriate for their
family. Sarada maintained an active performing and teaching career
after marriage. None of their daughters are married, so it is too soon
to evaluate how their association with the arts will be received by
their in-laws. Generally, playing the *vina* has for some years been

accepted as suitable for "respectable" women, so it was not unusual for Sarăda to have learnt this skill. Many brahmin women play this instrument.

Children

Between them, the older members of this tradition have a total of fifteen children but only one, P.M. Gopalakrishnan (born 1938), the eldest son[5] of P.M. Muthaiya, has been trained in dance and music. He took some training with his grandfather, P.S. Minakshisundaram. He was about sixteen years of age (1954) when his grandfather died and twenty when his father (1958) died. As a result, much of his training was with the non-hereditary dancer and teacher Leela Ramanathan (brahmin) who trained with his grandfather. Gopalakrishnan's uncle K.P. Kittappa, and father, P.M. Muthaiya have taught at her school in Bangalore where Gopalakrishnan now teaches along with her. Gopalakrishnan has an adopted son and daughter, both under age ten (in 1988). He would like to send his daughter to one of his students for training, as he does not feel that she would respond well if taught by him, a view shared by many teachers when considering their children's training.

Attitude towards the Nattuvanar Profession. K.P. Kittappa's father, T.K. Ponnaiya, was a professional vocalist who married both of P.S. Minakshisundaram's twin daughters. Ponnaiya trained his son in vocal music. He had aspirations for him to be a concert artist. Kittappa sang in various temples before his first big solo vocal recital at the age of nineteen (1931) at the Jagannatha Bhakta Sabha in Madras. This was his secular debut and it contributed to launching his professional career as a vocalist.

Ponnaiya actively discouraged his son from any association with dance. did not want his son to join the *nattuvanar* profession. He, however, made some concessions by allowing him to accompany the dance recitals conducted by his grandfather, P.S. Minakshi-sundaram. It was only after his father's death in 1945 that Kittappa started to conduct dance recitals and teach dance. His half-brother, K.P. Sivanandam, became a professional *vīna* player.

None of Kittappa's three sons and three daughters, received musical or dance training. Nor did the children of his cousin, P.C. Subbarayan, whose father A.P. Chokkalingam[6] trained with P.S. Minakshisundaram. Chokkalingam, after studying with Minakshisundaram, worked as his assistant when he was teaching, and also when he was working with Rukmini Devi at Kalakshetra. He conducted some of Rukmini Devi's solo dance concerts. His son, Subbarayan, supplied some of the vocal accompaniment before the family left Kalakshetra in 1943 to found their own institution in another part of Madras city (Sarada 1985: 49).

While Subbarayan was growing up in Pandanallur, P.S. Minakshisundaram spent considerable time there.[7] There were also the holiday periods when both he and his father, Chokkalingam, would return to the village where his grandfather continued to run an active dance school. Thus if Subbarayan was not training with his own father in Madras he was with his grandfather. Like his father, Subbarayan, chose to leave his three sons and one daughter in their ancestral village of Pandanallur, rather than bring them to Madras where he was teaching. By then there was no dance or music teaching being conducted in Pandanallur: consequently, Subbarayan's children were not exposed to it. His eldest son, S. Govindaswamy, at the age of thirty-four (in 1985) regretted this: "I wish I had studied my father's art but he was living with my grandfather, Chokkalingam, in a hotel. So we lived with our mother in the village. I would have liked to have learn this art but it is now too late."

P.S. Swaminathan, who grew up near P.S. Minakshisundaram's house and studied with him, gave the same reason for not training his son in the art. When he taught in Delhi he found it financially impossible to bring his two sons to the big city.

An interesting trend was beginning in 1988. Several of K.P. Kittappa's grandchildren were taking lessons in *mridangam* and dance. Their fathers stated: "We were the lost generation. Our children must return to our family's art."

Sarada, the wife of Sivanandam again commented on the fact that

Kittappa's granddaughter had studied dance, and presented an *arangetram* in 1988—an event that was no doubt precipitated by the fact that she grew up away from the orthodox influence of her family. This allowed her to "break our customs". "Padmavati [Kittappa's granddaughter] learnt dance but she will not be a professional dancer. ... My family is very orthodox ... our children should not show dance in public even though they know everything." Then she laughed and noted: "Her mother was very keen that some lady in our house should learn dance. ... That is why Padmavarti studied it. Her mother wanted her to."

This is the same reason given as the motivation for many girls to learn dance, regardless of caste. Mothers try to realise their ambitions and dreams through their daughters. This trend first appeared in the higher castes but has now reached the hereditary families. Sometimes the main driving force has been the father, as the daughter has been more likely to carry on his work. Some dancers from non-hereditary families have had the support of their fathers and, sometimes, their husbands, who have assisted their professional dance career in various capacities (impresario, musical accompanist). As yet husbands from the hereditary communities have not become directly involved in their wife's dance career.

Sarada gives a possible explanation for this: "Forty-five years ago, or perhaps even earlier, family women did not dance, only *dasis* did. Now anyone can dance."

Education of the Younger Generation

All the hereditary masters have chosen to encourage their children to pursue academic education. Out of the fifteen children, three have a B.A., one a B.Sc., one is studying for a B.Sc., one has completed the pre-university course (P.U.C.) while the rest have completed or nearly completed high school.

Although P.S. Swaminathan lamented that his son did not receive training in music and dance, he himself would like to have had a better education:

I had an interest in education. I wanted to be a doctor or something. I just wanted to study but it was difficult to get to school. In Pandanallur, in those days, the school only went up to the fifth class. To study further would have meant walking five or six miles. The head master in Pandanallur took ten of us privately and secretly to study in the morning. We studied till the ninth class.

The agitation against the *devadasis* dance was at its height then (1930s-40s), and non-hereditary persons were beginning to study the dance. Swaminathan said that he was pushed into his hereditary profession. His comments reflect the confidence that his grandfather (P.S. Minakshisundaram) had in encouraging his grandchildren to train in their family's profession:

I had so much interest in studies [academic subjects]. I wanted to do private study. *Tata* [his grandfather, P.S. Minakshisundaram] would beat me and say, if you want to learn English don't come into this house. Whatever *Tata* said we had to obey. I cried and joined the dance class, sitting with my grandfather.

Training Situation, Other Dance Styles

None of those brought up within the Tanjore Quartet families paid fees to learn dance. Instead they performed *seva* in return for knowledge. None of them studied additional Indian classical dance styles nor did any of the male teachers train to be dancers. This contrasts to many of the non-family members who were first dancers (some examples are: Mrinalini Sarabhai, Leela Ramanathan, U.S. Krishna Rao, Chandrabhaga Devi, etc.) and had studied other dance styles such as Kathak, Odissi, and Manipuri). Some of them had performed these other styles on the stage—(Mrinalini (Manipuri), Leela (Kathak) Krishna Rao (Kathak) and Chandrabhaga Devi (free dance). Non-family members had also studied several other *banis* of Bharata Natyam: Mrinalini (Muthukumar), Leela (Puttappa/ Gundappa), Krishna Rao (Puttappa/Gundappa) and Chandrabhaga Devi (free dance).

Most of the early non-hereditary dancers had some of their training either in Pandanallur or Tanjore. Later dancers relied on dance teachers who migrated to the major cities.

Future of the Hereditary Tanjore Quartet Bani

The Tanjore Quartet *bani* is often considered the most illustrious, because much of the Bharata Natyam repertoire was composed by this family. Until recently all the artistic skills needed to be a professional were passed on within the family. But because the last generation did not train their own children, most of the tradition will be passed on by non-hereditary members.

Some of those who studied directly with P.S. Minakshisundaram —Mrinalini Sarabhai, Leela Ramanathan, Tara Chaudhury, Shanta Rao, Ram Gopal, U.S. Krishna Rao and Chandrabhaga Devi, all non-hereditary dancers—have taught in their own schools. Krishna Rao and Chandrabhaga Devi did not train their sons, both engineering graduates, in dance. They have, however, presented their granddaughter, Anjali, in an *arangetram*. Anjali now performs and teaches dance. In 1986, she was planning to attend the university and have dance as a side-line. She did not see a dance career as a financially viable occupation; perhaps this has changed. Neither Mrinalini nor Leela trained their sons in dance. Both of them were university graduates. Their daughters they did train—Mallika Sarabhai and Mallavika Ramanathan. Both presented *arangetrams* and continued dance while obtaining educational qualifications.

1B: Non-Hereditary

T. (Tiruvalaputur) Swaminathan (1883-1972)

T. Swaminathan was the son of the *devadasi* S. Kalyani Ammal. His two sisters, Rajalakshmi and Jivaratnam, were also *devadasis*. Swaminathan studied dance with P.S. Minakshisundaram and with his mother's brother, Ponnuswamy:[8] no one was able to give me details about the latter's training. None of Swaminathan's children were involved in music and all died young. His student, Radha Srinivasan (brahmin) remembers:

Swaminathan had one son, who was a politician in Kumbakonam.

Swaminathan in his prime was not a dancer. He had a lot of hope for his two sisters, Jivaratnam and Jayalakshmi, from whom everyone, including Balasaraswati and Rukmini Devi, got inspiration. He and his master, P.S. Minakshisundaram did *nattuvangam* for them. Unfortunately Jivaratnam died suddenly ... of tetanus I think, so the whole family stopped dancing.

In the late 1950s he resumed his career: "For a while T. Swaminathan was in self-exile, looking after his fields and other things. Only after all that he came to Madras (late 1950s) and started his career teaching."

Like many of the *nattuvanars* whose teaching careers were in the 1950s he missed the big boom that came later.

He used to talk a lot about how his prime period was lost. I did not meet his mother, Kalyani, as when I started to study with him he was about sixty, so his mother must have been eighty. He said that she was fat, but used to sit and do *abhinaya*. I never saw her. He did not teach many pupils. He was self-contained, he would not go out much.

V. Sadasivan (1921-1990)

V. Sadasivan was a brahmin. Between the ages of fifteen and twenty-one, he trained as a vocalist, after which he gave a solo public recital in a temple. He then went to Madras and provided vocal accompaniment for at least two *nattuvanars*—T. (Tiruvala-putur) Swaminathan and T. (Tiruchendur) Minakshisundaram. He worked with both of them from 1949-53 and they influenced his interpretation of Bharata Natyam. Sadasivan performed *nattuvangam* for the first time in 1956. Until 1959 he continued to give vocal accompaniment while T. Minakshisundaram performed *nattuvangam*. Sadasivan had a practical knowledge of the dance, having danced the basic steps with T. Swaminathan. Sadasivan reported that he never performed dance but he did augment his earnings as an actor in the 1950s, before the increased demand for dance accompanists.

Sadasivan's style was also shaped by working with the top dancers of that period: Kamala Lakshman and Yamini Krishna-murti. These dancers could rightly claim to have had an important influence on his training as they taught him their repertoire. In the case of Kamala Lakshman this came from V. Ramaiya, and K. Muthukumar, and in the case of Yamini Krishnamurti from Kalakshetra and K. Ellappa.

Four of Sadasivan's five sons completed secondary school. The youngest, S. Satyanarayan, has an M.A. in Economics. He studied singing from the age of seven (1968). He gave his first solo vocal recital on the concert stage—not in a temple as his father had done. He started to sing for dance recitals in 1982. He is also studying violin. When I spoke with him, in 1988, he was hoping to take up music full-time, giving up his work in a private company: "I know typing, and various computer programs such as s-basic. I work 9 to 5 for a private company. I want to quit. My musical talent has been given by god and I must use it before I am forty. After fifty I can work in the company."

None of Sadasivan's sons underwent practical dance training. Even so, one of them, S. Ayyapan, teaches dance. He plays *mridangam*, and is following a path similar to that of his father, providing accompaniment for many of the top professional dancers. He also established a reputation as a *nattuvanar*, having first performed *nattuvangam* in 1982. At the same time he proved himself a versatile musician, and continued to play *mridangam*— a practice not very common, as a *nattuvanar* is generally accorded higher status than an accompanist.

Sadasivan's wife, Thangammal, was a trained singer. Before she was married she gave solo vocal recitals. In the 1970s she sang for Sadasivan's students' recitals, but she subsequently gave that up. It is not unusual that as a brahmin she received musical training (L'Armand 1978). Less common is the fact that after marriage she sang for a dance recital conducted by her husband. Whereas the majority of female vocalists who accompany dance are brahmins, their husbands are not usually *nattuvanars*.[9]

Sadasivan's two sons worked with many *nattuvanars*, but gave first preference to their father's recitals, thus ensuring that he was able to supply a cohesive orchestra for performances that he conducted. After his father's death, Ayyapan became more active as a *nattuvanar*.

Direct Influence on other Banis. The Tanjore Quartet *bani* was also
the foundation for the Kalakshetra *bani*, Rukmini Devi, its founder
having studied directly with P.S. Minakshisundaram.

2. TANJORE QUARTET *BANI*: T.(TANJORE) N.(NARAYANASWAMY)[10] PICCHAIYA (?-*c*. 1949) BRANCH

All the teachers from the T.N. Picchaiya *bani* in this chapter were
isai vellala. Picchaiya was the only member of the Tanjore Quartet
family.

The T.N. Picchaiya *bani* includes the late T.M. Arunachalam and
his wife Jayalakshmi, his youngest brother, the late T.M. Vasudevan,
the late K.J. Govindarajan, the late Lakshmi Kantham[11] and her
student, the late R.S. Rajendran. R.S. Rajendran was originally
from Tiruvidaimarudur and was not from a *nattuvanar* family (pers.
comm. B.M. Sundaram). Picchaiya died before 1950. His son, P.
Narayanaswamy[12] did not perform *nattuvangam*, instead he had a
successful career as a solo vocalist along with K.P. Kittappa, his
cousin.

T.(TANJORE) M. ARUNACHALAM (1922-1980)[13] AND A. JAYALAKSHMI (1934-)

Arunachalam was the nephew of the *devadasi*, Saradambal.[14] I was
not able to obtain details of his musical and dance training before he
joined T.N. Picchaiya to study and accompany dance.

Arunachalam's wife, A. Jayalakshmi, trained as a dancer and in
1942, at the age of nine, performed as part of a temple festival. This
was after about two years of training with both Picchaiya and her
future husband. She attended daily class at the home of Picchaiya.
She did not pay fees, but later, when she gave many recitals, her
teacher took a certain portion of the performance fee as payment for
the early training he gave her. After her marriage she continued to
perform. In the 1980s she taught at home and in the Karnatic
College of Music where her husband had been the principal. All

their three sons studied music and dance. The eldest, A. Hemnath, born in 1958 trained in vocal. After his father's death he conducted dance recitals. He also danced on the stage. The other two sons, A. Natarajan, born in 1961 and A. Chandrashekar, born in 1962, trained in *mridangam*. Both of them play for dance. All of them completed school. A. Hemnath has a B.A. His wife, Mallika, received dance training before marriage in another *bani*, that of Kutralam Ganeshan. She also taught in their school, but did not perform as her children were too young.

Arunachalam's youngest brother, T.M. Vasudevan (1929-1987) also studied in T.N. Picchaiya's school. He did not give a solo music concert and after Picchaiya's death (*c.* 1949) continued to work with Arunachalam both in Tanjore and later in Madras where they moved in the 1960s. Before his brother Arunachalam's death in 1980, Vasudevan had a close association with his in-laws and used to teach along with his brother and his brother's wife, Jayalakshmi. In 1985, Vasudevan was working as an assistant to P.C. Subbarayan of the P.S. Minakshisundaram branch of the Tanjore Quartet *bani*, teaching dance to beginners.

Vasudevan gave his children some musical training; each of his three sons has taken lessons in *mridangam*, flute and violin but none has accompanied dance or performed professionally. One of them, V. Subramaniam, born 1962, holds an M.A.; another, V. Swaminathan, born *c.* 1964 has completed a B.Com.: while the youngest, V. Murugananandam, born 1969 is still studying. Vasudevan's only daughter, born in 1960 is married.

K.(KIRANUR) J. (JAYARAMAN) GOVINDARAJAN (1935-1994)

Another example from the T. Picchaiya *bani*, the late K.J. Govindarajan[15] began to study dance after a successful vocal career. Govindarajan began his vocal training at age ten, living in the home of his teacher and performing *seva* in lieu of fees. His first solo vocal recital in 1950, at age fifteen, was in a temple. He then joined the T. Picchaiya school of dance, accompanying dance programmes until 1959. When he joined the school, Picchaiya had died, but T.M.

Arunachalam, who was working, there trained Govindarajan in this *bani*. In 1960 he moved to Delhi where he sang for Sikkil Ramaswamy, a *nattuvanar*, and studied his *bani*. In the same year, at the age of twenty-five, he conducted his first dance recital and in 1963, at age twenty-eight he conducted his first *arangetram*. He travelled and worked with several leading dancers, in particular Indrani Rehman. He gave her credit for inspiring him to train all of his children in different musical genres. The eldest, G. Vasudevan, born in 1961, has a B.Com. and has trained in *mridangam*. He first accompanied one of his father's students in 1974, four years after his first public recital on *mridangam*. He knows how to perform *nattuvangam* but has not done so in public. Vasudevan now lives in Canada where he teaches *mridangam* as well as holding down a full-time job outside the dance.

G. Ilangovind, born in 1964, has a B.A. and has trained in violin and flute. He sings for dance recitals in both the Karnatic style for Bharata Natyam and the Odissi style. His father had started to train him in *nattuvangam*. The third son, G. Raghunathan was born in 1969, and in 1986 was in the second year of a B. Com. He gave a solo flute recital in 1982 and one year later started to accompany dance. Both Ilangovind and Raghunath have broadcast on All India Radio's Youth section, *Yuva Vani*. Raghunathan plays flute for many Bharata Natyam recitals.

Govindarajan and his three sons are able to provide a complete orchestra. He also trained his daughter, G. Vani, born in 1972, in dance, vocal and *nattuvangam* and she assisted him in teaching dance. Vani has performed in public but, up to 1988, had not given a full solo recital. Govindarajan told me that they had no objection to her performing an *arangetram*, but that they had not done so because of the expense.

Children

The three examples from the T.N. Picchaiya school, T.M. Arunachalam/Jayalakshmi, T.M. Vasudevan and K.J. Govindarajan have in total eleven children, nine sons and two daughters. All except one daughter received musical training. The eldest son, Hemnath, from the T.M. Arunachalam/A. Jayalakshmi family conducts dance recitals and teaches dance. There are a total of three professional *mridangists* who accompany many dancers, a singer who sings for both Bharata Natyam and Odissi, a flautist who accompanies dance and one daughter and one daughter-in-law, who have performed and teach dance. Two of Govindarajan's sons and his daughter perform *nattuvangam*.

None of the older generation paid fees to study dance. Both Arunachalam and Govindarajan were trained vocalists and "picked up the dance" while accompanying it. Only Jayalakshmi was a trained dancer. While Vasudevan trained with his brother Arunachalam, all of the younger generation received much of their knowledge about dance from their own family, working with their fathers (Arunachalam and Govindarajan) and—in the Arunachalam/ Jayalakshmi family, their mother (Jayalakshmi). None of the sons restrict their activities to their family, and all have accompanied many dancers and *nattuvanars* from different *banis*. In 1985, A. Natarajan was the permanent percussionist for Swarnamukhi (Sampati Bhoopal *bani*), one of the most popular dancers in South India in the 1970s and 80s. G. Ilangovind (K.J. Govindarajan's son) has provided vocal accompaniment for Kiran Segal, a dancer who gives performances in two styles of dance, Bharata Natyam and Odissi. His willingness to diversify and sing for Odissi illustrates that he is adapting to the needs of the times.

Govindarajan is the only one from this sample who has created his own musical repertoire for Bharata Natyam. It includes all of the pieces for a full evening of Bharata Natyam.

Some other *isai vellalas* who studied and performed the T.N. Picchaiya *bani* are: Lakshmi Kantham who taught in Tanjore until her death in about 1954, the late R.S. Rajendran who taught in Tanjore and at the College of Music in nearby Tiruvarur, and R.S. Rajendran's wife who teaches dance in Tanjore. None of Rajendran's children teach dance.

DIVISION II: HEREDITARY TEACHERS WITH *DEVADASIS* IN THEIR LINEAGE

The only element that distinguishes the hereditary exponents of this group from those of Division I is that their founding families have included *devadasis* in the family tree for many generations. This was an important distinction within the *isai vellala* community. It is interesting to note that today many *banis* are now being sustained as hereditary professions by their female members. Some of these women were dancers, others musicians who later turned to dance. Many were brought up in music and dance households and are now successful teachers by exposure than by systematic training.

Among the *banis* being maintained by blood relations, five derive from male teachers: K.N. Dandayudapani, B. Gundappa, Baroda Kubernath Tanjorkar, T.P. Kuppaiya and V. Ramaiya, all members of hereditary music and dance families. Eight other *banis* are maintained by non-relatives, only a fraction of whom are *isai vellala*. The *banis* are named after their *isai vellala* founders: K.(Kattumannarkoil) Muthukumar, K.(Kutralam) Ganeshan, V.(Vaidisvarankoil) Minakshisundaram, B.(Bombay) Chandrashekar, S.(Sikkil) Ramaswamy, T.(Tiruchendur) Minakshisundaram, S.(Seyyur) Mannikam, and T. (Tanjore) Kannappa.

With the exception of the Baroda/Tanjore *bani* all these eight *banis* are named after *isai vellala* male *nattuvanars*.

1. BARODA/TANJORE *BANI*

KUBERNATH TANJORKAR (1917-)

Kubernath Tanjorkar's parents moved from Tanjore district to Baroda at the invitation of the Gaekwad. His father, Appaswamy (1862-1935) was born in Nagathinagar, a village near Tanjore, where his family had served in the temple. Appaswamy was a *nattuvanar* who trained in *mridangam* with Kumbakonam Alanganambi Pillai. He studied violin with Tirukodikaval Krishna Iyer, a brahmin, and was trained in singing by his father, Thangam

Pillai who also played the *mridangam*. Kubernath's mother, Kantimati (1872-1953), was a dancer. Kubernath believed that his father had studied with Kannusamy, a member of the Tanjore Quartet. Kannuswamy also taught Kantimati; she also studied with another *devadasi*, Saradambal, of Tiruvarur.[16] Consequently, their family has close artistic links with the Tanjore Quartet *bani*, and they may be regarded as an offshoot of it. Kubernath's brother, Janardan,[17] was a violinist in Bombay and his son, J. Venugopal, was trained in dance by Parvati Kumar, a non-hereditary teacher.

Training

From the age of twelve Kubernath studied *mridangam* with Kumbakonam Alaganambi Pillai. He lived with his teacher and his *seva* included washing clothes and bringing water from the well: "The students lived like servants. It was a barter system. We did not give money, just some grain every year." T.K. Marudappa, one of Kuppaiya's sons (T.P. Kuppaiya *bani*) was also living and studying *mridangam* in Kumbakonam with the same teacher.

Kubernath presented his *mridangam arangetram* in Tanjore in the Kaliamman temple before he was eighteen. He then studied *mridangam* accompaniment for Bharata Natyam recitals with his father. He played *mridangam*, and his father performed *nattuvangam* for his mother's recitals. He studied Karnatic music with Balakrishnan Pillai in Tanjore and Bharata Natyam with Minakshisundaram (Tanjore Quartet *bani*). His mother had also received training from this *bani*. Her teachers included Kannuswamy *nattuvanar*, and Kannuswamy's younger brother, Vadivelu.

Kubernath studied dance with his parents and in 1939 he started to teach in Baroda. That year his father died and he and his mother went to teach at the Bhatkhande College in Lucknow. This they did until 1942 when, like many *nattuvanars*, he went to south India to work in the film industry. He worked in two films with the director, T.R. Sundaram: "In those days Bharata Natyam in the films was pure; now it is mixed."

In the 1930s, Kubernath gave a dance recital which he described as an *arangetram* in female costume in the Brihadisvara Temple,

Tanjore. He danced the *varnam*, *Mohamana*, and several *padams*, in particular, one by Kshetrayya in *Bhairavi* (*Ituvanti*) and an *ashtapadi* from the *Gita Govinda* (*Haririha*). For his recitals his father, Appaswamy, did *nattuvangam* and his uncle's son Tambuswamy played *mridangam*. He also gave dance recitals dressed in female costume in several cities in north India such as Kanpur and Lucknow. When his father died, his mother performed *nattuvangam* for his dance recitals. This continued until 1941, when at the age of twenty-four he gave up performing on the concert stage.

The Gaekwad Sahaji Rao III, who ruled Baroda from 1942 until 1949, did not offer patronage to the family, but his successor, Maharana Pratap Singh, called the family back. From 1949 until 1951 Kubernath taught dance in the Music Department in the Palace Kalavan, which was later absorbed into the M.S. University of Baroda. From 1951 until 1981 he taught at the Music College. He recalls that in 1951 only four or five students were studying music there. At that time he studied Hindustani music with Faiyaz Khan and Atah Hussain.

In 1984 he opened his own school in his home. Since then, he reported, there has been a boom in Bharata Natyam in Baroda. His children are interested in the arts. Two of his daughters have given Hindustani vocal concerts and one of his sons, Ramesh (born 1943, B.Com.) although a trained chartered accountant, plays the *sitar*, and can perform *nattuvangam*. He assists his father in teaching. He is married to Leela, who is related to the K. Muthukumar *bani*. Her grandfather, Raghavan Pillai, played the *tavil*. Ramesh and Leela have two sons; the elder, Rajesh (about thirteen in 1986) was "really keen" and had just started training in their institution, *Tanjore Nrityasala*. The younger (about nine) had not begun dance training. Ramesh began studying *nattuvangam* at the age of twelve. From 1984 he began to teach in his father's school, which had over one hundred students in 1989. One of Kubernath's students, Madhu Patel, a Gujarati, started to study dance with him in 1961 and six years later he gave his *arangetram*. In 1988 Madhu Patel was running a very successful dance school in Baroda and continued to honour his teacher on public occasions when he was presenting his own students.

2. K.(KARAIKKAL) N. (NATESHA) DANDAYUDAPANI *BANI*

K.N. DANDAYUDAPANI (1921-1974)

K.N. Dandayudapani studied vocal music from his father Natesan, who was a singer. He started at the age of seven. K.N. Dandayudapani's granduncle, Ramakrishnan, was a *nattuvanar* attached to the Sani temple at Tirunallar. Dandayudapani had his first exposure to Bharata Natyam with him. Dandayudapani's brother, Pakkiriswami, married Girija. Her grandmother, Pranambal, had been dedicated as a *devadasi* in the same temple. Mohan Khokar reported that Dandayudapani first worked as a vocalist with K. Muthukumar and in 1938-39 he toured with the dancing sisters, Selvamani and Saroja Khokar. Thereafter he was employed at Kalakshetra to sing for Bharata Natyam programmes with the *nattuvanar* A.P. Chokkalingam (Tanjore Quartet *bani*). It was there that he picked up much of his knowledge. In 1949 he left Kalakshetra to work independently.

Initially, Dandayudapani taught the Kalakshetra repertoire but he soon started to choreograph his own dances. He later composed his own music and lyrics in Tamil, mostly on non-erotic themes. The pieces appealed especially to teachers who were training the new younger dancers. These were published in 1974 in a book entitled *Aadalisai Amutham*.

Hereditary and Non-Hereditary Exponents

The hereditary component from the older generation is represented by two of K.N. Dandayudapani's brothers, K.N. Dakshinamurthy and the late K.N. Pakkiriswami, and by Dandayudapani's niece K.J. Sarasa.[18] Non-family members from the *isai vellala* community are R. Nadanam and K.M. Nagarajan, and three brahmins, P. Venkataraman, Malati Srinivasan, and Vanaja Narayanan. Musicians from this group who studied dance by working in K.N. Dandayudapani's orchestra were: K.N. Pakkiriswami and P. Venkataraman on violin, K.N. Dakshinamurthy and M. Nagarajan on *mridangam* and Malati Srinivasan and K.J. Sarasa who sang.

Their vocal accomplishment varied. Vanaja Narayanan had given solo vocal recitals, K.J. Sarasa had previously sung for dance recitals conducted by V. Ramaiya (V. Ramaiya *bani*), and Malati Srinivasan's exposure to music had been at Kalakshetra (Kalakshetra *bani*) in conjunction with her dance training. Dandayudapani had been one of her teachers and she left Kalakshetra when he died. Her first public recital was conducted by him in 1949 after she had studied a total of about five years. Sarasa first trained in dance with V. Ramaiya, to whom she was also related. She trained for seven years before he conducted her first public recital which was also held in 1949. While studying dance and music she lived in his household and performed household duties in return for classes. One of her duties was to escort R. Samraj, V. Ramaiya's son (now a *nattuvanar*) to school.

The late K.N. Pakkiriswami (died 1989) started to train in violin at age thirteen (1941) and after five years of training gave a solo recital, in a secular setting (for a private party), and later in a temple. His younger brother, K.N. Dakshinamurthy started to train in vocal at the age of twelve but after three years changed to *mridangam*, which he studied for three years. In 1946 he gave a solo *mridangam* recital in a temple. Both brothers studied with non-family members, living with their teacher and performing *seva*. Their father Natesan, who trained their elder brother Dandayudapani in vocal, died before they were ten years of age.

The close kin taught by Dandayudapani have a total of eight children. Among these, one of Pakkiriswami's three children, a daughter, P. Minakshi had studied dance with her father, her mother, Girija, and A.P. Chokkalingam (Tanjore Quartet *bani*). Minakshi had given her *arangetram* and was teaching dance. Girija was from a traditional family and had studied dance in Kumbakonam with Shanmugan Sundaram, grandson of Pandanallur Nataraja *nattuvanar*. Girija gave many recitals before and after her marriage. Among Dakshinamurthy's five children, only the youngest daughter, D. Venu was encouraged by her family to study and perform. She said that her training was more by exposure than systematic study. She gave her *arangetram* in New Delhi in 1988 and her mother,

Naga, sang on this occasion. Although she was still too young to decide what profession she would take up, she stated that she would like to be a dancer and dance teacher. Dakshinamurthy's twin daughters, D. Amrita and D. Varshini, had danced for school functions, but neither was particularly interested in the dance; their parents did not encourage them. They have since married. The eldest son, D. Natarajan (born c. 1961), was sent to Madras to live with his uncle, Dandayudapani to be exposed to the dance, but he soon returned to live in Delhi with his parents. D. Natarajan stated that he too might have picked up the dance, like his cousins Uma and Kalyani, if his father had maintained an established school in their own home rather than visiting student's homes to give dance tuition.

Uma is K.N. Dandayudapani's adopted daughter,[19] Kalyani Shekar is his niece. Uma has a flourishing school in Madras and is totally committed to teaching dance as a profession. Although she had not performed dance solo on the stage she had taken part in group dances for her father's school. After her father's death she started to work in an office but within three years had founded her own school and was improving her musical skills by taking vocal lessons. Her training in the dance with her father was more by exposure than by systematic lessons. She attributes this to the fact that teaching was done in their home. She did not start to teach dance while he was alive, and it is clear that he did not particularly encourage or direct her towards adopting dance as a profession. Kalyani Shekar's career was similar. She had picked up the dance while living in her uncle Dandayudapani's home. In the mid-1980s her school in Delhi was smaller than Uma's: fifty students compared to several hundred. They now have many more students. While Uma taught in her own home, Kalyani also went to students' homes to teach.

Both these women had selected their own husbands, someone they met through dance. Uma was married to a brahmin, the brother of one of the assistants in her dance school. Kalyani was also married to a man from another caste, from another region in India, Kerala. Neither husband was involved in the arts.

Children

Kalyani Shekar hoped that her eldest son would undergo systematic training in *mridangam*, her own mother, Anjukam's specialty. She was considering sending him to a master to study *mridangam*, as she felt he would not get the proper discipline needed if his grandmother taught him.

The only sons of Dandayudapani's two female brahmin disciples (Vanaja Narayanan and Malati Srinivasan) were studying *mridangam*, one had given a solo recital but the parents of neither encouraged their sons to take up full-time dance accompaniment. Vanaja's brother, a professional *mridangist*, lived with them and worked as a dance accompanist but, for the same reasons as given by Kalyani, Vanaja had engaged a teacher from outside the family to teach her son. Although there appears to be some reluctance to engage family members to teach relatives, Vanaja herself studied vocal with an uncle.

The eight teachers in the K.N. Dandayudapani *bani* had a total of sixteen children (eleven girls and five boys). Three of the younger generation of women are teaching dance. Their fathers taught dance to two of them while one of them was introduced to the dance via her maternal uncle. Two of the younger girls could become professional dancers. Both they and their parents see this as a possibility.

Unlike their fathers all the children had either completed school, or were studying; three had completed college and one was combining study at college with studying *mridangam*. While all but one from the older generation had received their training living with their teacher away from the family, the younger generation had lived at home pursuing full-time academic education along with dance or musical training.

Nattuvangam

Among the older generation all but two, P. Venkataraman and R. Nadanam had presented solo recitals either in music or dance. All had undergone long apprenticeships, either as musicians or dance assistants, before performing *nattuvangam*. Among the three in the hereditary younger generation, all began teaching and performing *nattuvangam* without a long apprenticeship as musicians. Only one had presented a solo dance recital and none had performed a solo music concert. This can be contrasted with the older generation: Dandayudapani and his sister, K.N. Rukmini, gave solo vocal concerts; another sister, K.N. Anjukam, and a brother, K.N. Dakshinamurthy, gave solo *mridangam* recitals; another brother, K.N. Pakkiriswami, gave solo violin recitals; still another brother, K.N. Vaidyanathan was a *nagasvaram* player. All of them had performed in temples very early in their career, something not experienced by the younger generation.

Amongst the family members, the K.N. Dandayudapani *bani* will be passed on by three women—Uma Dandayudapani, Minakshi Pakkiriswami and Kalyani Shekar. In addition to the teachers that I have discussed there are many dancers who were taught by K.N. Dandayudapani or his relations who are now teaching his *bani*. Amongst the dancers, Usha Srinivasan spent a long time studying with him and made a systematic study of the *adavus* he taught. She studied all but one of his original compositions with him. She commented on his *bani*.

It is attractive, and fast. Many people are against the dance being done in the second and third speeds (*kalam*) but I think slow dance, no matter how beautifully it is done does not sustain your interest. Maybe this is a reflection of the times. His *adavus* are clear, vibrant and have a lot of life and movement. The *abhinaya* can be slow because then it can be enjoyed. He did not give much importance to *abhinaya*. The most important reason for this is that the students came at about age five and gave their *arangetram* at ten, so he did not have the right students for *abhinaya*. Frankly speaking his forte was *nritta*, not *abhinaya*. It was left to dancers to use their own imagination for the *abhinaya*. We learnt the *mudras* from him but the expressions we mainly had to do ourselves. It is easy to work with other members of his family as they have the same style. If I were to go to another *nattuvanar* he might say—this is wrong, I want you to do it like this. That is because each *nattuvanar* has his own way. The death of my master has not hampered his way of doing Bharata Natyam. He has become more popular after his death.

Usha's statement confirms that the Dandayudapani *bani* is firmly established as an important component of Bharata Natyam.

Usha has one son, Vivek, who has studied *mridangam* and violin but will not pursue an artistic career. None of the non-hereditary members had children who were planning a professional career teaching dance.

3. GUNDAPPA[20] (MYSORE) AND K. (KOLAR) PUTTAPPA/J.(JATITAYAMMA)[21] *BANI*

GUNDAPPA (?-c.1968)

Gundappa's grandmother, Rangamma, was a dancer attached to the Venkataramasvami temple at Basavanahalli.[22] He trained with both his maternal uncle, Kittappa,[23] and his own mother, Jatitayamma, a dedicated *devadasi* who danced in the Parthasarathy Temple in the village of Nelamangalam (about 18 kilometres from Bangalore).[24] Gundappa trained the *devadasis* who performed in the Mysore palace—an illustration of the interconnection between the temple and court traditions. There were then at least three dance masters in the palace: Gundappa, his maternal uncle K. Kittappa[25] and K. Puttappa.

H.R. Keshavamurthy, a non-hereditary teacher trained in this *bani*, explained: "The differences between the Mysore and the other *banis* are that in the Mysore *bani nritta* was not so important." He stressed the secular role of the Mysore *bani*:

Devadasis had to dance when the Raja went out .... most of the *devadasis* attached to the palace had to dance. I used to see hundreds. On the elephant they set up a proper platform and they had to dance solo. But it was only *abhinaya*. The instruments were on another elephant. The dancers had to sing. In those days *tabla* accompanied Bharata Natyam, but they stopped this and now only *mridangam* is played.

He noted the group choreography and rich costumes: "I have seen *devadasis* dancing in a group. They all performed to one song. They wore very heavy jewellery: diamonds and gold. Venkatalakshamma used to wear so much jewellery—just look at her photographs."

C. (CHINNAYYA) N. (NAIDU) RADHAKRISHNAN (1928-) AND
H. (HOCHIHALLUR)[26] R. (RAMASWAMY) KESHAVAMURTHY (1928(?)-)

The two examples from the Gundappa *bani*, Radhakrishnan and
Keshavamurthy, were contemporaries. They both studied with
Gundappa in Bangalore during the same period. Gundappa's wife,
who was not a dancer, died very young and they did not have any
children. Thus the hereditary component is represented by
Gundappa's nephew, C. Radhakrishnan.[27] Neither of Radhakrishnan's parents had studied music or dance. H.R. Keshavamurthy
was a brahmin. He had an uncle who was an actor, so it was perhaps
not so unusual that he should have decided to be a dancer. H.R.
Keshavamurthy first performed in his uncle's troupe, but dance was
still regarded with suspicion:

It was not permitted in those days to learn this art. Somehow I was
stealthily able to do this without the knowledge of elders. My uncle did
not know that I was studying dance. We would be scolded if we even saw
the performance.... I went to the Mysore palace and watched. Jettitayamma
the *devadasi* performed there.

Training/Seva

Although Radhakrishnan and Keshavamurthy underwent instruction
during the same period they had separate classes. Neither lived with
his teacher, Gundappa, while training. As a relative, Radhakrishnan,
did not pay fees but was required to perform service for his teacher/
uncle in lieu of fees. Keshavamurthy on the other hand paid fees.
Radhakrishnan remarked: "I had to meet his daily expenses and
give him fruit and drinks (alcoholic beverages)." C. Radhakrishnan
also qualified for a non-artistic job:

I combined studying dance from the age of twenty (1948) with work as a
practical instructor at an Engineering College. In 1959, at the age of thirty-
one, when I received the prestigious award, Bharata Kalamani in Madras,
I resigned my job and took up teaching dance full time.

Artistic Training

Radhakrishnan studied and performed only Bharata Natyam. On the other hand, Keshavamurthy, after a very brief introduction to Bharata Natyam with a teacher who was employed in the palace in Mysore, switched to the Kathak style of dance which he performed. Later, when he started to concentrate on Bharata Natyam, he abandoned performing in the Kathak style and devoted himself to teaching Bharata Natyam. Like Radhakrishnan he too combined teaching dance with another profession; he taught in an elementary school until he retired in about 1980.

Both men had given solo music recitals—Radhakrishnan vocal and Keshavamurthy flute.

Children

Of Radhakrishnan's three daughters, two learnt dance but only the eldest had performed solo. Radhakrishnan stressed that she did not perform an *arangetram* because for their community, an *arangetram* was still regarded as a *devadasi* ceremony of dedication. Keshavamurthy presented an *arangetram* for both his daughters. The elder daughter's *arangetram* in 1962 marked the first time that he conducted a dance recital. Both daughters are qualified to teach dance but the younger has since had to abandon teaching because her husband disapproved. The elder continues to teach dance, both in her own home and in her father's school. Keshavamurthy's two sons had also been trained in dance; the elder had given an *arangetram*.

Keshavamurthy sent his elder daughter to Kalakshetra, primarily to learn dance theory, but also to expand the dance repertoire beyond that which he had learnt from his teacher, Gundappa. When his eldest son, Shyamprakash, presented his *arangetram* he included several dances from the Kalakshetra repertoire. Keshavamurthy was able to provide a full orchestra: three of his family were able to perform *nattuvangam*: himself, his elder son, Shyamprakash, and his elder daughter. Shyamprakash also played *mridangam*, Shyamprakash's wife played *vina* and Ravishankar, the younger son sang. In the families of both Radhakrishnan and Keshavamurthy, the artistic training for the children was done in conjunction with academic studies.

Academic Qualifications

Six of the seven children from the two families had completed college. One was in school but intended to attend college. Radhakrishnan and Keshavamurthy had completed school and both held other jobs as well as teaching dance. Radhakrishnan as a draughtsman, and Keshavamurthy as a school teacher. Radhakrishnan took up teaching dance full-time in 1959; while Keshavamurthy worked as a school teacher until he retired in the 1980s.

Keshavamurthy's elder son combined working in an aerospace factory with teaching dance. His personal preference was to teach dance and give up his other job, but his father will not allow him to do so.

Future of the Bani

The Gundappa/K. Puttappa *bani* is marked by several interesting features. In particular, the generally accepted fact that there is a preference for imparting knowledge to a blood relative does not seem to apply. Both examples from the older generation were from different castes, brahmin and *isai vellala*. They studied dance as day scholars, and did not live with their teacher. Radhakrishnan's wife (*isai vellala*) had been a dancer and danced in the dance troupe of the non-hereditary dancer, Ram Gopal. Her training and performing were done just before, and just after, the passing of the *Devadasi* Bill in Madras. She now teaches dance. Keshavamurthy's brahmin wife is not involved in the dance. Radhakrishnan's wife's performances were well received in Madras and other centres and he said they were profitable. Both men trained their daughters but only Keshavamurthy (brahmin) presented three of his children (two daughters and one son) in an *arangetram*. Keshavamurthy, after training his elder daughter and conducting her *arangetram* sent her to Kalakshetra. He also gave his children a good musical training so that he has been able to form a family orchestra. Whereas until recently, wives of any caste did not dance, Keshavamurthy's family were upset by the restrictions imposed on his daughter by her husband's family, who prevented her from teaching dance. Both Keshavamurthy and Radhakrishnan have completed school and combined another occupation with teaching dance. Both men have been able to support themselves by teaching dance since the 1980s.

This Mysore *bani* of Bharata Natyam is distinct and many of Radhakrishnan's students told me that they were "dedicated to saving and propagating it". All of my examples from the other Mysore *bani*, that of K. Puttappa (Leela Ramanathan, U.S. Krishna Rao, Chandrabhaga Devi, Ram Gopal, Mrinalini Sarabhai) later took training from the Tanjore Quartet *bani*. They acknowledged it as more important than that of Puttappa in their own artistic development. This leaves Keshavamurthy and Radhakrishnan as the only examples in my sample of the Mysore *bani* of Bharata Natyam as represented by the T. Gundappa *bani*. To treat this as "pure" would, however, be unrealistic. Not only has Keshavamurthy's daughter introduced the Kalakshetra *bani* to her family, but both families are exposed to a wide variety of interpretations and influences. After C. Radhakrishnan, the Mysore Tradition will probably be passed on by non-family members.

4. T.(TIRUVIDAIMARUDUR) P.(PANCHAPAKESHA)[28] KUPPAIYA *BANI*

T.P. KUPPAIYA (1887-1981)

The family of the late T.P. Kuppaiya, *isai vellala*, was associated with the dance for several generations and was given patronage by the Tanjore Court between 1798 and 1832 (*Marg* 1979: 134). Kuppaiya began his training with his father Panchapakesha (1842-1902) at the age of ten and worked with him for five years. His father died when he was only fifteen. He then trained with T. Kannaiya Pillai, a *nattuvanar* from Tanjore. In 1917 he moved to Tiruvidaimarudur after he was offered a position in the temple there to serve as a dance master and conduct dance during the temple rituals. Kuppaiya's first son, T.K. Mahalingam, was born the same year. Mahalingam remembers that there were seven or eight *devadasis* who would come to their home as day scholars and study with his father.

In return for studying dance, they all worked in the house. Some of the students also paid cash, but I cannot remember how much. In those days *devadasis* danced when they brought the deity out but it was only for about fifteen minutes. They were all on the payroll of the temple. Their duties also involved cleaning the vessels,[29] lighting the lamps and helping the priests.

Hereditary Component

There are nine examples, all but one of them are from the *isai vellala* community. Most are related to Kuppaiya either by blood or marriage. Two exceptions are T.A. Rajalakshmi a former *devadasi* who now teaches Bharata Natyam in Kumbakonam, and a brahmin, Sudha Chandrashekar who now teaches in the United States. She is one of many students trained in this *bani*, which continues to have a strong hereditary component. The T.P. Kuppaiya *bani* has been passed on by his three sons: the late T.K. Marudappa, T.K. Mahalingam and T.K. Kalyanasundaram.

Kuppaiya's daughter, K. Karunambal and her late husband A.T. Govindarajan (1914-84), who was Kuppaiya's student, also taught Bharata Natyam. Mythili, the wife of T.K. Kalyanasundaram, T.P.'s youngest son, also teaches.

K. Mahalingam (1916-)

K. Mahalingam trained in vocal from the age of nine to the age of twenty-one, with Gnanasundaram Pillai. He was a day scholar and paid fifty rupees per month. In addition he gave his teacher a gold sovereign and some clothes annually on Vijayadasami day (the day on which teachers are honoured). At the age of ten, guided by his father, he started *nattuvangam*, accompanying the eight or nine girls in his father's dance class. He first performed *nattuvangam* on the stage in 1930, when he was twenty-four, and in 1945 conducted the recital of the first dance student, entirely trained by him.

In 1942 Mahalingam married[30] Mangala, and his sister Karunambal married Mangala's brother, A.T. Govindarajan. Govindarajan had been training with Kuppaiya, in *nattuvangam*. The only son of a *tavil* player, he came to Kuppaiya as a trained vocalist, having studied previously with three teachers.

T.K. Karunambal (1923-   )

Karunambal told me that she did not receive any formal training in either music or dance, but because she "watched and listened" she was able to teach dance. Although the family feels that women should not perform *nattuvangam* in public, she has conducted dance recitals.

Children

Govindarajan and Karunambal had two sons and four daughters. Both sons trained in music. The elder son, G. Vasant was born in 1949 and studied violin with Narayanaswami, from the age of twelve to the age of thirty. Vasant studied vocal at the same time. Narayanaswami played for their family dance orchestra. Vasant gave his first solo violin recital in 1973 and has played for some dance concerts. When he was fifteen, he started to train in *nattuvangam* with his grandfather, Kuppaiya, and his uncle, Mahalingam. He told me that it was usual in their family to begin training with someone other than their own father.

Since his father's death Vasant has given up violin and concentrates on conducting dance recitals and teaching dance. His wife, Lalita, is the niece of Venugopal Pillai, his father's vocal teacher. Lalita did not learn dance or music. Their daughter, who was nine in 1984, studies dance in the family school and they would eventually like to present her *arangetram*. None of the daughters of the other family members has done this, although they have danced for school shows.

Govindarajan's second son, G. Gopalakrishnan, born in 1957, learnt *mridangam* and *ghatam* (mud pot used as a percussion instrument), probably with his uncle K. Kalyanasundaram. He uses *ghatam* to accompany dance and first performed *nattuvangam* in 1984. Both sons have completed high school.

All Govindarajan's daughters married. Although they learnt to dance they did not present *arangetrams*. They all taught dance before they married but only the youngest, G. Rajeshwari, married to a factory worker and living in Delhi still taught in the 1980s.

Women Involved in the Bani

The career of the women in the Kuppaiya family is particularly interesting. While both T.K. Karunambal, T.P. Kuppaiya's daughter and Mythili, K. Kalyanasundaram's wife teach in the family school, the *Rajarajesvari Kala Mandir*, only Mythili has had formal dance training.

MYTHILI KALYANASUNDARAM (1940-)

Mythili, was adopted by her aunt, Kamalambal,[31] a *devadasi*, and studied dance with her. In 1947, at the age of seven, she presented an *arangetram*, in Tanjore in the home of K. Ponnaiya,[32] whose son, K.P. Kittappa (Tanjore Quartet *bani*), now teaches dance. Mythili thinks it was because Kamalambal studied with Kannuswamy *nattuvanar*, K. Ponnaiya's father, that the *arangetram* was held in their home.

As she was adopted by her aunt, she lived and trained with her and did not have to pay fees. At fourteen she danced in the Tanjore Palace. In 1957, at seventeen, Mythili married T.P. Kuppaiya's youngest son T.K. Kalyanasundaram. They were related as T.P.

Kuppaiya's father, Panchapakesha, had adopted Mythili's grandfather who later became a businessman. Mythili's father was also a businessman and her mother knew some dance.

Mythili and T.K. Kalyanasundaram had five children—Kannaki (born 1963), Vasuki (born 1966), Bharati (born 1970), Sumati (born 1973) and Harikrishnan (1975). In 1984 all of them were involved in music or dance. Kannaki qualified as a chartered accountant and was employed as one; she also studied vocal and *vina*. Vasuki studied banking and music: vocal, violin and *vina*. Bharati was learning violin, Sumati vocal and Harikrishnan *mridangam* and vocal. All of them were still at school. Mythili said: "I think our son will teach dance. All the girls teach when our school is very busy on Saturdays and Sundays."

T. (TIRUVIDAIMARUDUR) A. (AMMANIAMMAL) RAJALAKSHMI (1917-)

T.A. Rajalakshmi trained with T.P. Kuppaiya. She was from a *devadasi* family living in Tiruvidaimarudur. Her family had been associated with the Mahalingesvara temple in Tiruvidaimarudur for several generations. Her mother Ammaniammal had also been a dancer. Her grandmother Kamakshi had not been a dancer but had been dedicated to the god. Rajalakshmi began her dance training at the age of seven. Kuppaiya's son, Mahalingam, was then an apprentice and helping his father. She remembered: "There were about fifteen girls studying dance ... The classes lasted for one or two hours."

Kuppaiya taught her everything, including *abhinaya* and singing. She never gave a solo vocal recital but knew the music necessary for dance. In 1928-29, at age eleven or twelve, she was dedicated to the Mahalingesvara Temple in Tiruvidaimarudur and gave her *arangetram*.

Thereafter she gave as many as twenty-four dance programmes a month, in Bombay and for several maharajas of small princely states.[33] She also reported performing as a duo with another dancer also called T. P. Rajalakshmi, but nicknamed Chidambaram Papa. In 1987 they had not seen each other for twenty years.

Rajalakshmi's last programme was in 1956 in Ootacamund, a hill station in south India. She then left for Calcutta where she stayed from 1956 to 1971, beginning at an institution and later teaching privately. In about 1963 she first performed *nattuvangam* for one of her students. In 1971 she returned to Tiruvidaimarudur where she taught privately, having about ten students. From 1984 she travelled by bus every second day to teach in nearby Kumbakonam, in the Jana Ranjani Sabha. When I met her again in 1993 she was recovering from a broken leg which she suffered when she fell from the bus while trying to get down on her way to teaching in Kumbakonam. She did not marry and had no children.

5. V. (VAZHUVUR) RAMAIYA *BANI*

V. RAMAIYA (1910-1994)

The late V. Ramaiya's ancestral village was Vazhuvur, a town near Mayavaram which is associated with the legend of *Gajasurasamharamurti* (Gaston 1982). Before his death, Ramaiya told me that he was trained by his mother's (Bhagyammal)[34] brother, Manikka *Nattuvanar*, the son of Samu *Nattuvanar*. He studied *abhinaya* from Madhurantakam Jagadambal. Jagadambal was one of the many *devadasis* who trained under Samu *Nattuvanar*, some of the others who were studying at that time were: Alarmelu, Nagammal and Rukmini (*Marg* 1982: 132). Ramaiya's artistic lineage begins with Nagappa *Nattuvanar*, who predated the Tanjore ruler Sarfoji II (AD 1798-1832), the patron of the Tanjore Quartet *bani*. The oral history of the family relates that Nagappa *Nattuvanar's* grandson, Veerappa, declined the patronage of the Tanjore Court. Veerappa's daughter was Samu *Nattuvanar's* mother.

Ramaiya also worked with K. Muthukumar. Later, Muthukumar sent his pupil Kamala Lakshman to work with him.

Hereditary Component

Ramaiya had five children. Of his three sons, the eldest, Samraj, born in 1938, became a *nattuvanar*, another, Gurunathan, an officer in a bank, and the last, Vinayakam, a freelance music director. Of his two daughters, Bhagyalakshmi, born in 1942, danced on the stage, when eight years old. Later, she taught dance in his school, but gave up after she married.

Ramaiya trained Samraj in *nattuvangam* and vocal. As recently as 1985, Vinaiyakam, Ramaiya's youngest son was trained by both his father and brother, Samraj to perform *nattuvangam*, for the English tour of one of Ramaiya's students. Samraj has trained both his sons, Palaniappan, born in 1961, and Kumaraguru born in 1972, in *nattuvangam*. The elder conducted recitals and taught full-time, while the younger was still at school. All of Samraj's four daughters have been involved in the dance. The first two, Balanagammal, born in 1962, and Rajam, born 1960, taught dance, although they never had formal training, or danced on the stage. Both of them gave up teaching when they got married. Kala, born in 1969, does *nattuvangam*, and Shri Devi, born 1973, had an *arangetram* and in 1988 was still giving dance recitals.

The V. Ramaiya *bani* remains largely hereditary and the family appears to have encouraged some of their children to be involved in dance. All the daughters, however, limited their involvement after marriage. While some only gave up performing, for teaching, others severed all links with the dance.

Other Artistic Expertise: Vocal and Mridangam

All dance training for this family was with relatives. Vocal and *mridangam* training was with non-relatives as well. None of Ramaiya's children, nor those of his son Samraj, have performed solo music recitals. S.K. Rajaratnam, who married into the family, performed his first solo vocal recital at the age of thirteen (1944), in a temple. Kamala Lakshman, best known as a dancer, also gave her first solo vocal recital in the Parthasarathy Svami Temple in Triplicane, Madras.

Non-Hereditary Apprentices

The two male apprentices in this survey, the late S.K. Rajaratnam, an *isai vellala* and S.K. Kamesvaran, a brahmin, were both trained vocalists, and both picked up the dance while acting as accompanists. Kamesvaran worked for one year as an apprentice with V. Ramaiya. Earlier he assisted another *nattuvanar*, Mahadevan Pillai, as a vocalist. Rajaratnam had a much longer association, working with V. Ramaiya for fourteen years, from age seventeen. In 1960 he married V. Ramaiya's niece. Neither of Rajaratnam's two sons have studied dance or music. One of them, Vijayakrishnan, born in 1961 is a chartered accountant, while Shankar, born in 1962 holds an M.B.A. (Master of Business Administration). Rajaratnam's daughter, Jayakamala, born in 1963, is a B.Sc. graduate, who combined academic studies with teaching dance with her father. She did not give an *arangetram*. She married in about 1988 and initially stopped teaching dance.

Dancers who Trained with V. Ramaiya

The women who worked with V. Ramaiya all trained as dancers. He trained both *isai vellala* and brahmin girls and was one of the most popular teachers, both before and after the passing of the *devadasi* bill. His best known dance student was a brahmin, Kamala Lakshman. She founded her own dance school in the 1960s. In the 1980s Kamala was living in the USA, where she performed and taught dance. Her only son was a college graduate but also studied *mridangam*, with a view to accompanying her dance recitals.

Another student, K.J. Sarasa, *isai vellala*, started her training before 1947 and presented her *arangetram* in 1949. After an apprenticeship with V. Ramaiya, she founded a dance school in Madras.

Academic Education

None of V. Ramaiya's immediate family are college educated, but the children of S.K. Rajaratnam and Kamala Lakshman have all completed higher education. Kamesvaran is encouraging his daughter, Mahalakshmi, to combine training in dance with a university correspondence course. According to her father she had little formal instruction in the dance but was able to pick up most of her technique by observation. She joined Kalakshetra for further studies in dance and theory.

Kamesvaran's wife, Saroja, assists him in teaching. She was his student and he conducted her *arangetram* before they married. They conducted their daughter's *arangetram* together.

6. K. (KATTUMANNARKOIL) MUTHUKUMAR *BANI*

K. MUTHUKUMAR (1874-1960)

K. Muthu-kumar was an *isai vellala*. His father was a bookkeeper; his mother, Yogam Ammal, had studied dance and music. She had performed *seva* in the Kartumannarkoil Temple (pers. comm. B.M. Sundaram). Muthukumar's sister, Kannambal, was a dancer attached as a *devadasi* to the Siva Temple in Kartumannarkoil. Muthukumar trained initially with his mother. In 1880, at the age of six he began training with P. (Pandanallur)[35] Nataraja (Pillai) and gave his first public recital. His mother wanted him to be a dancer and he continued to dance at weddings and other secular celebrations.

In 1895, at nineteen, he started to teach dance in Kattumannarkoil but he also travelled around the south giving dance classes in various towns and cities (Khokar 1964). Muthukumar was active in Madras in the 1930s and 40s, just before the upsurge of interest that led to the current dance boom. Thus he was too early to reap the financial rewards that came later. The dance scholar and critic, Mohan Khokar tells a pathetic story of how in 1959, Muthukumar wrote to the Government of India requesting a pension of one hundred rupees per month and it was refused. He died the following year.

Because many of his students went on to study with other teachers, and only then became famous, K. Muthukumar's contribution has often been overlooked. In the 1930s, the musicologist, Sambamoorthy helped Muthukumar by arranging for him to teach folk dance (*kummi*) in a school. At that time a Mudaliar family engaged him to teach their two daughters: Selvamani and Saroja. In return he lived with the family. Saroja became the famous dancer known as "baby Saroja". In 1934 and again in 1938-40 he taught Rukmini Devi, the founder of Kalakshetra (Sarada 1985: 48).[36] During the 1930s he taught many young brahmin girls: in particular Kamala Lakshman, Radha and Anandi, K. Lalita and Mrinalini Sarabhai. He conducted the classes in their homes. The late K. Lalita recalled: "All his students credit him with giving them a strong foundation in the basics, in particular being able to hold their arms extended to the side parallel to the floor without drooping elbows."

At his suggestion, several of his students (Kamala Lakshman, Anandi and Radha) later studied with V. Ramaiya when he retired to his village of Kattumannarkoil. It was there that the male dancer Nala Najan (an American) trained with him in 1949-53. Muthukumar's other important male student, Ram Gopal, brought him to Bangalore where he taught in his school.

Interrelationship with Other Banis

K.N. Dandayudapani sometimes sang for K. Muthukumar's students. In particular he accompanied Saroja Khokar's dance recitals. In this capacity he was able to learn his *bani*.

Other Musical Skills

K. Muthkumar played and taught the violin which he studied from Minakshisundaram of the Tanjore Quartet *bani*. Nala Najan reported that he would play the violin and sing during his *padam* classes.

Children

None of K. Muthukumar's family was directly involved in teaching the dance. He had one daughter. Neither she nor any of her children has been involved in the dance. Consequently there are no hereditary exponents of this *bani*.

Non-Hereditary Exponents of the Bani

Five teachers who were teaching his *bani* in the 1980s were: the late V.S. Muthuswamy (*isai vellala*, the late C.S. Kunchitapadam (non-brahmin, goldsmith), and the late K. Lalita (brahmin). Two were teaching and performing: Nala Najan (American) and Saroja Khokar (Mudaliar).

V. (VAIDISVARANKOIL) S. (SETHURAMU) MUTHUSWAMY (1921-1992)

V.S. Muthuswamy was the son of V. Sethuramu, a singer and *devadasi*. All his knowledge about his mother was second-hand as she died when he was four. She was formally married to Lord Vaidisvarasvami in Vaidisvarankoil. Although his guardian, V. (Vaidisvarankoil) Minakshisundaram was a *nattuvanar* and a distant relative of his mother, he did not study with him.

Instead, he began to study dance with K. Muthukumar at the age of fifteen (1936). He studied with him until 1940, living in his teacher's home, along with five or six other boys, none of whom stayed on to complete their training. There were also ten-fifteen girls. He described their marital status: "All the girls were married to the god and were attached to various temples around Kutralam. Some of them were married even before their dance training began." None of them paid fees. Muthuswamy remarked about their *seva*: "All of us had to wash clothes, massage the guru, and clean the articles for worship. I once broke an ancient conch shell. The girls mainly worked in the kitchen." He later studied with V. Ramaswamy *Nattuvanar*, and married his daughter, Valambal.

Before acquiring dance training Muthuswamy began vocal training when he was eight with a distant uncle. A year later he went to live in Mayavaram with Chidambaram Mahadevan Pillai with whom he studied vocal music for seven years. He did not pay him fees, nor did he give a solo vocal recital. He began his dance training with Muthukumar after becoming a fully-trained singer.

In 1941, at the age of twenty, V.S. Muthuswamy arrived in Madras and started to teach. In 1953, he conducted the first *arangetram* of two of his students, Sai and Subbalakshmi. They were cousins from a hereditary dance family. The *arangetram* was held in the Rasika Ranjani Sabha and S.K. Rajaratnam (V. Ramaiya *bani*) sang. In the latter part of his life many of his students came from outside India, in particular from France. He received the Sangeet Natak Akademi Award in 1990 for excellence in Bharata Natyam.

Relationship with Other Dance Families

S.K. Rajaratnam, the dance teacher and *nattuvanar* is a distant relative by marriage to Muthuswamy's guardian, V. Minakshi-sundaram. V. Minakshisundaram's daughter, Paruvan, married V. Ramaiya's brother, Nataraja Sundaram, a *mridangam* player and their daughter, Nagalakshmi married S.K. Rajaratnam.

Children

Muthuswamy had three sons and four daughters. Prior to his premature death, his eldest son received an M.A. degree in Social Sciences and was a lecturer in an Arts College. He married the daughter of the dance teacher and *nattuvanar*, K. (Kutralam) Ganeshan. She had taught dance at one time, but gave it up to work in jobs unrelated to dance.

Muthuswamy's second son, M. Selvan, lives in Mayavaram and combines working in the Education Department of the Government of Tamil Nadu with teaching Bharata Natyam in Kumbakonam. His dance training was not with his father, who lived and taught in Madras, but with his maternal grandfather, V. Ramaswamy in Kutralam where his mother lived. M. Selvan did not study vocal and spent only short periods with his father in Madras. The youngest son, born in 1965 looked after the family lands and was studying tailoring. All of four daughters married; none studied dance.

C. (Chidambaram) S. (Subbaiya) Kunchitapadam (1928-1991)

C.S. Kunchitampadam was from the goldsmith community. All of his brothers as well as his father (Subbaiya) worked as goldsmiths. Kunchitampadam's mother, Jagadambal was a singer. In 1941, at age thirteen, he started to study vocal from T.P. Narayanaswami (Tanjore Quartet *bani*) in Chidambaram, his native place. He studied as a day scholar and could not recall whether or not he had paid fees. At eighteen he gave a solo vocal recital in the Nataraja temple at Chidambaram. He was therefore a trained singer when he began to study dance with K. Muthukumar, in Kattumannar from age nineteen to twenty-five (1947-53).

He conducted the *arangetram* of his first dance student in Chidambaram in 1953. In 1955 he moved to Madras where he taught until his death in 1991. His wife's family were also goldsmiths. They had no children, nor did he teach any relatives.

K. Lalita (1918-1992)

K. Lalita, a brahmin woman, began learning Bharata Natyam with K. Muthukumar in 1931, at age thirteen in Madras. He went daily to her home to teach. She paid him fifty rupees a month and helped with his living expenses by purchasing meal tickets for him at a lodge. On completion of her training she did not give a formal *arangetram*. Her family would not allow it because in the 1930s it was still regarded as a *devadasi* tradition. In 1934, at the age of sixteen, she opened her own dance school "Sarasvati Gana Nilayam" in Triplicane in Madras.

Lalita studied vocal for ten years with Venkataraman Iyer, and *vina* from Subramaniam Sastrigal. She did not give a vocal *arangetram* but acquired her music diploma from Madras University. Her father died when she was fifteen and her brothers respected her wish not to marry, but to devote herself to dance. She formally adopted L. (Lalita) Ranganayaki Jayaraman, the daughter of the secretary of her dance institution, in 1934, and trained her to be a dancer. In 1948, at the age of thirteen, Ranganayaki gave her *arangetram*, which K. Lalita conducted. At that time it was unusual for a woman to do *nattuvangam*. Lalita had many students and most were brahmins. One of her most successful students, Saroja Vaidyanathan (brahmin) studied with her from age seven (c. 1945) and had her *arangetram* at the age of twelve (c. 1950). Marriage at sixteen interrupted her dance career but in 1974 she returned to performing and teaching and now has a school in New Delhi. Saroja has a diploma in vocal music from Madras University. Her only child, a son, is a graduate and is not involved in the dance.

In 1950, Ranganayaki danced in the *praharam* of the Nataraja Temple in Chidambaram after receiving special permission from its priests (*dikshitars*) who control the temple. This is an early example of a brahmin woman dancing in a temple. Ranganayaki has been trained by her mother in flute, violin, harmonium, *mridangam*, and *vina*. She plays *vina* and sings on both television and All India Radio.

Ranganayaki married one of K. Lalita's nephews and they have two sons: one lives and works in the USA, another works as a computer programmer, plays *ghatam* (mud pot) and runs a light music troupe.

SAROJA KHOKAR (*c.* 1930-)

Saroja Khokar, a non-brahmin (*mudaliar*), studied with K. Muthukumar from the age of six in 1936. About one year later, she gave her first public recital, conducted by him. She and her sister, Selvamani, toured extensively while very young and gave many programmes. Saroja still performs and teaches dance in Madras. Her father was a businessman and she married the well-known authority on dance and critic, Mohan Khokar. Mohan Khokar studied and performed Bharata Natyam as well as various other classical, and less classical dance styles. An excellent photographer, he has written extensively on dance. He was the Dance Secretary for the Sangeet Natak Akademi for many years. Saroja did not teach Bharata Natyam to any of her sons. One of them, Ashish learnt Odissi with Mayadhar Raut but did not pursue it professionally. He is a dance critic in Delhi for one of the major newspapers.

Hereditary Component of the Bani

This *bani* is being passed on by non-family members. Except for K. Lalita, who taught her daughter Ranganayaki, none of those who trained directly with K. Muthukumar have trained their own children.

All except K. Saroja took musical training before they began their dance training (V.S. Muthuswamy, C.S. Kunchitapadam) or afterwards (K. Lalita). The two men sang first for K. Muthukumar, thus assisting him when his students performed. K. Lalita did not assist her teacher, but began teaching independently. It is a common pattern for women to study the dance, perform and begin teaching, but without undergoing any formal apprenticeship as teachers or *nattuvanars*.

7. K. (KUTRALAM) GANESHAN *BANI*

K. GANESHAN (c. 1918-83)

The late K. Ganeshan studied and taught in Kutralam, Tanjore district. None of his students knew who his teacher was. He moved to Madras in 1955 where he taught until his death. Rajalakshmi Kalanidhi, a student of his, stated that when she was studying with him, his singing voice was "not good" but she was too young to comment on the level of classical training that he had had. He sometimes played on the *mridangam* to demonstrate its use in a dance recital. She felt he played it to concert standard. His teacher was Kutralam Kuppuswamy Pillai (pers. comm. B.M. Sundaram).

Hereditary Component of the Bani

K. Ganeshan's only daughter did not train in dance, hence the K. Ganeshan *bani* is represented by non-relatives all women: Rajalakshmi Kalanidhi (non-brahmin), T. Muthulakshmi, Indira

Rajan, and P.R Thilagam (*isai vellala*) and Malati Dominic whose mother was *isai vellala*.

T. Muthulakshmi and Indira Rajan both trained as dancers with him and stayed in his home while undergoing training. Indira Rajan is currently teaching and conducting recitals. T. Muthulakshmi teaches dance and can perform *nattuvangam*. She was permanently employed for several years as a singer by the professional dancer Swarnamukhi (Sampati Bhoopal *bani*), who was giving frequent recitals throughout India and abroad. Swarnamukhi is discussed later in this chapter. Up to five years ago Muthulakshmi sang for the recitals conducted by Indira Rajan. As both these women had trained with K. Ganeshan this would tend to reinforce the passing on of his teaching. P.R. Thilagam[37] was a professor of vocal music in Tiruvayyar and runs a dance school in her home in nearby Tanjore, known as the Sri Kamalambal Vidyalaya. She is assisted by her daughter, Kamalambal, who studied dance with the late T.S. Shanmugamsundaram (*isai vellala*) who taught in Kumbakonam.

Devadasis *in the* Bani

T. Muthulakshmi's older sister, T. Kalyani, was a dancer; their mother, T. Tillai Ammal, was a famous singer. She died in 1945 when Muthulakshmi was about eight years of age; Kalyani, who was twenty-one years older, brought her up. In 1929, at the age of thirteen, Kalyani was dedicated to the deity of the Ratnapurisvara temple in Tiruvalaputtur where she gave her first dance recital.

Muthulakshmi is three years older than Kalyani's son Navanita Krishnan, with whom she was living. Navanita allowed his own daughter to study dance for a month but then changed his mind because he said he wanted her to get married.

Muthulakshmi never married. She supports herself by accompanying dance recitals as a vocalist and teaching dance. She remarked: "I am happy I did not marry as I am free."

Neither Kalyani nor Muthulakshmi had much formal academic education but T. Kalyani had other plans for her son, Navanita. He said: "My mother wanted me to be a graduate so I completed my

B.A. in economics and now I work for the Tamil Nadu Housing Society as a Liaison Officer."

Teaching Situation/Seva

In 1945, at the age of eight, just after her mother died, T. Muthulakshmi went to Kutralam to live and study in the home of her teacher. In return for his teaching she paid fifty rupees per month and performed *seva* or service. She reported being lonely at times: "Master did not have a favourite, but at one time or other we could be beaten or scolded. I would sometimes go to the back of the compound where we lived and cry. We did not have our own room. Each of us kept all our belongings in a small box."

His other students such as Rajalakshmi Kalanidhi trained with him after he moved to Madras. She lived at home and her classes took place after school. She had more sentimental feelings towards her training.

Arangetram *and Professional Career*

In 1949, after three years of training, Muthulakshmi gave her first solo dance recital at the age of eleven. It was held in their family home in Tiruvalaputtur and was organized by her sister, T. Kalyani. Another *nattuvanar*, Kutralam Ramaswamy, was the second singer on this occasion. He was the father-in-law of the late *nattuvanar* V.S. Muthuswamy. During her performing career, T. Muthulakshmi performed in the temple premises as part of festivals, but not as part of temple rituals. She remembered performing frequently, about eight or nine times a month and she was paid for her recitals, starting at the age of thirteen. The payment was always given to her teacher to distribute and she remembers that he was "fair and generous".

Muthulakshmi gave her last public dance recital in 1954 when she was sixteen. In 1955 she went to Madras with K. Ganeshan and assisted him by teaching and singing until his death in 1983. One of their students, Mallika, later married Hemnath (non-hereditary Tanjore Quartet *bani*). She now teaches in the dance school run by her in-laws. Muthulakshmi also sang for the *arangetrams* and other dance concerts for K. Ganeshan's students: Indira Rajan (1952) and Rajalakshmi Kalanidhi (1959). Muthulakshmi trained in vocal with K. Ganeshan. Her first solo vocal recital was in 1955 at the age of eighteen, in a temple.

INDIRA RAJAN (1942-)

Indira Rajan is the cousin of K.N. Dandayudapani (K.N. Dandayudapani *bani*). Her mother, Sundara Kamakshi was Dandayudapani's paternal aunt. Indira is also related to K.J. Sarasa (V. Ramaiya *bani*), whose father, Jagadisan was another of her mother's brothers. Their common grandfather, Tirunallar Ramaswamy was a *nattuvanar*, Indira's mother, Sundara Kamakshi, was a professional singer[38] and her father, Pakkiriswami, a businessman. Her formal education was up to the third standard. She remarked: "From the time I was six, I wanted to be a dancer. I was not interested in studies. Now I only know dance." Indira Rajan started to study dance in 1949, at the age of seven. Like Muthulakshmi she lived in K. Ganeshan's home and did not pay fees. Although Muthulakshmi is her senior they would have been there at the same time. Indira commented:

If you do work in return for learning dance you don't get the same respect as if you pay fees. The students who paid fees did not have to do any work. I had to do housework such as grinding rice for *idli*, *dosai*, washing the guru's wife's clothes, drawing *kolams* (decorative designs painted on the doorstep), massaging and fanning the guru. It was very hard work.

This contrasts with the observations made by K. Ramaiya (Balasaraswati b*ani*) who believes that one gets better, and more sincere artistic training if one "pays" for it with service *seva* rather than money.

Debut Recital

Indira Rajan's dance training lasted for three years. In 1952 she gave her first solo recital at the age of ten, in the Jyothi Theatre in Karaikkal, her native village. K. Ganeshan conducted it and T. Muthulakshmi sang. Indira continued to study and perform with K.

Ganeshan for three more years during which time she was paid for performing. Indira's account of the division of the professional fee after a dance recital contrasted from that of Muthulakshmi's given in Chapter Four. While both state that the teacher received payment for the whole group, Indira stated that the dancer got half, the *nattuvanar* a quarter and the orchestra divided the remaining quarter between themselves.

In 1955, at the age of thirteen, she moved to Madras and started to teach. She had no formal vocal training, but as her mother was a well known professional singer she was exposed to a great deal of music while growing up. She taught herself *nattuvangam*. In 1958 she conducted an *arangetram* for the first time for one of her own dance students, Udaya Chandrika. It was held in the Museum Theatre in Madras and her mother, Karaikkal Sundara Kamakshi, sang. In 1958 it was still unusual for a dance recital to be conducted by a female *nattuvanar*, accompanied by a female singer.

Her marriage to a photographer was "self-arranged". The birth of her son, Praveen Kumar, in 1959 did not curtail her teaching dance and conducting recitals. She said: "My art always came first. My mother had to take care of our son."

But three years later she abandoned her performing career because of "marriage responsibilities", a common enough reason.

Her son completed a B.A. in Economics. She taught him dance and in 1985 stated that she would like him to be a great dancer and *nattuvanar*. He was, however, interested to act in films. In 1985, she was arranging for his marriage and was actively seeking an educated dancer.

P.(PARVATAVARDINI) R. (RAMATHILAGAM) THILAGAM (1926-)

P.R. Thilagam belonged to a hereditary family. She began to study dance at the age of seven (1943). She continued this for two years, travelling four times a week to Kutralam to study both dance and vocal with K. Ganeshan while living at home. Besides the basic training, she learnt three dances: *alarippu*, *jatisvaram* and *tillana*. She paid monthly fees of one hundred rupees for dance and the same amount for vocal instruction. In those days that was a significant amount.

Her mother, Parvatavardani Ramathilagam (a dedicated *devadasi*) had been singer. She died when P.R. Thilagam was two years of age and she was brought up by her grandmother, Kamalambal,[39] who was a dancer. This could account for the name of P.R. Thilagam's dance school, the Sri Kamalambal Vidyalaya, in Tanjore where she and one of her daughters, also called Kamalambal were teaching in 1988. Kamalambal, Thilagam's grandmother, had Tiruvarur Gopalakrishnan as her dance teacher and *nattuvanar*. She had learnt both *abhinaya* and abstract dance from him. Thilagam had not seen Kamalambal perform but reported that she had performed both in the temple and on secular occasions. Kamalambal owned land and a house. She died at the age of seventy-five. She had encouraged Thilagam to concentrate on singing rather than dance. Thilagam's vocal teacher, a brahmin, Srirangam Iyengar, was from the Puchi Srinivasan Iyengar *bani* and his brothers had been the vocal duo known as the Madurai brothers. Shrirangam Iyengar took the one-hour bus trip to Tanjore from Mannargudi four times a week to teach her at home. She reported that he gave her intensive training for three hours in the morning (8 a.m.-11 a.m.) and again in the evening (6 p.m.-9 p.m.). As he was a brahmin he ate only fruit and milk in her home. Her vocal *arangetram* was held in 1942, when she was sixteen years of age, in the Murugan temple in Swamimalai. She gave many vocal concerts, about five-six a month.

Thilagam still performs some ritual functions in the Tyagarajasvami Temple at Tiruvarur. Her family has the "right" to offer flowers to the deity before it is taken out in its chariot (*vahana*). When the image is travelling outside the temple she also has the "right" to fan it with a peacock *chamara* (Kersenboom 1984: 246-47).

Future of the Kutralam Ganeshan Bani

The Kutralam Ganeshan *bani* will be passed on by non-family members. The mothers of both T. Muthulakshmi and Indira Rajan were professional hereditary singers. Despite the campaign to ban the dance from the temples, T. Muthulakshmi began her training in 1945, only two years before dance in temples was officially forbidden; and Indira Rajan began in 1948, one year after the ban became law. Their actions suggest confidence in the dance. Both of them have been professionals and supported themselves solely through the dance. Indira's son, Pravin Kumar has been trained in dance and might take up the profession although he sees dancing in films as more lucrative.

Links in the Bani to Other Musical Families

There are several links to other musical families. T. Muthulakshmi was the youngest of three children. Her brother, a *nagasvaram* player married his daughter Chandra to the late K.J. Govindarajan, a dance teacher and *nattuvanar* (non-hereditary Tanjore Quartet *bani*). The late V.S. Muthuswamy's (K. Muthukumar *bani*) eldest son was married to a daughter of Kutralam Ganeshan.

8. S.(SEYYUR)[40] S.(SUNDARESAN) MANIKKAM *BANI*

S.S. MANIKKAM (?-1952)

S.S. Manikkam was an *isai vellala*. His father, S.S. Sundaresan, was also a dance teacher and *nattuvanar*. Both taught several *devadasis*; in particular S. (Seyyur) Jagadambal, was taught by the father and Jagadambal's daughter, Rukmini, by the son, an example of a *nattuvanar* family teaching several generations of *devadasis* from the same family. Another example of a *nattuvanar* family teaching several generations is P.S. Minakshisundaram (Tanjore Quartet *bani*) who taught both P. Kalyani and her daughter P. Jivaratnam (chapter 8).

P.S. Ramaswamy Iyer, a brahmin, studied with S.S. Manikkam in Madras and reported singing for the *devadasi*, Rukmini's, dance classes. Ramaswamy will carry on the S.S. Manikkam *bani* because, although Manikkam had one daughter born in 1939, she did not have any connection with the dance. Thus there is no hereditary component in this *bani*.

P. (PATTAKUDI) S. (SWAMINATHAN) RAMASWAMY IYER (1927-)

P.S. Ramaswamy, a brahmin, was born in Pattakudi, Tamil Nadu. He was not from a family of traditional musicians and stated that he "picked up" vocal music while listening to his sister's vocal class; a common occurrence for many young brahmin boys.

Ramaswamy's father, Swaminathan worked for the French government because at that time Pattakudi was governed by the French.[41] In 1943, Ramaswamy completed college, inspired by watching a performance by Kamala Lakshman, he then decided that he wanted to learn Bharata Natyam. He approached two *nattuvanars* from different *banis*: V. Ramaiya and T. Minakshisundaram. They wanted him to pay a monthly tuition fee of one hundred rupees, which was more than his salary at the time.

In 1945, supported by his father, Ramaswamy began dance training with S.S. Manikkam. Prior to that he had a job in Madras which he continued to do for about two years. His teacher urged him to quit his job and devote himself full-time to studying dance. In the 1940s, he saw a lot of dance concerts. One of the *devadasis* he saw perform was Ambhujan, a dancer who V. Sadasivan (brahmin, non-hereditary Tanjore Quartet *bani*) later accompanied for several years. He remembers that in the 1940s there were many dance programmes in conjunction with marriage celebrations. In 1948, he danced at a wedding, in male costume, along with a brahmin girl. A convention followed by some other male dancers of that time was to wear a female costume (e.g. K. Muthukumar).

Ramaswamy was a good singer and Manikkam was eager to teach him so he could assist him with his dance recitals. When Manikkam died in 1952, Ramaswamy took over teaching his students. His abilities as a singer and his relatively flexible attitude persuaded several dancers to employ him as a *nattuvanar*. He told me why another teacher's students, Uma and Jaya, hired him: "They wanted a teacher to travel around but as their teacher was old, he did not want to travel out of Madras. I went to Egmore and asked their teacher's (A.P. Chokkalingam) permission, which he gave."

Uma and Jaya danced together. They gave many recitals all over south India during the 1940s. At the same time he also taught cinema actresses. He recalled that Kutralam Ganeshan, V.S. Muthuswamy, T. Minakshisundaram, K. Ellappa, and the *devadasis* M.D. Gauri were also teaching in Madras at that time. In 1953 he learnt some *padams* with M.D. Gauri, who was by then virtually blind.

In 1969, he left Madras for Ahmedabad to teach Bharata Natyam at Darpana, the dance school founded and run by the dancer, Mrinalini Sarabhai. He said that one of the factors that encouraged him to leave Madras was that he had been sick with typhoid and had to stop taking his dance tuitions for seven months. This caused many of his students to study with other teachers.

Children

Neither of Ramaswamy's sons learnt music or intended to follow a career in dance. It was their own choice. One was an engineer working in Bombay; the other was going to study commerce. Ramaswamy had an arranged marriage, and his wife was not involved in music or dance.

D. MOHANRAJ (1929-)

D. Mohanraj came from the non-brahmin, Nayakar community. He was born in Madras. His parents died when he was very young. His father's brother worked in the Kapalisvara Temple, in Mylapore, setting up the lights. From the age of fifteen (1944), Mohanraj trained as a singer under Ramamurthy Sharma, a brahmin, for five years. His teacher did not charge him for classes and he reported that he later repaid him by teaching vocal classes for him. The teacher came to his home. Mohanraj gave vocal concerts, some of which he described as including "light songs". M.K. Thyagaraga Bhagavatar sang for the first half and he sang for the second half of the programme.

Mohanraj learnt dance while working as a vocalist in an dance orchestra. Initially he worked for V. Ramaiya. Later he worked for P.S. Ramaswamy. Mohan Raj stated that it was the *bani* of Seyyur

Manikkam which he studied with P.S. Ramaswamy, that has had the greatest influence on his approach to the dance: Mohanraj made himself available for dancers who needed a *nattuvanar*: "Whoever calls me, I will go".

He worked and travelled with the dancer Chitra Vishveshvaran for many years and hence he knows her repertoire, which is that of T.A. Rajalakshmi (T.P. Kuppaiya *bani*) and V. Ramaiya. Initially he also worked with the latter. He also conducted recitals for Lakshmi Vishwoinathan and so became acquainted with the K. Ellappa/T. Balasaraswati *bani*. Another dancer, Srinidhi Rangarajan used him to conduct the repertoire she studied with Kamala Lakshman (V. Ramaiya *bani*) and S.K. Rajaratnam. For twenty years Mohanraj has been giving dance instruction. He travels by bus to students' homes and does not have a main centre or central gathering point.

Children

Mohanraj had two daughters by his first wife, the eldest born in 1957. Both daughters completed high school. He regretted not training them in dance, as he now has asthma. Had he done so they could have assisted him. He intended to train his son by his second marriage, born in 1977, and had already begun to teach him some of the basic steps and some *nattuvangam*. He wanted his son to be a *nattuvanar*. When I met him, in 1988, his son was studying in an English medium school. He was teaching him vocal and was planning to enrol him in the *mridangam* class at the Bharatiya Vidya Bhavan, "because then his *nattuvangam* will be better".

DIVISION III: *DEVADASI BANIS*

This division comprises purely *devadasi banis*. Transmission within these *banis* has taken place by two main routes. In the first, female dancers taught their repertoire to their own female members or to *devadasis* from other families. In the second, they taught their concert repertoire to musicians who performed with them, especially *nattuvanars*.

1. M. (MYLAPORE) D. (DORAIKANNU) GAURI *BANI* (*c*.1900-1970)

M.D. Gauri had been a dedicated *devadasi* attached to the Kapilesvara Temple in Mylapore a suburb of Madras. She had a vast repertoire of descriptive songs (*padams* and *javalis*). Gauri had received training in *abhinaya* from her mother Doraikannu and in dance from two *nattuvanars*; one was Nellore Munuswamy (pers. comm. B.M. Sundaram). Gauri also taught the other *devadasi* in this division, T. Balasaraswati.

Gauri trained both hereditary and non-hereditary female dancers. The men she trained were only from non-hereditary families. Some of them were: T.V. Venkataraman, Nana Kasar, Parvati Kumar, and U.S. Krishna Rao. All of them taught dance and some of them became dancers. All the *nattuvanars*, who studied with her said that their training in the basic steps (*adavus*), abstract dance (*nritta*), and most dance compositions, had been with a *nattuvanar*; Gauri had given them training only in *abhinaya*.

2. T. (TANJORE) BALASARASWATI *BANI*

T. (TANJORE) BALASARASWATI (1918-1984)

T. Balasaraswati belonged to a *devadasi* family of musicians and dancers. Her ancestor, Papammal, was a dancer in the Tanjore court in the eighteenth century and Papammal's granddaughter, Kamakshi (1810-90) was also a court dancer. The training of Balasaraswati's family was linked to that of the Tanjore Quartet *bani* because it is said that Gangamuttu and Papammal were contemporaries (*Marg* 1982: 126). Balasaraswati's musical lineage is also important. Her grandmother, T. Dhanammal, played the *vina* and her mother, T. Jayammal, was a vocalist. Balasaraswati's dance *arangetram* took place in the Kamakshi Amman Temple in Kanchipuram in 1925 when she was seven.

Balasaraswati was trained in dance by N. Kandappa (1899-1941) and her *bani* evolved from this. Kandappa was trained by, and was related to, the Tanjore Quartet *bani*. Balasaraswati added the musical expertise of her family to the dance tradition of Bharata Natyam she had been taught, and passed it on to three male *nattuvanars*: K. Ellappa,[42] who had originally sung in her orchestra, T.K. Ganeshan, the son of her teacher, T.N. Kandappa, and K. Ramaiya, a trained vocalist. Her *bani* was also passed on to her own daughter, Lakshmi Shanmugan-Knight. Other important students were Nandini and Priyamvada, the daughters of one of the former Secretaries of the Madras Music Academy, V. Raghavan. The latter were brahmins. An example of the interdependence of *isai vellala*, and brahmins in this *bani* was recounted to me by Nandini Raghavan regarding T.K. Ganeshan's funeral in 1987. Nandini had been paying for Ganeshan to live in an ashram and when he died she was one of four persons at his funeral. K. Ramaiya (*isai vellala*) was the only male present and lit the funeral pyre. The bond between K. Ramaiya, T.K. Ganeshan and Nandini Raghavan was not as blood relatives but as recipients of the same artistic tradition.

T. (Tanjore) K. (Kandappa) Ganeshan (1923-1987)

T.K. Ganeshan's great-grandfather, Jagannathan married one of the daughters of S. Ponniah (one of the original founders of the Tanjore Quartet *bani*), but a good deal of his training was with qT. Balasaraswati's family. While he was young his father, T.N. Kandappa, did not teach in their home, but travelled to his students' homes to teach. Kandappa travelled a great deal, working in Uday Shankar's school in Almora for some time. Consequently, his son was not with him for long periods of training. He died when Ganeshan was eighteen. Ganeshan was encouraged to pursue academic study and he completed high school. He was able to sing and play the *mridangam* as his father had also done. He explained how he was taught:

My great grandfather was a *nattuvanar* and a good composer, so was my grandfather, and my father Kandappa, but none of my musical training was conducted in a formal manner. You see, it is our family tradition. Whenever my father played I would watch and listen. I also listened to concerts when I was young. I was inspired by great artists. One *mridangist* in particular, Palani Subramaniam Pillai, was my ideal, so despite being left handed I play *mridangam*.

Although Ganeshan has never played *mridangam* for dance recitals in public, one of his foremost disciples, Nandini Raghavan (brahmin) remembers that he would often play for her classes. When I interviewed him in 1986 he was ambivalent about his profession. His comments illustrate the importance of coming from a hereditary family for gaining exposure to the dance.

When my father died there was no other goal or choice for me. People forced me to learn music and dance, so that my father's name would carry on. After my father's death I went and stayed first in Madras with (T.K.) Ponnaiya, (K.P.) Kittappa's father and later in Tanjore and Pandanallur from the age of twenty to twenty-two (1943-45).

He described his training at that time with P.S. Minakshisundaram:

I helped Minakshisundaram,[43] both in Tanjore and Pandanallur, with practical things, not with music. He was pretty old then, but still teaching.[44] As far as my training went, Minakshisundaram forced me to watch the class and see things, that is all. The dancers, [U.S.] Krishna Rao, Shanta Rao and the *nattuvanars*, [P.S.] Swaminathan and [K.P.] Kittappa were also there. At that time Kittappa was not involved in the dance profession.

In 1945, he went to Madras to live in the home of his father's most famous student, T. Balasaraswati. He described it as "living as a family member", but in return he was training to replace his father as Balasaraswati's *nattuvanar*. "Jayammal, Bala's mother, forced me to sing in their style. Jayammal would advise me, she didn't teach me and after training from 1945 for six years I conducted Bala's recitals from 1959 until 1972."

K. (KUMBAKONAM) RAMAIYA (1941-)

In 1972, K. Ramaiya replaced T.K. Ganeshan as T. Balasaraswati's *nattuvanar* and accompanied her on her foreign tours. Ramaiya was born in 1941 in Kumbakonam, where he studied *nagasvaram* from the age of seven to twelve. He lived with his teacher and performed *seva*. In 1953, he began to learn violin which he did for four years, once again living with his teacher. His teacher did not teach his own son. In 1957 at the age of sixteen Ramaiya went to Madras with the intention of becoming a soloist. A chance meeting with Balasaraswati's brother, T. Vishwanathan, the flautist, and the opportunity of a Government of India scholarship to study dance with Balasaraswati, at her school in the compound of the Music Academy, changed his career.

At Balasaraswati's school, T.K. Ganeshan instructed him in the basic steps. In 1964, when I studied in Balasaraswati's school we both shared the same class. That year he joined Balasaraswati's dance orchestra as the second singer while T.K. Ganeshan conducted the recitals. He did this for five years (1964-69). In 1969, he left "with Bala's permission" to teach in Bombay, in the dance school of the dancer, Vyjayanthimala Bali. Leaving with the permission of his teacher meant that he still had the option to return to work with her later.

At the age of twenty-eight (1969), he performed *nattuvangam* for the first time in public for one of Vyjayanthimala's school shows. Balasaraswati was in the audience and, in 1972, she invited him to tour abroad with her. He worked with her until her death in 1984. After that, he combined teaching dance at the Music Academy School, in Madras, with giving private instruction. In 1989 he was teaching dance at Annamalai University in Chidambaram, Tamil Nadu.

While K. Ramaiya is from the *isai vellala* community and many of his relatives are musicians, principally *nagasvaram* players, none of them has been *nattuvanars*. His career is unusual in that he has trained with two of the most important traditional families: the one a *devadasi* family (T. Balasaraswati) and the other, the Tanjore Quartet *bani* (K.P. Kittappa). He started to work with the latter in 1985. Ramaiya was eager to expand his knowledge and not be limited to one *bani*. His comments showed the importance of being chosen by a teacher and given the opportunity to watch, listen and observe:

Kittappa is training me. He asked me to go with him and sit. Kittappa has never trained anyone. He said to me. You are the right person. I don't pay him but I run errands. I have a motor scooter. If he needs to meet someone I go on my scooter and inform that person. I do any tasks that he requires. In Madras, Kittappa stays in the Karpagam Lodge which is just near my house. As he is old he often needs some assistance.

He was confident that Kittappa would not withhold any of his "special knowledge" and would teach him all the musical and dance skills unique to the Tanjore Quartet family.

Children

The late T.K. Ganeshan never married. K. Ramaiya is married and has two sons. Both attend school, but are taking musical training as well. One, born in 1973, is learning vocal, the other born in 1975, *mridangam*. The music teachers come to their home. Ramaiya is taking both the academic and musical training of his children very seriously.

Academic Education

K. Ramaiya studied to the eighth standard. He commented:

Studies are important. I take my children to school every day and pick them up. I also like to be present during my eldest son's vocal lessons so that I know the type of training he is getting. I am reducing the number of tuitions I give in dance so that I can supervise their studies. I want my children to be graduates and have music as a side-line. I want them to be government officers. There is no security in music. If you get a "job" you will get paid whether or not you work hard or are intelligent.

In 1987, a year after he had made the above comment, Ramaiya was offered K.P. Kittappa's job as a professor at Annamalai University in Chidambaram. It was tempting, with a fixed salary every month, sick leave, pension, etc. but he refused. He gave the following reasons:

I thought a lot about it but I won't take it. Firstly there are mainly boys studying the dance so there will not be much opportunity for me to conduct recitals and build up students ... I would be forgotten if I left Madras. But more important, I want my sons to come up in music and how is that possible in Chidambaram? There is very little cultural activity in Chidambaram. All the good musicians and music teachers are here in Madras. My sons can train with the best, and besides, when the time comes for them to appear on stage they will do that in Madras and then they can launch their career. They can listen to good music here in Madras. They are exposed to more artistic activity than being stuck away in Chidambaram.

His final comment sums up the decline of the temple towns as cultural centres. Nevertheless, in 1989, when I met him at the Madras Music Academy, he had accepted the job in Chidambaram. He said: "My sons will go to the university there, I can come back to Madras often".

K. (KANCHIPURAM) ELLAPPA (1913-1974)

K. Ellappa was from a family associated with music and dance. His grandfather was Pachaimuttu *nattuvanar* He had his initial vocal training from his uncle and used these skills to accompany the dance students of another relative, his uncle, Tiruvengadam[45] *nattuvanar*. Hence he traces his dance training to him. The actual details about his artistic training are unclear. When he was hired as a singer by T. Balasaraswati she trained him in her repertoire and a lot of his dance training was augmented by watching her recitals. This experience was invaluable for him as later, in about 1959, when they no longer worked together he was able to attract important professional dancers. These included Yamini Krishnamurthy, Mrinalini Sarabhai, and Ram Gopal as well as others who wished to be exposed to T. Balasaraswati's repertoire. I remember in 1964 when I was studying with him that he could, and would, stand to demonstrate some of the dance movements.

Children

K. Ellappa had three sons and three daughters. When I was studying with him (1964-67, 1969-70), one of his daughters was married and one was "at home" waiting to be married while the third was

attending school. Only the eldest son E. Gnanaprakasham studied
Bharata Natyam and assisted his father by singing during recitals.
In the 1960s, E. Gnanaprakasham moved to Calcutta to teach, but
he died in the 1970s. The second son became a mechanic and the
youngest son, Palani, did not study music, although his father tried
to encourage him to come and watch the classes. I do remember that
for dance recitals conducted by his father, Palani often pumped the
sruti box or drone. His three daughters did not study dance, watch
the classes, or assist him while he taught.

U. (UDIPI) LAKSHMINARAYANAN (1926-)

Lakshminarayanan is a brahmin and began learning Bharata Natyam
with K. Ellappa at the age of twenty-one. He had learnt some dance
before that in Dharwar (Karnataka). He studied with K. Ellappa for
seven and a half years, performing *seva* for his teacher and paying
no fees. He picked up music and *nattuvangam* informally. He began
teaching Bharata Natyam in 1957.

Because of his association with K. Ellappa, he conducted the
recitals of several of K. Ellappa's former students.

Children

Lakshminarayanan had five children. All were being educated;
only his youngest daughter, Madhumati was learning Bharata
Natyam. She combined this with studying for a B.A. in music at
Queen Mary's College. Two of his daughters completed a B.Com.,
another a B.A. One was studying *vina*. All the daughters said that
they would have liked to have studied dance. Madhumati was the
only one who had been allowed to do so. Although she had not
presented an *arangetram*, she performed in their ancestral town of
Udupi, in the Krishna Temple "in front of god". Before about 1981
Lakshminarayanan did not have enough room in his home, or a
central spot where the students could gather for classes. This may
be the reason why he did not teach his elder daughters. All this
changed when he started to teach group classes in the Narada Gana

Sabha. Madhumati began her dance lessons there and soon began assisting her father by teaching the junior classes. Because he wants her to be a professional, she is also studying vocal music so that she can become a *nattuvanar*. Lakshminarayanan is also teaching dance to his brother's two daughters.

Lakshminarayanan's son was in his final year of B.Com. and was studying *mridangam*. He intended to give a solo recital in a year. Lakshminarayanan did not want his son to be a professional dance teacher or musician, but his son had other ideas. He said: "Life may be difficult but music and dance are great art".

DIVISION IV: RECENT *BANIS*

1. THE KALAKSHETRA *BANI*

This division includes all those who trained at Kalakshetra, the dance school established by Rukmini Devi in 1936[46] at Adyar, just outside Madras city. There is no hereditary component in this group, as Rukmini Devi had no children. Many of her former students, however, have children who are being trained as dancers and teachers, so a hereditary component may emerge. Kalakshetra is an important institution for training students in all aspects of Bharata Natyam. The majority of this group are brahmin and female, although there is a significant number of both male and female non-brahmins including Nairs, Christians and a Jew. The group includes only one *isai vellala* (T.R. Devanathan).

RUKMINI DEVI (1908-1984)

Rukmini Devi trained in vocal music as a child, as was the custom for most brahmin girls in southern India. Her dance training began in 1934. Her first teacher was the *devadasi*, M.D. Gauri, the second, P.S. Minakshisundaram, and the third, K. Muthukumar. After Kalakshetra was founded, the *devadasi*, Karaikkal Saradambal taught there. Saradambal was well known for her *nritta*: "She polished the *adavus* and made these graceful" (Sarada 1985: 20). Saradambal's contribution was significant as she "taught special traditional exercises for the students before the regular class hours" (ibid: 21). At the time of her death, M.D. Gauri was employed to teach *abhinaya* at the school.

Another hereditary master, A.P. Chokkalingam of the Tanjore Quartet *bani*, also taught there until 1943. His departure "because of monetary considerations" (ibid: 49), marked a turning point for Kalakshetra and a complete break with the hereditary *isai vellala nattuvanars* (Sarada 1985: 50). Most of the staff who had received their training before joining the school left eventually because they could earn more as independents. Among those who trained at the school, artistic considerations were also important. Some believed that they were not given sufficient opportunity to perform and create their own work within the context of the institution.

Rukmini Devi took several Bharata Natyam *banis*, which she studied from hereditary practitioners, and evolved her own interpretation based on those elements which she felt were most aesthetically pleasing:

Rukmini [Devi] was particular that there should be no unnecessary movements of the foot [sic] or any limb of the body ... This resulted in the Kalakshetra style of dance concurring with the descriptions contained in the ancient treatises of Dance. A new Kalakshetra style developed (Sarada 1985: 20-1).

Artistic Training of Senior Teachers at Kalakshetra

Among the teachers who were trained by one or all of the original trio of M.D. Gauri, P.S. Minakshisundaram, and K. Muthukumar, only two remained at Kalakshetra in the 1980s: Sarada Hoffman and Jayalakshmi. Two others, Lalita Shastri and Malati Srinivasan had their own institutions. Malati left Kalakshetra in 1949 at the same time as K.N. Dandayudapani. I have included her in the Dandayudapani *bani*. All four of these women were brahmins. Indeed, all of the women teachers and all but two of the men were brahmins. Only one member of the *isai vellala* community came to

Kalakshetra to train, rather than teach (T.R. Devanathan). He joined in the early 1960s.

Offshoots of the Kalakshetra Bani

The *bani* of K.N. Dandayudapani is often cited as an offshoot of Kalakshetra because its founder, K.N. Dandayudapani, received additional training in dance and *nattuvangam* while working there as a vocalist.

I talked with several teachers who had received significant influence from Kalakshetra. All of them had trained there. Some of the early male students received scholarships from Kalakshetra to study there (Adyar Lakshmanan, his elder brother K. Ramarao,[47] V.P. Dhananjayan). C.V. Chandrashekar and V. Ramani did not. All, except V. Ramani, came as young boys and were educated and grew up there. Narasimhachari and the late T.R. Devanathan were already trained vocalists when they joined Kalakshetra and Narasimhachari had been performing another style of dance, Kuchipudi, from the age of five.

C.V. Chandrashekar, V. Ramani, Adyar Lakshman, K. Ramarao, V.P. Dhananjayan and Shanta Dhananjayan, and Narasimhachari were all taught dance by Rukmini Devi and Sarada Hoffman, as well as others. All of this group now operate their own schools and all are very much influenced by the Kalakshetra *bani*.

V.P. Dhananjayan, Narasimhachari, and Vasantalakshmi all completed university degrees by correspondence. They did this in the early 1970s as a "precaution", but from the late 1970s both their dance schools and performing careers flourished, giving them confidence to pursue dance full-time.

None of my examples from the Kalakshetra tradition presented their first solo recitals of either dance or music in a temple. During their period of training they all lived at Kalakshetra and all of them studied dance and vocal and danced on the stage prior to teaching dance. K. Ramarao and Adyar Lakshmanan were both professional musicians, performing on All India Radio. Ramarao has also given a solo *gottuvadyam* recital. Adyar Lakshman worked for many years as a *mridangist* for both dance and music concerts. V.P. Dhananjayan and Narasimhachari took tuition in *mridangam* after leaving Kalakshetra.

The only *isai vellala* student who was trained by the Kalakshetra school was T.R. Devanathan. He brought with him previous training in *mridangam*, *konnakol* (speaking drum syllables) and vocal— all skills that he acquired from his father. "Pure" Kalakshetra school products (i.e. those that can attribute all their training both in music and dance to that institution) to date have been limited largely to upper caste students.

Narasimhachari comes from a traditional brahmin family of entertainers and was taught vocal and dance by his father and began performing in his father's troupe at a very early age. He taught dance to his wife Vasantalakshmi.[48]

Children

The late Rukmini Devi did not have children. Nor did two of the important teachers at Kalakshetra, S. Sarada and Jayalakshmi. Sarada Hoffman's son and daughter studied at university in America. Her daughter studied some dance at Kalakshetra but did not give an *arangetram*.

Adyar Lakshmanan's daughter studied dance with him and the other teachers in his school. His twin sons were learning *mridangam* with someone outside the family, despite the fact that their father and his half brother, Gopi, play *mridangam*. Ramarao's eldest daughter has learnt dance at the same school run by her uncle where her father teaches but she has not performed an *arangetram*. She wants to be a chartered accountant. Both daughters of the late Lalita Shastri studied dance with their mother and performed *arangetrams*, which were conducted by their mother. One teaches dance in Hyderabad and both would like to perform more. They both graduated with a B.A. Lalita's son did not learn dance; he took a secretarial course.

Both of V.P. Dhananjayan and Shanta's sons have learnt some dance and *mridangam*. In 1989 the eldest was more interested in studying engineering. V.P. Dhananjayan hoped that the younger one Satyajit, would take over the school, as he was an accomplished performer. Both of Narasimhachari's daughters performed dance, having been taught by him and his wife, Vasantalakshmi, who is also a dancer and teaches along with him in their school.

Of the nine brahmin children, two were in the USA studying (Sarada Hoffman), one wanted to be a chartered accountant (Ramarao), one was studying engineering (Shanta and V.P. Dhananjayan), two were studying *mridangam* (Adyar Lakshmanan), six were learning dance (Adyar Lakshmanan's daughter, Shanta and Dhananjayan's younger son, Vasantalakshmi and Narasimhachari's two daughters, K. Ramarao's two daughters), and both of Lalita Shastri's daughters had given *arangetrams*.

T.R. Devanathan, the only *isai vellala*, had five children. He trained one of his daughters to dance and she presented her first dance recital in a temple in 1980 as part of a festival. He was adamant that it was not an *arangetram*. His eldest daughter was a typist, while the third was studying at school, as were his two sons. One of the sons (D. Gnanapanditam) studied some flute, but was studying *mridangam* in the 1980s, and another (D. Kumaraguru) was studying violin. T.R. Devanathan said that he would teach one of his sons *nattuvangam* later. Two of the daughters whose parents studied at Kalakshetra, one a brahmin, (Lalita Shastri's daughter) and the other from a traditional family (T.R. Devanathan's daughter, Abhirami), teach dance.

The Kalakshetra Legacy

The Kalakshetra *bani* is an example of a school that was founded on the training of *devadasis* and *isai vellala* teachers, but was "liberated" from the control of traditional masters, when the school began to train its own dance teachers and *nattuvanars* (Sarada 1985: 50). The artistic vision of the founder, Rukmini Devi, has been the paramount influence. Essentially, she selected dances and themes from the traditional repertoire, but made adjustments according to her perception of how the dance should be taught and performed. These reflected her own aesthetic criteria. Many of the Kalakshetra graduates continue to perform and teach the repertoire that they studied at Kalakshetra but they also choreograph their own dances. The standardized repertoire of Kalakshetra has been taught and disseminated all over India by teachers and *nattuvanars*. This is an advantage for dancers who travel away from Madras, because it is relatively easy to assemble an orchestra that is familiar with the Kalakshetra repertoire. There are many persons from the younger category who continue to make important contributions to teaching and performing, including: Jayalakshmi Eshwar (Delhi), Leela Sampson (Delhi), V Gayatri (Bombay), etc.

2. RE-CREATION/INNOVATION BANIS

Here I have included three examples named after persons who have re-created a dance tradition that is closely associated with Bharata Natyam.[49] Some have based their movements on dance postures (*karanas*) carved on temples and described in texts such as the *Natya Sastra*. Two examples are Padma Subrahmanyam (dancer) and Sampati Bhoopal (*nattuvanar*) who taught his daughter Swarnamukhi. Others, such as Parvati Kumar dancer (dance teacher and *nattuvanar*), have reconstructed a form of Bharata Natyam that was performed several hundred years ago, but survives only in fragments described in texts (Parvati Kumar 1989; *Marg* 1982: 125). Another, M. Durairaj Iyer, *bhagavatar*, dancer, teacher and *nattuvanar* developed a technique that incorporated movements from a closely related dance style, Bhagavata Mela, which has an affinity with Bharata Natyam and shares a common history. He also reconstructed several styles of dance identified as *Perani* and *Sudha Nrittam* which are described in the *Natya Sastra* and a thirteenth century Sanskrit text, *Nrittaratnavali* (Raghavan 1965: 138; Parthasarathy 1989: 23-24).

There is only one case of hereditary transmission in this sample; the dancer/teacher Swarnamukhi, daughter of Sampati Bhoopal. Among the other representative, M. Durairaj and Padma

Subrahmanyam do not have children, and Parvati Kumar's children are not professionally involved in teaching dance. All of this group looked to the past for their inspiration, finding it in carvings on temples, descriptions from early texts, or pre-existing dance styles. They all evolved in the 1960s.

2A. SAMPATI BHOOPAL *BANI*

SAMPATI BHOOPAL (1927-1975)

Sampati Bhoopal was a Telugu Naidu, originally from Naidupetta in Nellore district, Andhra Pradesh. He was brought up in Rangoon (Burma), where his father, S. Narayanaswamy lived and worked as an advocate. As Sampati was fond of dance, he went to Tanjore and stayed with Doraiswamy, a traditional dance master and studied the traditional Bharata Natyam repertoire. He did not pay for his classes but did *seva* in return. He was the only one student of Doraiswamy to become famous.

In the 1950s, Sampati Bhoopal began to create his own style of Bharata Natyam which incorporated dance postures (*karanas*) described in the *Natya Sastra* and carved on the temple gateways of many south Indian temples (Gaston 1982). He also integrated yoga postures and developed different basic steps (*adavus*) from those in use at that time.

Sampati Bhoopal trained his daughter Swarnamukhi and conducted her *arangetram* in their native village when she was eight years of age (1958). She was teaching his *bani*; hence the *bani* may be regarded as hereditary. Swarnamukhi, however, did not confine herself to her father's repertoire. Like most professional dancers today, she has studied, and continues to study, with *nattuvanars* from different *banis*, "I learnt a full set of dances from each teacher so I could know about their individual styles. The difference is very slight. Some *adavus* are different and the look is different. Every recital I include compositions by different masters."

She belongs to the group of professional dancers who believe that ultimately each will evolve their own interpretation and in time create their own *bani*. As with many professional dancers her background is eclectic. Two of her teachers were from the K. Muthukumaraswamy *bani* (C. Kunchitapadam and V.S. Muthuswamy), and one from the Tanjore Quartet *bani* (P.C. Subbarayan). She also studied *abhinaya* with Kalanidhi Narayan (Kanappa *bani*) and studied the north Indian style, Kathak, from Vishnu Vazakar, for the highly developed rhythmic component. Her father taught her *nattuvangam* and she studied vocal with a family friend, Harihar Iyer, a brahmin. He played harmonium in Sampati Bhoopal's troupe of forty-five dancers and musicians. Her mother, Ranjini Bhoopal, had been a dancer, trained by her future husband, when he was teaching dance in Madurai. Swarnamukhi's elder sister, Devika Rani, sang and also performed *nattuvangam* for her, as did a former *isai vellala* dancer, T. Muthulakshmi (Kutralam Ganeshan *bani*). Swarnamukhi stopped performing in the 1990s.

This *bani* is very fluid and continues to be influenced by others. It has similarities with the Padma Subrahmanyam *bani* in that both have incorporated *karanas* into their dance, but they have integrated them differently. Whereas in the 1980s, Swarnamukhi combined creating her own *bani* with studying various *banis* with several teachers, Padma Subrahmanyam is not known to have augmented her training after she began her research into the greater possibilities of movement within the structures of Bharata Natyam.

2B. PADMA SUBRAHMANYAM *BANI*

PADMA SUBRAHMANYAM (1941(?)-)

One of Padma Subrahmanyam's first teachers was V. Ramaiya. He conducted her *arangetram* in 1959. After several years as a professional performer, she started to develop her own style of Bharata Natyam, using the *karanas*, as they are carved on the gateways of the temples of south India and described in the *Natya Sastra*. She studied the various *karanas* with the archaeologist, T.N.

Ramachandran. Her doctoral thesis for Annamalai University discussed movements which she believed disappeared from performance several hundred years ago. For her dance recitals, Padma does not use a *nattuvanar*; her sister-in-law provides vocal accompaniment. The unique repertoire which she has developed is not being performed by a lot of students. The influence of her movements is more likely to be disseminated laterally, through their effects on other dancers. Certainly arbitrary movements which imitate Padma's insight into the integration of sculptural poses on temples are now interspersed in the work of many dancers. Everyone recognizes the originality of her contribution, but whether it will be maintained intact as a lasting *bani* in the sense that I have used the word, remains to be seen.

2C. PARVATI KUMAR\MARATHI *BANI*

PARVATI KUMAR (1921-)

Parvati Kumar's dance background is eclectic. He started to study dance at the age of eighteen. The style he chose initially was Kathak, which he studied for three years. He gave his reasons for discontinuing Kathak: "I was not satisfied with Kathak. It is only *tala* (rhythm), there is not the same scope."

Between 1939 and 1944 he learnt Kathakali.[50] In 1942 he presented his first dance drama, "Dawn of a New Era". In 1947, he started to study Bharata Natyam with Chandrashekar, in Bombay. Chandrashekar's family originally came from Tanjore and he is related to Kubernath Tanjorkar (Tanjore/Baroda *bani*). Chandrashekar and Kubernath trace their lineage to the city of Tanjore, and the dance tradition of the *devadasi*, T. Kantimati. She had been sent there as part of the royal dowry.[51] Her relations, of whom Chandrashekar was one, are still teaching in Bombay and Baroda.

Chandrashekar charged Parvati Kumar forty rupees a month to teach him Bharata Natyam. The classes were held three times a week in the room where Parvati Kumar lived in Bombay. In order to finance his Bharata Natyam lessons, Parvati Kumar taught dance, and choreographed and presented dance dramas. Several other teachers: Nana Kasar, and J. Venugopal and his wife, Jayshri, were all initially trained by Parvati Kumar and danced in his dance company. Sumati, Parvati Kumar's wife, was formerly his student and a dancer in his company, which he dissolved in 1965.

In 1947 Parvati Kumar went to Madras to study *abhinaya* with the *devadasi*, M.D. Gauri. In 1956 he, his wife, and their one year old daughter returned to Madras. They remembered that "it was not easy". They paid Gauri fifty rupees for each dance composition that she taught them.

Parvati Kumar has studied some *mridangam* and another drum, the *khol*. Neither he nor his wife have had formal Karnatic vocal training, but she has sung for him when he was composing new dances, and on occasions when he was teaching. In 1985 she said that she no longer had the patience to teach but continued to assist him by singing. All of Sumati Kumar's training in abstract dance was with her husband.

Parvati Kumar is a *kshatriya* from the weaver community. He took up dance despite his family's objections. He is best known for his dance dramas and his pioneering work in reviving and reconstructing the Marathi dance repertoire, which fell into disuse when it was replaced by the repertoire created by the Tanjore Quartet.

Social Background of Exponents of this Bani

The examples include: Sumati Kumar, Nana Kasar, J. Venugopal and his wife Jayshri, and Sucheta Bhide (Chapekar). Like their teacher, all were dancers before they started to teach. Sucheta Bhide, a brahmin dancer, combines teaching with giving professional solo dance recitals. All were from non-traditional families, except J. Venugopal. Though an *isai vellala* he chose to train with a non-traditional dance teacher. Nana Kasar belonged to the *kasar* or bell making community and the others—Sumati, Jayshri and Sucheta Bhide—were *brahmins*.

NANA KASAR (1930-)

Nana Kasar began his training with Parvati Kumar in 1950. He was about twenty at the time. He described how he went to Bombay:

I had learnt *tabla* (north Indian drum) in my village of Malgaon (in Maharashtra State). My father died when I was eighteen so I had to work as a compounder in a dispensary. I did this for two years. I felt it very insulting doing this job. I thought, "I cannot go on filling these medicine bottles". I had learnt *tabla* but had failed my matric so when my brother allowed me to go to Bombay I went.

His comments illustrate the importance of having a variety of artistic skills to be able to survive as an artist and the difficulty of finding accommodation in Bombay:

Through some friends I met Bhargava Ram Pande, and got work playing *tabla* for dance dramas. Bhargava Ram Pande was a bachelor and shared his room with several of us involved in the theatre. It is a great thing to get a room in Bombay. All the Marathi actors would gather and rehearse there.

He remembered meeting Parvati Kumar and how he was able to start taking dance classes and finance his studies: "One day, when I was playing *tabla*, Parvati Kumar came in. After several days I dared to ask him for some *tabla bols*, which he gave me. Later, Parvati Kumar agreed to teach me, and I started my classes in 1950, on the first day of *Nava Ratri*." His comments indicate that teachers learn by teaching:

After six months of training with him I started to give dance tuitions. This helped me to pay my tuition fees of about thirty rupees to Parvati Kumar, and helped pay the rent for the room Parvati and I now shared. I studied with Parvati Kumar for four years. I did not present a formal *arangetram*, but I did dance on the stage. This has helped me in my teaching.

In 1954, Nana Kasar, encouraged by Parvati Kumar, went to Madras to study with A.P. Chokkalingam from the Tanjore Quartet *bani*. He was assisted by a Government of India scholarship of two hundred and fifty rupees per month. One hundred rupees went to Chokkalingam for dance tuition fees, thirty rupees for Karnatic vocal lessons with Kittamani Iyer, and ten rupees for *mridangam* lessons with Chandra Mauli. He sent fifty-five rupees a month to his family in Malgaon and the remaining fifty-five rupees on his living expenses. He lived and ate in the same hotel as his teacher. The classes were conducted in a nearby elementary school when regular teaching was not going on. Nana Kasar studied with A.P. Chokkalingam for four years (1954-58), after which he returned to Bombay and continued to live with Parvati Kumar. Their accommodation consisted of one room and Nana Kasar slept in the hall after Parvati Kumar married Sumati.

Nana Kasar then took some classes with Parvati Kumar's teacher, Chandrashekar, and started to teach. He presented his first student's *arangetram* in 1963. He moved to New Delhi in about 1979 to teach at Triveni Kala Sangam, an art institution, until about 1987. Thereafter he taught privately in his own home in the Asian Games Village in New Delhi.

J. (Janardhan) Venugopal (1940-)

In 1947, from the age of seven, J. Venugopal began his Bharata Natyam studies in Tanjore with Kantimati, his grandmother, a former *devadasi*. Venugopal's grandfather was Appaswamy, a *nattuvanar*. He was discussed under the Baroda/Tanjore *bani* of Kubernath Tanjorkar to whom J. Venugopal is also related. Venugopal studied with Kantimati for two years. In 1957, at age seventeen, he began to study with Parvati Kumar, in Bombay. After two years of training, he began to teach, and in 1969 he presented his first student's *arangetram*.

Venugopal received vocal training from age fifteen from his father, Janardhan, a violinist and vocalist. He learnt both Hindustani and Karnatic vocal. He did not give either a dance or a vocal *arangetram*.

Jayshri Venugopal (1943(?)-)

Jayshri Venugopal studied Bharata Natyam with Parvati Kumar and appeared in his dance dramas. She did not give an *arangetram*, because of the expense. She started to study Karnatic vocal after her marriage to J. Venugopal in about 1978. Jayshri performed *nattuvangam* for the first time in 1978 although her husband, J. Venugopal remarked: "My grandmother, Kantimati, never did *nattuvangam*. Women should not do *nattuvangam* on the stage."

Traditional Families and Non-Traditional Teachers

Although J. Venugopal is an *isai vellala*, his father Janardhan chose to send him to Parvati Kumar for training. This was also the case with J. Venugopal's younger brother, J. Dhyanand. The rationale for this appears to be that Parvati Kumar's teaching would be better and he would impart all he knew, rather than withhold some knowledge, out of jealousy. This reiterates the widely held belief that perhaps some teachers do not teach as sincerely as others.

Payment

Because Parvati Kumar had studied with Chandrashekar he did not charge Venugopal fees as he felt that he was returning the family heritage to him. Venugopal reported that Parvati Kumar had treated him like a son and said: "I have taken from your *bani* and now I am returning it."

Neither did J. Venugopal's wife, Jayshri pay fees. In her case it was because her father did not want her to study the dance and refused to pay. Instead she contributed by performing in Parvati Kumar's dance company, as did her husband. They never forgot Parvati Kumar's generosity. Every Vijayadasmi day (the day on which teachers are honoured) they present him with a gift of some gold. They also honour him by inviting him to their students' *arangetrams* and on these occasions present him with a gift.

Education

Although Parvati Kumar's formal education ended at the fourth class, he has published his research on the dance repertoire that had fallen into disuse. The lyrics for these dances are attributed to the Maratha rulers, Shahaji and Sarfoji II (1798-1832). Parvati Kumar conducted his research in the Saraswati Mahal library in Tanjore and reconstructed the dances, which predate those written by the Tanjore Quartet (1798-1832). While the Marathi pieces attracted some attention they did not make a substantial comeback. Among his students, only J. Venugopal and Sucheta Bhide (Chapekar) use the Marathi repertoire.

Support from their families was rather mixed among members of this *bani*. The families of Parvati Kumar and Nana Kasar were against their taking up dance as a profession. Jayshri's parents also objected. The family of Venugopal, who was the only hereditary exponent, actively encouraged it.

Marriage

Parvati Kumar is from the weaver community, his wife and former student is a brahmin. Since their families did not approve of their marriage they eloped, and thereafter received no support from either family. Nana Kasar's wife was from the same, non-brahmin community; it was an arranged marriage. J. Venugopal is an *isai vellala* and Jayshri, his wife, is a brahmin. Their families have not objected to their marriage and both are teaching dance.

Children

Parvati Kumar and Nana Kasar each had three daughters,[52] J. Venugopal and Jayshri had two, making a total of eight girls. In 1985 none was studying music. Two of Parvati Kumar's daughters learnt dance but neither presented an *arangetram*. All of Nana Kasar's daughters studied dance and his eldest daughter presented an *arangetram*, which her father conducted. One of J. Venugopal's daughters studied dance, the other was to start when she got a bit older.

One of Parvati Kumar's daughters had an M.A. and two had a B.A. Two of Nana Kasar's daughters had a B.A. and the other was still in school. In 1986, none of the children was teaching dance. This may change after they complete their academic education. The *bani* as a whole was being passed on by non-family members and therefore is non-hereditary.

Important Features of the Bani

The Parvati Kumar *bani* includes present day teachers of Bharata Natyam who were members of his dance company. The trajectory of Parvati Kumar's and Nana Kasar's life-style illustrates a conscious choice, made as adults, to follow an artistic career with all its financial and familial strains. They made many sacrifices for their art, travelling to the source (Madras), to study with teachers resident there (A.P. Chokkalingam, M.D. Gauri). Two of the sample married dancers who have assisted them in their career. In both instances the wives were from a higher caste than their husbands. The decision of J. Venugopal's father to choose Parvati Kumar as his son's teacher, rather than one of his *isai vellala* relations, seems surprising.

The *isai vellala bani* of Chandrashekar and the *devadasi bani* of M.D. Gauri were passed on to Parvati Kumar who was from a non-traditional family. He in turn, passed it on to those from both traditional and non-traditional families.

The future of Parvati Kumar's original research in uncovering a repertoire that predates that of the Tanjore Quartet is uncertain. It appeared that it would be passed on by Sucheta Bhide, his student with whom he collaborated when he did the reconstruction, and J. Venugopal, to whom he taught it. Whether this repertoire survives depends to some extent on the demand by the public to see it and just how easy it is to train accompanists in this new repertoire which uses the Hindustani mode of music. It is probably too early to assess its impact.

OTHER *BANIS*

A *bani* develops and evolves over a period of time. The beginning is unconscious. Some *banis* derive from teachers who, having studied within pre-existing ones, decide to strike out on their own, either by developing their own choreography for existing repertoire, or more commonly, by composing their own music and lyrics for dances within the accepted classification of Bharata Natyam pieces. In some cases they were experienced musicians and composed the music for a full set of dances (*margam*: *jatisvaram*, *sabdam*, *varnam*, *tillana*). As more and more dance teachers begin to compose, we may expect the repertoire to increase.

Dancers training with a teacher who has developed a unique musical and rhythmic repertoire may be somewhat restricted in their options for performing. Whereas most teachers share a core repertoire of dances, based largely on the music composed by the Tanjore Quartet, training with a teacher with dances not from this group can limit a dancer's options in selecting accompanists for her recitals. In most cases these teachers are just beginning to establish their own distinctive *banis* by training students, including their own children. The late K.J. Govindarajan is a case in point. He composed his own repertoire for many years. I have, however, placed him in the Picchaiya Pillai division of the Tanjore Quartet *bani*, because his initial training was in that one. He began to teach his compositions to his sons and daughter less than ten years before he died. When they and others begin to teach them we may consider his *bani* fully established. This is how the K.N. Dandayudapani *bani* became established.

Many dancers also teach dance. A few have studied with several teachers, from a variety of *banis*. Their teaching is influenced by the combination of what they studied with their teachers and their own ideas about the dance. Some dancers also perform *nattuvangam* and are therefore self-sufficient; they can conduct the recitals of their own students. Others employ a *nattuvanar* for their students' recitals. These dancers teach both the abstract dance (*nritta*) and descriptive dance (*abhinaya*). Most dancers in this group are also actively performing. It is from this group that there is the potential for new *banis* to emerge.

There are a number of female teachers, who, like the earlier hereditary dancers such as T. Balasaraswati and M.D. Gauri, specialize in giving training in *abhinaya*. Most of them come from non-traditional families. There were very few of them at first but the number is growing. Some of these specialists are: Kalanidhi Narayanan, Lakshmi Vishwanathan, Nirmala Ramachandran, Jamuna Krishnan and others. In effect, these women are replacing the void caused by the death of hereditary dancers who used to teach. An added impetus is that since the late 1970s there has been a resurgence of interest in *abhinaya*. The *abhinaya banis* have the potential to be non-hereditary and hereditary, as some of them are teaching members of their own family. These women undoubtedly have an important influence on the presentation of descriptive dances, and their impact on the evolution of Bharata Natyam should not be overlooked.

DISCUSSION

Biologists prepare charts of evolution that show the ancestors and descendants of organisms, demonstrating the course of biological evolution as branches from a single stem. The dance tradition of a particular dancer or teacher may have several ancestors. Using the same analogy for dance we would end up with interlocking roots, trunks and branches more like a banyan.

I have described the careers of only some teachers to illustrate the diversity of learning trajectories and artistic influences that have gone to make up present day Bharata Natyam. It is clear that many *banis* crossed the boundary from the traditional arena of *sadir/dasi attam* to the Bharata Natyam of the post-independence era. In most of what has been written on Bharata Natyam, the Tanjore Quartet/ Pandanallur *bani* of teachers appears central to the transmission of Bharata Natyam, through the enormous impact of P.S. Minakshisundaram. But, as I have shown, there were many other *banis*. Some branches are presently (1990) producing many shoots (students), whereas others have withered entirely.

Methods of teaching have changed a great deal. Most students now live at home and study in dance schools in large classes. Dancers of the older generation usually trained in their teacher's home or the teacher came to their home. Whereas both dancers, teachers and dance musicians of the older generation were mainly trained in dance orientated activity, many younger ones have also had academic education to the post-secondary level. It is noticeable, that many traditional families continued to train their children in music, even when they discouraged them in dance. Many of them later started to teach.

Some dancers over the past two to three decades have opted to move among teachers and augment their repertoire and movement vocabulary. Some, when they come to teach and/or perform, select the repertoire of one particular teacher, whereas others may select pieces from several. The technique for each dancer and teacher is a synthesis of the movements that they were originally taught and those modifications that they themselves originated, or selected by imitation, according to their own artistic vision.

I have dealt only with who studied with whom and the extent to which they have trained their children. My classification of a *bani* is approximate and makes no claim to be comprehensive. My selection is based mainly on those with whom I had an opportunity to speak, or about whom I was able to obtain reliable reports. I hope the information provided here will encourage others to document further the artistic training of those who brought Bharata Natyam into the modern era. The comments made by an important non-hereditary dancer, teacher and choreographer, Mrinalini Sarabhai, whose career began in the revival period, summarize the situation:

A true dancer is not one who unquestioningly copies her guru's style but one who evaluates each movement, finds its essence and integrates each movement with a physical and emotional response (*India Today*, 30 April, 1987).

NOTES

1. *Sruti*, an important journal devoted to south Indian dance and music, periodically publishes accounts of the lives of teachers and musicians.
2. There are a few exceptions pers. comm. B.M. Sundaram.
3. T.N. Picchaiya's father was Narayanaswamy. Narayanaswamy's sisters married Ponnaiya and Vadivelu.
4. Mahadevan, his relative, gave this information.
5. According to B.M. Sundaram, P.M. Muthaiya had three sons: Gopalakrishnan, Suryamurthy and another.
6. The wife of one of the founders of the Tanjore Quartet, Chinnaiya was from

Ammachatram. A.P. Chokkalingam married the aunt of P.C. Swaminathan who taught in New Delhi for many years (pers. comm. B.M. Sundaram).

7. B.M. Sundaram the musicologist was also there.

8. Ponnuswamy was a *mridangam* player who studied dance and dance accompaniment with Arunachalam *nattuvanar* the son of Kumaraswamy *nattuvanar*. Arunachalam was the cousin of P.S. Minakshisundaram (pers. comm. B.M. Sundaram).

9. For some other examples of wives providing vocal accompaniment while their husbands perform *nattuvangam* see T. Venkataraman, U.S. Krishna Rao and Parvati Kumar.

10. Two of the original Tanjore Quartet, Ponnaiya and Chinnaya, married Narayanaswamy's aunts (pers. comm. B.M. Sundaram).

11. Ganapathy Iyer was Lakshmi Kantham's patron. She did not have any children. She was about forty-five when she died and her last rites were performed by R.S. Rajendran, her disciple. There were three sisters: Lakshmi Kantham, Revati and Sivakamu. All three were dancers. Sivakamu stopped dancing after she married. Lakshmi Kantham taught herself *nattuvanagm* and conducted recitals (pers. comm. B.M. Sundaram).

12. Narayanaswamy pre-deceased his father Picchaiya.

13. For a photograph of T.M. Arunachalam see Kothari (1979: 34).

14. Saradambal's brother was Arunachalam's father.

15. K.J. Govindarajan was first a *nagasvaram* artist and later began to study vocal and dance (pers. comm. B.M. Sundaram).

16. According to B.M. Sundaram, Kannuswamy's father was Mahadevan the one who first introduced clarinet as part of the dance orchestra.

17. Janardan's daughter is the wife of B.M. Sundaram's brother-in-law. He is the brother-in-law of B.M. Sundaram's second wife. His first wife died (pers. comm. B.M. Sundaram).

18. K.J. Sita, K.J. Sarasa's sister is also a dance teacher.

19. Uma was adopted by her paternal uncle, K.N. Dandayudapani, in her infancy. K.N. Vaidyanathan, Uma's father, played the *nagasvaram*.

20. According to H.R. Keshavamurthy, K. Gundappa spoke Telugu. In his village of Kolar, Telugu is common, but Kannada is also spoken. Another *devadasi* from Mysore, Venkatalakshamma also spoke Telugu. She belongs to another community.

21. Jatitayamma is also often referred to as Taiyamma. She originally trained with Sadasivan *nattuvanar* from Kanchipuram in south India. Sadasivan went to Mysore for that purpose (pers. comm. B.M. Sundaram).

22. Basavanahalli is on the outskirts of Nelamangala (*Marg* 1982: 122).

23. This Kittappa is not to be confused with K.P. Kittappa in the Minakshisundaram branch of the Tanjore Quartet *bani*. B.M. Sundaram stated that Kittappa was also known as Kittanna (pers. comm.).

24. For Jatitayamma's service in the temple she was given a considerable amount of land. With the passing of the *Devadasi* Bill, however, it was taken

away from her. Another dance teacher, H.R. Keshavamurthy reported that Jatitayamma's son, T. Gundappa took the matter to court as his mother had no other means of support, but lost the case.

25. K. Kittappa and K. Puttappa were related. Kittappa was the "head of that family", according to H.R. Keshavamurthy.

26. Hochihallur is in Kadur District, Karnataka.

27. Radhakrishnan's father and Gundappa were brothers.

28. The Tamil spelling is Panchapagesha but it is pronounced Panchapakesha; therefore I have spelt it the latter way.

29. Cleaning vessels was not one of the duties of *devadasis* noted by Kersenboom (1984).

30. See Gonda 1975 in the *Diksa* section where it states that a student is forbidden to marry his teacher's daughter, according to the Sanskritic convention of studying with a teacher for twelve years. See also A. Srinivasan (1984) who states that a principal way for a family to maintain an artistic stronghold was to have daughters marry their father's most prominent students.

31. In 1989 Kamalambal was living in Chidambaram with one of her daughters. None of her daughters has been trained in dance.

32. This house is on West main Street in Tanjore and is still occupied by K.P. Kittappa and his sons. It has many photographs as well as the original ivory violin given to Vadivelu, one of the original Tanjore Quartet brothers, by the Maharaja of Travancore. Kannuswamy was a *nattuvanar* as was his son T.K. Ponnaiya. During the anti-*nautch* campaign, Kannuswamy encouraged his son to pursue a vocal career and give up *nattuvangam*. Ponnaiya did not allow his son K.P. Kittappa to perform *nattuvangam*.

33. This type of unreported activity continues on a large scale. I found that many of the new Bharata Natyam dancers in regional centres would appear to have a low profile in Madras or other large urban centres but they were travelling and giving many shows locally.

34. Bhagyammal had at least five children. The eldest, a daughter was Doraikannu. She was a *harikatha* artist, and a *devadasi*. The youngest, Radha was a dancer and a *devadasi*. She danced in films. Ramaiya was the eldest son and he had two other brothers, one Natesan was a *mridangist* (pers. comm. B.M. Sundaram).

35. Nataraja Pillai was from Pandanallur but was not related to the members of the Tanjore Quartet *bani* who also lived in Pandanallur.

36. Rukmini Devi invited K. Muthukumar after she had studied with M.D. Gauri and P.S. Minakshisundaram. B.M. Sundaram stated that Muthukumar only conducted the classes and performances at Kalakshetra and he did not teach Rukmini. Radha and Anandi were mainly taught by V. Ramaiya.

37. P. stands for her mother's name Parvatavardini and R. for her father's name Ramathilagam. P.R. Thilagam was attached to the Amman Koil at Tiruvayyar (pers. comm. B.M. Sundaram).

38. Sundara Kamakshi was dedicated to the deity in Tirunallar (pers. comm. B.M. Sundaram).
39. Kamalambal was from Tiruvarur and was the granddaughter of the famous *devadasi* from that temple Kamakshi (pers. comm. B.M. Sundaram).
40. Kersenboom (1984: 124) refers to a tradition of Bharata Natyam in Seyyur.
41. Karaikkal was also governed by the French at that time and is the ancestral village of another important founder of a *bani*, K.N. Dandayudapani.
42. Kandappa's second wife was Ellappa's cousin (pers. comm. B.M. Sundaram).
43. P.S. Minakshisundaram was his relative. Through the female side of his family they are related to T.S. Sivanandam, one of the original Tanjore Quartet brothers.
44. It is interesting to note that T.K. Ganeshan described P.S. Minakshisundaram as "old"; yet it was at this time that he trained most of his students who are active now.
45. Tiruvengadam *nattuvanar* conducted the *arangetram* of the hereditary dancer, R.(Rajamani Ammal) Swarna Saraswati (1921-85). She also trained with her grandmother Amrita Ethiraj Ammal, Kutralam Narayanaswamy, Pandanallur Arunachalam and Mylapore Gauri. When Swarna Saraswati moved to Delhi to teach dance in the 1950s she was assisted by Chokkammal, the niece of Mylapore Gauri. See also *Sruti* (16: 5).
46. Sarada (1985: 3). Kalakshetra was first called the International Centre of Arts.
47. K. in Ramarao's name stands for Kuppam, his family's ancestral village in Andhra Pradesh. Although they were brought up in another village in Tamil Nadu, Ramarao affixes a K. before his name indicating that he is from Kuppam. His younger brother, Adyar Lakshmanan, on the other hand, has been teaching in Adyar, a suburb of Madras, since the 1960s so he has chosen to affix Adyar to his name.
48. Another example of a teacher marrying his student is S.K. Kamesvaran who married Saroja. Both of them trained in the V. Ramaiya *bani*.
49. Several individuals have digressed from the norm and created new forms. I have made no attempt to include their work. The examples are numerous. One choreographer, Chandralekha integrates martial arts and other techniques with Bharata Natyam.
50. He studied Kathakali in Bombay with two teachers: Karuna Panniker and Narayananswamy.
51. Two dancers were sent—T. Kantimati and T. Gauri. This Gauri is not to be confused with M.D. Gauri from whom many dancers, including Parvati Kumar studied *abhinaya*.
52. Nana Kasar had four daughters but the eldest died.

6 Learning Bharata Natyam in the Modern Setting

DANCE CLASSES

Bharata Natyam may be studied privately with a teacher or in a group. Classes can take place in the teacher's home, the student's home or in one of the numerous institutions or schools. For the majority of students dance training begins in a group class. The parents generally select a dance school close to home.

Some teachers conduct classes in their own home. For teachers, living in the right locality counts when it comes to attracting students. Many hereditary *nattuvanars* do not usually live in the more affluent neighbourhoods where their upper middle class students do. Those students who wish to study with a traditional teacher may have to travel considerable distances to attend class. Most travel by car.

If a child shows promise and interest, or if the parents are anxious that she or he should appear on the stage quickly, they will engage a private teacher, for concentrated tuition. Some students reported that initially, while undergoing intense individual classes the dance training was regular and done earnestly. As time passed, the classes tended to become irregular, with the teacher shifting his attention to newer students. Months might go by without classes. For the parents this was naturally a source of annoyance. The outlook of the teacher, on the other hand, is that he has to ensure that he has work. Tempers may flair but in the end both parties know that the teacher's success rate in completing one full set of dances and getting the student on the stage for an *arangetram* is of utmost importance. For the teacher, there is considerable financial incentive in it. Moreover, each success has the potential to attract new students. Eventually, therefore, the teacher would definitely honour his commitment.

THE ROLE OF DANCE INSTITUTIONS

Most major cities now also boast one or more large academies of dance run by professional administrators. Usually these institutions employ teachers on fixed salaries. There are also institutions which rent space to teachers for a fixed fee or charge a percentage of their earnings. On the surface it might seem ideal to study dance at an institution. The disadvantages are that the classes are for a fixed period of time and the teacher does not have the freedom to devote extra time for individual attention.

For professional or established dancers there are specific problems training or working with a teacher in an institution. Several dancers complained:

I have tried institutions in several cities but everywhere the director refused to admit me. This is partly because they do not want teachers going on tour to accompany my recitals, but also because the principals do not want potential competition for their offspring. The daughters of many school principals train for careers as professional dancers.

Her comments reflect the fears of those running institutions. In particular, as the teachers were on a fixed salary, they might use this opportunity to ignore their teaching responsibilities and continually try to augment their salaries by travelling around the country accompanying the dance recitals of their professional students.

There were advantages to institutional employment. Some institutions provided free or subsidized housing, paid vacations, and medical care. Such incentives are hard to turn down in an otherwise precarious profession. Hence the schools are able to exercise fairly tight control over the teachers in their employ. One dancer explained: "Teaching in an institution could, I suppose become tedious, but at least the chances of becoming destitute are reduced".

At the same time the teacher has no incentive to push the student to become a professional dancer. Sometimes money earned through performances goes to the school rather than the teacher, which is a disincentive to the teacher to produce top quality dancers.

COST OF CLASSES

Dancers were conscious of the cost of classes: "In 1984, the actual expense for a group class, twice a week, in Delhi, might be no more than one or two hundred rupees. But that is not negligible considering that this may be the monthly salary of a maidservant." This limits a serious pursuit of Bharata Natyam to the upper middle class. The growing international demand to learning Bharata Natyam has also contributed to the inflationary costs of studying Bharata Natyam:

I am flabbergasted how much people are paying. The other day (1985) a little Indian kid from USA was to be in Delhi for ten days and her mother wanted her to learn two dance items. A *nattuvanar* charged her a considerable amount for them. He taught her in ten days. He devoted every morning to her and then for the last two days he worked entirely with her. He then made a professional recording for her and charged five thousand rupees.

Her conclusion was that while it was expensive by local standards, for an ex-patriot Indian living and working in the USA it was not. This demand from abroad was also inflating costs in India.

The financial stakes may be high but teachers generally work very hard to get their students on stage. The student's suitability is hardly ever questioned, it is up to the teacher to make anyone who presents themselves into a dancer.

Some parents are so anxious to see their daughters on stage that teachers report: "Even before they have attended their first class the parents want to know exactly how long it will take for their daughters to perform."

ARANGETRAM

The *arangetram* is the formal presentation of the first full dance performance. It is regarded as the culmination of the training phase for a Bharata Natyam dancer, and a landmark in her/his dance career. The term *arangetram* is widely used for any debut recital. Because historically the *arangetram* was an important validation ceremony for a *devadasi* during the early revival period, when its association with the *devadasi* tradition was still strong, early non-hereditary dancers preferred not to call their first recital an *arangetram*.

The complete suite of dances in a concert programme is known as a *margam*. This suite consists of certain dances performed in a particular order. Until about 1960, the order in which these compositions were danced in a recital was more or less fixed; *alarippu, jatisvaram, sabdam, varnam,*[1] *padams/javalis, tillana,* and *sloka*. This order is not generally followed today, nor are all these dances still included in a dance recital.

FINANCIAL CONSIDERATIONS
FOR THE *ARANGETRAM*

Most dancers agreed with these comments: "An *arangetram* was originally the teacher presenting the student and asking knowledgeable people to come. Now it is how much you pay, and who knows your family, not how much you know." Some masters now quote an all-inclusive fee for the dance classes and the *arangetram*. They then take a sizable advance before beginning the task at hand, thus committing both parties to a stake in the venture.

A non-hereditary dancer-teacher commented on the boom in *arangetrams*: "Since the late 1960s an *arangetram* has been a daily affair. At one time the *arangetram* in Madras was at its height. In the 1980s it was Bombay. All one needed was six months of training to study a whole *margam*."

On the other hand, some students complained that they were required to study for an *arangetram* far longer than was necessary, so that the teacher could continue to earn through the tuition fees. By the same token, it was generally accepted that a student who learns quickly or is taught a considerable amount of the teacher's repertoire in a short period should be required to pay more. Teachers, therefore, charge more for an *arangetram* that takes place after a short period of training. The cost of an *arangetram* is open ended: It can cost as much as a wedding, by the time the family hires the hall, prints a brochure, and specially printed invitations. It is the time to make a big fuss over the dance teacher. He or she is given cash and the female musicians are given *saris* and males *dhoti*. Eminent personalities are invited.

Initially the practice of giving the teacher cash, some clothing and another gift, was to compensate the teacher for teaching for "free". Certainly the student contributed with his or her *seva* but this event was a time to reward the teacher financially. Despite the fact that today, teachers charge tuition fees, the tradition of giving presents continues. Of course the teacher also works considerably harder and devotes a lot of extra time to the student, so the presents can be seen as compensating for that. A dancer explained:

Even if he has been teaching her for a long time and taking a sizable monthly tuition fee, the day of the *arangetram* he would get *dakshina* (present). At the time of the *arangetram*, the practice has been to give a generous present not only to the teacher but to the musicians. The musicians are paid more than for a regular concert and usually given a piece of clothing as well.

The sheer cost of an *arangetram* is astounding: "It has been so commercialized. This situation will continue as long as people think that Indian dance is easy and easily picked up and paid for. It could cost anything."

A father detailed some of the financial considerations for an *arangetram*: "In addition to paying for the classes over several years we had to pay for costumes, a sizable monetary gift to the teacher, a silk *sari* for his wife, a *dhoti* plus *angavastram* for him and all the members of the orchestra." A high caste girl remarked: "In the 1980s an *arangetram* would cost more than my marriage did. This is even with all the jewellery and dowry a marriage involves. The amount that people will spend now is so vulgar." The financial side can be straightforward or left to the student's family's generosity. A non-hereditary dancer commented: "In 1975 my *arangetram* cost about nine thousand rupees. My teacher didn't demand, we just gave it to her. She was not a very avaricious person."

There were several reactions regarding presents and the extra payment involved. Often the financial circumstances of the family were taken into account. A non-hereditary Delhi based teacher explained:

They give what they can. I don't demand more as it is my job to teach and then at the end conduct their *arangetram*. I shouldn't ask for a present as I have so many things. I am comfortable. For example this next one will be by a Bengali girl who has been learning for six years. Her father works for the Railways. They will only pay as if it is for a show. It is wrong to ask for guru *dakshina*. Some teachers even ask for a television.

Another non-hereditary male dancer/teacher also saw an *arangetram* as a logical extension of his professional obligations without burdening the family economically: "I am opposed to *arangetrams*. Yes, I have done them but I never force them. I am paid per month. I don't like the system where the student gives you a ring, *dhoti* and money." The importance of an *arangetram* in launching a dance career may be considerable:

First you learn and then you have to attract the public eye. To do it properly the *arangetram* should cost at least ten-fifteen thousand rupees (in 1982). This includes hiring a good hall, decorating it, printing invitations, and a programme, taking photographs for the brochure to be handed out at the event as well as those photographs to be taken during the recital to document the occasion. Presents and money for the teacher and some extra payment for the musicians are also called for. The dance jewellery, costumes and make-up are expensive. *Saris* are costly and you need at least two for two costumes. If the girl is young she will outgrow her costumes, otherwise with all the wear and tear they will last for only three to four shows. The family might even have a party for the critics and other people involved in the art world so that they can meet their daughter and assist in her career.

In the late 1980s and early 1990s the costs have escalated even further and must include a professional video of the recital. This is often later shown to the families of prospective bridegrooms. Many men consider the ability to dance an important asset for a wife.

INSTITUTIONS AND *ARANGETRAMS*

The choice of whether or not to have an *arangetram* may not wholly be in the hands of the dancer's family. This is often the case when a dancer studies at an institution. One of the students at Kalakshetra in the 1960s and 70s recalled:

I certainly was ready for an *arangetram* and entitled to a diploma but it didn't work that way with Rukmini Devi. If she thought you were mature enough then you gave your *arangetram* and you got your diploma. Now it is all unionized (i.e. more regularized) and after four years you get it but in those days it depended on her personal stamp of approval.

At Kalakshetra, by and large the girls who did their *arangetram* had to be a certain age. One dancer-teacher recollected:

There are many girls who have not done their *arangetram* in Kalakshetra. They are usually about eighteen when they do it. Rukmini did not like the girls to do it at fifteen or sixteen, but later. Eighteen to twenty years of age was normal.

In the case of an institution the motivation behind actually presenting an *arangetram* was often the family, not the dancer: "Those that presented an *arangetram* did it because their parents were keen and their families felt that it was good to do it as they had spent so many years studying dance."

The flexibility regarding having a formal *arangetram* is evident in the career of many top dancers when they first completed their training. Yamini Krishnamurti remembered:

I didn't have an *arangetram*. My first public show was after three years of study at Kalakshetra. It was in Chidambaram along with Rukmini Devi's troupe at a festival. It was part of the *Kuravanji* drama. I was one of the *sakhis*. I felt it was quite enough because it happened in the temple.

It was generally acknowledged that an *arangetram* was necessary. "Outside (i.e. not at Kalakshetra), an *arangetram* is more important." For some it was equivalent to graduating: "The *arangetram* is a culmination of your training, you reach a certain proficiency. Your guru and your parents decide that you should display what you have learnt."

CHANGES OVER THE PAST SIX DECADES

When the *arangetram* was a validation ceremony for a *devadasi* it marked the entry into the profession. Now it is just another qualification for the dancer along with her college degree. Over time the number of non-hereditary dancers and teachers involved in *arangetrams* has increased. Whereas before dance was done only by women, men now give *arangetrams*. The age of the dancer at this debut recital has gradually increased. I have obtained information on one hundred and thirty-six first performances, which are only a very small fraction of the *arangetrams* carried out over the past sixty years. I concentrated on obtaining information on *arangetrams* during the early part of the revival (up to 1950). I probably recorded a significant proportion of those that took place then. For later periods, especially after 1970, I have information for only a small fraction of *arangetrams*, which have become very frequent. I have, however, made no attempt to select, choosing to record all those that came to my attention (Table 6.2). This information illustrates

TABLE 6.1: CASTE COMPOSITION OF TEACHERS AND DANCERS PRESENTING *ARANGETRAMS*, BY DECADE, AN ANALYSIS OF SAMPLE GIVEN IN TABLE 6.2

Teachers	Isai Vellala*	Brahmin	non-Brahmin	Male	Female
Up to 1940	12(100%)	0	0	12	0
1941-1950	19 (90%)	2 (10%)	0	18	3
1951-1960	22 (85%)	5 (15%)	0	25	2
1961-70	17 (57%)	10 (33%)	3 (10%)	23	7
1971 (onwards)	12 (48%)	11 (44%)	2 (8%)	18	7
Dancers	*Isai Vellala**	*Brahmin*	*non-Brahmin*	*Male*	*Female*
Up to 1940	7 (58%)	3 (25%)	2 (17%)	3	10
1941-50	6 (19%)	22 (71%)	3 (10%)	4	27
1951-6O	6 (21%)	15 (54%)	7 (25%)	2	30
1961-70	3 (8%)	26 (72%)	7 (20%)	0	37
1971 (onwards)	6 (19%)	19 (61%)	6 (20%)	1	30

*Includes members of other castes belonging to traditional dance families, e.g. Telugu *naidus*.

especially the transition of the teaching and performing of Bharata Natyam from the *isai vellala* to other communities and its acceptability as a ceremony for male dancers as well as duets for men and women.

ARANGETRAMS BY DECADE

ARANGETRAMS UP TO 1950

Among those I interviewed, most *arangetrams* which were presented up to 1950 were conducted by male *isai vellala nattuvanars* (Table 6.1). There were very few women: one *isai vellala* and two brahmins. At that time it was unusual for women from either community to perform *nattuvangam*. Among the dancers, one-third were *isai vellala/naidu*, and the majority of the remainder were brahmins. There were very few from other castes. There were seven male dancers: two *isai vellala*, three brahmins and two non-brahmins.

Five *arangetrams* presented two dancers simultaneously. Of these, three involved girls from non-hereditary families (brahmin and non-brahmin), and two involved male/female duos, both of whom were brahmins. One of the duos was a husband and wife team, the other team was not married. The tradition of dancing as a duo began with the *devadasi*s but was also adopted by non-hereditary dancers. The majority of dancers (all but one *devadasi* and ten brahmins) were less than fifteen years of age. The non-traditional dancers were older; seven were in their late teens or twenties; two were in their thirties.

ARANGETRAMS 1951-60

In this decade also, most *arangetrams* were still being conducted by *isai vellala nattuvanars* but there were some brahmin teachers. Three *arangetrams* were conducted by a duo of *nattuvanars*, both male. There were four women *nattuvanars*, one *isai vellala* and three brahmins. Only one quarter of the dancers were *isai vellala*. The rest were non-hereditary and included seventeen brahmins and seven non-brahmins (three men and four women). Both from the hereditary and non-hereditary communities there was still a predominance of young girls presenting an *arangetram*. Except for two female brahmin dancers in their twenties, all others, whether *isai vellala* or brahmin were below the age of fourteen. The non-brahmins were generally older. In that group two dancers were below age fourteen, and four were in their late teens or twenties. Among the upper caste girls who presented their *arangetram*, twelve were still actively performing and teaching dance when I interviewed them in 1987. Three of them had not married. The other nine continued with dance after their marriage. While all the *isai vellala* female dancers had stopped performing, two taught dance, and one also became a *nattuvanar*. One of the non-brahmin dancers stopped for a while to pursue her profession as an architect but later became a part-time dance teacher in a school. Two others stopped dancing after marriage.

More than half of the brahmins continued as professional dancers after their *arangetram*. Many had their own schools, acted as *nattuvanars* for their students and conducted their students' *arangetrams*. The fact that many non-hereditary dancers continued to be involved in the dance after marriage indicates that by the 1950s dance was not, as Singer (1959) suggested, limited to unmarried young girls. Those who had severed their association with dance after marriage had generally done so in the face of objections from in-laws.

ARANGETRAMS 1961-1970

In the 1960s *arangetrams* conducted by traditional *isai vellala/ naidu nattuvanars* was lower than during the preceding decades, less than two-thirds. The rest were mainly conducted by brahmins (thirteen), and three by non-brahmins. Most of the dancers were brahmins, nearly three quarters, with only five *isai vellala/naidu* and five from other communities.

More than half of the brahmin dancers, and two *isai* v*ellala/naidu* went on to teach the dance. Several teachers and students left the dance school, Kalakshetra, where they had received their training, and taught independently. Some of them stayed on in Madras—a bold step, to establish themselves in the same city as the mother institution. Prior to this decade most graduates of Kalakshetra had joined the staff. Only those Kalakshetra graduates who had moved away from Madras had established their own schools. The boom in Bharata Natyam began in this decade and gave some teachers the necessary confidence needed to establish their own centres. Whereas many dance teachers taught dance only as a side line by the 1970s the trend was to become full-time dance teachers as they could now earn a good living through teaching dance.

In this decade two teachers, one a brahmin, another from the hereditary dance community,[2] presented their own daughters in an *arangetram*. For a *nattuvanar* from a hereditary family to do this was particularly interesting, because traditionally these families discouraged their females from any association with the arts, unless she was being groomed for a career as a *devadasi*. Also, whereas previously the dancer and the *nattuvanar* had no filial ties, we now see more fathers becoming directly involved in teaching, encouraging and promoting their own daughters' dance careers. Initially there were more examples from non-traditional families, but in the 1980s this became acceptable for all communities, even the *isai vellala*.

An increasing number of women, mainly brahmins, were teaching and performing *nattuvangam*.

One non-brahmin male, in his twenties gave an *arangetram*; although it was not a frequent occurrence, men were becoming more active in studying and presenting Bharata Natyam solo.

ARANGETRAMS 1971-1980

By this decade only half of the twenty-eight *nattuvanars* in my sample were *isai vellalas*, the others being brahmins. Nearly two-thirds of the dancers were brahmins (twenty), with six *isai vellala*, and six non-brahmins. The majority of the dancers from all communities were under the age of sixteen. There were, however, a few examples from all communities of mature women presenting their first public recital. One was Lakshmi Shanmugan-Knight, daughter of T. Balasaraswati, *isai vellala*. She was well into her twenties when she performed her first full programme, a clear indication that until the 1970s the family had some reservations about presenting her in a public recital. This was the decade when many *isai vellalas* abandoned their reservations about their daughters' involvement with music and dance, in particular performing dance. Brahmin *nattuvanars* such as T.V. Venkataraman who conducted his daughter Rani's *arangetram*, had no such reservations.

Twenty of the dancers who gave their *arangetram* in this decade were still actively involved in the dance in the late 1980s as dancers or teachers. Those who gave up cited a variety of reasons, especially having children and looking after their home. For some at least, their withdrawal may only be temporary. Many will return to the field, encouraged by the growing demand for Bharata Natyam teachers.

ARANGETRAMS IN THE 1980s

My sample for this decade is small because I chose to concentrate on dancers and teachers who had a long association with the dance and therefore their *arangetrams* were earlier. Among my sample, three of the *nattuvanars* were brahmins, and three *isai vellalas*. Among the dancers, too, three were brahmins, and three *isai vellalas*. The fact that my sample was evenly divided between the *isai vellala* and brahmin communities suggests that both these communities continue to support, and be involved in the dance.

Five of the *arangetrams* were conducted by a member of the family—three *isai vellala* and two brahmins. For the three *isai vellala* examples, the father conducted the recital of his daughter; in two cases it was their youngest daughter. There were examples of a grandfather conducting the recital of his granddaughter from both the brahmin (U.S. Krishna Rao) and *isai vellala* (K.P. Kittappa) communities. Both these families, each from different castes, had missed a generation training any of their own children.

LAUNCHING A DANCE CAREER

Once the first recital has been given, the aspiring professional dancer reaches a critical stage in her career. At this point continued financial backing is necessary to achieve success. To establish a career a dancer must be prepared for the first few years to pay for her own concerts: hiring the hall, printing the programmes, paying the musicians, and the teacher for the rehearsals and the recital. Only if she is prepared to do this can she expect to develop a reputation sufficient to get shows that will pay later.

At this stage, working with her original teacher may also become difficult. There were, however, some exceptions as recorded by a non-hereditary dancer:

Up to the *arangetram* all is fine. Then the teachers start feeling that they are indispensable. I know that my master exploited many students but I had a very good experience. For fifteen years he charged me the same moderate fees. When I moved to Bombay, he wrote to me a week before his death and said, "Come to Madras and live with me and be my assistant. All that I know I will teach you." I felt it was a genuine offer. It is that sort of rapport you should have. I have never had that since. He was a true master for me. Now relationships with such teachers is based on money and it is expensive.

As the dancer matures she usually prefers a more mature relationship with the teacher, which may be hard to achieve. There are many reasons why working with one's initial teacher becomes more difficult. Performing involves travelling all over India. This requires the teacher to leave home for several days at a time with a consequent loss of teaching income. Some dancers were sympathetic and realistic: "It would be great if your guru could conduct all your recitals but he cannot spend all his time with you. That is why they do not work with famous dancers."

Even when teachers are prepared to travel it is rare that they are willing to learn a student's choreography in order to conduct a recital. The dancer's dilemma is illustrated clearly in the following remarks: "I would hope that after so many years of training I would be able to create. Surely it is the purpose of the training and we are being penalized for it." Another complained: "As soon as you start to create for yourself the guru-student relationship, which is based on dependency, breaks down." While another explained: "It is at best difficult and often impossible to collaborate with a guru. If you have a go-between such as an influential father or husband, or if a member of your family is in the orchestra, then collaboration might be possible." Because of the present financial incentives, which make it more profitable for teachers to work with new students, it seems unlikely that the situation will change. As one dancer announced: "The masters are behaving like despots".

This may be true in certain cases, but it is likely that the teachers simply continue to behave in the way they have always done. Those dancers who wish to perform may adopt the following strategy:

I use a musician as a *nattuvanar* even though the big gurus add charisma. They add a lot, they wear a silk *jubbah* (shirt), and chew betel, but the amount of trouble and begging! Who has the time? They continually want guru *bhakti*. The man I have trained knows my repertoire and we can work together.

It is the dancers who have changed, with the increasing preponderance of highly educated emancipated young women. They see the art as being enriched by many teachers: "Dancers can outgrow their teacher. They want to add to what their gurus have taught them. Every dancer must remember with gratitude what she has learnt from the person who has taught her. This is guru *bhakti*." While the dancers feel grateful for the knowledge the apparent lack of loyalty amongst teachers was lamented.

" The gurus do not feel sorry when a good dancer has gone off as there are so many more coming up."

All the dancers reported that as they became better known they were charged more. Some dancers left a master because his fees had become too expensive. One dancer reported that she was anxious to expand her repertoire and learn from several teachers but felt that their charges were too high: "When I approached him a couple of years ago he wanted three thousand rupees for a varnam, and one thousand rupees for an *alarippu*. Even if I accepted the offer, he wouldn't create it just for me but might teach it to others as well."

For this individual the cost was too much, especially since the piece would not be unique in her repertoire. She felt that the teacher demanded too much credit: "Although it is the *nattuvanar* who teaches the piece it is the dancer who makes it famous."

The teachers see it differently: "Once a dancer knows my piece she can perform it many times. There is no royalty and over the years the dancer can earn a great deal from it. At the same time, she may teach it to other *nattuvanars* and to her own students, and hence people will not have to come to me to learn it."

Previously, when only *nattuvanars* taught, everyone had to go to the source to learn their special compositions. Now that these pieces are taught by several teachers, some do not even remember who the original choreographer was. Acknowledgement for artistic endeavours was not always given equally One dancer said: "The press can be held responsible for many a guru-dancer split, kindling jealousy by giving more, if not all, importance to the dancer, and often omitting to mention the teacher When this happens, it is terrible." The reverse case seems unlikely.

Dancers are very cautious about severing the relationship with their teacher since they rely on him not only for teaching and conducting the orchestra, but for the claim they can make on his pedigree which affirms their status within a *bani*.

Most professional dancers choreographed their own items; yet the majority of them would like to learn from others. One explained: "One mind can repeat itself and new teachers give fresh ideas."

Although many dancers had studied with more than one master, changing masters was not easy. Some had tried to balance working with two *nattuvanars*, but human nature is such that there was jealousy and suspicion of possible divided loyalties. Usha Srinivasan, a non-hereditary dancer wanted to give credit where it was due: "I still do the *tillana* that I learnt from my teacher Dandayudapani, but there is something of me in it. For that item I can't be anyone else's disciple. Another *nattuvanar* I was working with said, you should mention me. These jealousies get really bad." Some dancers objected to continually acknowledging their teacher: "After some time a dancer feels that she does not need to say that she is a disciple of someone. But if she doesn't the guru feels let down. A really good guru should not feel hurt. The mark on his disciple's dance should be so strong that the audience knows that he trained her." The same dancer believed that dancers should be judged on their own terms: "It is the dance that counts. If I am good, people should come up and ask, 'Who taught you?' My guru died ten years ago. How long can I go on cashing in on his name? Ultimately it is the dancer who should get the credit. Of course this does not happen right after the *arangetram*."

If the break comes, the dancer has no choice but to train a new *nattuvanar*. After spending hours drilling the *nattuvanar*, she rarely reaps any long-term rewards. Very soon the dependency/dominance roles are reversed. Since the new *nattuvanar* trained by her, is not contractually bound to work for her, other professionals can snap up the new expert by offering more money or other inducements. The first dancer would then be doomed to once again expending hours of her talent and energy training another. The process could well repeat itself. The dancer has more to loose from a breakdown of the relationship. Consequently if the *nattuvanar* demands to be treated as a guru she must be prepared to act subordinate. A leading dancer, who earned her entire income from the dance, lamented:

In the 1970s I could afford to keep a drummer, singer and *nattuvanar* on a monthly salary and they would accompany me for all my programmes. All that is now impossible because there are just so many dancers that the musicians can earn much more by free-lancing. Now, when I have a programme, I often have to spend more time teaching the new orchestra than on my own practice. This situation is not very satisfying artistically but I have no choice.

If, instead of training someone, the dancer decides to try to study with a new master and perform his items, this brings other problems. Because the teaching is usually one to one, the teacher-student relationship is very intense and the trauma of changing teachers is charged with emotion and suspicion. Most partings have been so bitter there can be no reconciliation: "Once you have studied with someone and then break off, to return is an avenue that is sealed off forever." The same dancer described the difficulties in selecting musicians who would perform together:

There is a very intricate network and your relationship with one can affect who will work with you and who you can approach. A mistake can follow you around for years. Of course it can sometimes be overcome, but it takes a lot of negotiations to get an orchestra of five together, particularly if they don't usually work together, and if you want the best musicians.

Many dancers felt that they should be able to deal with their teachers on equal terms. This was particularly noticeable where the dancer had trained for many years with another teacher and regarded herself as professionally qualified as her new teacher. The dancers regretted that teachers were suspicious of any training other than their own, or of their family or institution. "Learning with a new master can be very humiliating and frustrating. Any differences between the old and new style must be eradicated. Whatever small nuances appear are certain to be objects of ridicule." Many dancers felt that the situation was absurd: "All the styles in Bharata Natyam are very similar and conform to the rules in the *Natya Sastra,* so I would hope that after so many years of previous training I would be able to start in and learn pieces and not waste time going over the basics." Most of them recognized that the student-teacher relationship needed to be redefined and were well aware of the problems facing the dance.

For some dancers learning different traditions of Bharata Natyam did not pose many problems. Yamini Krishnamurti remembered leaving Kalakshetra, where she initially trained: "I was supposed to continue with them but I thought I would learn something else from different people." As with many dancers, after their initial training she wanted to broaden her experience of Bharata Natyam: "My father felt that Ellappa's style should also be learnt because he comes from Bala's school." In 1956-57, when she had completed her training with K. Ellappa she presented a full recital in the Children's Theatre, Madras. She noted that it was not announced as an *arangetram*, but it was a full performance and it was the first time that K. Ellappa conducted it for her.

The possibility of becoming a professional is very slim as Usha Srinivasan noted:

To be very frank no-one calls a dancer. She has to try herself to get programmes. The television or *sabha* (cultural organizations) will never call you, you have to go to them. It does not mean your dance is bad but that is the way it is. You have to write a letter, phone, pull some strings, know some officials. There are many good dancers so there is a lot of competition. Unless you and your family are pushy and influential you will be left behind.

DISCUSSION

In examining the evidence from *arangetrams* over the past few decades, the trend towards increasing involvement in the dance by communities other than the *isai vellala* is clearly illustrated by both teachers and dancers (Table 6.1). Up to 1940 all teachers, and more than half of the dancers involved in *arangetrams* were *isai vellala*. After 1947 there was a sharp fall in the number of *isai vellala* women who underwent dance training, with the result that after 1960 *isai vellala* dancers made up only a small proportion of dancers having *arangetrams*. There is a suggestion from my information that the numbers from the *isai vellala* community giving *arangetrams* rebounded somewhat after 1970, perhaps because of increased interest among *isai vellala* teachers to have their daughters or grand-daughters trained in dance: several of these *arangetrams* involved fathers or grandfathers. Involvement with the dance once again became a family concern. The most noticeable change is that, in the past, most hereditary dancers (*devadasis*) did not have fathers from within the *devadasi* community. The fact that by the 1980s, *isai vellala* dance teachers and *nattuvanars* were prepared to conduct their own daughters' *arangetram* indicates that the hereditary community no longer recognized the stigma attached to dance. Presenting their daughters in an *arangetram* was no longer seen as a *devadasi* rite of passage. Rather, dance was one of their many educational activities and a universal accomplishment.

After 1970, less than half the teachers presiding at *arangetrams* were *isai vellala*. The trend towards increased involvement by non-hereditary teachers in teaching the dance shows no sign of slowing down. The biggest change occurred between the 1950s and the 1960s. In the earlier decade most *arangetrams* were presided over by hereditary *isai vellala* teachers, but by the 1960s other communities provided *nattuvanars* for almost half of the recitals. This change reflected the arrival of the first generation of non-hereditary dancers/teachers, trained over the previous two decades by the *isai vellala* community and in particular by the dance school, Kalakshetra. There were also several musicians who became *nattuvanars*.

By the 1980s teaching Bharata Natyam had become a viable profession. Because there were many dance students, the celebration of *arangetrams* increased. The *arangetram*, once an important validation ceremony restricted to hereditary persons, had been democratized. Presenting an *arangetram* was no longer determined by community but rather by financial considerations, the cost of which continued to escalate.

The old relationship between *nattuvanars* and dancers, as exemplified by the early *devadasi* performers, broke down fairly quickly. Originally, activities within the profession were determined by gender—with the women dancing, and the men teaching and conducting recitals. After the revival, schools were set up mainly by individual female dancers, and this single person very often performed three roles: performer, teacher and *nattuvanar*. Some dancers trained their students as *nattuvanars* and accompanists, to ensure that the means of performance were readily available. Those dancers who did not have a sizable number of well trained senior students to assist them, trained musicians or percussionists to be their *nattuvanar*. Permanent relationships between dancers and *nattuvanars* have largely become a thing of the past. Although some deference is still paid to artistic lineage, it appears that non-hereditary dancers have much more control than before over the direction of the dance.

NOTES

1. In a music concert, *tana varnam* is the first item. This order was established in the century by Ramanuja Ayyangar (Ramakrishna 1991).

2. My sample included examples from both the non-hereditary, brahmin and hereditary, *isai vellalal naidu* communities. H.R. Keshavamurthy, a brahmin, conducted the *arangetrams* for two of his daughters (Saroja and Sumitra). Sampati Bhoopal, from the traditional *naidu* dance community, conducted the recital of his daughter Swarnamukhi.

TABLE 6.2: SELECTED LIST OF *ARANGETRAMS* REFERRED IN TABLE 6.1

Date	Teacher Nattuvanar	Dancer	Place	Additional Styles	(approximate age)
1883	(P. Nataraja(IS))	(K. Muthukumar (IS))	Pandanallur?		M (9)
1920s	(+T. Appaswamy(IS))	+Kubernath Tanjorkar(IS	Tanjore		M (teens)
1925	N. Kandappa(IS)	(T. Balasaraswati(IS))	Kanchipuram	KU	(7)
1925	P. Vadivelu(IS)	K. Bhanumati(IS)	Kumbakonam		(7)
1929	T.P. Kuppaiya(IS)	T.N. Rajalakshmi(IS)	Tiruvidaimarudur		(11)
1931	(K. Thiruvengadam(IS))	(+Swarna Saraswathy(IS))	Madras	(?)	(10)
1933	male (IS)	T.P. Ranganayaki(ND/IS)	Tirutani		(17)
1930s	P.S.Minakshisundaram(IS)	Ram Gopal(OT)	Tanjore	KA, KK	(20s)
1934	K. Muthukumara(IS)	*K. Lalita(BR)	Madras		(teens)
1935	N. Kandappa(IS)	Radhanamalai(NA)	Madras		(9)

Date	Teacher Nattuvanar	Dancer	Place	Additional Styles	(approximate age)
1936/38	K. Kannappa(IS)	*Kalanidhi Narayan(BR)	Madras		(10)
1936	P.M. Muthaiya(IS) A.P. Chokkalingam(IS)	(Rukmini Devi(BR))	Madras		(30s)
1937	K. Muthukumar(IS)	Selvamani(a) (OT)	Madras		(10)
1941	K. Muthukumar(IS)	Kamala Lakshman(BR)	Kutralam	KA	(7)
1941	V. Ramaiya (IS)	Vyjayanthimala(BR)	Madras	MO	teens
1943	V. Minakshisundram(IS)	Yogam(BR) & Mangalam(BR)	Madras		(20) (16)
1943	Picchaiya(IS)	Jayalakshmi(IS)	Tanjore	Arunachalam	(9)
1943	Rukmini Devi(BR)	Sarada Hoffman(BR)	Madras	KK	(teens)
1944	P. Vadivelu (IS) T.S. Shanmugansundaram (IS) K.N. Pakkiriswami (IS)	Girija(IS)	Kumbakonam		(8)

Date	Teacher Nattuvanar	Dancer	Place	Additional Styles	(approximate age)
1944	A.P. Chokkalingam(IS)	Lalita Shastri(BR)	Madras	KK	(12)
1944	A.P. Chokkalingam (IS)	U.S. Krishna Rao(BR) Chandrabhaga Devi(BR)	Tanjore/Madras	KK	(30s) (20s)
1945	V. Ramaiya(IS)	Anandi(BR) Radha(BR)	Madras		(12) (12)
1946	T.S Govindarajan(IS)	C.V.S. Vasanta(BR)	Tanjore	BM	(12)
1947	T.Kamalambal(IS)F	Mythali Kalyanasundaram(IS) P.M. Muthaiya(IS)	Tanjore		(7)
1948	+V. Ramaiya (IS)	+E.V. Saroja(IS)	Madras		(12)
1948	S.S. Manikkam (IS)	P.S. Ramaswamy Iyer(BR) & Sri Kala(BR)	Madras		(20s) (20s)
1948	+K. Lalitha (BR)(F)	+L. Ranganayaki (BR)	Madras		(13)
1949	V. Ramaiya(IS)	K.S. Sarasa(IS)	Madras		(14)

Date	Teacher Nattuvanar	Dancer	Place	Additional Styles	(approximate age)
1949	K. Ganeshan(IS)	Muthulakshmi(IS)	Tiruvalluptur		(12)
1949	V. Ramaiya(IS)	Viyaya Rajan(BR) & & Hema(OT)	Madras		(12) (13)
1949	A.P. Chokkalingam(IS)	Indrani Rehman(OT)	Madras	MO,OD,KU.	(teens)
1949	S.Thiruvengadam[3] (IS)	Komala Varadan(BR)	Madras		(10)
1949	K.N. Dandayudapani(IS)	Malati Srinivasan (BR)	Madras	KK	(18)
1940s	K.Ellappa(IS)	Tara Ramaswamy(BR)	Madras	KK	(12)
1940s	P.S. Minakshisundaram(IS) and P.M. Muthaiya(IS)	Shanta Rao(BR)	Madras?	KK, MO	(20s)
1940s	B. Puttappa(IS)	*Leela Ramanathan(BR)	Bangalore		(teens)
1940s	T. Swaminathan (IS)	*Nirmala Ramachandran(BR)	Madras		(pre teens)
1950	Kalakshetra(BR)	*Chandrashekar(BR)	Madras	KK	(20s)

Date	Teacher Nattuvanar	Dancer	Place	Additional Styles	(approximate age)
[1950]	K. Ellappa (IS)	Bhaskar(OT)(M)	Madras	KK]	(20s)
1951	Kausilaya(IS)	Lakshmi Vishwanathan(BR)	Madras	KU	(7)
1951	A.P. Chokkalingam(IS)	Subbadra(BR) and Sundari(BR)	Madras		(14) (16)
1952	K. Ellappa(IS)	Chandralekha(BR)	Madras		
1952	Chandrashekar(IS)	Parvati Kumar(OT)	Bombay	KA,KK,M	(20s)
1952	K. Ganeshan(IS)	Indira Rajan(IS)	Karaikkal		(10)
1953	V.S. Muthuswamy(IS)	Sai(IS) and Subbalakshmi(IS)	Madras		(11) (11)
1953	P.M. Muthaiya(IS) and P.C. Subbarayan(IS)	Lakshmi Rajan (?)	Tiruvidaimarudur		(teens)?
1953	U.S. Krishna Rao(BR) Chandrabhagadevi(BR)	Sudharani Raghupaty (BR)	Bangalore		(9)

Date	Teacher Nattuvanar	Dancer	Place	Additional Styles	(approximate age)
1953	A.P. Chokkalingam(IS)	Rita Devi (OT)	Madras	OD,KU	(20s)
1953	K. Muthukumar(IS)	Nala Najan(OT)(M)	Kartumunar	CH	(teens)
1956	S. Ramaswamy(IS)	S. Vasanta Kumari(BR)	Sikkil		(9)
1956	V. Ramaiya(IS)	Padma Subrahmanyam(BR)	Madras		(pre teens)
1956/7	K. Ellappa(IS)	Yamini Krishnamurti(BR)	Madras		(teens)
1957	Lakshmi Rajam	Vasanta Rani	Tanjore		(teens)
1957	P.S. Ramaswamy(BR)	Ganga(BR)	Tanjore		(teens)
1958	K.N. Dandayudapani(IS)	Chamundeswari(ND/MU)	Madras		(10)
1958	T. Balasaraswati(IS) T.K. Ganeshan(IS)	Priyamvada Raghavan(BR)	Madras		(9)
1958	Indira Rajan(IS)	female student	Madras		(pre teens)?

Date	Teacher Nattuvanar	Dancer	Place	Additional Styles	(approximate age)
1958	V.Ramaiya(IS)	Malati Dominique(IS)	Kumbakonam		(pre teens?)
1958	T. Swaminathan (IS)	Radha Srinivasan (BR)	Madras		(10)?
1959	K. Ganeshan(IS	Rajalashmi Kalanidhi(MU)	Madras		(8)
1959	T. Bhavu(IS,MH)	Kalayani(IS) and Vasanta(IS)	Tanjore		(teens?)
1959	Kalakshetra(BR)	Shanta Dhananyajan(OT) & Krishnaveni Laxmanan(BR)	Madras	KK KK	(teens) (teens)
1959	Janaki Raman	Bharati Shivaji(BR)	Jamshedpur	OD,MO.	(pre teens)
1959	T.P.Kittappa/	Punitavadi⁴(IS) P.M. Muthaiya (IS)	Tanjore		(12)
1950s	K. Lalita(BR)	Saroja Vaidyanathan(BR)	Madras		(12)
1960	V. Ramaiya(IS)	Kanaka Srinivasan(BR)	Madras		(13)
1960	Kalakshetra (BR)	Ambika Buch (OT)	Madras	KK	(teens)

Date	Teacher Nattuvanar	Dancer	Place	Additional Styles	(approximate age)
1961	T.K. Marudappa (IS)	Sareswati Sundaresan(BR)	Calcutta		(12)
1961	K.N. Dakshinamurthy(IS)	Savitri Mahadevan(BR)	Delhi		(14-15)
1961	K.N. Dakshinamurthy(IS)	Prema Ganapathy(BR)	Delhi		(?)
1961	U.S. Krishna Rao(BR) Chandrabhagadevi(BR)	Sonal Mansingh(OT)	Bangalore		(late teens)
1962	K.N. Dandayudapani(IS)	Savitri Balasubramanium (BR)	Madras		(13)
1962	+H.R. Keshavmurthy(BR)	+Vasantalakshi Murthy(BR)	Bangalore		(15)
1962	+ S.K. Kamesvaran(BR)	+Saroja Kamesvaran(BR)	Madras		(15)
[1963	K. Ellappa(IS)	Lakshminarayanan(BR) along with a female dancer	Madras]		(29)
1963.	Malati Srinivasan (BR)F	Saroja Vanchi(BR)	Madras		(13)

Date	Teacher Nattuvanar	Dancer	Place	Additional Styles	(approximate age)
1964	Padma Subrahmanyam(BR)	Jayalakshmi(BR)	Madras		(teens)
1964	Chandrashekar(IS)	Krishnakumari Narendran(NB)	Madras		(?)
1964	Parvati Kumar(NB)	Suchita Bhede(BR)	Bombay		(16)
1964	Kunchitapadam(NB)	Bragha Guruswamy(BR)	Chidambaram		(teens?)
1964	Kunchitapadam(NB)	Brinda Guruswamy (BR)			(teens)
1964	Mani	Chitra Sundaram(BR)	Bombay		(?teens)
1964	Kalakshetra	Gayatri Venkataraman(BR)	Madras	KK,OD	(teens)
1965	K.N. Dandayudapani(IS)	Usha Srinivasan(BR)	Madras		(14)
1965	+H.R. Keshavamurthy(BR)	+Sumitra Murthy(BR)	Bangalore		(15)
1965	U.S. Krishna Rao(BR)	Kamadev(OT)	Bangalore		(20s)
1966	P.C. Subbaroyan(IS)	Alarmel Valli(MU)	Madras		(12)
1966	K.J.Sarasa(IS)	Sarala(IS)	Madras		

Date	Teacher Nattuvanar	Dancer	Place	Additional Styles	(approximate age)
1967	Padma Subrahmanyam(BR)	Sundari Santanam(BR) Usha Shriram (BR)	Madras		(teens)
1967	T. Balasaraswati(IS) T. K. Ganeshan(IS)	Nandini Raghavan(BR)	Madras		(18)
1968	M. Durairaj(BR)	Revati Ramachandran(BR)	Madras		(8)
1968	Rama Rao(BR) P. Ramaswamy(BR)	Mallika Sarabhai(BR)	Ahmedabad		(14)
1969	Malati Srinivasan(BR)	Pushkala Gopal(BR)	Madras		(teens)
1960s	T.P. Kittappa(IS)/ +Kamalambal(IS)	+Angarkani(IS)	Tanjore		(teens)
1960s	+Sampati Bhoopal(ND)	+Vasanta Lakshmi(BR)	Madras		(10)
1960s	P.C. Subbaroyan (IS)	Minakshi Sabhanayagam(MU)	Madras		(?12)
1960s	+Sampati Bhoopal(ND)	+Swarnamukhi(ND)	Nellore		(8)

Date	Teacher Nattuvanar	Dancer	Place	Additional Styles	(approximate age)
1960s	T.A. Rajalakshmi(IS)	Chitra Visweshwaran(BR)	Calcutta		(teens)
1970	T.R. Devanathan(IS)	Lalita Baskaran	Delhi		(?)
1970	K. Sadasivan(BR)	Swatimahalakshmi(BR)	Delhi		(teens)
1970	Kalakshetra(BR)	Jayalakshmi Eshwar(BR)	Madras	KK	(teens)
1970	A.P. Chokkalingam(IS)	Minakshi Pakkiriswar..i(IS)	Madras		(14)
1970	K.N. Dakshinamurthy (IS)	Tarveen Mehra (OT)	Madras		(20s)
1970	K.N. Dakshinamurthy (IS)	Anjali (Anne-Marie Gaston)(OT)	Delhi	OD,KU,KK	(20s)
1971	Lalita Shastri(BR)	Rasika Khanna(OT)	Delhi		(teens)
1971	Kalakshetra (BR)	Leela Sampson(OT)	Bombay		(20)
1971	Dhananjayan (NR) Shanta (NB)	Catharine Kuniraman(CR)	Madras	KK	(20s)

Date	Teacher Nattuvanar	Dancer	Place	Additional Styles	(approximate age)
1971	C. Radhakrishnan(IS)	Avanti Meduri(BR)	Madras	KU	(10)
1972	T.K.Kalyanasundaram(IS)	Mallika Sarrukai(BR)	Bombay	OD	(12)
1972	Kalakshetra(BR)	C.S. Thomas(CR)	Madras	KK	(28)
1972	+Venkataraman(BR)	+Rani(BR)	Tirumuruganpudi (Tirumurugan temple)		(10)
1973	P.C. Subbaroyan(IS)	Prema Sadagopalan(BR?)	Madras		(teens)
1973	Lalita Sastri(BR)	Uma Kumar(BR)	Delhi		(teens)
1973	T.K. Ganeshan(IS)	Lakshmi Shanmugam-Knight (IS)	Madras		(20s)
1974	K. Sadasivan(BR)	Kiran Seigal(NB)	London,UK	OD	(20s)
1974	Kamala Lakshman(BR)	Shoba Natarajan(BR)	Madras		(10)
1975	Swarna Saraswati(IS)	Gita Ramakrishnan(BR)	Delhi	MO	(teens)

Date	Teacher Nattuvanar	Dancer	Place	Additional Styles	(approximate age)
1976	T.P. Kalyanasundaram(IS)	Vijalakshmi Prakash(BR)	Bombay		(16)
1976	Malati Srinivasan(BR)	Naganandini Ramachandran(BR)	Madras		(16)
1977	Chitra Visweswaran(BR)	Sujata Srinivasan(BR)	Madras		(12)
1977	Kamala Lakshman(BR)	Srinidhi Rangarajan(BR)	Madras		(10)
1970s	K.J. Govindarajan(IS)	Jamuna Krishnan(BR)	Delhi		(20s)
1978	K. Ganeshan(IS)	Shymala Mohan(NB)	Madras		(20s)
1978	T. Arunachalam(IS)	S. Umamaheshwari(IS)	Madras		(12)
1979	V.P.Dhananjayan(NB)	Radhika Natarajan(BR) Shanta(NB) Gayatri Natarajan (BR) Shobana Natarajan (BR)	Madras		(12) (11) (10)
1979	+ S.K.Kamesvaran(BR)	+Minakshi Kamesvaran(BR)	Madras		(pre-teens)
1980	+ K.J. Govindarajan(IS)	+Kalaivani(IS)	Delhi		(12)

Date	Teacher Nattuvanar	Dancer	Place	Additional Styles	(approximate age)
1981	Saroja Vaidyanathan(BR)	Mythali Sivakumaran(BR)	Delhi		(14)
1982	+ T. J. Nagarajan(IS)	+Nargis Natarajan(IS)	Tiruvarur temple		(9)
1985	+ US Krishna Rao(BR)	+Anjali Rao(BR)	Bangalore		(14)
1987	Chitra Vishweshwaran(BR)	Sanjukta[5](BR)	Madras		(12)
1980s	+K.N. Dakshinamurthy(IS)	+Veenu(IS)	Delhi		(12)
1989 +	T.P. Kittappa(IS)	+Padmavati (IS)	Tirunevelli		(teens)

ARANGETRAMS

ABBERVIATIONS

Community

IS	:	*isai vellala*
BR	:	brahmin
NB	:	non-brahmin
MU	:	*mudaliar*
ND	:	*naidu*

Dance Styles

KA	:	Kathak
KK	:	Kathakali
KU	:	Kuchipudi
MO	:	Mohiniattam
BM	:	Bhagavata Mela

NR	:	*nair*[2]	CH	:	Chhau
CR	:	christian	OD	:	Odissi
OT	:	other			

(In parentheses indicates style studied, but not performed)

GENDER

M= male. In the case of *nattuvanars* the sex is male unless indicated.

F= female. In the case of the dancers the sex is female unless indicated.

*= was not called an *arangetram*

+= related to each other, either their child, their wife, or distant relation.

[ ] indicates it was celebrated as an *arangetram* but was a full first recital of dance

@ *arangetram* was performed in a temple

(In parenthesis indicates that the dancer or *nattuvanar* died prior to 1989)

NOTES

1. Information regarding his career was obtained from his wife Karunambal and his sons.

2. The Suchindram temple refers to accepting *devadasis* from this community (Pillay 1953).

3. S. indicates that he was from Seyyur. There is also a K. which indicates Kanchipuram Thiruvengadam.

4. Punitavadi was the grand-daughter of Kamalambal a *devadasi* who had studied with P.S. Minakshisundaram

5. Granddaughter of Leela Shekhar who studied music with T. Dhanammal and T. Jayammal and later accompanied T. Balasaraswati's dance recitals.

7 The Structure and Repertoire of Bharata Natyam

CLASSICAL INDIAN DANCE

Within the various *banis* of Bharata Natyam, the difference in technique is minimal to the untrained eye. Although it is easier to detect differences in the different styles of Indian classical dance, the comments of India's first Prime Minister, Pandit Jawaharlal Nehru, reflect a common perception: "I am unable to distinguish one style from another" (Gopal 1957: 134). This confirms the need to have informed exposure to the basics of the various styles since each stresses certain movements and postures more than others. At the same time, it also illustrates just how subtle the differences may be. In particular it is indicative of the fact that the different styles of Indian classical dance share certain common features. These include the use of hand gestures (*mudras/hastas*),[1] stylized facial expressions (*abhinaya*), and extensive use of the rhythmic beating of the feet.[2] All the classical styles contain a repertoire of some traditional compositions. In addition it is acceptable in most styles to choreograph new dances set to appropriate musical compositions. Most classical dance movements and gestures are choreographed and any improvisation occurs within a strict classical framework.

NRITTA/NRITYA/NATYA

Bharata Natyam includes three components: abstract dance (*nritta*), descriptive or expressive dance (*natya/abhinaya*), and *nritya* which is a combination of the two. The terminology used by present-day

practitioners to describe the various movements and body positions
has been taken largely from Sanskrit texts:[3] the two most important
being the *Abhinayadarpana* and the *Natya Sastra*. There are, in
addition, some Tamil and Telugu words used to describe the various
dance steps and body positions. A systematic study of the theory of
Bharata Natyam was begun by Rukmini Devi, and her staff at
Kalakshetra. Theory has been taught there since the late 1940s.
Rukmini Devi chose selected portions from several Sanskrit texts,
in particular the *Natya Sastra* and *Abhinayadarpana*, with emphasis
on material in the latter. She remarked: "Traditional *nattuvanars*
were not keen on theory. I just got interested in theory because I
wanted to understand the meaning of everything."

Although most traditional dance masters are fully conversant
with the context in which various parts of the body are to be used,
they are not always familiar with the textual references. The
theoretical and practical aspects of the dance were, and continue to
be, largely separate. It is possible to be a dancer or dance teacher
without systematic knowledge of the textual tradition. While the
majority of the traditional teachers and dancers looked upon technical/
theoretical knowledge, devoid of practical application, with
suspicion, there were exceptions. The late K. Muthukumar is an
example of a traditional dance teacher who had a good grounding
in the theory of the dance (Khokar 1964). Mohan Khokar very
kindly showed me the various texts in his possession that K.
Muthukumar owned. Mannargudi Durairaj Iyer, a brahmin dance
teacher, was also very familiar with dance texts (Parthasarathy
1989). Parvati Kumar, a non-brahmin who teaches in Bombay, re-
created a form of Bharata Natyam that had survived to the present
day only in texts.

The basic stance (*ardhamandali*) for Bharata Natyam is with
both feet turned outward, heels slightly apart (as in first position in
ballet), knees bent,[4] arms extended and held parallel to the floor.
The wrists are slightly bent so that the fingers point forward. The
hands are held in a flexed position, the thumb is bent and tucked in,
the fingers extended and touching each other.[5] This basic stance is
earth bound and gives some indication of the parameters of acceptable
movement. The torso is not used much and remains mostly upright.

The position with the arms parallel to the floor is one from which many of the basic steps (*adavus*) are executed.

The beating of the feet is one of the most important components of Bharata Natyam. The sole of the foot, heel, and ball of the foot are used to accent the rhythm. Leg movement is minimal.[6] Hand positions (*hasta/mudra*) are an integral part of the choreography, and the hands are never allowed to remain relaxed. The same hand signs may be used in both abstract dance (*nritta*) and the expressive portions (*natya/nritya/abhinaya*). In abstract dance the hand positions are decorative and devoid of meaning. In the descriptive portions during which the lyrics are sung, the hand gestures provide a sign language, partly symbolic, and partly specific. The hand signs, aided by facial expressions (*abhinaya*) express the meaning of the text to which the dances are choreographed. Lyrics are basic to the performance of descriptive pieces of Bharata Natyam and the *abhinaya* tends to follow them rather closely the first time they are sung. When the same lyrics are repeated several times, the dancer employs her imagination to suggest ideas and situations inherent in the text. This is known as *sanchari bhava*. The hand gestures are subdivided into single and double hand positions. All have names which vary according to different texts (Gaston 1982: 36-46). Amongst the older generation of teachers it was the context in which the hand signs were used rather than the actual names of the positions that was important. Texts also list the variety of uses for the same hand sign. Some are very versatile and may be adapted for different situations, others have a limited application. For example, *pataka*, the hand sign with the fingers closed has more than fifteen different uses.

All joints, such as wrists, which assist in the movements of the hands, shoulders and knees, form part of the accepted movements.

NRITTA

The basic steps (*adavus*)[7] of the pure dance (*nritta*) are the building blocks of Bharata Natyam. Each dance teacher has his/her own combination of *adavus*. In every *bani* the *adavus* have the same basic structure but differ in execution and minor embellishments

(*Sruti* January 1985: 43). Thus it is the manner in which *adavus* are executed and their minor variations which determine the different *banis* of Bharata Natyam. *Adavus* that share similar characteristics are divided into groups. The number of groupings varies anywhere from nine to fifteen (Vatsyayan 1963, 1974: 17; Bhavnani 1965: 32; Khokar 1963: 17-23).

Groups of *adavus* are referred to either by the particular movement that is performed, or by the mnemonic syllables (*solkattus*)[8] to which they are danced. Two examples of *adavus* that are identified by the names of movements are *sarrukal* which means sliding or slipping, and *tattu* which means to strike, pat or slap, indicating that the foot is to be slapped (Marg 1963: 18). Some of the mnemonic syllables by which *adavus* are identified are: "tai ya tai hi", or "ta tai tai ta" etc. The spoken rhythmic component for each *adavu* dictates the accents in the movement and suggests the movement. Thus hard sounds such as "ta", "di", "gi", "na", "tom", call for direct percussive movements. Softer sounds such as "longu" suggest other movements such as turns or jumps. This codified integration of rhythmic mnemonic syllables and the dance movements themselves underlies the strong rhythmic structure in the dance. Several *adavus* performed together are known as *korvai*. The syllables that accompany both *adavus* and *korvais* are known as *solkattus*.

New *adavus* are being developed within the accepted parameters of Bharata Natyam[9] and new complex combinations of *adavus* which are known as *jatis* are constantly being created. This has increased the rhythmic complexity and is one of the most noticeable innovations in recent Bharata Natyam. The rhythmic syllables (*solkattus*) for *jatis* are taken from the *mridangam* (drum) repertoire (Brown 1965; Higgins 1973). Certain combinations are considered more appropriate than others. Such decisions are based on the musical quality of the spoken sound and the choreographic feasibility of one *adavu* joining another. *Jatis* are spoken by the *nattuvanar*, who is accompanied by the *mridangam*. At that time there is usually no melodic accompaniment. Each *jati* combination concludes with a *tirmanam*[10] which is the same rhythmic structure repeated three times. This convention allows the musicians to anticipate the end of the rhythmic passage. The successful conclusion of a *jati* must be supported by the entry of the singer and the other musicians who join with the music at the same time as the *jati* concludes. This intimate link between the rhythmic structures of the dance and the music emphasizes the importance of training in music for teachers and *nattuvanars*. The music determines how the dance is taught and performed.

Although basic principles define what movements and body positions are accepted as Bharata Natyam, each tradition sanctions certain movements. For example, some omit jumps; others make maximum use of them, although they are not intended to free the dancer from what is basically an earthbound form (Gaston 1971). Lunges[11] and kicking movements of the feet feature in some Bharata Natyam *banis* and not in others (Gaston 1971:26; *Sruti* January 1985: 7). The use of space is another area over which there is controversy. Opinion on just how much of the stage a dancer should cover with leaps, glides and movement varies. While the lineage of a *bani* can be traced to a common teacher, even among dancers trained in the same one there may be disagreement regarding how a movement is executed.

Van Zile (1983), commenting on the T. Balasaraswati *bani* states that turning the back on the audience is allowed for only very brief movements. Here it is worthwhile to note that in the sculptures of dancers in the frieze in the Amman court of the Nataraja temple in Chidambaram in Tamil Nadu there are examples of dancers with their backs facing outward (Vatsyayan 1968). This sculptural evidence tends to support those Bharata Natyam *bani* that permit turning the back to the audience. It also suggests that as a living tradition, the movements and conventions of Bharata Natyam continue to evolve and change.

ABHINAYA: NATYA/BHAVA/RASA

Indian dance was created as an adjunct to drama (*natya*). For that reason the expression of the emotions remains an important component of the dance. The execution of the theatrical component of Indian dance (*natya*) is more commonly called *abhinaya* and is expressed according to strict rules. What the artist projects through *abhinaya* is known as *bhava*: what the audience feels is known as *rasa* (literally, flavour). The ability to express feelings is often more highly regarded and stressed than the technical virtuosity of the abstract dance (*nritta*) when judging the excellence of a Bharata Natyam recital. The delineation and appreciation of the nine emotions— *sringara* (romance), *hasya* (contempt), *bibhatsa* (disgust), *soka* (sorrow), *bhayanaka* (fear), *raudra* (anger), *vira* (bravery), *adbhuta* (wonder), and *santa* (tranquillity)—is central to the presentation of Indian dance and drama. The depiction of *sringara*[12] or romantic love underlies most of the main themes in Bharata Natyam. The convention that is used to depict *sringara* is of eight (*ashta*) heroines (*nayikas*) in different states of love. Dance shares this convention with all other Indian classical artistic traditions such as literature, theatre, music, and painting (Vatsyayan 1968; Randhawa 1981). Because there are several conventions and symbols in Indian classical dance that are found in the plastic arts, in particular painting and sculpture, an introduction to one facilitates appreciation of the other. To fully appreciate this integration one must be familiar with the conventions and the symbols common to them and recorded in Sanskrit texts (Vatsyayan 1968; Sivaramamurthi 1970).

IDENTIFYING THE REPERTOIRE

Many of the principal compositions that make up a *margam*, the complete suite of dances in a concert programme, were first composed specifically for dance in the early nineteenth century by Ponnaiya Pillai (born 1804), one of the Tanjore Quartet, who was both a musician and a dance master. The repertoire in modern Bharata Natyam can be said to date from that period, their repertoire being regarded as the most traditional. Higgins states that the "infusion of creative energy marks the early nineteenth century as one of the most innovative periods in the history of Indian dance" (Higgins 1973: 4).

The full classical Bharata Natyam recital is divided into six or more discrete pieces, each of which belongs to a well-defined category on the basis of its music, and the content of the dance. The name of each dance piece usually identifies the musical form to which it is set. For example, *varnam*, *jatisvaram*, *sabdam*, *padam*, *javali*, and *tillana* are the names of musical forms and also of the dances choreographed to that music. These pieces are identified on the basis of their musical content and the choreographic conventions to which dances are set. All these are generic terms; thus, for example, there are many *jatisvarams*, *varnams*, etc. While the dances have the same name, the choreography for each of them varies. There are numerous options, but the dance steps must be structured to conform to the established general patterns. Within each category, the musical compositions can have a different *tala* (rhythmic structure), *raga* (musical structure), and *sahitya* (lyrics, where they are present). The songs are generally in Telugu, Sanskrit, Tamil or Kannada. Recently songs in various regional languages such as Marathi, Hindi and Bengali have been set to dance. This is an expanding area, as the dance is becoming popular all over India and the world. Naturally audiences are more appreciative if the songs are in languages that they understand. For that reason English is also used. A brief description of the concert repertoire in Bharata Natyam established at the beginning of the nineteenth century follows.

ALARIPPU

Alarippu,[13] the first dance, is an abstract piece, with little or no musical accompaniment. But if music accompanies *alarippu*, it is a selection from the Tiruppuhal (Tiruppukal) by the fifteenth century composer Arunagirinadar. This convention was often followed by the T. Balasaraswati *bani* and is the way I learnt my first *alarippu* from K. Ellappa in 1964. Higgins believed that this music was appropriate both for its formal devotional content (an auspicious beginning for the recital) and for the highly repetitive metrical rendering of the text. He illustrated the suitability of several poems from the Tiruppuhal (Higgins 1983: 114). The musical basis of *alarippu* is the fixed composition of mnemonic syllables (*solkattus*) that are spoken by the *nattuvanar*. The rhythmical element (*tala*) predominates.

JATISVARAM

Like *alarippu*, *jatisvaram* is a piece of abstract dance. The melody for a *jatisvaram* is sung to solfege syllables (*svaras*) (Higgins 1973: 73-102). A *jatisvaram* includes rhythmic sections of pure dance (*korvais*) which come to a climactic end. These discrete sections are repeated anywhere from five to nine or more times. The choreography for each *korvai* is different. The dance begins with *solkattus* of the first sequence of dance steps (*korvai*) which are spoken by the *nattuvanar* while the song is sung. The *korvais* that follow are executed without spoken *solkattus*, while the *nattuvanar* beats his *talam* (cymbals) to accent the beats of the dancer's feet. The dance consists of rhythmic passages with an interlude between each of these sections during which the dancer walks to each side, then backward before proceeding to execute the next *korvai*. The footwork, movement and *svaras* increase in complexity. The *jatisvaram* musical form is unique to the dance repertoire. Unlike some of the musical compositions to which dances have been choreographed, *jatisvaram* is not part of the solo Karnatic vocal repertoire sung on the concert stage, perhaps because it does not allow for musical elaboration. *Sabdam* is the name of a musical piece found in the Bharata Natyam, Bhagavata Mela, and Kuchipudi repertoires. The manner in which it is rendered differs slightly in the various styles (Raghavan 1949). *Sabdam* is distinguished from all other dance pieces except *varnam* in having sections of pure dance alternating with mime. The music, rhythmic patterns, and choreography are simpler than for a *varnam*. The text of the song that accompanies a *sabdam* generally describes and eulogises the qualities of the hero. These include his superhuman feats and generosity. Many *sabdams* are in *kambodi raga* and *misrachapu tala*, although there are others in *raga mallika* (Iyer 1963b: 42;

Higgins 1983: 103-104). The *raga* and *tala* in a *sabdam* are less varied than in the other compositions.

VARNAM

Varnam is the name applied to both the musical form and to the dance piece. The dance opens with a rhythmic section of pure dance which is followed by descriptive dance in which the dancer enacts the lyrics and incidents related to them using symbolic expression and gesture. This alternating format repeats another three times in the section known as *pallavi*. This is followed by the *anupallavi* which is introduced by the most complicated rhythmic section in the whole *varnam*. Next there are *svaras* (solfege syllables) which are first choreographed as abstract dance, and then used as the musical form for poetry which elaborates on the theme begun in the *pallavi* (see Ramakrishna 1991).

Varnam contains the most complicated rhythmic patterns and descriptive poetry which suggests, rather than dictates, a literal depiction. The dance is intended to challenge the dancer's command over the rhythmic component of the dance, her stamina and her ability to evoke feeling. Only a limited number of *varnams* are considered suitable for dance, so that, with repetition, critics have a convenient yardstick by which to judge the standard of a performance. A common *varnam*, such as *Manavi* or *Rupamu Jootsi*, can be equated with the solo of the dying swan in Swan Lake in ballet. This is confirmed in Arudra's review of two variations of a particular *varnam* (Arudra 1986: 7). After *varnam*, the most common practice in the period 1934-85 was to have an intermission during which the dancer changed her costume. From about 1985 many performers dispensed with both an interval and a costume change as audiences were inclined to leave.

ABHINAYA

The second half of the recital is dominated by the rendering of *abhinaya*, which is choreographed to poems set to music. The rhythmic component of these dances is generally very understated, although it has been the practice in some Bharata Natyam *banis* to augment the rhythmic component either by portraying the descriptive sections with a rhythmic beating of the feet or by inserting rhythmic passages (Sarada 1985: 9).

Most of the dance compositions in which *abhinaya* is the main component belong to the genre of song poems known as *padams*, and *javalis*. The differences between a *padam* and a *javali* continue to be debated but it is generally agreed that the only difference is that the music of a *javali* is more up tempo.[14] A translation of the term in various languages emphasizes the form. *Java* means speed in Telugu, a song of lewd poetry in Kannada, a gesture of the eyes in the language of "love" in Marathi; the Tamil lexicon states that it is an Urdu word *jhali*. *Javali* came into use during the time of the Maharastrian kings who ruled Tanjore in the eighteenth and nineteenth centuries (Rao 1964: 46, 224). The *javali* form can be traced to some dance compositions which were important in processions of kings or deities on festive occasions. The content of both *padams* and *javalis* is erotic but, according to Arudra (1986) *javalis* are "lascivious". Rao (1964) noted that they tended to be obscene and treat amorous themes with levity. Nevertheless there is a growing trend amongst dancers to discover and perform many of the same *javalis* and other dance compositions branded as provocative when performed by *devadasis*.

The themes of both *padams* and *javalis* usually involve the portrayal of a young woman (*nayika*) in a variety of moods and amorous predicaments. While the erotic component dominates the repertoire, devotional and descriptive poems are also set to dance. All of the imagery, situations, and reactions to them are codified and are usually highly predictable.

TILLANA

Tillana, the penultimate dance, is also the name of a musical form. This dance consists predominantly of abstract movement with a few simple lines of text, usually included near the end of the composition.

Tillana music utilizes drum *solkattus* in the main body of the music. These *solkattus* are not usually spoken, a convention also followed in the *jatisvaram* after it opens with the speaking of only one set of *solkattus*. Uttering the *solkattus* in some sections of the *tillana* has recently been featured in several *tillana* compositions of K.N. Dakshinamurthy in 1993. The musical form, *tillana*, developed from the *tarana* form in north Indian music. V. Subramaniam and Arudra (personal communication) believe that it entered the Bharata Natyam repertoire at the beginning of the nineteenth century during the time of Swati Tirunal, the ruler of the princely state of Travancore. As well as being a composer of dance and other music, he provided considerable patronage to music and dance. Numerous *tillanas*, which are constantly being absorbed from the vocal and instrumental concert repertoire, have been choreographed for dance. Many prominent musicians, Bharata Natyam teachers and vocalists have composed *tillanas* for dance which are regarded as "musically simple" (Higgins 1983: 105).

SLOKA

In the accepted order, a recital should conclude with a *sloka*, which is danced to a piece of free verse addressed to a god or goddess. *Slokas* are generally in Sanskrit. If sung in Tamil, a similar poem is known as a *viruttam* and if in Telugu a *sisapadya* (Higgins 1983: 105). This concludes the dance. To give an auspicious ending to the dance programme a short piece of music known as *mangalam* is played. The dancer often enters and standing centre stage alternately stamps her feet, squats in a deep *plié* and offers obeisance to mother earth by touching first the floor, and then her eyes. She may then walk towards the orchestra and place her palms near their instruments, returning her hands to the prayer position known as *anjali* each time. These concluding conventions are not always followed.

From the 1940s until the 1970s, the second half of the recital generally included several other dances: a gypsy dance (*kurathi*) (KU), and a dance on the theme of the wedding of an important

female Tamil saint, known as *Andal* (AN). The events surrounding
the marriage of Andal to Vishnu are described in the *Tiruppavai*
from which the lyrics of the dance are taken (Hardy 1983: 414-17;
Dehejea 1988: 118-29). Another new dance was a peacock dance.
Indrani Rehman (non-hereditary) told me that her mother, Ragini
Devi, created this dance in the 1930s for Gopinath, a male dancer.
He wore a tail of real feathers that could spread in a lifelike manner.
A snake dance (*naganrittam*) (NN), and a piece on the theme of
Siva's cosmic dance, *natanam adinar* (NA) were also added to the
dance repertoire. All but the latter were considered semi-classical
because their choreography incorporated many movements from
various folk traditions. Four of them, [(gypsy (*kurathi*), *Andal* (AN)
and the Peacock dance] called for a change of costume to correspond
with the theme. The inclusion of these dances in performances
presented at the Madras Music Academy, 1931-88, gives some
indication of how they became accepted and absorbed into the
traditional repertoire (chapter 8). The Madras Music Academy's
festival is regarded as the most prestigious and most traditional
venue for presenting south Indian classical arts. It has been an
important force in the preservation of traditional performing arts in
south India.[15] Its associated experts committees provide some
uniformity of standards, and encourage dancers to justify their
innovations against some recognized aesthetic norm. Many
performing artists are invited by the Academy to lecture about their
art and some of the major controversies surrounding Bharata
Natyam, especially in maintaining the traditional repertoire of
sadir, have been the subject of heated debate. Consequently,
dancers and choreographers working within the style are very
conscious of the demands of connoisseurs (*rasikas*). Because the
economics of the dance do not depend on attracting a mass audience,
the views of such intellectual gatherings are very important in
determining the form of the dance and its presentation. The influence
of the Academy, and other similar cultural groups (*sabhas*), may
have created a greater self-consciousness among artists than would
be typical of performing arts elsewhere in the world.

　　Various folk dances termed "light" or "popular" have also been re-introduced: *pinnal kollatam*, a folk dance was taught at Kalakshetra (Sarada 1985: 11). This dance was an important part of the *devadasi* repertoire according to several *nattuvanars*. Seetha (1981) refers to *pinnal kollatam* being performed at the court of one of the Tanjore kings.

CHANGES IN THE TRADITIONAL REPERTOIRE

The innovations addressed are those that have evolved within the framework accepted as classical Bharata Natyam since the 1930s. Although there have been changes, the original repertoire, presented in the traditional order has been retained for most *arangetrams*.

Opinions vary about the importance of maintaining the traditional order and the composition of the repertoire. The hereditary dancer, T. Balasaraswati, was an ardent advocate for presenting the dance pieces in the prescribed manner: "I believe that the traditional order of the Bharata Natyam recital viz. *alarippu, jatiswaram, sabdam, varnam, padam, tillana, sloka* is the correct sequence in the practice of this art" (T. Balasaraswati 1980: 100).

This order is not, however, generally followed today, a fact noted by the late V. Sadasivan a non-hereditary brahmin dance teacher. He represented the older generation who conducted the recitals of both *devadasis* and many of the top performers from other communities. He recalled: "The *devadasis* danced according to the 'rule'; they kept the order of the items. Now dancers open with a *tillana* and put the dances in any order."

Shanta Rao was one of the early non-hereditary dancers to abandon the traditional order in favour of selecting particular dances. She believed in presenting, "fewer items which could still encompass the entire range of expression available in Bharata Natyam ... this lead, for example to a frequent substitution of a traditional opening with invocatory pieces of a richer dramatic content" (Chatterjee 1979: 16).

She did not, however, shorten her recital. Instead, she added variety by presenting several styles of dance, a practice that is now common.

TABLE 7.1: CHANGES IN COMPOSITIONS: PERFORMED IN
A TRADITIONAL BHARATA NATYAM RECITAL

1950	1960	1991
ALARIPPU		pushpanjali/kautvam todaiya mangalam arangetram and occasionally at a recital
JATISVARAM		arangetrams only
SABDAM	started to disappear	arangetrams only
VARNAM	important	important
INTERMISSION		
PADAMS/JAVALIS	variety has increased	variety has increased
NATANAM ADINAR	Hindi bhajan	arangetrams only in north India
TILLANA	important	important
KURATHI	arangetrams only	arangetrams only
SLOKA		rare

ALARIPPU

T. Balasaraswati believed that it was important to open a dance recital with *alarippu*. Her comments highlight that even a seasoned dancer requires to focus her attention at the beginning of a recital.

In the beginning, *alarippu,* which is based on pure rhythm alone, brings out the special charm of pure dance. The movements of *alarippu* relax the dancer's body and thereby her mind. They loosen and co-ordinate her limbs, and prepare her for the dance. Rhythm has a rare capacity to concentrate the mind. The *alarippu* is most valuable in freeing the dancer from distraction and making her single-minded (Balasaraswati 1980).

The well-known non-hereditary dancer, Yamini Krishnamurti, agreed: "I like to start with an *alarippu* as it is a traditional warm-up for the eyes, neck and arms. I like the concept of *alarippu*."

All the same, it has been the practice for many years to dispense with an *alarippu* after the first public recital. Table 8.1 illustrates that even the conservative Madras Music Academy were willing to accept recitals that dispensed with *alarippu*. *Alarippu* is often replaced with a *kautvam* or poem addressed to one of the eight guardians of the quarters (Visweswaran 1985). Other options are: *pushpanjali*,[16] *nrittanjali* (which includes *svaras* and *jatis*), *todaiya mangalam*, or *mallari* (a piece of *nagasvaram* music still played in temples).[17] All of these pieces are adaptations of music or dances that were part of the temple tradition. Yamini Krishnamurti again commented on these innovations: "There is nothing to learning a *kautvam*. One must just know the song and its meaning. The whole rhythm is in the song and the *jatis* (rhythmic patterns) are in the music."

Padmavati, granddaughter of the hereditary teacher K.P. Kittappa,[18] and a descendant of the Tanjore Quartet family, included the *Vayu*[19] *kautvum* prior to *alarippu* when she presented her *arangetram* in 1989. This would indicate that reviving *kautvams*, after not being presented for many years, has become acceptable even to hereditary families.

TODAIYA MANGALAM

Todaiya mangalam is from the repertoire of ritual temple music (Higgins 1973; *Marg* 1982; Kersenboom 1987). It was also danced in the Bhagavata Mela dance style, which has close affinity to Bharata Natyam (Parthasarathy 1989). The non-hereditary brahmin dance teacher, Durairaj Iyer (1900-80) borrowed heavily from Bhagavata Mela. It is not surprising that in his tradition of Bharata Natyam, *todaiya mangalam* is danced. Nevertheless, support for this dance varies. Yamini Krishnamurthy frequently opened her recitals with *todaiya mangalam* followed by *alarippu*. T. Balasaraswati and her daughter, Lakshmi never performed it.

Todaiya mangalam is in the repertoire of several teachers including the hereditary teacher, V. Ramaiya, and the non-hereditary teacher, Adyar Lakshman, from whom I learnt it. According to many dancers it is the choreography by the late *nattuvanar* Kalyana-sundaram that is used by many *nattuvanars*.

JATISVARAM

Jatisvaram was one of the first dances to disappear from the concert repertoire. This was to cut down on the length of recitals and allow the dancer to concentrate on *tillana* which is also a piece of abstract dance, but more spectacular and with more appealing music (Rukmini Devi 1985: 18).

SABDAM

Sabdam, like *jatisvaram* began to disappear from the concert repertoire of Rukmini Devi from the 1940s. Her decision to omit *sabdam* was not to cut down the length of the recital, but to add variety.

I found *sabdam* musically uninteresting as it depended on the *manodharma* (artistic imagination) and the quality of the singer to make it good. Good singers were also difficult to find because good musicians, even from the *nattuvanar* families, thought it was undignified to sing for the dance and, therefore, had given up the profession completely (Rukmini Devi, 1985: 19).

Her remarks are important, as most innovations have come from choreographing musical compositions already in the concert music repertoire. The debate around their suitability continues. She filled the traditional third spot with several songs from the classical music concert repertoire (Sarada 1985: 45).

From the 1960s onwards, *sabdam* has often been omitted even for *arangetrams*. This is significant because an *arangetram* is that one moment in a dancer's career when she is expected to demonstrate that she is competent in the full traditional repertoire. It also means that many dancers will not be familiar with the *sabdam* form. With the exception of the T. Balasaraswati *bani*, best exemplified in the 1980s by her daughter Lakshmi, *sabdam* has hardly been performed by an established dancer since 1970. Lakshmi told me that for both herself and her students it was still an important part of the concert repertoire. Nevertheless, T. Balasaraswati herself omitted *sabdam* for her concert at the Music Academy in 1950 (Table 8.1). In the 1950s and 1960s, V. Raghavan, the Sanskritist and authority on Bharata Natyam, and Secretary of the Madras Music Academy at the time, composed several *sabdams* which T. Balasaraswati performed. This added to the list of *sabdams* that had been previously performed[20] and gave some variety in the repertoire.

The tendency to drop *sabdam* is not recent. Venkatachalam lamented that, even in the 1940s, *sabdam* was often omitted. He justified the inclusion of *sabdam*: "*Sabdam* is often omitted in the ordinary Bharata Natyam recitals but is of great help to a conscientious dancer who intends to render the long *varnam* that follows without any stop or break as it gives her sufficient rest for the feet and time for the mood" (Venkatachalam 1946: 13). Yamini Krishnamurti, who began her career in the 1950s, hardly ever included a *sabdam* in her recitals. She summed up the general attitude towards this piece and the reason why it can be dispensed with: "*Sabdam* has neither the vitality of *jatisvaram*, nor the power of *varnam*."

No doubt this was why K. Ellappa did not include *sabdam* in the first *margam* that I studied with him in 1964. I subsequently studied several *sabdams* with Adyar K. Lakshmanan, K. J. Govindarajan and V. Gayatri, but at my request.

VARNAM

For many dancers the fourth dance, *varnam*, must be included. In the 1980s it lasted anywhere from about fifteen minutes to one hour. Opinion varies about how long a traditional *varnam* should be. Although it is generally accepted that a *varnam* should be "at least an hour", many traditional dancers such as K. Bhanumati and

Swarna Saraswati stated that when they were performing, their *varnams* never exceeded half an hour. Swarna Saraswati continued to follow this practice. When I studied with her, both *varnams*, *Dhanike* and *Manavi* lasted about twenty-five minutes. The fact that *varnam* is considered important says much about its musical and dance content. Where a concert needs to be kept short a *varnam* can be edited: sections can be cut out, or abbreviated, in particular the descriptive portions. When a great deal of compression is required, the solfege syllables (*svaras*) in the second half of the *varnam* are included but their accompanying text can be omitted. This maintains the musical integrity of the piece, at the expense of the poetry. For some, the very formalized descriptive content of the *varnam* can be highly repetitive with little significance (Subramaniam 1985). Since the 1960s, the rhythmic abstract dance sections (*jatis/tirmanams*) have continued to increase in complexity and length. In contrast, the *varnam* in the *sadir* style, performed in the Tiruttani temple tradition in the 1930s and early 1940s, was very simple and made use of only one choreography for the five rhythmic passages (*tirmanams*) (Kersenboom 1987: 172).

Varnams are of two varieties: *pada* and *tana*.[21] *Pada varnams* (also known as *chauka varnams*) have been composed for dance and hence it is generally agreed that they are best suited for a Bharata Natyam recital. *Tana varnams* have been composed for music recitals but have also been used as music for dance. Despite the objections made against including *tana varnams* as part of the Bharata Natyam repertoire, several eminent traditional teachers, most notably P.S. Minakshisundaram, whose in-laws included the composers of most *pada varnams* in the Bharata Natyam repertoire, have choreographed *taha varnams* (Chatterjee 1979). Many dancers perform them, among them Shanta Rao (non-hereditary) who studied with P.S. Minakshisundaram, and Yamini Krishnamurti (non-hereditary), who studied with one of his relatives, K.P. Kittappa. Most "traditionalists" consider that the repertoire is large enough and that *tana varnams* are unsuitable. Yamini Krishnamurti and Shanta Rao, however, both told me that *tana varnams* were their favourite. As *tana varnams* are in a medium or fast tempo, it is very easy to accelerate (increase the *laya*), a fact noted by Yamini Krishnamurti who was ecstatic about learning a *tana varnam* with K.P. Kittappa, but added: "The only problem is that he has to be present to conduct it. He has to do the *talam* to control the *laya*."

Many, including Rukmini Devi, believed that for dance recitals *tana varnams* were inferior to *pada varnams*: "... *tana varnams* should be learnt only as a sample and should not take the place of the *pada varnam* which is more ideally suited for the dance. I regret to say that even the *pada varnam* which is meant to be done in slow tempo is often ruined by too much speed" (Rukmini Devi 1985: 19). Rukmini Devi was against "speed" but expanded the traditional repertoire of *varnams* by adding rhythmic patterns to various pieces of music and adapting them to the *varnam* format.[22] She also commissioned original *varnams* by eminent living musicians and scholars (Sarada 1985:46, Devi 1985:18). Her main reservations about conventional *varnams* were to their erotic themes.

EXPANDING THE REPERTOIRE

Although the male dancer Ram Gopal performed dances from the traditional repertoire, he also adapted them and had dances composed for him which reflected the *tandava* or masculine element of Bharata Natyam. One of these dances was *natanam adinar*, based on the dance of Siva. He accounted for the creation of this dance: "*Natanam adinar* was composed specially for me by [P.S.] Minakshisundaram. I was the first to perform it. Now they don't do it properly. It should be danced by a man. At the beginning of the dance I often preferred to do a few Siva poses and get into a sort of trance." Others such as Shanta Rao also claimed that *natanam adinar* was composed for them. There is no doubt that this dance was a new creation in the 1940s. *Natanam adinar* appeared in the concert repertoire for several decades and was very popular until the 1960s. It is a very energetic dance. While it was often presented in addition to the traditional finale, *tillana*, it was also used to replace it. In the 1980s, *tillana* continued to be popular, but *natanam adinar* almost disappeared from the repertoire.

Several semi-classical pieces once common in the Bharata Natyam repertoire, were dropped. No doubt this was because the audience became bored with them and musically they were not of a high order. The gypsy dance (*kurathi*), which did not make great demands on the technical skill of the performer, was usually considered more appropriate for younger girls. The dancer, Yamini Krishnamurthy, performed a gypsy dance when it was in fashion, but told me that it was in "classical style", choreographed by A.P. Chokkalingam. Indrani Rehman, another non-hereditary dancer, also included the gypsy dance choreographed by A. P. Chokkalingam as part of her repertoire in the 1950s and 1960s. Some of these recitals were held at the Madras Music Academy, noted for its conservatism, which underlines that at one time the gypsy dance was acceptable but there was a change in public taste.

Beginning in the 1970s, audiences and dancers have placed increasing emphasis on classicism and reviving old forms. As a result some earlier innovations have been dropped and others created.

SOME CHANGES IN *ABHINAYA*

The enthusiasm for some new pieces suggests that traditional dancers and musicians have always expanded their repertoire. Hereditary musical/dance families, with their musical excellence and personal contact with contemporary composers were sometimes involved in the direct creation of the dance repertoire. Much of the repertoire for *abhinaya* then came to be regarded as the preserve of the family.[23] Particularly noted in this respect was the family of T. Balasaraswati. Neither she, nor another hereditary dancer, Swarna Saraswati, approved of the tendency to increase the rhythmic portions in the dance.

Opinions varied about choreographing different musical forms. Balasaraswati objected to *kritis* being added to the Bharata Natyam repertoire, especially those of Muthuswami Dikshitar which become popular in the 1970s. In her view the lyrics and the musical rendering of his songs were unsuitable for dance. In contrast, Rukmini Devi and others considered them suitable if in moderate numbers (Rukmini Devi 1985: 19). Rukmini Devi's decisions regarding addition or omission to the repertoire centred on the content of the lyrics and the rendering of the descriptive passages (*abhinaya*).

... there was much that was undesirable not only in the actual movements and *hastas* but even in the subtle *abhinaya*, eye movements, lip movements, etc. It was not difficult for me to convince my teacher, Meenakshisundaram[24] Pillai that I would not be able to learn such an aspect and so my dance took another turn and I worked entirely for the spiritualization of the art (Rukmini Devi 1985: 18).

The *abhinaya* in the *devadasis'* dance was usually direct and uncluttered, in contrast to the highly choreographed and complex depictions of today's dancers. This is best seen in the part of the descriptive dance where the same line of the song is sung repeatedly while the dancer elaborates using hand and facial gestures (Vatsyayan 1968; Narayan 1989). This is known as *sanchari bhava*. The dancer, Yamini Krishnamurti, commented on the *abhinaya* of the *devadasi* M.D. Gauri: "Gauri did not have much *sanchari bhava*. What she did was direct and it was not necessary for her to elaborate."

Another non-hereditary dancer, Gita Ramakrishnan said of the *abhinaya* of Swarna Saraswati, also a former *devadasi*: "Swarna did exactly what the line said and not much *sanchari*, she did the literal meaning in one hundred different ways.... Dancers today drift away and depict stories around the exploits of various deities, whether or not they are relevant."

I studied with Swarna Saraswati at about the same time (1971-72) and also found her *abhinaya* clear, direct and uncluttered. She taught me several Kshetrayya *padams*, including some with highly erotic content, and I never once felt that she had transgressed the bounds of good taste. There was a simple majesty to her exposition.

Although change is inevitable, some, such as K.S. Srinivasan (1985), a well known dance critic, argue that *abhinaya* should continue as an essential component. He believes that *abhinaya* "reaches for the mind" and the "cultural consciousness of the viewer". For him, audiences should be connoisseurs (*rasikas*), and therefore not only receptive, but familiar with Sanskritic theory of aesthetics (Sivaramamurti 1970; Chari 1980). He lauds the close association of *abhinaya* with the poetry. Krishna Chaitanya (1987), however, has a different view. "Mimesis is murderously strong in our tradition. The choreography is shackled to the libretto in *Nritya* ... the body cannot speak in its own language if it is compelled to illustrate the text slavishly" (Chaitanya 1987: 5).

K.S. Srinivasan appreciates the traditional repertoire, and V. Subramaniam, a radical among dance connoisseurs laments the standardization of the Bharata Natyam recital in particular the *abhinaya* of the central piece, *varnam*: "Always a declaration of love by a lovelorn maiden, pining for union with her lord who may be a deity (Krishna, Nataraja or Ranganathan) or a king or a local chieftain" (Subramaniam 1985: 28).

Both V. Subramaniam and Krishna Chaitanya believe there is little potential for artistic creativity. On the other hand, K.S. Srinivasan, and those who share his opinion, argue for reviving the older repertoire. K.S. Srinivasan's approach presupposes familiarity and exposure to the dance and related traditions such as literature, painting and music (Vatsyayan 1968). Chaitanya, on the other hand, believes that the traditional repertoire has outlived its usefulness, and is no longer relevant. For him the themes have become repetitive and boring. He would also no doubt challenge whether the over emphasis on *abhinaya* could, in fact, still allow for it to be called dance ... rather theatre with some dance. The contrast in these two approaches may be characterized as indigenous/traditional (K.S. Srinivasan) versus modern/creative (Chaitanya, V. Subramaniam).

ADDITIONAL STYLES

I have not discovered any examples of *isai vellala* dancers performing more than one style. Some of them, however, did augment their *abhinaya* repertoire by working with a Kuchipudi master, but it would seem that not many *devadasis*, trained in the *sadir* tradition, followed this practice. With the non-*devadasi* dancers, however, it was different and some immediately saw the potential in studying several classical styles. This allowed them to expand the variety of movement and expression in their dance recitals. They also needed new vocabulary if they were to choreograph themes not dealt with in the Bharata Natyam repertoire. As each dance style has its own unique strengths, beauty and charm, the dancers and the audiences found it stimulating. The innovation began with including one or more additional styles, such as Kathakali in a Bharata Natyam dance programme. There are instances of two or more dancers sharing an evening, with each performing a different style. Many of the early non-hereditary dancers, such as Uday Shankar, Ragini Devi, Ram Gopal and Indrani Rehman performed as part of a troupe which presented several dancers and several styles, including solo and group dances.

By performing other styles alongside the better known Bharata Natyam, the new dancers gradually educated audiences to accept the new styles in their own right. Mohini Attam was the first style to be presented sharing half a programme with Bharata Natyam, initially by Ragini Devi in the 1930s and later by Shanta Rao. By the 1950s, a number of dancers were offering performances in which the two halves of the evening were devoted to different styles. Odissi had not, as yet, been granted classical status. Two other dance styles, Kuchipudi in the mid 1960s and Odissi in the late 1950s were also introduced to share a programme with Bharata Natyam. Full solo programmes in Odissi, Kuchipudi and Mohini Attam have been developed only since the 1960s. Recitals in the 1980s have been dominated by a single dancer rather than a troupe, the same dancer performing two styles, usually devoting one half of a programme to Bharata Natyam and the other to another style.

Among the various styles of Indian classical dance, Bharata Natyam was originally most closely related to Kuchipudi. Both are set to classical Karnatic music. Swapnasundari, a non-hereditary professional exponent of both styles commented: "[Bharata Natyam] is restrained and perhaps geometric, while Kuchipudi is freer, more flexible and essentially a *natya*, or expressive form."

In Bharata Natyam the dancer is the medium through which the story is told. In Kuchipudi the dancer becomes the character. One convention to indicate that the dancer has changed characters is to make a full turn (*Sruti* 13: 17-34). During the early period of increased interest in Bharata Natyam it was considered appropriate for Bharata Natyam dancers to study the *abhinaya* of the more theatrical traditions of Bhagavata Mela, Kuchipudi[25] and Kathakali. Until about 1947 these three styles were a male preserve. Rukmini Devi brought a celebrated exponent of the Bhagavata Mela tradition, Balu Bhagavatar from the village of Melatur to Kalakshetra to assist her in recreating the main dance dramas using the technique of his style. Today the dancer, Revati Ramachandran, who is continuing the work of her teacher Durairaj Iyer, as well as others, are trying to enrich Bharata Natyam by encouraging contact with the Bhagavata Mela tradition. The *abhinaya* of Kuchipudi is particularly rich. Though the style was originally performed only by men, it was studied by both *devadasi* and non-*devadasi sadir*/Bharata Natyam dancers. Two *devadasis*, T. Balasaraswati and M.D. Gauri enriched their *abhinaya* by studying with one of the greatest Kuchipudi masters, Lakshminarayanan Sastri. Their skill in *abhinaya* must have been influenced by their contact with this style as this report from Madras in 1943 confirms: "(Lakshminarayanan Sastri) taught Balasaraswati a whole set of *padams* and *javalis* and she publicly declared that Sastri's art had opened her eyes to a new world of dance and beauty, of which she had been unaware till then" (*Marg* 1963: 32).

According to the hereditary Kuchipudi dancer and teacher, Vempati Chinnasatyam, between 1943 and 1952 Lakshminarayan Sastri taught several high caste, non-traditional dancers such as Tara Chaudhury (*Sruti* Dec.-Jan. 1989; *Marg* 1963). Another important Kuchipudi master, Vedantam Satyanarayan also taught T. Balasaraswati (*Sruti* 1984: 23). *Abhinaya* is more adaptable and easier to integrate into various dance styles than abstract movement.

Another style studied by Bharata Natyam dancers was Kathakali. Because of the highly codified, and varied way in which the emotions are portrayed in Kathakali, many non-hereditary dancers such as Ragini Devi, Shanta Rao, Ram Gopal, Uday Shankar and Rukmini Devi included Kathakali dances in recitals primarily devoted to Bharata Natyam. Kathakali training was also important for men at Kalakshetra who combined it with studying Bharata Natyam. Rukmini Devi used to present several dances in the Kathakali style using the rhythmic instruments available rather than the ones traditionally used. Sarada writes that it was only later, "we learnt that Kathakali had music of its own, full of *bhava* for the various stories" (Sarada 1985: 8).

CHANGES AND INNOVATIONS

The revival of interest in Indian classical dance in general and Bharata Natyam in particular began in the 1930s. By then there was already a form of Indian dance that had received international recognition. Created by Uday Shankar, these dances were culturally Indian, but innovative. They drew from art forms such as Indian painting and sculpture, as much as from the various classical styles of dance. Uday Shankar wished to create a style that was relevant to his time: "A cultural revival cannot be achieved simply by offering so-called finished products of art, especially those dealing with subjects of past periods. It can only be achieved when there is a real breakdown [*sic*] of feeling" (Uday Shankar, quoted in Banerji 1982: 73).

Uday Shankar's dances were created outside of India, and first performed to western music.[26] He then returned to India, founded his art centre at Almora (Banerji 1982: 45) and increased his repertoire by working with classically trained teachers in various dance styles. This was a period when many *nattuvanars* and other classically trained dance masters in most of the classical styles needed work. Uday Shankar recruited many of them, including K.N. Kandappa, T. Balasaraswati's *nattuvanar* and dance teacher. Uday Shankar selected those aspects of the various styles that he wished to incorporate into his own work. In that respect his approach differs from many innovations in the 1980s where the approach has been to master a particular classical technique and innovate within its conventions.

Since Uday Shankar, there has been no other creative dance movement in India that has been so universally accepted. In the quest for purity and authenticity, Uday Shankar's work later came under attack. Kapila Vatsyayan accounted for this: "Naturally there was a reaction to his contributions because the very fact of his having brought to light the rich resources of the tradition meant a re-establishment of the tradition and a decrying of the eclectic approach" (Vatsyayan 1978: 7). Perhaps this, more than anything else, explains the timidity of dancers and teachers towards innovation up until the 1980s.

Another important dancer from the early period was Ram Gopal. Although he kept within the traditional guidelines of Bharata Natyam he was not afraid to examine critically the traditional forms:

I want to see something that does not bore me or embarrass me with the endless repetition of the Indian dancer's movement. And can you blame me, or the vast Indian public? You see we have changed too. Oh, I know you are going to tell me that the traditions must be kept pure and all that. The dance of the temples and village is only a fragment of the Sanskrit drama and theatre that has come down to us. Besides the temple theatre and the ancient dance in India were created for another rhythm of another age, long since dead. Don't you think we should step forward and create something that is understandable in terms of today (Gopal 1957: 53).

His objections addressed the fact that most of the descriptive dances fit into a standard format in which the dancer enacts a plea for union with her lord, chides him for his callousness, criticises him for his attentions to the other woman, flatters him for his heroism and physical beauty, and lauds his great compassion. Whether the dancer addresses a potential patron or a deity the poetic conceits are the same, as is the imagery. There is a formula for the choreography, with no surprises. It is the subtle nuances which make a memorable recital and this requires an audience that is extremely knowledgeable.

DISCUSSION

In the past thirty years there has been a resurgence in Indian dance both in India and abroad. Some dances, once exclusively performed by a particular sex, are now done by either. These are all minor changes, and most of the movements remain recognizably the same. The idea that the dance is a timeless, never-changing art is, however, easily refuted. This statement is reiterated on many brochures and other promotional material produced by Bharata Natyam dancers in India and abroad. The very fact that it is necessary to repeat the historical pedigree of the dance as frequently as is customary today, qualifies Bharata Natyam to some extent; as an invented tradition. No secure and unmodified custom would need to reiterate its claims to antiquity so frequently (Hobsbawm and Ranger 1989).

Nevertheless the concert repertoire of *sadir* still forms the basis for presentday Bharata Natyam. Most students today learn the full traditional programme before progressing to newer material.

Two camps have emerged among adherents of modern Bharata Natyam; those who extol the virtues of the "older" Bharata Natyam, and those who believe that the traditional form has outlived its artistic usefulness. We may characterize the traditionalists as being inventors of traditions, while the modernists lean towards a concept of "creative" art. Both streams have many adherents and the clamour of their artistic discourse makes Bharata Natyam a lively art form. In the long run these two streams can only help to keep it vibrant.

NOTES

1. Dance masters use both the terms *hasta* and *mudra*.
   It may be of interest to note that many of the hand signs used in dance are also used in iconography, see Gaston 1982: 26.
2. The one exception is the Manipuri style of dance where the foot rhythms are not continuous as in the other styles.
3. The Sanskrit texts relating to dance have been dealt with in detail by K. Vatsyayan 1968: 25-301; Bose 1970,1989.
4. Four styles (Bharata Natyam, Kuchipudi, Mohini Attam, and Odissi) adopt a position that incorporates bent knees, Bharata Natyam would be regarded as the most angular of all the styles.
5. This hand position is known as *pataka hasta*. For an illustration see Gaston 1982: 42.
6. See Subrahmanyam 1979, where she describes how she has incorporated leg movements into her style of Bharata Natyam.

7. Raghavan (1973: 251) identifies *adavu* as a Telugu word. According to the Tamil lexicon, *atavu* is correct, but as *adavu* is the more common spelling I have used it here.

8. *Sol* in Tamil means word and *kattu* means put together. *Solkattu/Sholkattu* indicates any fairly lengthy combination of rhythmic syllables.

9. Van Zile's (1983) comment, that the number of *adavus* is fixed for the T. Balasaraswati *bani*, does not apply generally. See Higgins (1973: 52) where he states that T Balasaraswati would not disclose her particular *adavu* patterns to him to record while he was conducting his research.

10. In practice the terms *tirmanam* and *jati* are used interchangeably for a long rhythmic passage.

11. Lunges are used in the *adavu* known as *sarrukal/sharrukal*. In discussing the V. Ramaiya tradition of Bharata Natyam, one of his disciples Radha states that it is essential to stretch the leg backward while in a full *mandi* or deep plié position (*Sruti* January 1985:42).

12. *Sringara* is not the dominant emotion in the *Natya Sastra*. In the *Natya Sastra*, the two dramas described, for which dance was created: Siva's destruction of *Tripura*, or the triple cities of the demons and the churning of the Ocean of Milk by the Gods, are dominated by *vira* and *raudra* (V. Subramaniam 1985: 29).

13. Higgins 1973: 27 notes that in Ponnaiya's day two additional musical items, *melaprapti* and *todaiya mangalam*, were performed behind a closed curtain before the dancer performed *alarippu*.

14. *Javalis* were sung as the curtain was raised and as relief during tense scenes in the Bhagavata Mela tradition. Some composers of *javalis* are Dharmapuri Subbarayar. T. Pattabhiramayya, Dasu Sreeramulu, Patnam Subrahmanya, Tirupathi Narayana Swami. *Javalis* are in bright *rakti ragas* like *khamas*, *behag*, *junjhuti*, *kafi*, and *mohana*.

15. When the Indian National Congress met in Madras 1927-28 and national independence was declared for the first time the surplus funds collected at that time were used to found the Madras Music Academy. See also Baskaran 1981.

16. Satyanarayan (1966) discusses the antiquity of the *pushpanjali* dance. The Mysore *bani* of Bharata Natyam has always had *pushpanjali* as an important dance in its repertoire (*Marg* 1982).

17. Kersenboom (1984: 249) lists the usual compositions performed by *devadasis* as *nalanku*, *unjal*, *lali*, *ootam*, *kappal pattu*, *nottu svarams*, *astapadi* (*ashtapadi*) *nattupatti*.

18. *Navasandhi kautvams* were included in the book of dances in the traditional repertoire of the Tanjore Quartet, edited by K.P. Sivananda (1961). See also Kersenboom 1987.

19. *Vayu* is the wind god.

20. The Souvenir of the Madras Music Academy, 1955 stated: "Srimati Balasaraswati's recital (December 25, 1955) includes a new *sabda* (*sabdam*) in Sanskrit by Dr Raghavan on Goddess Kalpakambika at Mylapore".

21. The most celebrated *tana varnam* is *Viriboni* by Pachimirayam Adiyappaiyya. See Seetha 1981: 178.

22. While Rukmini Devi performed *varnams* from the repertoire of the Tanjore Quartet such as *Sakhiye* by T.S. Ponnaiya Pillai she also choreographed others using the music of Swati Tirunnal, such as *Sami Nine Nami Nanu*, and songs such as *En Palli Kondeerayya* by Arunachala Kavi Rayer, *Ela ni daya radu*, and *Rama Sita* of Thyagaraja, *Oh Jagadamba* by Shyama Shastri and several from Jayadeva's *Gita Govinda*.

23 V. Subramaniam notes that Arikudi Ramanuja Iyengar pleaded with Dhanammal, Balasaraswati's grandmother to allow her to study dance because their family was the "storehouse" of most *padams* (Seetha 1981; Sankaran 1984).

24. This is an alternative spelling for Minakshisundaram.

25. While Kuchipudi and Bhagavata Mela are often considered to be the same style, there is some controversy over this.

26. Uday Shankar's first dance experience was with Anna Pavlova's ballet troupe. The music was set to a written score, so that he was able to tour with the dancers, recruiting musicians locally.

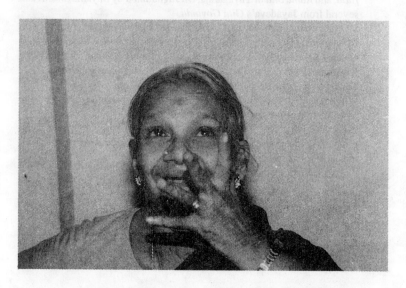

Plate 7.1: Abhinaya: T.A. Rajalakshmi

T.A. Rajalakshmi, a former *devadasi* is demonstrating the hand and facial gestures used to show a beautiful face (1985). Her left hand is in *alapadma hasta*; she is looking upward smiling. Because she is singing at the same time her mouth is slightly open. Her make-up includes the symbol of marriage, the red dot in the centre of her forehead, even though she never married a mortal. As a dedicated *devadasi* she was married to the deity of the temple in Tiruvidaimarudur.

Plate 7.2: Abhinaya: T.K. Mahalingam

T.K. Mahalingam (*isai vellala*) demonstrating *abhinaya* in his school in Bombay 1985. His right hand held over his head is intended to represent a window, his left hand is held in a relaxed posture at the centre of his body. He depicts a heroine looking anxiously out of her window for her beloved. His expression mimics expectation.

8 Dance Performances at the Madras Music Academy, 1931-1988

Since the 1930s, dance has been presented as part of the Madras Music Academy's music festival. This festival is regarded as the most prestigious and most traditional venue for presenting south Indian classical arts. Consequently, we can regard all those artists appearing at the festival as having the recognition and approval of this important group of connoisseurs.[1] By reviewing chronologically the artists presented by the Madras Music Academy we can trace the public profile given to the different *banis* of Bharata Natyam, as well as the various styles of classical dance that were presented at the Madras Music Academy. It also documents the repertoire giving us some indication of the dances considered traditional or innovative. Thanks to the Secretary of the Academy, T.S. Parthasarathy, I was able to inspect, in their library, their records of their programmes for practically all festivals since 1931.

The Madras Music Academy has been an important force in the preservation of traditional performing arts in south India. The history of the Academy given in the 1935 Conference Souvenir records:

Very early the Academy set its hand to the taste [sic] of dispelling the cloud of prejudice that hung over the ancient institution of Bharata Natyam. By refining the performance and issuing an enlightening programme it has brought the classic Indian dance within the limits of intelligent appreciation, and has thus rescued it from the danger of extinction. It has now a bright future before it as an important branch of *sangita* (music).

The Academy has been educating the public as one of its functions: "The performances arranged by the Academy on classical lines have exerted a chastening influence on public taste ... the publication of an educative programme."

The Academy, with its associated expert committees, gives south Indian music and dance a centre for intellectual debate and a body which sets artistic criteria. This has the twin effects of maintaining some uniformity of standards, and encouraging artists to justify their innovations against some recognized aesthetic norm. Many performing artists are invited by the Academy to lecture about their art. Some of the major controversies surrounding Bharata Natyam such as the depiction of *sringara* and maintaining the traditional repertoire of *sadir* have been the subject of heated debate. Consequently, dancers and choreographers are very conscious of the demands of connoisseurs (*rasikas*) for maintaining the classical rigour of Bharata Natyam.

Because the economics of the dance do not depend on attracting a mass audience, the views of such intellectual gatherings become very important in determining the form of the dance and its presentation. The influence of the Academy, and other similar cultural forums (*sabhas*), may have created a greater self-consciousness among artists than would be typical of performing arts elsewhere in the world.

The annual music conference of the Madras Music Academy, held in late December to early January each year, has included some dance performances practically every year since 1931. I have used the details of these performances (Table 8.1) to look at the development and evolution of Bharata Natyam.

It is impossible to obtain an exact picture of the number of dancers, both hereditary and non-hereditary who were active at the time of the revival. The Madras Music Academy presented several programmes, which were important as they were some of the first to be presented to the general public that were not part of marriage festivities or other private celebrations.[2]

To give some idea of the level of activity at the Madras Music Academy, the recitals held there will be discussed by decade.

1930s

All the dancers who performed at the Music Academy in the 1930s were *devadasis*. With the exception of M.D. Gauri (1890-1974), who was then forty-two, all the dancers were in their teens.

The first recorded recital by a *devadasi* for the Academy was on March 15, 1931 by P.K. Jivaratnam and P.K. Rajalakshmi, daughters of P. Kalyani (1873-1938), a *devadasi* from Pandanallur. Kalyani had trained with the Pandanallur-based teachers, P. Kumaraswamy and his cousin, P.S. Minakshisundaram, who later taught Rukmini Devi and other important non-hereditary figures of the revival. Kalyani had studied with two other *devadasis*, S. Chellammal, from the town of Seerkashi and M. Meela from Madras. This is an example of a *devadasi* teaching a non-family member, as M.D. Gauri was to do later. M.D. Gauri's pupils, however, comprised both *devadasis* and brahmins.

In 1933, on December 28, two *devadasi* cousins from Kumbakonam, K. Varalakshmi and K. Saranayaki, danced. In 1934, on December 31, and again in 1936, on December 27, K. Varalakshmi danced with another of her cousins, K. Bhanumati. These three girls had three other cousins who were also *devadasis*: K. Gauri, K. Pattu and K. Sulochana. The Kumbakonam dancers were very popular and after the untimely death of K. Varalakshmi in 1937, K. Bhanumati was invited to perform alone in 1940. All the Kumbakonam *devadasis* studied with P. (Papanasam) Vadivel,[3] another of P.S. Minakshisundaram's students.

Other *devadasis* from Pandanallur also performed. In 1935, on June first, two daughters of P. (Pandanallur) Nagamma, P.N. Sabharanjitam, and P.N. Nagaratnam, gave dance recitals. The next year, on December 29, P.N. Sabharanjitam gave a solo recital. P.N. Sabharanjitam used to demonstrate the dance for Rukmini Devi when she was studying with P.S. Minakshi-sundaram.

The Madras *devadasis*, who danced at the Academy, were represented by M.D. Gauri and T. Balasaraswati. In 1932, on the third of January, M.D. Gauri danced. T. Balasaraswati performed at the Madras Music Academy for the first time in 1933, when she was fifteen; thereafter, her performances at the Academy were presented frequently until 1971. Balasaraswati continued to perform elsewhere until her death in 1984.

The *devadasi* T. (Tirunelveli)[4] N. Muthuratnambal, performed at the Academy on December 27 1937. Her family had been dancers for four generations: her mother, T. Nallanayikam, had studied with Subramaniam, son of Sabhapati *Nattuvanar*. Muthuratnambal trained with the Ettayapuram court teacher, as well 'as with Subbaraya *Nattuvanar*, and with Sabhapati *Nattuvanar* from Chidambaram. Muthuratnambal trained her daughter, T.M. Bala Rukmini, who also studied with Tiruchendur Subramaniam *Nattuvanar*.

No programme notes were available for the first recorded recital at the Academy in 1931 by P.K. Jivaratnam. I was only able to find information on programmes beginning in 1933.[5] There were ten performances altogether, involving nine different *devadasis* (P.K. Jivaratnam, M.D. Gauri, K. Varalakshmi, K. Saranayiki, P.N. Sabharanjitam, T. Muthuratnambal, K. Bhanumati, T. Balasaraswati, K. Nagarangitam). T. Balasaraswati performed twice. Three of the presentations included joint dances by P. Varalakshmi and P. Saranayaki; K. Varalakshmi and K. Bhanumati; and P.N. Sabharanjitam and K. Nagarangitam. No *nattuvanars* or accompanists were listed in the programme notes. All the dancers presented the traditional order of items, but T. Balasaraswati omitted *sabdam* on both occasions that she performed, and also dispensed with *sloka* at the end of her recital. There were no additions to the repertoire, nor styles other than Bharata Natyam presented. No men were invited to perform nor were any dance dramas presented. During this decade most of the *devadasis* were living in temple towns and only three were based in Madras. The fact that eleven different *devadasis* were invited to perform suggests that in this decade there were still many *devadasis* active whose dance was of a high calibre.

1940s

Twenty-one dance recitals by twenty different dancers were presented by the Music Academy in the 1940s. Three of the dancers were *devadasis*: K. Bhanumati, T. Balasaraswati (twice), and P. Jayalakshmi. Another dancer, Bhavani, is believed to have been a *devadasi* but despite extensive inquiries I was unable to obtain exact details about her. The fact that there were only three, or possibly four, *devadasis* for the 1940s and the remaining were non-hereditary dancers, is in contrast to the previous decade when there were eleven *devadasis* and no non-hereditary dancers. Of the fourteen non-*devadasis*, twelve were brahmins. This decade also included presentations by so and so "and party". Because the composition of the party has not been given and details are not available, it is impossible to give a comprehensive list of all the dancers. Duos were still popular; in this decade they were presented by three sets of young high caste girls: Yogam and Mangalam; Kausalya and Kalyanasundaravalli, and Radha and Anandi. Kausalya also presented a solo recital on another occasion.

The traditional order was followed by all the dancers, except that *sabdam* (SA) was not danced by Kausalya or by Mrinalini Sarabhai. Other deviations from the traditional programme were that *sloka* (SL), which was included by Shanta (Rao) and party, and Hemamalini Vijayaraghavan was dropped by two *devadasis* T. Balasaraswati, and P. Jayalakshmi (twice), and seven brahmins: Yogam and Mangalam, Kausalya (twice) and Kalyanasundaravalli, Anandi and Radha, and Hemamalini Vijayaraghavan.

Natanam adinar (NA), the cosmic dance of Siva and his consort (1981: 105-6, 124, 225, 524, 544, 554) was danced by one *devadasi*, (P. Jayalakshmi), and five brahmins (Yogam and Mangalam, Hemamalini, Kamala, Anandi and Radha). Each of the brahmins included it twice in their programme. The popularity of this composition is seen by the fact that it was in the repertoire of at least three *nattuvanars*—P.S. Minakshisundaram, V. Ramaiya and V. Minakshisundaram. G. Venkatachalam observed in 1946: "*Tillana* is usually the last item though dancers like Rukmini Devi and Srimati Shanta dance *natanam adinar*. That is only an innovation." (Venkatachalam 1946: 13).

The semi-classical dance called *naganrittam* (NN) or snake dance was first presented at the Madras Music Academy by

Hemamalini Vijayaragavan. It was in the repertoire of V. Ramaiya and was made famous by his student Kamala Lakshman who presented it at the Academy several times. The snake dance as part of the repertoire was recorded by Seyyur (Ceyyur) Cenkalvarayya Sastri 1810-1900 (Kersenboom 1987: 62).

Tara Chaud/uri presented some Bharata Natyam dances, as well as those from three other styles: Kathak, Kathakali and Mohini Attam. In her Bharata Natyam presentation she omitted *varnam* and *sloka*. The omission of *varnam* is something unusual, this dance being regarded as the most complete of all the dances in the Bharata Natyam repertoire. Gopinath presented Oriental dances twice in 1941. He is the only male to have danced for the Academy during this decade. He did not perform Bharata Natyam.

Three *nattuvanars* are mentioned: A. P. Chokkalingam (twice), V. Ramaiya (five times) and K. Ellappa (once). Chokkalingam conducted the recitals of two of his students, Kausalya and Kalyanasundaravalli when they danced together and also when Kausalya danced alone. V. Ramaiya conducted the recitals of Hemamalini Vijayaraghavan (twice), Kamala Lakshman (twice) and the duo of Radha and Anandi. V. Minakshisundaram was not given in the programme notes but he was the teacher and *nattuvanar* for Yogam and Mangalam at that time. K. Ellappa conducted the recital for Mrinalini Sarabhai, who was not his student. Mrinalini had studied some of the dance items that she performed with K. Ellappa but acknowledges P. S. Minakshisundaram as her Bharata Natyam teacher, and the teacher who shaped her dance style. This was one of the first examples of the *nattuvanar* serving in the capacity as orchestra conductor and not as the teacher who shaped the dancer's basic style. Initially V. Ramaiya conducted the repertoire that Kamala had studied with her first teacher K. Muthukumar, but by the 1940s she was performing only those dances that she had studied with V. Ramaiya. We may conclude that both A.P. Chokkalingam and V. Ramaiya continued to serve the traditional role of *nattuvanar* as both teacher and orchestra conductor for those dancers that they had trained. The distinction, however, is not always clear-cut.

1950s

The Madras Music Academy presented thirty-one dance programmes, by at least fifteen different dancers, all females. It is impossible to give an exact number as one dance group was simply listed by its name as "Nandikesvara Natyalaya".

Two of the dancers were *devadasis*: P. Jivaratnam and T. Balasaraswati. The latter gave ten recitals, about one-third of the recitals in this decade. Eight of the dancers were from non-traditional families; seven were brahmins, one a non-brahmin (Anglo-Indian, Indrani Rehman).[6] The background of another dancer, Sarala, is unknown. Kamala Lakshman's (brahmin) dance was presented five times, once in a duo with her sister Radha. Except for T. Balasaraswati and Kamala Lakshman, all of the other dancers appeared only once. One of those non-hereditary dancers, Hemamalini Vijayaraghavan, had appeared before in the 1940s.

The traditional order of items was generally followed, with a few minor changes. *Sabdam* (SA) was omitted by T. Balasaraswati in only one of her ten programmes. *Natanam adinar* (NA) was performed by one of the *devadasis* (P. Jivaratnam) and seven of the non-*devadasis* (Kamala Lakshman, her sister Radha, Hemamalini Vijayaraghavan, Chandralekha, Sarala, Chitralekha and Indrani Rehman). In the 1950s *natanam adinar* was presented in nearly half (thirteen) of all the performances. The *nattuvanars* who conducted *natanam adinar* were V. Ramaiya, T. Swaminathan (who probably studied it with P.S. Minakshisundaram) and K. Ellappa.

Two other innovative dances appeared; *kurathi* (gypsy dance) was presented seven times, and *Andal*[7] (excerpts in the life of the saint *Andal*) was presented eight times. *Kurathi* was danced by one of A.P. Chokkalingam's students (Indrani Rehman), one of Gopalkrishnan's students (Sarala) and two of V. Ramaiya's students (Kamala Lakshman and her sister, Radha). *Andal* was presented by one of K. Ellappa's (Chitralekha), one of Gopalakrishnan's students (Sarala) and on several occasions by Kamala and Radha. This indicates the popularity of these new pieces with the students and the willingness of several teachers to choreograph them.

The 1950s saw Kathak, a north Indian dance style, presented three times: twice as a full evening recital and once sharing an evening with two other styles: Bharata Natyam and Manipuri.

K. Ellappa and V. Ramaiya conducted eight recitals each. Six other *nattuvanars* conducted recitals only once: A.P. Chokkalingam, T. Swaminathan, P. Muthaiya and P.C. Subbarayan, K.N. Dandayudapani and M. Gopalakrishnan. Four of them belonged to the Tanjore Quartet *bani*. Another, K.N. Dandayudapani, was acting largely as a *nattuvanar* but by the next decade he could be regarded as having established his own *bani*. I was unable to find out which *bani* M. Gopalakrishnan had been trained in.

V. Ramaiya, A.P. Chokkalingam, and T. Swaminathan performed in the traditional capacity of *nattuvanar* as they had also trained the girls whose recitals they conducted. Five of the *nattuvanars* (K. Ellappa, T.K. Ganeshan, P.M. Muthaiya, P.C. Subbarayan, K.N. Dandayudapani) had not taught the dancers, but were acting only in the capacity of *nattuvanar*. P. Jivaratnam, a *devadasi*, employed *nattuvanars* who had trained with her teacher, P.S. Minakshisundaram (P.M. Muthaiya and P.C. Subbarayan, both relatives of P.S. Minakshisundaram). Both dancer and *nattuvanar* would therefore have been familiar with the same compositions. In contrast, T. Balasaraswati had to train *nattuvanars* after her teacher, T.N. Kandappa, left Madras in 1939, for Almora to teach in Uday Shankar's school. She first trained K. Ellappa, who subsequently became a dance teacher. He presented two of his own students at the Madras Music Academy: Chandralekha, and Chitralekha later in the same decade. K. Ellappa therefore falls into two categories: that of a hired *nattuvanar* (for T. Balasaraswati) and as a *nattuvanar* in the traditional sense, because he conducted the recitals for two of his own students. After K. Ellappa began teaching on his own T. Balasaraswati trained two other *nattuvanars*: first, her teacher T.N. Kandappa's son, T.K. Ganeshan, and later, K. Ramaiya. All of those she trained were *isai vellala*.

Vyjayanthimala had been trained by V. Ramaiya who also

conducted her *arangetram* in 1941. But to conduct her recital at the Academy she hired K.N. Dandayudapani. The relationship between Dandayudapani and Vyjayanthimala was different from that between K. Ellappa and T. Balasaraswati. Initially Ellappa was not a *nattuvanar*, but a singer who had worked in that capacity with T.N. Kandappa when he conducted recitals. Later Balasaraswati gave him additional training to be her *nattuvanar*. Although originally a singer, K.N. Dandayudapani was a trained *nattuvanar* before he worked with Vyjayanthimala. Thus the interaction was different. Dandayudapani would have had power in the relationship as he was also a dance teacher with his own students and his own repertoire. Initially K. Ellappa was in a subdominant position, as he was being trained in the dance repertoire of one of the most famous musical families. As he mastered Balasaraswati's repertoire he became less dependent on her for work and more able to train his own students and direct their careers.

This decade marked a change in the meaning of the term *nattuvanar*, which came to be applied to all those who conducted dance performances, irrespective of whether or not they had actually taught the dancer involved. In practice, the distinction was often blurred. Dancers who used *nattuvanars* other than those with whom they had received their initial training might study the repertoire of the new *nattuvanar*, or teach him their own repertoire. In either case there might be an exchange of knowledge across *banis*. Dancers often preferred to study the new *nattuvanar's* items as they generally found that they could learn them faster than they could teach theirs to a new *nattuvanar*.

No men danced Bharata Natyam at the Madras Music Academy and no dance dramas were presented during this decade. Nevertheless, Kathak was danced by a male, Birju Maharaj, and perhaps the group, Nandikesvara Natyalaya, also included male dancers; they may also have presented a dance drama.

The exceptional amount of dancing that flourished in the 1950s prompted the experts' committee of the Madras Music Academy, in 1955, to discuss the need to start an institution for training dance teachers and the necessity to collect data:

To pool together the teaching resources available for turning into proper [sic] and on correct lines, the learning of Bharata Natyam in which the public were now evincing great interest ... Mr Krishna Aiyar referred to the demand for teachers all over the country and need to train teachers (*Journal of the Madras Music Academy* XXVII, 1955-56).

The Academy had actually founded a dance school in 1953 in which T. Balasaraswati taught. In 1955 Mr Krishna Aiyar referred: "to a number of defects in the quick training and an *arangetram* at a very early age, now so common in Bharata Natyam."

1960s

Thirty-three dance programmes were presented by the Madras Music Academy. The only hereditary dancer to perform was T. Balasaraswati, who danced seven times. In 1961 Balasaraswati also performed in Japan and later at the Edinburgh Festival. This was the first time she performed abroad. She would have been about forty-three years old at the time. All the other dancers who performed at the Academy were female brahmins. Kamala Lakshman presented three programmes with her two sisters Radha and Vasanti, one programme only with Radha, and one solo recital. Vyjayanthimala Bali danced alone three times and twice with her "party". The Travancore sisters, Padmini and Ragini, danced three times.

The traditional repertoire was presented by T. Balasaraswati, Kamala Lakshman and Vyjayanthimala, but with omissions on some occasions. Both Vyjayanthimala and Kamala omitted *jatisvaram* and *sabdam* on two occasions while Balasaraswati, whose forte was *abhinaya*, omitted the vigorous abstract dance, *tillana*, because of ill health. The practice of omitting *jatisvaram* and *sabdam* gained momentum. These two dances were rarely performed in the 1980s. *Natanam adinar* was presented only three times, twice by Kamala, and once by Vyjayanthimala. Adyar Lakshmanan conducted this dance when Vyjayanthimala performed. When Kamala presented it no *nattuvanar* was listed in the programme notes. She probably employed V. Sadasivan, as he was her *nattuvanar* during this period. No doubt both these dancers taught their respective *nattuvanars* the choreography for *natanam adinar* which they had both studied with V. Ramaiya.

Andal was less popular. Vyjayanthimala danced it twice. She was the only dancer who maintained this dance in her Madras Music Academy programmes until the 1980s. *Kurathi*, the gypsy dance, was not presented at all, and has never been performed since at the Academy.

This decade marked the beginning of the popularity of the dance drama. These were danced either by several sisters or by a group of dancers who had been taught in the schools founded by famous dancers, such as Vyjayanthimala. Some of these dance dramas included stories on mythological themes: *Ramayana, Nowkacharitham, Dasavatar, Rukmini,* etc. The popularity of dance dramas increased noticeably from the late 1960s onwards. They have the advantage of allowing schools to present all of their students on stage. Most such dance dramas feature the dancer-teacher in the lead role.

Kamala Lakshman had been a film star since the late 1930s. Other film stars such as Vyjayanthimala and the Travancore sisters also danced at the Academy. As noted above, early films included classical Indian dance and music, in contrast to later practice.

In 1960 a *kautvam* was first presented by Vyjayanthimala. When she performed it again in 1963 she presented it along with *alarippu*. In the 1960s and 1970s, *kautvam* was danced at the Academy by Vyjayanthimala who had three different *nattuvanars* for her recitals: Adyar Lakshmanan (Kalakshetra *bani*), T.P. Kittappa (Tanjore Quartet *bani*) and K.P. Krishnamoo (*bani* unknown). Kamala Lakshman was the only dancer during the 1960s to present another piece of temple music, *pushpanjali* along with a *kautvam*. She continued to do this in the 1970s. Both *kautvam* and *pushpanjali* were danced often by many dancers in venues other than at the Academy.

Yamini Krishnamurti, who presented both Bharata Natyam and Odissi in her recital, and Sonal Mansingh, who presented only dances in the Odissi style, appeared once each during the 1960s.

Both dancers were based in Delhi, where they dominated the field of classical dance over the next two decades. They presented different *banis* of Odissi. It was only in the late 1960s that a sufficient Odissi repertoire was composed to occupy a full evening's recital. The popularity of this style and the re-creation of it in terms of both movement and repertoire gained momentum in the 1970s.

Styles other than Bharata Natyam were presented by various dancers: the most unusual were Kuchipudi by T. Balasaraswati, and Mohini Attam by Vyjayanthimala. Two full recitals of Manipuri, one by a group of traditional dancers from Imphal, Manipur, and another by the non-traditional Jhaveri sisters, from Bombay, were presented. Two Kathak recitals were given, one by Roshan Kumari from a non-traditional family, the other by Birju Maharaj from a hereditary family who had been involved in the dance for several generations.

There were six *nattuvanars* identified: V. Ramaiya, Adyar Lakshmanan, T.K. Ganeshan, V. Sadasivan, K.P. Krishnamoo, and Jyoti Krishnamurti. Jyoti was a trained vocalist from a non-hereditary family. She conducted the recital for her sister Yamini Krishnamurti. Even in the 1960s it was still unusual for a woman to conduct a recital. Jyoti is an example of a relative who took an active role in a dancer's career and of a musician who trained to act in the capacity of *nattuvanar* without extensive dance training. This trend intensified later.

Three of the *nattuvanars* were from non-traditional families: Jyoti, Adyar K. Lakshmanan and V. Sadasivan. V. Ramaiya was the only one who had trained all the dancers for whom he performed *nattuvangam*; all the other *nattuvanars* were hired as orchestra conductors. Vyjayanthimala was now performing with Adyar K. Lakshmanan whereas in the 1950s K.N. Dandayudapani had conducted her recitals for the Academy. The three sisters, Kamala, Radha and Vasanti still performed together but V. Sadasivan had replaced V. Ramaiya as their *nattuvanar*. The *banis* represented by the *nattuvanars* were: V. Ramaiya *bani* (V. Ramaiya), Kalakshetra *bani* (Adyar Lakshmanan), Tanjore Quartet *bani* (T.K. Ganeshan, V. Sadasivan).

V. Sadasivan's artistic career is eclectic and interesting. His first exposure to the dance after training as a vocalist was with T. Swaminathan (Tanjore Quartet *bani*). By working with two non-hereditary dancers, Kamala Lakshman and Yamini Krishnamurti, who trained him to conduct their repertoires, he was able to learn both the K. Muthukumar and V. Ramaiya *banis* in which Kamala was trained, and the Kalakshetra and K. Ellappa *banis*, in which Yamini Krishnamurti was trained. This is an excellent example of the dissemination and absorption of *banis* and illustrates the difficulty in establishing an exact classification for them. His career and that of K. Ellappa are examples of musicians being trained to be *nattuvanars* by dancers. With the growing number of dancers and the shortage of *nattuvanars* this trend is increasing.

1970s

There were fewer recitals (twenty) in the 1970s than in the previous decade. This number included the mid-year series as well, which indicates a much smaller number during the December-January festival season. Eighteen dancers were involved and nine *nattuvanars* were named: Adyar Lakshmanan, K.N. Dandayudapani, K.P. Kittappa, P.C. Subbarayan, S.K. Rajaratnam, T.K. Ganeshan, Indira Rajan, Sitaram Sharma and Aravindakshan. Two of the *nattuvanars* were brahmins, and seven were *isai vellala*; one of the latter was a woman, Indira Rajan. Those *nattuvanars* who conducted recitals by their own student were: Adyar Lakshmanan (Anita and Prita Rathnam), K.N. Dandayudapani (Sri Vidya), and P.C. Subbarayan (Meenakshi Sabhanayagam). The *banis* represented were: three from the Kalakshetra *bani* (Adyar Lakshmanan, Sitaram Sharma, Aravind Akshan), three from the Tanjore Quartet *bani* (P.C. Subbarayan, K.P. Kittappa, T.P. Ganeshan) and one from the Kutralam Ganeshan Pillai *bani* (Indira Rajan).

Sitaram Sharma was an employee of Kalakshetra, the institution where both he, and the dancer Krishnaveni Lakshmanan, whose recital he conducted, trained. He was from a hereditary dance family in the Kuchipudi dance style. He was working in Kalakshetra as a singer and *nattuvanar* for all Bharata Natyam recitals of that institution. Unlike the majority of *nattuvanars* from Kalakshetra, he was not a trained Bharata Natyam dancer. All the other *nattuvanars* listed in 1970 were hired by dancers to conduct their recital: T. Balasaraswati was still working with T.K. Ganeshan; Vyjayanthimala hired two new *nattuvanars*, K.P. Kittappa for three recitals and Indira Rajan for two others; Kamala Lakshman employed three new *nattuvanars*: S.K. Rajaratnam, Aravindakshan and Jayanathan (*bani* unknown).

For seven concerts the *nattuvanar* was not named, a practice common in the 1930s as well, but for reasons that were probably different. In the 1930s there was a strong link between a dancer and her *nattuvanar* and information about the *nattuvanar* was probably considered redundant. By the 1970s the omission was more likely because the dancer did not know with whom she would be working far enough in advance of the programme being printed. The competition for good *nattuvanars*, who were now in short supply, had begun. It was this shortage that encouraged many musicians, percussionists and dancers to become *nattuvanars*.

During this decade Vyjayanthimala performed six times, Kamala Lakshman twice solo, and once with her sisters Radha and Vasanti. T. Balasaraswati, by then in poor health, performed only once, as did ten other dancers. Balasaraswati and a young dancer, Sri Vidya, were the only *isai vellala* dancers.

Anita and Pritha included some dances in the Mohini Attam style as part of their presentation. Three dance dramas were presented: *Rukmini*, *Prahalad* and another. The traditional repertoire, in the usual configuration, was presented by Hemamalini, Anita and Pritha Rathnam, Minakshi Sabhanayagam, Krishnaveni Lakshmanan, Vyjayanthimala (three times), Sri Vidya, and Kamala Lakshman (twice). Only very minor additions and omissions were attempted. Innovation centred around replacing *alarippu* with either a *kautvam* (Radha and Vasanti) or a *pushpanjali* (Padma Subrahmanyam). Kamala Lakshman danced a *kautvam* twice and Padma Subrahmanyam once. T. Balasaraswati dropped the two abstract energetic dances, *tillana* and *jatisvaram*. Chitra

Visweswaran did not dance *jatisvaram*. Vyjayanthimala dropped *jatisvaram* and *sabdam* for all three of her recitals while Kamala Lakshman dropped *sabdam* twice and Padma Subrahmanyam omitted it for her recital. *Sabdam* and *jatisvaram* were on the way out.

Varnam remained the most important composition and several *varnams* new to the dance repertoire were presented. *Varnam* and *tillana* had become firmly established as the most important dances in the core repertoire; *varnam*, because it combined both aesthetic movement and the dramatic elements of the dance, and *tillana* as a vehicle to show off the dancer's skill in pure dance.

1980s

More than forty-four recitals, by thirty-two different dancers were presented by the Academy. Brahmins (twenty-two) predominated among dancers; I could not determine the caste of five. There was no *isai vellala* dancer. Some dancers performed more than once. Those who performed three times in that decade were: Padma Subrahmanyam (brahmin), who had performed once in the previous decade; Lakshmi Vishwanathan (brahmin), Sudharani Raghupati (brahmin), and Chitra Visweswaran (brahmin). Alarmel Valli (non-brahmin), Sujata Srinivasan (brahmin), Vyjayanthimala Bali (brahmin) and Shoba Naidu (non-brahmin), all performed twice. Malavika Sarukkai (brahmin) gave two full recitals, one in Odissi, the other in Bharata Natyam. Kamala Lakshman (brahmin) and her sister Radha danced once, as did twenty-two others. Kuchipudi was performed by Ratna Papa (brahmin) and Swapnasundari (brahmin).

No males presented solo dances, but several men danced in the dance drama, *Devi Mahatmya*. It was choreographed by the dancer and teacher V. Chandrashekar (brahmin) who also danced and conducted portions of the work. Combining the two professions of dancer and *nattuvanar* in one evening was not unusual in the 1980s. Padma Subrahmanyam (brahmin) presented solo dance dramas, and Vempati Chinnasatyam (brahmin), from a hereditary dance family, presented a dance drama in the Kuchipudi style. This decade included a lot of Kuchipudi; seven performances altogether.

The *nattuvanars* listed were: U. Lakshminarayan (Lakshmi Vishwanathan, Sujata Srinivasan), D. Mohanraj (Chitra Visweswaran once and Lakshmi Vishwanathan twice), Padma Gopal (Sudharani Raghupati twice), V.P. Ram Doss (Vyjayanthimala), Indira Rajan (Alarmel Valli), Rajashekaran (Chitra Visweswaran twice), V. Krishnamurthy (Kanaka Srinivasan), Aravindakshan (Malavika Sarukkai), S.K. Rajaratnam (Srinidhi Rangarajan). S.K. Rajaratnam and Indira Rajan, were *isai vellala*, U. Lakshminarayan and V. Krishnamurthy were brahmins, while D. Mohanraj belongs to the goldsmith community. The *nattuvanars* and their *banis* represented were: D. Mohanraj (a combination of the V. Ramaiya *bani* and S.S. Manikkam *bani*), S. K. Rajaratnam (V. Ramaiya *bani*), Indira Rajan (Kutralam Ganeshan Pillai *bani*), V. Krishnamurthy and Aravindakshan (Kalakshetra *bani*), Padma Gopal via her teacher Sudharani Raghupati (Tanjore Quartet *bani*) and U. Lakshminarayan (T. Balasaraswati/K. Ellappa *bani*). Only one of the dancers, Srinidhi Rangarajan, was trained by the *nattuvanar*, S.K. Rajaratnam who conducted her recital. All the other *nattuvanars* were hired to conduct recitals for dancers who had received their training elsewhere. Two of them (V.P. Ram Doss, Aravindakshan) earned their living almost exclusively by conducting recitals and did not teach dance.

During this decade, many new musicians trained in *nattuvangam*[8] made their appearance. The decade also marked the decline and virtual disappearance of *nattuvanars* with a strong hereditary dance connection. The fact that in many instances the *nattuvanar* was not named is also significant, suggesting that his/her importance was much diminished from earlier decades, or had not been finalized before the programme notes went to press. All the *nattuvanars*, except V. Krishnamurthy who lived and taught in Delhi, were working in Madras.

Lakshmi Vishwanathan and Alarmel Valli danced *alarippu, jatisvaram, varnam* and *tillana*, and only omitted *sabdam* and *sloka* from the core repertoire. Most of the dancers included *varnam* and *tillana*. A great deal of innovation continued to be centred around the opening dances *kautvam*, and *pushpanjali* which had been presented in earlier decades. Mallavika Sarukkai presented *kautvam* and *pushpanjali* while four other dancers—Sudharani Raghupaty, Jayanthi Rajagopal, Srinidhi Rangarajan and Padma Subrahmanyam presented *pushpanjali* alone. In 1983 Chitra Visweswaran introduced *mallari,* a piece of music used in temple ritual. She set this to dance and presented it along with *kautvam*.

DISCUSSION

The number of dance recitals and the number of dancers involved increased over the period considered. The dancer's caste shifted from *isai vellala* to those for whom dance was not a hereditary profession, especially brahmin women, duplicating the trend seen for *arangetrams* in chapter 6. *Nattuvanars* were not listed in the 1930s but were usually included in the later programmes, although some were omitted in the 1980s. Where they were not, it sometimes indicated that the dancer worked with several *nattuvanars*. Duos continued until the 1980s, when Vani and Meera performed together, but they were not as important as they were in the earlier decades.

Many early *isai vellala* dancers were in their teens when they performed. This demonstrates that the community was continuing to train young girls, at the same time as the anti-dance movement was at its height, and there were clear indications that dancing in temples would soon be abolished.

During the period before 1950, most dancers from a non-traditional background were also very young when they first performed: Rukmini Devi, who was in her forties being the notable exception. Other mature persons, such as U.S. Krishna Rao, Chandrabhaga Devi and Mrinalini Sarabhai were also performing from the 1930s. To look at the Music Academy programmes alone does not give a complete view of the events at that time. The fact that the Academy invited these young girls shows its desire to support and encourage girls to dance. G. Venkatachalam wrote concerning this trend:

Child dancers are a common phenomenon in this art. Every child is a prodigy in this art, so it is always claimed. Instead of being condemned and discouraged as a national disgrace and senseless exploitation it is usually being encouraged. Even such learned bodies as the Music Academy and other allied art associations welcome them and even specialize in them (Venkatachalam 1946: 16).

Probably the most striking feature to emerge from a consideration of the Music Academy programmes is the change in the role of teachers. At first, the dancer's teachers also accompanied her dance recital. But from 1970 onwards, most performers were accompanied by a *nattuvanar* other than their teacher, one who had been trained for the occasion. In part, this was because some *nattuvanars* died. Both T. Balasaraswati and Kamala Lakshman performed regularly over more than thirty years, and changes over such a long period seem inevitable. At the same time, even fairly young dancers performing in the 1970s and 1980s appeared with *nattuvanars* other than their original teacher, a clear symptom of increased mobility within the field.

The core repertoire was never presented invariably, even by T. Balasaraswati who consistently advocated it. Many new invocatory dances were introduced, some inspired by temple ritual and music (*kautvams* and *mallari*). Other dances were choreographed from the Karnatic classical music repertoire. Despite the innovations, most recitals opened with a devotional song.

The gradual disappearance of two dances characteristic of the early repertoire (*jatisvaram*, *sabdam*), has enhanced the central importance of *varnam*. Both the rhythmic intricacy of *jatisvaram* and the descriptive elaboration of *sabdam* were concentrated and embellished in *varnam*. Because *varnam* contains both elements of the dance, the rhythmic and the descriptive, it has come to be the test of any Bharata Natyam dancer. Despite the changes going on around it, the inclusion of *varnam* has remained fairly constant. Although some new *varnams* have been introduced, many of those popular in the 1930s and 1940s were just as likely to be seen in the 1980s.

The trend towards shorter recitals, in keeping with the needs of audiences increasingly bound to fixed timetables of work, public transport, etc. meant that something had to be cut. Because the music and choreography of the popular *varnams* tends to be of a very high quality, they have retained their place in the repertoire. The obvious solution was to excise those pieces which duplicated, to some extent, the effects of *varnam*. Hence the demise of *jatisvaram* and *sabdam*. Likewise those dances which required a time-consuming costume change (*Andal, kurathi*) were also dispensed with. The elimination of these two pieces, and the lack of interest in *naganrittam*, was pretty well complete by the 1960s.

Certainly *kurathi, Andal* and *natanam adinar*, which were popular at one time, were no longer danced by established dancers in the 1980s. Vyjayanthimala and others continued to perform *Andal* until the early 1980s, although no one else presented it at the Music Academy after 1961. *Kurathi* was not performed at the Music Academy after 1957 and *natanam adinar* after 1968. At *arangetrams*, however, these dances were still sometimes danced.

The recent popularity of Kuchipudi dances probably reflects several tendencies: a feeling that the dance programmes need to be diversified: the emergence of a modern Kuchipudi technique, properly adapted to performance by females (especially the students of Vempati Chinnasaytam); and a strong Andhra representation in the Madras artistic community. It remains to be seen whether the prominence of Kuchipudi in the 1980s will be maintained. Another style, Odissi, first performed at the Madras Music Academy in the 1960s did gain considerable popularity in Madras during the 1970s and early 1980s. This is not reflected in the programmes presented at the Academy, where only one full Odissi recital, that of Mallavika Sarukkai, was presented in the 1980s. There were, however, some individual dances in the Odissi style and several occasions where it was half of a recital.

This analysis reflects innovations, additions and omissions of repertoire for recitals held at the Madras Music Academy. Because a certain dancer introduced a particular dance at the Music Academy, she should not necessarily be credited with this particular innovation. The number of recitals and the number of dancers documented by the Academy records is very limited when compared with the level of activity all over India, or even in Madras. Because of the relatively conservative nature of the Academy, it is likely that most innovations appeared there after they had become firmly established elsewhere. Nevertheless, there seems no reason to think that the trends discernible in the repertoires presented at the Academy are not valid for the whole field of Bharata Natyam.

TABLE 8.1: REPERTOIRE PERFORMED AT THE
MADRAS MUSIC ACADEMY CONFERENCES, 1931-89

Year	Dancer	Nattuvanar	Items Performed
1931	P.K Jivaratnam	?	?
1932	M.D. Gauri	?	?
1933	Varalakshmi,Saranayaki	?	AL,JA,SA,VA,TI,SL
1933	T. Balasaraswati	?	AL,JA,VA,TI
1934	K. Varalakshmi & K. Bhanumati	?	?
1935	T. Balasaraswati	?	AL,JA,VA,TI
1935	Sabharanjitam, Nagaratnam	?	AL,JA,SA,VA,TI,SL
1936	K. Varalakshmi & K. Bhanumati	?	?
1936	P.N. Sabharanjitam	?	?
1937	Muthuratnambal (Tirunelveli)	?	?
1940	Kumbakonam Bhanumati	?	?
1941	Bhavani	?	VA,TI
1941	Gopinath and Tangamani (2)	?	"Oriental Dances"
1941	T. Balasaraswati	?	?
1941	Gopinath		"Oriental Dances"
1941	Swarna Saraswati	?	?
1942	T. Balasaraswati	?	AL,JA,SA,VA,TI
1942	Shanta & party	?	AL,JA,SA,VA,TI,SL
1943	Pandanallur Jayalakshmi	?	AL,JA,SA,VA,TI
1943	Rukmini Devi and party	?	?
1944	Yogam, Mangalam	?	AL,JA,SA,VA(S), TI,NA
1944	Pandanallur Jayalakshmi	?	AL,JA,SA,VA,TI,NA
1945	Hemamalini Vijayaraghavan	V. Ramaiya	AL,JA,SA,VA(S),TI, NA,SL
1946	G.Kausalya, Kalyan Sundaravalli	A.P. Chokkalingam	AL,JA
1947	Tara Chaudhari	?	AL,JA,SA,TI, + Other styles
1948	Anandi, Radha	V. Ramaiya	AL,JA,SA,VA,TI,NA
1948	Kamala	V. Ramaiya	AL,JA,SA,VA,TI,NA

Year	Dancer	Nattuvanar	Items Performed
1948	Kamala	V. Ramaiya	AL,JA,SA,VA,TI,NA
1949	G.Kausalya	A.P. Chokkalingam, P.M. Muthaiya	AL,JA,VA,TI,
1949	Hemamalini Vijayaraghavan	V. Ramaiya	AL,JA,SA,VA,TI,NA
1949	Mrinalini Sarabhai	K. Ellappa	AL,JA,VA,TI,SL
1950	T. Balasaraswati	K. Ellappa	AL,JA,VA,TI,
1951	T. Balasaraswati	?	AL,JA,SA,VA,TI
1951	Kamala	V. Ramaiya	AL,JA,VA,TI,
1951	T. Balasaraswati	?	AL,JA,SA,VA,
1952	Kamala	V. Ramaiya	AL,JA,SA,VA,TI, NA,KU
1952	T. Balasaraswati	K. Ellappa	AL,JA,SA,VA,TI
1953	Hemamalini Vijayaraghavan	V. Ramaiya	AL,JA,SA,VA,TI, NA,KU
1953	Kamala	V. Ramaiya	AL,JA,SA,VA,TI, NA,KU
1954	T. Balasaraswati	K. Ellappa	AL,JA,SA,VA
1954	Indrani Rehman	A.P. Chokkalingam	AL,JA,SA,VA,KU,SL
1954	Nirmala Ramachandran	T. Swaminathan	AL,JA,SA,VA(S), TI,NA
1955	T. Balasaraswati	K. Ellappa	AL,JA,SA,VA(S),SL
1955	Kamala	V. Ramaiya	AL,JA,SA,VA,TI, NA,SL,NN
1955	Birju Maharaj, etc	-	Kathak, Manipuri
1956	Chandralekha	K. Ellappa	AL,JA,SA,VA,TI,NA,SL
1956	T. Balasaraswati	K. Ellappa	AL,JA,SA,VA
1956	R.K. Jivaratnam	P.M. Muthaiya & P.C.Subbarayan	AL,JA,SA,VA, TI,NA
1956	Kamala	V. Ramaiya	AL,JA,SA,VA,TI, NA,KU
1957	Sarala	Gopalakrishnan	AL,SA,VA,TI,NA,KU
1957	T. Balasaraswati	K. Ellappa	AL,JA,SA,VA
1957	Kamala	V. Ramaiya	AL,JA,SA,VA,TI, NA,AN,SL
1957	Chitralekha	K. Ellappa	AL,JA,VA,TI,NA, AN,KU
1958	Kamala, Radha	V. Ramaiya	AL,JA,SA,VA,TI, NA,AN
1958	Sambhu Maharaj, Briju Maharaj		Kathak
1958	Vyjayanthimala	K.N.Dandayudapani	AL,JA,VA*,NA
1959	T. Balasaraswati	K. Ellappa	AL,JA,SA,VA
1959	T. Balasaraswati	T.K. Ganeshan	AL,JA,SA,VA
1959	Damayanti Joshi		Kathak
1959	Nandikesvara Natyalaya	?	AL,JA,SA,VA,TI,SL
1959	Kamala, Radha	V. Ramaiya	AL,JA,SA,VA*,TI,AN
1960	Vyjayanthimala	Adyar Lakshmanan	AL,JA,SA,VA*,TI, NA,AN,KA

Year	Dancer	Nattuvanar	Items Performed
1960	T. Balasaraswati	T.K. Ganeshan	AL,JA,SA,VA,TI
1960	Kamala	V. Ramaiya	AL,JA,SA,VA*,TI
1960	Manipuri, Imphal	?	
1960	Vyjayanthimala	Adyar Lakshmanan	AL,JA,SA,VA,TI
1961	Kamala, Radha	?	AL,JA,SA,VA*, TI,NA,AN
1961	T. Balasaraswati	T.K. Ganeshan	AL,JA,SA,VA
1961	Travancore Sisters	?	Ramayana Dance Drama
1962	Kamala, Radha, Vasanti	(In aid of building fund)	
1962	Ragini and party	?	Ramayana Dance Drama
1962	Kamala, Radha, Vasanti	V. Sadasivan	AL,JA,SA,VA,TI
1962	Ragini (Sept and Dec)	?	Ramayana Dance Drama
1963	T. Balasaraswati	?	?
1963	Vyjayanthimala and party	?	?
1963	Kamala, Radha, Vasanti	?	AL,JA,VA,TI, Rukmini DD
1963	Vyjayanthimala Bali	K.P. Krishnamoo	AL,VA,TI,KA
1964	T. Balasaraswati	T.K. Ganeshan	AL,JA,SA,VA,TI
1964	Roshan Kumari		Kathak
1965	Jhaveri Sisters		Manipuri
1965	T. Balasaraswati	T.K. Ganeshan	AL,JA,SA,VA
1966	T. Balasaraswati	T.K. Ganeshan	AL,JA,SA,VA,TI,SL
1966	Birju Maharaj and party		Kathak
1967	Padmini and party		Dasavatar DD
1967	Vyjayanthimala Bali	?	VA,TI,Mohiniattam
1968	Kamala, Radha, Vasanti, etc	V. Sadasivan	Nowkacharit DD
1968	Kamala, Radha, Vasanti	?	AL,JA,SA,VA*,TI,NA
1968	T. Balasaraswati	?	?
1968	Yamini Krishnamurti	Jyoti & V. Sadasivan	?, Odissi
1968	Vyjayanthimala and party	?	?
1968	Kamala	?	JA,VA,TI,KA,PU
1969	Padmini, Ragini, &party		Shakuntalam DD
1969	Sonal Mansingh		Odissi
1969	Kamala, Radha, Vasanti	?	VA,TI,SL,PU,NN
1970	Hemamalini	?	AL,JA,VA(S),TI
1970	Anita, Pritha Rathnam	Adyar Lakshmanan	AL,JA,VA*,TI, Mohiniattam
1970	Vyjayanthimala	?	JA,VA,TI,SL,KA
1971	T. Balasaraswati	T.K. Ganeshan	AL,SA,VA,SL
1972	Sri Vidya	K.N. Dandayudapani	AL,JA,SA,VA*, TI,SL
1972	Vyjayanthimala Bali	T.P. Kittappa	VA,TI,KA
1973	Kamala, Radha, Vasanti	?	Rukmini DD
1975	Meenakshi Sabanayagam	P.C. Subbarayan	AL,JA,VA*,TI
1975	Vyjayanthimala Bali	T.P. Kittappa	VA*
1976	Chitra Visweswaran	?	AL,JA,VA*,TI,

Year	Dancer	Nattuvanar	Items Performed
1976	Vyjayanthimala Bali	T.P. Kittappa	AL,VA,TI,KA
1978	Kamala	S.K. Rajaratnam	Prahalad DD
1978	Padma Subrahmanyam	?	JA,VA*,TI,PU
1978	Vyjayanthimala Bali	Indira Rajan	AL,VA,TI,SL
1979	Shobana Vedanarayanan	mid year series	
1979	Anuradha Jagannathan	mid year series	
1979	Jayanthi Rajagopal	mid year series	
1979	Kamala	Aravindakshan, Jayanathan	Parvati Kalyanam DD
1979	Krishnaveni Lakshmanan	Sitaram Sharma, Prabhavati	AL,JA,VA*,TI,SL
1979	Vyjayanthimala Bali	Indira Rajan	AL,VA*,TI,AN,KA
1980	Meena Raman	mid year series	
1980	Kamala and Radha	mid year series	
1980	Matangi Varadan	mid year series	
1980	Lakshmi Vishwanathan	U. Lakshminarayan	AL,JA,VA,TI,
1980	Sudharani Raghupati	Padma Rajagopal	VA,TI,SL,PU
1980	Chitra Visweswaran	D. Mohanraj	SA,VA*,TI,SL
1980	Vyjayanthimala Bali	Indira Rajan	VA,TI,AN
1981	Vani, Meera	?	VA(S),TI
1981	Vyjayathimala Bali	V.P.Ram Doss	VA(S),TI,AN
1981	Shoba Naidu (Kuchipudi)	mid year series	
1981	Uma Sriram, Sundari S	mid year series	
1981	Shoba Radhakrishnan	mid year series	
1982	Alarmel Valli	Indira Rajan	AL,JA,VA,TI,
1982	Jayanthi Rajagopal	?	AL,VA*,TI,NN
1982	Padma Subrahmanyam	?	JA,VA*,TI,PU
1982	Padma Subrahmanyam		Kamban Ramayana, solo DD
1982	Chitra Chandrashekar	mid year series	
1983	Lakshmi Vishwanathan	D. Mohanraj	SA,VA,TI,SL
1983	Chitra Visweswaran	Rajasekharan	VA*,TI,KA,MA
1983	Sujata Rajan	?	VA*,TI
1983	Nirmala Ramachandran	?	AL,JA,VA,TI
1983	Sudharani Raghupathy	?	VA,TI
1983	Malavika Sarukkai		Odissi
1983	Nityakalyani Vaidyanathan	mid year series	
1983	Sujatha Srinivasan	mid year series	
1983	Kausalya Narasimhan	mid year series	
1983	K. Shylaja	mid-year series	
1983	C. Bharathi	mid year series	
1984	Alarmel Valli	?	AL,JA,VA,TI
1984	Kanaka Srinivasan	V. Krishnamurthi	AL,VA,TI,SL
1984	Swapna Sundari	?	Kuchipudi
1984	Lakshmi Vishwanathan	D. Mohanraj	VA,TI
1984	Shobha Naidu	?	Kuchipudi
1984	Chitra Visweswaran	Rajashekaran	VA*,TI,SL,MA

Year	Dancer	Nattuvanar	Items Performed
1985	Padma Subrahmanyam	Jaya Jaya Shankaran	DD
1985	Sudharani Raghupathy	Padma Rajagopal	VA*,TI
1986	Kamala Reddy		Kuchipudi
1986	Malavika Sarukkai	Aravindakshan	SL,KA,PU
1986	Ratna Papa	Chinnasatyam	Kuchipudi
1987	Uma Balasubramanium	?	AL,TI
1987	Shobha Natarajan	Chinnasatyam	Kuchipudi
1987	Sujatha Srinivasan	U. Lakshminarayan	AL,VA,TI,PU
1988	Vempati Chinnasatyam company	Kuchipudi DD	
1988	Srinidhi Rangarajan	S.K. Rajaratnam	SA,VA,TI,MA
1989	Chandrashekar & company		Devi Mahatmya DD

Abbreviations: AL = *Alarippu*, JA = *Jatisvaram*, SA = *Sabdam*, VA = *Varnam* (* = not Tanjore Quartet, S = *Svarajati*), TI = *Tillana*, SL = *Sloka*, KU = *Kurathi*, NA = *Natanam Adinar*, NN = *Naganrittam*, KA = *Kautvam*, PU = *Pushpanjali*, MA = Mallari, DD = Dance Drama

NOTES

1. See L'Armand 1978 for a list of other cultural organizations in Madras that present dance and music recitals.
2. Additional information regarding early dancers is given by R. Nagaswamy who gives a list of dancers and musicians in his article "Rajarajachola and the Dance", in *Sruti* November 1984: 7.
3. Papanasam Vadivel married the daughter of P.S. Minakshisundaram's sister-in-law. He became a member of the Tanjore Quartet by marrying into the family.
4. The Tanjore Quartet family originally came from Tirunelveli before they moved to Tanjore.
5. Singer (1972: 173) states that his informant KVR believed that the first public recital of Bharata Natyam was held in 1933, all the others were in private homes and at weddings.
6. Indrani's mother, Ragini Devi, was an American, Ragini Devi was one of the first foreigners to perform Indian dance and receive international recognition. Indrani's father was a Bengali.
7. The incidents in the life of Andal were set to a dance drama by Rukmini Devi and presented in 1961 at Kalakshetra. See Sarada 1985: 138-43.
8. Some of these new *nattuvanars*, such as V. Krishnamurthy had also trained as dancers and performed. V. Krishnamurthy had lived and worked in Madras before moving to Delhi.

9   Vestiges of Religion in Bharata Natyam

During the initial stages of the revival, the originators of modern Bharata Natyam sought to suppress those aspects which linked it most firmly with the person of the *devadasi*. In those early days, therefore, many of the rituals and ceremonies associated with the *devadasi* dance tradition were not performed because of the stigma attached to that institution.

More recent trends make an interesting contrast. For example, some of the validation ceremonies of the *devadasi* tradition, conferring the rights and obligations associated with being a hereditary dancer, have been adapted to the needs of modern Bharata Natyam and are now firmly established as "traditional". Other innovations of a quasi-religious type have also appeared. As a result, Bharata Natyam has more rituals and ceremonies attached to it today than it had during the period of its revival, when strenuous efforts were made to dissociate it from *sadir*. I shall describe some of these recent changes and examine the role of religious ritual in modern Bharata Natyam. I shall show that some rituals and symbols now associated with Bharata Natyam can be traced to earlier practices, while others are recent creations. Generally, there has been an attempt to validate the antiquity of the dance by emphasizing the religious rather than the secular. This increasing religiosity in the dance relates to social changes affecting dancers and dance audiences.

In the context of the takeover of the dance by non-traditional groups, it is important to remember that many dancers and teachers who were part of the hereditary tradition of the *devadasi*, as well as others from non-traditional families, such as critics, are still alive. To exemplify the changes taking place, I explore the attitudes of dancers, teachers, and critics from both hereditary and non-hereditary families, towards a range of phenomena. First, I examine the reintroduction of two of the validation ceremonies for the *devadasi*, the *arangetram*, and the pre-*arangetram* ceremony, called *gejjai puja* ("worship of the ankle bells"). Then I discuss the presence of an icon on the concert stage, in particular the Nataraja. I also consider the performance of acts of worship (*puja*) in front of that icon as part of the dance recital, and the use of hand signs similar to those used by the *devadasi* when dance was part of temple ritual. I then explore the significance of menstruation for performers and teachers of dance, and their perception of the dance as ritual or entertainment. Finally, I consider the question: to whom is the dance addressed?

THE TEMPLE TRADITION

Those *devadasis* who participated in religious ritual were required to be initiated with six ceremonies, two more than those whose function was largely secular. The two additional ceremonies were marriage (*kalyanam*) and dedication (*muttirai*) (Kersenboom: 1984, 1987). Three ceremonies essential for all *devadasis*, whether their function was secular or religious were: the first dance lesson, the *gejjai puja* and the *arangetram*. All of them have appeared, in a modified form, as part of accepted practices within modern Bharata Natyam. The fourth, the selection of a patron, is no longer relevant because the financial basis of the dance has changed and it is now possible and acceptable for dancers to marry.

WORSHIPPING THE ANKLE BELLS (*GEJJAI PUJA*)

One of the rites of passage for a *devadasi* was the ritual worship of the ankle bells (*gejjai puja*) (Kersenboom 1987: 187, 191; Srinivasan 1984). This ceremony was intended to mark the conclusion of the

dancer's mastery over the first piece from the dance concert
repertoire, *alarippu*. In some instances, where it was intended to
mark the completion of her dance training as a whole, worshipping
the ankle bells appears to have been included in the ceremonies of
the *arangetram*.

The incorporation of a mini-recital known as *gejjai puja*, into
Bharata Natyam training was unknown until recently. Present-day
celebrations of it include a public or semi-public recital in which
several dances—at least *alarippu*, *jatisvaram* and *sabdam*, and
sometimes *varnam* and *tillana* as well—are danced, leaving only
the descriptive dances—*padams* and *javalis*—to be mastered before
the *arangetram*. The rationale for such a mini-recital is that it
constitutes an intermediate stage, which allows the dance student to
gain performing experience before she goes on to the taxing full
programme of a formal *arangetram*. Another, less charitable,
explanation is that it provides the teacher an additional opportunity
to receive the customary gifts (*guru-dakshina*), besides those that
are given at the time of the *arangetram*. Not all teachers present
their students in such a mini-recital. The "custom" is an innovation
that has become common in Bharata Natyam only since 1980.

ARANGETRAM

The *arangetram* was perhaps the first *devadasi* ritual to be adopted
into modern Bharata Natyam. Its importance has increased so much
that other dance styles, which did not have this tradition, such as
Odissi and Kuchipudi, have also adopted it.[1] As dance becomes
more and more popular, no expense is spared in preparing a
daughter's *arangetram* (chapter 6).

At the beginning of the dance revival, during the 1930s and 40s,
dancers from non-*devadasi* families gave a debut solo public dance
recital, but did not usually call it an *arangetram*. The connection
with the temple tradition was evidently still too close, and high-
caste families did not wish to be associated with *devadasi* traditions.
For this reason, most brahmins who first performed in the 1930s,
were adamant that their debut recitals were not *arangetrams*. There

were exceptions such as the late Rukmini Devi who acknowledged that her first recital was an *arangetram*, on the grounds that she was dedicating her dance to god (Srinivasan 1984). Her earliest students reported that, for them too, the first recital constituted an *arangetram*. Rukmini Devi's decision probably contributed to the gradual acceptance of the term *arangetram*. Yet it took another twenty years for both the ritual, and the term, to become an essential part of modern Bharata Natyam. Some dancers still prefer not to give a formal debut recital although the reason is more likely to be the expense.

PRESENCE OF AN ICON
ON THE CONCERT STAGE

A bronze image placed at stage left is a common feature of a public recital of Bharata Natyam today. The image is usually that of Nataraja. Nataraja is Siva depicted dancing in the pose called "the wild dance of bliss" (*anandatandava*) (Gaston 1982). Recently a variety of images of deities have been included on the concert stage. From both oral and pictorial accounts, it is evident that the introduction of icons onto the concert stage is an innovation of the 1940s. Just as Rukmini Devi absorbed the *devadasi* rite of passage, the *arangetram*, she was also chiefly responsible for the introduction of a ritual object, or icon on the concert stage. She accounts for this: "People have Nataraja on the stage because I started it. People copy what I do. Dance is a form of worship. Why not have Nataraja? I am a person with devotion and a religious person; it is not just there as decoration." Hence, Rukmini Devi introduced the Nataraja image to assist in creating a temple on the stage. This practice was, however, at variance with that followed by *devadasis* who were performing on the concert stage during the same period. T. Balasaraswati's recitals were remembered by Nirmala Ramachandran, an early brahmin performer who also danced with her professionally: "Bala never had a Nataraja on the stage. She did not believe in that sort of thing, bringing the temple to the stage. She was opposed to this. She said, it is in the mind." None of

Balasaraswati's recitals that I saw from 1964 onwards included a Nataraja image, nor did her home have a large Nataraja on display, as many dancers have today. She preferred to create a devotional atmosphere by using *abhinaya* rather than by using ritual elements as stage props. Her daughter, Lakshmi Shanmugam-Knight, did not use icons on stage either, or have them prominent in her home, when I visited her. She explained: "It is not in our tradition to have Nataraja. I am carrying on my mother's tradition."

T.S. Parthasarathy, Secretary of the Madras Music Academy and dance critic of the *Indian Express* confirms this:

The older dancers like Bala never had a Nataraja or started with a *puja*. Now it is a stunt to attract the audience. When they see the Nataraja idol garlanded with coloured lights it sort of inspires some devotion in the audience. A true artist does not start the recital with a devotional thing. Bala was an artist in the true sense.

Two brahmin dancers active in the same period agree.

Chandralekha, who began performing in the 1950s, comments: "No, if I feel worshipful I will not make a stagey thing out of my religiosity. It is totally phoney to put Nataraja on the stage." Shanta Rao, a non-hereditary dancer, who started her career before 1947 declared: "I have a plain stage. I don't know why people do this [have Nataraja on stage]. It is a dance show not a *puja*."

Further evidence that an icon on stage is an innovation is provided by three brahmin women, who were also performing in the 1940s, Hema, Vijaya and C.V.S. Vasanta. They did not have Nataraja on the stage or "even own our own Nataraja image", an almost unthinkable situation today. Nirmala Ramachandran remembers otherwise, despite her recollection (see above) that Balasaraswati did not follow this practice. She told me, "It was fashionable even then". This is confirmed by two other brahmin dancers, Yogam and Mangalam, who had active careers in the late 1940s and early 1950s: "Yes we had Nataraja on the stage. We still have the one we used. This is because it is the cosmic dance of Siva. He is the symbol of our dance. It is also decorative and it shows others that you are artistic."

R. Nagaswamy, former head of the Archaeological Survey of

India (Southern Circle), and a dance connoisseur, bases his views on the reading of the texts (eg. *Natya Sastra* III. 1-10). He concludes: "Nataraja on the stage is a totally modern innovation. No text prescribes this. As a dancer you try to create the image." Although Nagaswamy had a personal bias towards reintroducing the dance into the Nataraja Temple in Chidambaram to revive the temple as a centre of art and culture, his views coincided with those who were opposed to the idea of icons and *puja* on stage. His remarks reinforce Balasaraswati's comment that, "it [religious devotion] is in the mind".

In general, dance critics were strongly opposed to the idea of icons and acts of worship on the stage. Only one critic, Subbudu, from the *Statesman* (New Delhi), was willing to be charitable towards the presence on the stage of a Nataraja image. All the others shared T.S. Parthasarathy's view quoted above. For example, Mohan Khokar, a well-known authority on the dance, commented:

I cannot stand those icons. Worship is your own personal business. I do not believe in having anything on stage which will distract. Often the Nataraja is so small no one knows what it is anyway. Nor do I agree to the practice of worshipping the image on stage. Worship is a private affair. Do it backstage before you go on. The worst is a dancer who prostrates herself in front of the image on the stage.

His remarks reveal an objection not only to public worship but also to elaborate declarations of devotion. Here his remarks echo those of another dance critic, Shanta Serbajeet Singh (*Hindustan Times*, New Delhi), in which she remarks on the difficulties encountered when the religious and secular meet:

Nataraja is put on the stage to remind the audience and the dancer that the dance came out of the temple. It is so embarrassing to see the Chief Guest walk on the stage with shoes on, something one should not do near a religious icon. Worshipping Nataraja should be private and should not be part of the show. The presence of Nataraja shows the confused state of mind of the dancers.

The same critic describes the dance simply as: "... neither ritual nor entertainment but an aesthetic search bound by rules."

Her definition brings it squarely in line with western ideas of art.

K.S. Srinivasan (former dance critic the *Times of India*, New Delhi), is, like R. Nagaswamy, nostalgic for the classical period of India, which he perceives as the "wonder that was India". He feels empty as the concert halls of today try to recreate the temple's atmosphere: "The outer atmosphere of the temple is on the stage: traditional music, icons of Nataraja and Jagannatha,[2] public prayers in front of the audience. But I regard all of this as exhibitionism."

Thus, it appears that most critics, as well as many of the dancers who began their careers at the beginning of the revival, are opposed to having an image of Nataraja on the stage.

In contrast, a considerable number of those recent dancers and dance teachers that I interviewed favoured the presence of an icon, usually Nataraja. Some dancers felt that a photograph of their dance teacher (if he or she had died) and their spiritual guru (e.g. Sai Baba, or Christ if the dancer was a Christian) should be placed at the feet of Nataraja. Here they differed with the practice followed by their own teacher, and their family tradition. S. Umamaheshwari (T. Balasaraswati's niece, but born well after the dance was banned from the temples), exemplifies this tendency: "Yes I have a Nataraja on the stage, because my guru says that I must, I do it. I don't know why. My relation, Bala, never had one on stage. We do the *puja* to Nataraja before the curtain is opened."

Some brahmin dancers believed that the presence of the Nataraja image, or other images, sanctifies the place where they teach. For one female brahmin teacher the image clearly had a spiritual significance: "When I or my students dance I carry Nataraja with me. I think of him when I dance and take his blessings. I think I am dancing in Chidambaram, the temple of Nataraja in Tamil Nadu."

The idea of creating the appropriate atmosphere for teaching the dance is considered particularly important by those who teach dance or perform abroad. As noted earlier, expatriate communities consistently place a greater emphasis on the religious or devotional elements of the dance.

Kamala Lakshman, currently working in the United States of America told me:

I carry a small Nataraja and Ganesha around to the various centres where I teach and place them in the classroom. I always keep Nataraja on the stage. This is because I feel that this dance is for him. It is not for human beings. We are born and we die, but we want some celestial power, something that is supreme. It is music and dance that has been given to us. It has all been given to us by him, so it is an offering to him.

The presence of a Nataraja image during a performance is not universal, it is a common feature today, especially when the performance in question is an *arangetram*. This too does not appear to have been part of the earlier tradition.

Mythili Kalyanasundaram, (*isai vellala*) recalled that there was no Nataraja image, at her *arangetram* in Tanjore in the home of T. Ponnaiya in 1947. Nor was there one for the first performance given by Chandrabhaga Devi and her husband U.S. Krishna Rao (both brahmins). He remembered the period when he was performing in the 1940s: "... there was no Nataraja on the stage. This must have started fifteen years ago. Now they make an entrance and drop flowers, we never did that. We just came to the stage, touched the feet of the teacher, and started."

However, he believed that it was appropriate to have an image of Nataraja on stage during an *arangetram* today, a belief he shared with many other teachers and dancers who might otherwise not have bothered: "The *arangetram* is the first stage. At that time you worship. At other times you just feel the presence."

Most dancers today do have Nataraja on stage, although they rationalize its presence in different ways. For example, Mythili Kalyanasundaram and Indira Rajan both believed that an icon conferred on the stage an aura of sanctity. They may have considered a visible link with religion important because they were teaching and living in large urban centres (Bombay, Madras).

Others considered the presence of an image to be purely decorative. This was reflected in its frequent absence while on tour, a point made by many dancers, who said it was impractical to carry an image with them; they installed one only for performances in their home city. Nevertheless, they usually worshipped privately before the performance. For one brahmin dancer/teacher, Usha Srinivasan, the image was a combination of talisman and stage prop. Her comments reflect her pragmatic approach.

It looks nice on the stage, but I have also danced without one ... in Japan for three months we did not have a Nataraja, nor did we do *puja*, and nothing happened. I do not do *puja* in the green room. It is all in the hands of god. There is faith that it will work. I do *namaskar* to the mother goddess, Nataraja, guru and orchestra—all that before the curtain comes up.

The notion of the image as a talisman is reiterated by Subbudu, dance critic of the *Statesman* (New Delhi): "It is just a symbol, it looks nice. It is a shield or good luck charm to help one not make mistakes. Worshipping the image is just an outward show. It is the same as breaking champagne over the bow of a boat when it is launched."

FORMS OF WORSHIP ON THE CONCERT STAGE

Many dance teachers believe that on entering the stage, the dancer should first drop flowers at the feet of the Nataraja image. She should then greet (*namaskaram*) her seated teacher in a reverential way by touching the floor in front of him/her (using *chatura hasta*), and then place her hands in a folded position (*anjali hasta*) (Gaston 1985: 37). Some teachers include touching the teacher's feet as part of the reverential greeting (*namaskaram*). Others are shocked that a girl, in particular a brahmin girl, should be expected to touch the feet of anyone other than her husband (Leslie 1989: 156ff). For the brahmin dancer, C.V.S. Vasanta, it was not the practice in the 1940s (when she was performing) to pay homage to their teachers on the stage: "In addition to the elaborate *puja* the dancers come on stage and do *namaskaram* to the teacher. We never did either on the stage. Instead, we used to do *namaskaram* and *puja* at home before we set out." According to her account, therefore, paying homage to one's teacher on stage is a recent innovation.

Whereas some dancers do not express the need to perform *puja* to the image, they do regard Nataraja as an important element of the dance. The presence of the image allows them to direct their spiritual energy towards it, which in turn gives them confidence. A brahmin dancer elaborates:

Of course it is very essential. I have a big Nataraja. First I do a big *namaskaram* to Nataraja, then to my gurus. Only then I start. It sets the mood and gives me a lot of confidence. The curtains are open when this happens. I then feel that the stage has become benevolent. It promotes *bhakti rasa* which is the basis and is being lost with professionalism. If you do a *Ganesha vandana* and don't mean it and don't understand it then all is lost.

There is an implication in her comments that the icon is in some sense necessary to counterbalance other changes in the dance. Those of my informants who were in favour of icons were mostly not particular about which one it should be. Some felt that it should relate to the themes of the items performed. The brahmin dancer/ teacher, Jayalakshmi Eshwar, explained:

When I did a show on Murugan, I had an image of Murugan on the stage. When I travel I have an image of Ganesha that I put on the stage. I do a *puja* backstage before the performance, not on stage. At Kalakshetra we have been trained to start with *alarippu*. We did *namaskaram* to the stage, to Rukmini Devi, if she was there. People trained outside Kalakshetra go and touch the cymbals and feet of the gurus.

An image of Krishna playing the flute is considered appropriate for dance recitals in the theatre of the Krishna Gana Sabha.

The variety of icons chosen is increasing. Indira Rajan, *isai vellala* commented: "Because the dance items are based on god the stage must be like a temple. Any god can be there—Nataraja, Ganesha. I have seen a Christian give her *arangetram*. I composed a *varnam* for her on Jesus. For a Christian student we had a Nataraja and Jesus on the stage."[3]

These comments suggest that the importance of icons, and in particular that of Nataraja, is increasing. On the occasion of an *arangetram*, it is now an almost universally accepted practice to have an image of Nataraja on stage and to offer homage to him there. As I have shown, an *arangetram* is a relics of the *devadasi* tradition that has taken a new form. We have thus moved from a time when the presence on stage of icons such as Nataraja was unusual, through an era in which the icon has become increasingly prominent (partly as a prop, partly as an object for the expression of overt religiosity), to reach a third stage. Now two of the more recent brahmin dancers can claim: "It is the tradition to have Nataraja on stage. We are keeping up the tradition. We have Nataraja on stage as he is the god of the dance. If we have another idol such as Krishna it just means that we are doing the recital on that theme, in his presence." This is the current situation.

USE OF HAND SIGNS

Once an icon was firmly established on the stage, new dance pieces were choreographed which took its presence into account. Much of the new choreography which related to the introductory portions of many modern Bharata Natyam recitals, recalled the ritual activities of the *devadasis* inside the temple. For example, it was the custom for traditional temple dancers to enact many of the same rituals as the priests, with hand gestures (*mudras*) to mimic the implements that they used such as the flywhisk (*chamara*) and lamp (*dipa*). The most important function of the *devadasi* was to circle the image in a clockwise direction while holding a pot-lamp (*kumbharati*, literally pot *kumbha*, light *arati*). Kersenboom (1987) states that "to wave the pot-lamp was synonymous with the *devadasi*". This makes the introduction of a similar activity on the concert stage by the late 1960s particularly interesting in the context of the re-ritualization of Bharata Natyam. It is now more the rule than the exception, particularly for the younger dancers, who are mainly brahmins, to include this symbolic representation. The offering of flowers (*pushpanjali*) at the beginning of a dance recital is another choreographic innovation that has been recently introduced, but with some modification. Whereas the *devadasis'* offering was a symbolic one, today many dancers offer real flowers, using the hand gesture appropriate for holding flowers (*pushpaputa*). Nirmala Ramachandran's comments reveal her awareness that this is an innovation: "When I started with Chokkalingam the first piece was *alarippu*. This was right after the orchestra sang a *stotra* to Ganesha. We never brought flowers etc. as they do now. If I had Nataraja on the stage it was just there. I never did *puja* to Nataraja on the stage."

Later, however, she altered her repertoire: she began with the invocatory *pushpanjali* dance and dropped flowers in front of the Nataraja image. Other dancers who were performing in the 1940s (Shanta Rao, U.S. Krishna Rao and Chandrabhaga Devi) and the 1950s (Yamini Krishnamurthy, Indrani Rehman) have not followed this trend.

The ritual offering of flowers (*pushpanjali*) precedes the first dance item, generally an *alarippu*. But while *alarippu* on its own was accepted as part of the traditional concert repertoire of *sadir*, no mention is made in that context of *pushpanjali*. Kersenboom describes it as part of the temple ritual, but not as part of the court tradition. T. Balasaraswati (1980: 98-108) never included *pushpanjali* as part of her repertoire. Today, however, this ritual offering of flowers has even been choreographed as a dance piece to be presented alone or in conjunction with the first dance piece, *alarippu*.

With the presence on stage of an icon, and the ritual offering of flowers, the first ten minutes of a modern Bharata Natyam recital encapsulate the earlier temple tradition, thus exemplifying the transformation of the secular venue into a religious one. In 1964 when I was taught *alarippu* by K. Ellappa, (*isai vellala*), the dance began by standing centre stage. There was no elaborate entry with flowers in hand. Until his death in 1976, K. Ellappa did not include any suggestion of rituals. K.N. Dakshinamurthy, *isai vellala*, when he taught me *alarippu* in the 1970s, prefaced it with hand signs (*mudras*) which mimicked various rituals used in worship. For example, two hands were held touching at the wrist and fingers open, in the gesture *alapadma*,[4] signifying the pot (*kumbha*), and then circled counter-clockwise in front of the image. This same counter-clockwise movement was repeated with the right hand in *kapittha hasta*, the left in *suchi* placed by the elbow, to indicate a lamp. Exactly the same hand signs but with the *pataka* or *arala hasta* shaken, indicated a flywhisk. These were also circled in a counter-clockwise direction. This elaborate imitation of certain temple rituals had begun by 1969. By the 1980s some, although not all, dancers followed this practice and it still remains an option. It continued to the 1990s.

SHOULD A MENSTRUATING DANCER DANCE?

According to Hindu social custom, menstruating women are impure and inauspicious (Altekar 1962: 194; Marglin 1985: 60-3; Leslie 1989: 283-90). In orthodox households, their activities are restricted. Regarded as extremely impure and temporarily untouchable, they are forbidden to enter temples, to cook, or to come into contact with others. According to Altekar, "even the sight of their person and the sound of their voice were to be avoided". In the context of the traditional dance, the *devadasi* had to be in a ritually pure state (*mati*) when she performed as part of temple ritual. The auspicious presence of a *devadasi* was important at life-cycle events (*samskara*) (Kersenboom 1987). According to some of my informants, the onset of menstruation is still celebrated by non-*brahmins* in south India. In earlier times, however, the ceremony included dance as an auspicious offering. For example, M. Gopalkrishnan, *isai vellala* dance teacher, notes that "dance was a part of the festivities around the first menstrual period celebration". The dancer herself would not, of course, be menstruating.

In talking to female dancers I explored the question of what activities associated with dance (teaching, studying, performing) were allowed during the menstrual period. The responses I received indicated that dancers were aware of their ritual impurity while menstruating: only one claimed never to have heard of such a taboo. The limits that this awareness put on their dance activities varied from person to person. There appeared to be two reasons for not performing: because of the perceived impurity, "We were impure on those days and we could not dance", or, for reasons of health, "god does not enter into it".

All the younger dancers I interviewed said that they performed publicly while menstruating, and none of them ever declined an invitation or cancelled a public recital on that account. One brahmin dancer commented: "Because you are already committed you must perform, but there was an idea of pollution so I kept some distance from the cymbals and the musicians. You will pollute them if you touch them. We would not drop flowers in front of the image, or bow down in front of the icon on the stage."

Well aware of the potential she has to pollute, this dancer avoids all contact with sacred objects, in particular flowers that would normally be offered to the image. The cymbals, too, are regarded as sacred. For example, a male, non-brahmin teacher explained how he changed his former liberal views after an event which he interpreted as inauspicious: "I made them dance as part of a group when I had a dance troupe but when it comes to solo Bharata Natyam I try to avoid having them dance. This is both for health reasons and religious reasons. Once my cymbals broke in my hand."

For him, there was greater potential for inauspicious divine intervention if it was a solo dance than when it was a group dance: presumably the effect of one ritually impure dancer could be diluted by the presence of others not in that state.

The *talam*, it may be recalled, refers to a stick which is beaten on a block of wood (*tattu-kal*) in the dance class, or to the cymbals that are played during a dance recital. In this context, a male *isai vellala* teacher explained: "No, one must not touch the *talam*. The monthly course is impure and the *talam* is holy. Now the girls take class and dance on those days but they really should not. Just as one should not do *puja* on those days, so one should not dance."

The importance of the *talam* is underlined when we appreciate that consistently, whether in class or on the stage, restrictions are imposed on dancers touching it when they are menstruating.

Some teachers prefer their students to stay away when they are menstruating but are unable to enforce their preference. "They used to be strict in the olden days", laments a female brahmin teacher. "Now we can't stop them from coming." Some dance teachers appear to have the situation under control. "They are not allowed in the teaching hall", a male *isai vellala* teacher in his early fifties insisted.

One female *isai vellala* teacher was just as strict with herself as she was with her students: "I will not allow my students to come into the dance hall. On those days I will not dance and when I teach I will not touch the *tattu-kal.*"

During her dance training as a *devadasi*, she remembered having to "eat and sleep outside". Others, (but not all) from the same community also said that they had to avoid all contact with people while menstruating. Despite their own experiences, several female *isai vellala* teachers did not appear concerned about their students dancing while menstruating. A male *isai vellala* teacher believed that a dancer who did not dance while menstruating "showed respect for the art". Another male *isai vellala* teacher expressed his reservations more forcefully: "No", he said, "it is wrong. It pollutes if the student comes into the hall."

But while several teachers abstained from dancing because they saw dance as the personification of god, others saw nothing wrong in it. They also had no objection to their students coming to class, although many of their students chose, of their own accord, to stop taking classes when menstruating. During their menstrual period the girls would often come to the dance class but sit to one side and watch.

The choice is not always left to individuals. One brahmin performer in her forties felt that the pressure to conform came from her female classmates:

We were just sort of told. It was hushed talk. If a girl came everyday then the tongues would wag that maybe she was polluting the classroom. This was only in the group classes, not in my private classes. My teacher never said anything, just the girls said this. My teacher had a huge Nataraja in the classroom and it was a sort of temple-cum-classroom. While I myself did not see the logic or reason in this I had no right to interfere with other people's beliefs, so I just stayed away on those days. It was out of deference rather than my own acceptance of this.

Another dancer, torn by her commitment to give a public recital, yet conscious of her impurity agonized: "When we have to give a public recital we must do it, but we apologize to god."

Sometimes the dancer is encouraged by her teacher to overlook the taboo, in particular when the training period is limited. In the 1940s when Chandrabhaga Devi took a three-month condensed course with P.S. Minakshisundaram, he insisted that she dance daily, to prepare for those occasions when she would have a professional engagement while menstruating. "Try to dance", he said. "It is only by dancing that you will get over your headaches at this time." A male *isai vellala* teacher was also willing to compromise when necessary: "If they have to give a programme they must do it, but they must not go to the Nataraja, touch the *talam*, or the guru." This view seems to be the most common.

The younger girls were more pragmatic and gave reasons such as, "it is not practical". Others made every effort to plan ahead and avoided accepting engagements on those days, or purified themselves with a ritual bath. A brahmin dancer, now in her fifties, remembered that previously not only performances, but dance classes were stopped. "There was no question about it. We would not dance, nor would we touch the *tattu-kal*."

Thus the majority of dancers were willing to disregard "pollution" when it came to performances, but were somewhat reluctant to attend class. Most refrained from going to the *puja* room, lighting the lamp, going to the temple, touching or going near others, and from personal religious practices such as meditation, for they "required more cleanliness". Whereas cooking was once forbidden to the menstruating woman, the decline of the joint family and the inability to get servants has forced many dancers to ignore this taboo as well.

In general, it appears that, in keeping with a general decline in religious taboos, abstention from dancing during the menstrual period is no longer as widely practised as it was twenty years ago. This decline in the religious observance of a private function is in marked contrast to the increasingly overt demonstrations of religiosity on stage. The implications of menstrual impurity are still observed with regard to temples and religious rituals; elsewhere, pragmatism has taken over.

While dancers, teachers and all connected with the dance recognize that a menstruating woman is unclean, a new set of rules have been devised. These rules are open to a variety of interpretations and may be relaxed for a variety of reasons. For some, dance class is possible, for others, not. For all concerned, however, a performance must be honoured. Some dancers isolate themselves by keeping their distance and not touching religious objects, or other people. This suggests that the dance itself is regarded as less than holy; but is the dance that she performs in her impure state religious? Perhaps the dancers consider the dance to be separate from their bodies and hence above pollution.

ARE DANCERS ADDRESSING GOD OR THE AUDIENCE?

In the temple, dance was one of sixteen offerings to the deity, who was addressed in terms appropriate to royalty (Appadurai 1981: 22). The same metaphors used in the dance were also used to flatter and describe wealthy patrons. The secular component of the dance was part of the courtesan tradition. Today we have new patrons, and new settings for the dance. Nevertheless, the historical perception of the dance permeates both the dancer's presentation and audience reaction to it.

One of the main underlying aesthetic principles of the dance is the dancer's ability to express *bhava* or feeling, which in turn is intended to evoke a response from the audience. That the dance is highly erotic, and dancers and critics are aware of it, is not in doubt. How can this eroticism be justified? If the dancer is perceived as addressing her erotic longings towards god rather than the audience it lends an air of "respectability".

The issue of whether or not the dance, as it is performed today, can be considered spiritual was posed in a different way when I asked dancers whom they addressed during performance—god,[5] or the audience. The diverse answers that I obtained substantiate that for some, the dance is religious, while for others, it is entertainment.

Two dance critics, Subbudu and T.S. Parthasarathy were adamant that the dance was not for god. Parthasarathy took a historical interpretation: "The dancers are dancing for the audience, not for god. The early dancers danced to attract the attention of kings and perhaps become his mistress."

For some dancers the transfer of the dance from the temple to the concert stage meant that they should make some concessions to the audience, and treat the dance as entertainment. For others, it was the ritual component of the dance and their expression of *bhakti* that underlined the motivation for their recitals. Those who believed that the audience played an important role in their performances were willing to consider reducing the length of time for particular dances, to enter into a relationship with the audience, and acknowledge that the primary purpose of being a performer was to communicate with an audience. The following comment from a brahmin dancer substantiates the importance of the audience: "I prune my items. If it is a cosmopolitan crowd I would not do a forty-minute *varnam*. If dance isn't entertainment what is it?"

A senior non-hereditary dancer took it one step further. He believes in a "relationship with the audience". This interchange was important for many dancers. A brahmin dancer in her late forties explains: "I cannot forget the audience. I need feedback. If I am dancing to god I could do it in a closed room. Communication should be there between the audience and the dancer, if it is for God you could do it alone." Another brahmin dancer, in her thirties agrees: "If you address just god, why do it in public?" A more recent brahmin professional dancer, however, weighted her response on the side of god. "Seventy to eighty per cent for God, but I do not forget the audience."

A non-hereditary dance teacher in Delhi was sceptical of the various reasons given by professional dancers. His remarks suggest that he was deeply aware of the dancers' competitive religiosity, their turning to the dance in an effort to compensate for losing their roots in the traditional culture. As a non-hereditary *nattuvanar* from the new generation and one who had worked with both established dancers as well as those from the younger generation, he had an exceptionally broad experience. His remarks may be more pertinent to the cosmopolitan city of Delhi than to Madras when he observes that for many dancers, their only link with Hindu traditions is studying Bharata Natyam. His remarks indicate that he views the dance as an extension of daily life: "They [the dancers] dance for themselves. I don't think many of the girls today know about god. Many dancers today are rich and live like Europeans; they don't wear the sari,[6] have forgotten the rituals. They do the dance for entertainment."

Another male brahmin dance teacher was also aware of the public and private persona of the dancers. He was sceptical about the dancers today. "Dancers don't say they are dancing for the audience, even though they are."

A male *isai vellala* dance teacher from the younger generation saw dancers as belonging to two groups and did not pass judgement on either approach:

Some want to please the audience, others want to dance as a dedication to god, or they feel something. You can see the difference on the stage. It all depends on the individual. There are two kinds of dancers: those who try to dance with dedication, *bhakti*, others who do it as entertainment. It depends on the attitude of each individual dancer.

Another important brahmin dancer, in her forties did not fall into his categories and obviously had thought about the issue before. Her answer revealed that she was very conscious of the various stages through which she had progressed.

At first it was for myself. I used to feel really kicked about being there and doing it all, and they were watching it. It gave me an innocent thrill. Then I went on to doing things the audience wanted, but doing it in a tasteful manner. Then I went on to a phase doing everything according to "the tradition"—classicism just the way the teachers said, I should not overstep— I went through all that. Then I went through a militant period and felt I should undo what others have done. Now I am dancing for myself. I know it sounds pompous. There is no god and no audience only a consciousness. I feel all my higher feelings and ideas focusing together ... but I need feedback from the audience.

Others report this same super-consciousness, but explain it differently. A very popular brahmin dancer in her thirties believed:

"If you address the audience you will be in a mess. It is the character at the moment that requires your total attention. When it is like that then it is transcendent."

Another non-hereditary dancer explained this is terms of being "involved in the theme". She was not dancing for god but tried "to evoke a response in the audience and engage their attention".

CONTENT OF THE DANCE REPERTOIRE

The lyrics in the songs of the Bharata Natyam repertoire describe deities and secular patrons. Dancers have a choice of selecting dances originally intended to describe a deity or a patron. Some choose to restrict their repertoire to only those songs that describe god, while others choose from both possibilities. But a dancer who would present a traditional Bharata Natyam recital without including a single song that addresses a deity would be a rarity. This is mainly because the repertoire contains relatively few secular pieces.

Several dancers included both god and the audience. In justification they said that the lyrics in the dance repertoire usually were in praise of a particular deity. While this group felt that the audience should also be considered, others, like this brahmin dancer in her thirties consciously chose only certain pieces which: "... mention only god even though there are such pieces that address patrons I don't use them. I address god."

Two other early brahmin dancers in their sixties agreed with her. One *isai vellala* dancer who no longer performed, was emphatic that she "thought only about god when she danced. I do not interact with the audience". Even though she had been a dedicated dancer and had had an active career on the stage and in films, she claimed to dance only for her spiritual satisfaction.

Dance as an offering to god was given as a reason for the dance by many Kalakshetra graduates. Some, such as one dancer in her late forties, were prepared to make concessions while planning their programme, although in the final analysis they were addressing god: "The audience is also important. Before I chart out the programme I consider the audience, but once on the stage I do not consider them. I address only god. I do each performance as an offering to god."

If we look for textual support, the *Natya Sastra* (NS I. 110) keeps the needs of the audience in mind: "This [*natya*] gives diversion to kings, and firmness [of mind] to persons afflicted with sorrow ... it brings composure to persons agitated in mind." For many, such as this brahmin dancer in her thirties, the purpose of their dance was similar to that given in the *Natya Sastra* (NS I. 108-10): "We try to get the audience to reach some heights, be elevated. They should forget all their troubles. We are working for a sublime experience. It is entertainment in that the audience and dancer should be one, and share joy."

Most of the songs in the Bharata Natyam repertoire are addressed literally to god. It is clear, however, that the majority of my respondents did not interpret my question literally, but rather interpreted it in a general sense to mean, "where was their main attention being directed during a performance".

One non-hereditary male dancer interpreted my question as popularizing the dance if one danced for the audience. He would not make any concessions. "We perform for god. We don't care how many are in the audience." A very early brahmin dancer in her early sixties felt one was able to evoke more feelings by performing for god. "Even though I dance on the stage I address only god. Only then will you have real *bhava* (feeling)." *Bhava* for another early brahmin dancer could be evoked by being involved in a theme: "If we cried they cried, if we laughed they laughed."

The god that they are addressing varies. For some it their iconographic representation, for others, such one non-hereditary male dancer in his late forties, it is: "a super-power. I personally do it to an abstract power, not to the audience." He did concede, however, that his "inspiration comes from the audience".

The critics in particular believed that dancers danced for the audience. Originally they did so to attract the attention and favours of wealthy patrons. It is equally important for today's dancers to please their audience in order to ensure future engagements. The late K.V. Ramachandran, a scholar and early dance critic, felt that the secularizing trends in the dance were unfortunate: "By secularizing it, we have converted it into an affair of the drawing room; and imparted the spirit of the market place into the tabernacle" (Singer 1972). Ramachandran saw all art as ancillary to religion (Singer 1972; Chari 1980; Coomaraswamy 1947, 1968; Lipsey 1977). This attitude is shared by many but makes a strong contrast to those I encountered.

I found that dancers in the 1980s were becoming increasingly aware of their own involvement in recreating the dance. Their comments showed that they were aware that the dance had served a ritual function, and many were keen to augment their own concert repertoire with dances that had been the exclusive preserve of the temple repertoire.

Two brahmin dancers held contrasting views about presenting ritual songs once used in the temple. One used the historical connection of the dance to ritual to validate the authenticity of her innovation, but held that the dance that she was presenting was basically entertainment: "I took songs from the Murugan temple that were used during the ritual. These are real ritual songs and although the stories are based on god the dance is entertainment."

For another non-hereditary brahmin dancer, although her introduction of new songs into the dance repertoire could be regarded as innovative, the devotional content of the songs defined the purpose of her dance: "... Especially last night as it was all about Ramana Maharshi. No part of it was entertainment. The mood of the songs was *bhakti* (devotional). Most of the songs were composed by Ramana Maharshi, the last two *padams* (songs) by two of his devotees."

This dancer's artistic vision is re-creating Rukmini Devi's perception of the original purpose of the dance: "The people who belonged to the temple performed at different times of the ritual. They were not just performers; they danced in praise of the deity."

IS BHARATA NATYAM AS PERFORMED
TODAY RITUAL OR ENTERTAINMENT?

When asked whether the dance was ritual or entertainment, opinion was fairly evenly divided. One third felt it was both, another felt the dance was entertainment, and another third believed the dance to be basically ritual. A non-hereditary male teacher redefined my question: "It is neither ritual nor entertainment it is tradition."

A female brahmin dancer also saw the dance as neither, but as a way that she could feel her Indianness. "It is self expression." Her response encapsulates a principal reason why most dancers begin, and pursue Bharata Natyam studies.

T.S. Parthasarathy, dance critic for the *Indian Express* (Madras), and Secretary of the Madras Music Academy, saw the dances performed today as:

All entertainment, purely to sell tickets and collect money. When the dance disappeared from the temples, so did ritual dance. If we look at the repertoire, while many songs mention god they also mention patrons. For example, "Manavi", a well known *varnam* in the Bharata Natyam repertoire addresses god in the beginning, but later it is all about love. Even Jayadeva[7] addressed his songs to Krishna but they contained a lot of love situations between a man and a woman, including physical acts.

Parthasarathy's response to the ritual/entertainment dilemma addressed several pertinent questions: first, the need to make a recital a financially viable proposition by selling tickets; second, the change in the function of the dance, particularly the loss of its ritual function; third the text of the songs to which the dance is set and the unclear division between a piece of music addressing a particular god or patron, or in some cases both. His fourth point, the graphic description of the *bhakti* tradition of personal surrender to god expressed through the metaphor of sexual union and its enaction on stage brought him to the conclusion that the dance was purely for entertainment.

His first two reasons—selling tickets and loss of ritual function—are echoed by many dancers. Nevertheless, there continues to be a debate over the function of the dance when the dance piece focuses on a particular god. The other area of confusion lies in the interpretation of *bhakti*. The sexual metaphor is central to this philosophical interpretation of ecstatic bliss.

A young dancer from one of the most prestigious *devadasi* families, young enough to be removed from the opprobrium attached to traditional dancers, still suffers from her hereditary connections with the profession. She observes that the dance is:

... purely for entertainment now, it is not a ritual at all. Dancers are more worried about their dress. My grandmother [Mukta, a professional singer, and member of the T. Balasaraswati family] too feels that the dance today is only entertainment. Even for the audience, if the girl is not beautiful they will not care for her, even if she is a good dancer. But if she is beautiful and even if she does not dance well they will appreciate it. This is because only about ten per cent of the audience know something about dance.

I shall give the last word on this subject to a non-hereditary dancer who, while believing that the audience wanted to be entertained, felt that she must give them something spiritual: "If it is entertainment then I have to compromise. I can never compromise."

RE-INTRODUCING BHARATA NATYAM IN THE TEMPLE

Following closely on the re-creation of the dance and its adaptation for modern audiences and venues, there has been a recent movement to re-introduce it into the temple. This does not involve rituals, or the *devadasis*, but is aimed at reviving artistic pursuits outside the large cities. It takes the form of annual dance festivals at major temples throughout India, including Khajuraho (Madhya Pradesh), Konarak (Orissa), Belur/Halebid (Karnataka), and Chidambaram (Tamil Nadu).[8] The temples at all the sites chosen for dance festivals are artistically very fine and these spots have been major tourist attractions for many years. These festivals have had a twofold effect: they have re-introduced classical culture, and they have brought urbanized artists to centres which they might not have visited otherwise. Artists have also been permitted to dance in front of the deity. For many, this was an added bonus and brought new life and validation into their art, especially at Chidambaram. Now, for a few weeks a year, the cultural life in certain temple towns is being re-created.

Chidambaram, where the Nataraja temple is located, is generally acknowledged as the great pilgrimage to be made by a dancer. Nataraja has become the patron deity of the new generation of Bharata Natyam dancers. It was not for the *devadasis*: those dedicated to a temple owed allegiance to the deity to whom they had been married, while the secular *devadasis* in many instances were partial to the worship of Murugan.[9] The whole cult, in which dancers worship Nataraja in his *anandatandava* form, is a recent creation. It is as if the term Nataraja ("king of dance"), has been extrapolated to mean that Nataraja is the patron saint of dance. The actual Nataraja cult at Chidambaram, as expressed in the *Chidambaram Mahatmya*, is very different (Zvelebil 1973, 1985). Moreover, there is no evidence that dance was any more important in the Nataraja shrine than in other temples in Tamil Nadu.

Reactions to re-creating the temple atmosphere on the concert stage varied. The majority of the dance critics were sceptical about reintroducing the dance to the temple complex, about introducing religious elements such as icons on the concert stage, and about a visible display of ecstatic emotion during recitals. Most critics shared Mohan Khokar's reaction, "the ecstasy at Chidambaram is exhibitionism".

All the same, it cannot be denied that the venue for the dance inspires a feeling of devotion in the dancers and assists them in projecting a religious feeling. Interestingly, the particular dance style is of no importance. Leela Venkataraman (a dance critic) commented on a dance recital in Chidambaram of a north Indian style of dance, Kathak, which owed much of its patronage to the secular courts of northern India, revealing her belief that the dance is more than entertainment:

To be a great dancer you have to have *bhakti* or devotion. You have to have a religious feeling. I have seen it in people who dance on stage but it is definitely there during the festival in the Nataraja temple at Chidambaram. The dancers dance the night before in the compound and the next day in the temple in the *sanctum*. The entire aura is different. You begin to realize that this is what it was meant to be. One dancer gave his bells to the priest who blessed them and when he danced [in the Kathak style] he forgot himself.

R. Nagaswamy, who founded the Chidambaram festival, agreed with Leela Venkataraman and saw more meaning when the dance, which "flowered in the context of the temple rituals", was performed there. He gave examples of certain dances, in particular *varugelamo*, in which an untouchable begs to enter the sanctum and see Nataraja, an experience that he is normally denied because of his low birth.

When the great compositions such as *varugelamo*, composed by Subrahmanya Bharati, are danced in front of the deity the emotion of the dancer is something supreme, it is considerably different than when she performs in the *sabhas* [cultural organizations in Madras city]. I have seen great dancers completely relate to god. With an audience the dancer is conscious of it. I think the art is a degree less when you dance for the art's sake.

His comments support Leela Venkataraman's observations given above on the influence of the venue.

DISCUSSION

Many dancers whose careers extended from the 1930s to the 1960s included only the simplest show of religiosity in their public performances. In contrast, some of the more recent dancers (1970-89) made a conscious effort to accentuate the religious spectacle. Even if a dancer is happy to exclude religious rituals, her teacher, or more important, her audience, may encourage it. Consequently, as time passes, some dancers, dance teachers and audiences seem increasingly to require that concert recitals include religious elements, in the form of rituals and symbolic gestures.

Before the "revival" some elements of the dance were regarded as appropriate for the temple, and others for secular occasions. Today, some dancers are re-ritualising the dance by introducing into the concert repertoire dances and ritual movements, that were originally intended to be part of temple ritual. While the initial stage performances of Bharata Natyam derived mainly from the court tradition (*sadir*), the incorporation of hand signs (*mudras*) once used in rituals, the performance of *gejjai puja* and an *arangetram*, and the presence of an icon on stage, emphasize the temple heritage of the dance. This trend removes Bharata Natyam from the realm of the strictly theatrical, making it increasingly a religious phenomenon. At the same time, the religious element in the dance is becoming more formalized. The dancer acts out the precise rituals of worship, while the audience watches very much as a *puja* is performed in a temple.

For some, introducing rituals to the concert stage confirms the historical link of the dance with temple ritual, for others it is "phoney". In both cases the attitude displayed appears rather different from that of, for example, the Tiruttani *devadasis* whose approach to her dance was "respectful, but matter of fact" (pers. comm. S. Kersenboom). Non-hereditary dancers who began performing in the early period of the revival generally tried to avoid association with *devadasi* rituals. The more recent reintroduction of *devadasi* rituals seems to signify that the dance has distanced itself sufficiently from the *devadasi* tradition to be immune from that stigma.

Among dancers, it appears that while private ritual observances (for example, the menstrual taboo) are declining, public displays of religion are increasing. This apparently contradictory development can be rationalized when we consider that most of the young women and men practising dance today have had a western education. Outside of their life as dancers, they have moved far from the traditional ways of their community. To obtain credibility as Bharata Natyam dancers, they need to establish their religious credentials. This can be done by public expressions such as acts of worship on stage and the presence of a visible icon.

No such practices were followed by the *devadasis*. But they are now taken so much for granted in Bharata Natyam that many dancers regard the presence of an icon as stemming from the *devadasi* heritage. Hence, when such displays of ritual are referred to as "traditional", we need not take the description at face value; rather, we should interpret this to mean, "affirming adherence to traditional values in the context of a changing society". This is surely a major function that Bharata Natyam performs for Indian society today.

Because the dance is an extremely competitive field, and the competition is increasing, the apparent need for religious credentials may have led to an escalation of these tendencies. I am inclined to believe that responses to my questions were coloured by whether my informants chose to refer to their own attitude to the dance, or to that of others. The comment, "'it' is entertainment" was common when referring to dance in general; and the opinion that other dancers cheapened their art by pandering to audiences cropped up frequently. Conversely, most who considered the dance as largely spiritual, did so in personal terms; "I approach my dance as ritual", or, "my dance is spiritual". There appeared to be an implicit assumption that the spiritual is superior to the non-spiritual.

Although self-expression was mentioned by only one dancer, self-fulfilment as part of a spiritual goal was mentioned by many. Apparently the dance functions for some dancers as a channel for spiritual experience. It seems likely, however, that the experience thus obtained is similar to that of other artists who might define their heightened state as an aesthetic experience.

Dancers who kept the audience in mind gave several reasons for doing so, the most important of which was that dance was primarily entertainment. Another reason was the feedback provided by an audience.

Dance teachers and critics were very sceptical of the dancers' motives. Some felt that the dancers were either unaware of their own motives, or deliberately misrepresented them in claiming that their motivation was mainly spiritual. The teachers felt that the dancers regarded the dance mainly as entertainment. Most seemed to base this on the fact that the dancers led a westernized way of life. If any dancers claimed that they danced for god, which the teachers suspected they would, this was probably untrue. The teachers felt that the audience was very important for the dancers. In fact, the dancers were more candid than either the critics or dance teachers suspected.

Bharata Natyam is a living art form, hence practices and

perceptions of what is correct are in constant flux. At present it appears that there is a trend to re-ritualize and romanticise the dance of the *devadasis*; but there is also a parallel tendency to question what is currently regarded as tradition and to call for new forms and new dances. Of all the arts (including painting, sculpture, and music), it appears that dance has been the least affected by outside influences or innovation. For that reason, recent developments in the dance provide an excellent insight into the tensions and contradictions created by the impact of the twentieth century. Only time will tell the extent to which Bharata Natyam will be re-ritualized.

NOTES

1. The Odissi equivalent is termed "stage entry", *manchapravesa*.
2. The icon of Nataraja is usually on the stage during a Bharata Natyam recital and during an Odissi recital that of Jagannatha. This reflects the regional origins of the two dance styles. See Gaston 1983.
3. For Christian themes in Bharata Natyam, see Barboza 1985: 29-32. Mary, Jesus' mother is also considered appropriate. In south India she is known as Velangani.
4. *Alapadma*, *kapittha pataka*, are the names of hand signs in the *Abhinayadarpana*: 146-9, 121-4. See also Gaston 1985: 36-43 where they are illustrated and other textual sources given. *Pushpaputa* is the name of the hand sign in which the flowers are held (*Abhinayadarpana*: 182-4).
5. See Neuman 1980 who commented on this.
6. Wearing the *sari* is considered to be appropriate for mature Hindu girls and women. His comments are more appropriate to Delhi than Madras where he teaches.
7. Jayadeva composed the *Gita Govinda*. Most of the descriptive dances in the Odissi style of dance are set to his poems. Subbudu comments on the erotic content of Jayadeva's work; he too is sceptical of its spiritual content.
8. At one time at Khajuraho, the temples were used as a backdrop but recently the Archaeology Survey of India banned this. See *India Today*, April 1990 for more details.
9. Murugan is the Tamil counterpart of the Sanskritic deity Subrahmanyam/Subramaniam/Skanda.

Plate 9.1: The Image of Nataraja on the Concert Stage

A decorated Nataraja image is placed on a table between two brass lamps. Beneath the table is a brass image of Nataraja surrounded by small brass lights. The lower image is garlanded and coconuts, bananas, incense sticks and other *puja* articles are placed in front of it. The dancer has just entered the stage and is performing *namaskaram* to the images. This photograph was taken in December 1989 at the Vazhuvur Dance Festival, organized by the family of V. Ramaiya, held at the Rasika Ranjini Sabha, Mylapore, Madras.

Plate 9.2: The Image of Nataraja on the Concert Stage

An image of Nataraja is placed on a table and garlanded. It is on stage left. Beneath the garland is a photograph of Sai Baba, a well known contemporary holy man. The presence of this photograph indicates that the dancer acknowledges him as her spiritual teacher (guru). On either side of the photograph are two brass lamps. On the right there is a tray with the regular *puja* articles: bell, bananas, fruits, etc. The two halves of a broken coconut signify that a *puja* has been performed on the stage.

Plate 9.3: The Image of Krishna on the Concert Stage

The image of Krishna playing the flute has been installed on the stage of the Krishna Gana Sabha for a Bharata Natyam recital. *Nattuvangam* and vocal is being performed by women. The *mridangam* is played by a man, as is the *vina*. The *vina* player is Kannan (brahmin).

Conclusion

Central to the original intentions of many artistic traditions that developed within the rituals of Hindu temples, was the presentation of royal honours to a presiding deity. These activities were carried out by hereditary specialists who belonged to specific professional groups. The artistic presentations evolved as part of *seva*, with the implication that there was a commitment of the artist to the presiding deity of the temple.

In the case of hereditary temple dancers, the girls were dedicated to the deity, and only women dancers could serve in the temple. The *nattuvanars* and musicians who accompanied the dance, with few exceptions, were all men. This group was known as the *cinna melam*. While dance was an essential component of temple ritual, most of the dancers and their accompanists were also free to accept secular performances, especially those patronized by royalty. The extent of this support and the repertoire varied according to what appealed to the patron. The celebration of many festivals and life cycle events usually included dance.

Music has a more universal ritual importance in Hindu temples than dance. The temple musicians of the *periya melam*, were distinct from the dance accompanists (*cinna melam*). In this century, the *periya melam* musicians continue to serve a largely ritual function, while many of the *cinna melam* were forced to become independent of temple patronage. The recent popularity of the dance has assisted the latter by making their profession reasonably well paid. Certainly, the majority are better off than those musicians who still serve in a largely ritual capacity.

Performance of ritual music, of the type that continues to be played by the *periya melam*, seems to provide many of the features cited as being attractive to dancers today: for instance, the opportunity to express religious devotion through art, as sanctioned by antiquity. However, it is most unusual for a person from a non-hereditary community to attempt to train and enter the musical profession of the *periya melam*. This contrasts with the *cinna melam* tradition, as most Bharata Natyam dancers, teachers and accompanists today belong to non-hereditary families and choose to enter this profession. One suspects that the ingredient lacking in the *periya melam* music is glamour. The dynamic world of Bharata Natyam makes a strong contrast with the generally codified presentation of arts which continue as part of temple ritual. Consequently, the profession of temple musician provides limited, and often diminishing, rather than expanding, prospects for employment.

Dance as part of temple ritual was banned but music was not. It is ironic that an art, which was subject to so much social opprobrium as the early concert component of Bharata Natyam (*sadir*), should continue to flourish. That it did, is largely because it was adopted by the urban upper-middle class as an accomplishment which, amongst other things, emphasized their Indian identity. Among the many classical Indian dance styles, Bharata Natyam has proved one of the most attractive. It also lends itself to evaluation in terms of aesthetic criteria. At the same time, the temple connection enabled the dance to maintain an aura of religious association which has reappeared on to the concert stage, although in a different form.

Most dance during the latter part of the nineteenth century existed as an entertainment lacking in respectability and tainted by its association with courtesans. To fill the vacuum, an existing dance tradition that could claim the twin sanctions of antiquity and religion was needed. It was the desire for a national classical dance that catapulted Bharata Natyam to its present position as the quintessence of Indian culture. That it overcame the prejudice associated with the institution of *devadasi* probably owes much to a small number of far-sighted individuals who recognized the aesthetic value of the style, and were not intimidated by its dubious past.

The leaders of the Indian independence movement saw the "revival" of Indian culture as being an integral part of their mission. If Indian culture was to be projected, both at home and abroad, it was necessary to provide a full spectrum of artistic activities. Classical music was already highly developed. In the field of dance, however, a vacuum existed in the early part of the twentieth century.

The "revival" of Bharata Natyam marked a watershed in the presentation of classical dance in south India. Popular conception today is that a defunct art was snatched from the brink of extinction by the zealous "revivalists". I believe it is more realistic to view the "revival" as a metamorphosis, in which an old artistic caterpillar changed into the butterfly of modern Bharata Natyam. A new interpretation of the dance was required for modern India, and arguments about what form it should take and the position of *sringara* and *bhakti* still continue.

An essential part of the rehabilitation of Bharata Natyam was the development of a historical view that saw the last phase of the *devadasi* system as a degenerate remnant of a once glorious past. This is very explicit in the writings of Muthulakshi Reddy, E. Krishna Iyer, Rukmini Devi and others. They used this view to justify the modifications that they made to the dance. Support for this stems from the perception that in the past the dance was entirely spiritual, and free from the taint of eroticism. Appeals to the past continue to be made by some innovators to justify changes in the basic thrust of the dance.

The more recent dancers and their families still affirm that they come from a "good" family, and claim purity for their art, but not as the early revivalists did, to distinguish themselves and their dance from that of the *devadasis*. Stylized dance has become one of the necessary adornments for marriageable girls, whose families are trying to attract a suitable husband.

The position of Bharata Natyam as a national treasure has led to intense pressure to conserve the dance in what is perceived to be its "traditional" form. The opposing desires of Bharata Natyam dancers to preserve, and innovate, have led both sides to seek historical justification for their positions. The two extremes—the innovators, who equate art with creativity, and the traditionalists, who wish to preserve it completely unchanged—are in the minority; the majority have taken the middle road and combine traditional repertoire with new compositions in their programmes.

In the process of being seen and performed, the dance is changing; any change can be considered modernizing. Whether we embrace the new trends, or reject them, the current processes will probably continue. As a living art, change has always been a part of Bharata Natyam and I see no reason to fear for the future. Seen in its historical perspective, the dance has undergone tremendous changes over its nearly two thousand year old history. The history of dance movements is recorded in temple sculptures. These carvings demonstrate that, while there is a clear continuity with modern traditions, changes have occurred in the past, as they continue to do today. What is happening now is no doubt accelerated by the great mobility of current dancers, and their musicians and teachers and the universal availability of its presentation on television and video. These factors have artistic repercussions such as the blending of previously distinct *banis*, and the creation of new ones. Nevertheless, the increasing penetration of the teacher's role by persons from outside the traditional community has brought an influx of new ideas and interpretations that continues to provide the necessary creative impulse within the style.

In examining the pedigree of the traditional dance families, it was clear that some *banis* were no longer being taught by members of the original family; some may have died out completely. Others may do likewise on the death of the limited number from the present generation trained in music and dance. There is a great danger that their contribution will disappear, leaving no record of their place in shaping the artistic heritage of Bharata Natyam. Some impoverishment of the tradition seems inevitable. Likewise, the gradual divorce of dance training from training in musical accompaniment creates a tendency towards greater emphasis on movement and less reliance on musicality. The increased concentration on movement and rhythmic complexity has resulted in a diminishing emphasis on *abhinaya*.

Considering the current state of Bharata Natyam, we can examine what it tells us about the role of classical arts in society. A number of points arise if we review the changes that have taken place since the revival:

(1) Control of the dance has mainly passed out of the hands of the *nattuvanars*/teachers into those of the dancers (now mostly from non-traditional families). It is the dancer, rather than the *nattuvanar* who is likely to negotiate for performances, and decide on the artistic content.

(2) The majority of dance recitals anywhere in India are built around the same core classical repertoire. Essentially it was, and is, the repertoire of *sadir*—although some dancers have built on, and expanded the technique. Others have mingled it with various indigenous (Kuchipudi, Odissi, Kathakali), or innovative styles, to create new forms. Most recitals, however, remain relatively conservative.

(3) Those changes in repertoire that occurred over the past fifty years, either revived pieces formerly associated with the temple music and dance repertoire, or introduced, and then dropped the items that were considered semi-classical. Others were discontinued for the more practical reason that they required a time-consuming change of costume. The proportion of an average programme devoted to the most complex and demanding item *varnam* has increased, indicating that the classical component is being increasingly emphasized. *Varnam* encapsulates the strongest representation of complexities in rhythm, *abhinaya* and choreography.

(4) Changes in staging and presentation increasingly emphasize the religious connections, such as bringing icons onto the stage, to which ritual offerings are made. In some cases subservience to the teacher is also publicized (e.g. by touching feet), and the antiquity of the artistic lineage is stressed by pictures of a founding figure, such as the teacher's father, or spiritual master. These innovations contrast with the increasingly cosmopolitan and emancipated character of the dancers themselves. It has been suggested that they

have been introduced to emphasize the dancer's adherence to, or respect for, traditional Indian values.

The attitude of the critics to such innovations was generally negative. They saw them as hypocritical. There is, however, no evidence that audiences object to overt religiosity and submissiveness. The opinions of the dancers were mixed and appeared to be fluid, perhaps in response to changing public moods.

(5) Parents of many aspiring dancers invest very large sums of money in training, costumes, publicity material, and the hire of halls. They may also make substantial donations to cultural organizations to encourage their collaboration in their daughter's recitals. Such investments are unlikely to pay a dividend in purely economic terms, as very few dancers make even a modest living from performing.

Many features of Bharata Natyam and its place in Indian society can be accounted for if we view its acquisition and presentation as relating mainly to social status. Status remains a potent force in Indian society, as elsewhere. As Hinduism is the majority faith, so Hindu arts are identified most easily with national arts. The dominant model for the urban elite is to combine western academic education and material comfort with traditional Indian (Hindu) values and aesthetics.

Bharata Natyam, and its numerous offshoots, project precisely that obeisance to India's cultural heritage which has become most important to a generation of Indians who find themselves, like their counterparts worldwide, adrift in a sea of global culture. Bharata Natyam seems to preserve a part of India that links the past and future; a vehicle by which the wonder of the Indian past can be carried forward to the next generation.

Because Bharata Natyam has moved a long way from its origins, both geographically, socially, and artistically, there has been some re-creation involved in the establishment of the dance that we now see. Bharata Natyam today has assumed many of the characteristics of an "invented tradition".

... a set of practices, normally governed by overtly or tacitly accepted rules, and of a ritual or symbolic nature, which seek to inculcate certain values and norms of behaviour, which automatically implies continuity with the past. (Hobsbawm 1983: 1).

I have explored the evidence for change in Bharata Natyam and examined the extent to which it represents the invention of tradition. The values and norms of behaviour of today's dancers and teachers are not unified and their diversity reflects the tension and confusion which surrounds the transmission and presentation of Bharata Natyam. Bharata Natyam remains an oral tradition.

Nor can we ignore the sheer momentum of a cultural predilection for dance, deeply rooted in the popular psyche, as dance is throughout India. The current popularity of Bharata Natyam seems no more than a reinstatement of dance as an important cultural phenomenon in Indian society, where, from at least the time of the *Natya Sastra*, dance has provided a universally recognized metaphor for the cycle of existence. A story from the *Rajatarangini* illustrates the power of dance as a medium for connecting past and present.

A king, riding alone on an untrained horse, travelled into the wilderness to break the animal in. Far from human habitation he came on two young women, one dancing, the other singing. He paused to ask them why they performed in such a lonely spot. "It is the tradition of our family", they explained, "Our mother danced here before us, and before her our grandmother. Why we must do this, we do not know. Simply we dance." Later the king returned with servants and commanded an excavation of the spot where the women had performed. Buried in the ground, they found the remains of an ancient temple. Such is the power of tradition; such is the nature of the dance (Stein 1900: 147).

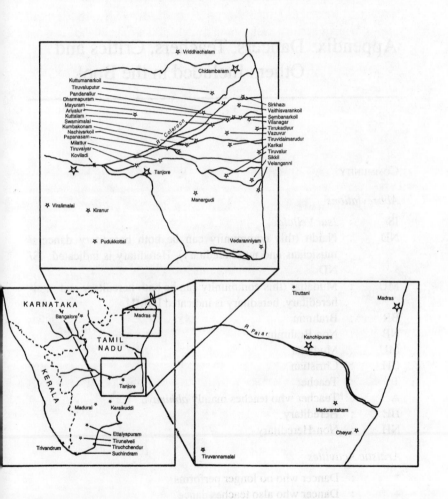

Vriddhachalam

Chidambaram

Kuttumanarkoil
Tiruvaluputur
Pandanallur
Dharmapuram
Mayuram
Ariyalur
Kuttalam
Swamimalai
Kumbakonam
Nachiyarkoil
Papanasam
Milattur
Tiruvaiyar
Koviladi

Sirkhazi
Vaithisvarankoil
Sembanarkoil
Vilanagar
Tirukadiyur
Vazuvur
Tiruvidaimarudur
Karikal
Tiruvalur
Sikkil
Velanganni

R. Coleroon

Tanjore

Manargudi

Viralimalai   Kiranur

Pudukkottai

Vedaranniyam

KARNATAKA

Bangalore

TAMIL
NADU

KERALA

Madras

Tiruttani

Madras

R Palar

Kanchipuram

Madurantakam

Cheyur

Tanjore

Madurai   Karaikuddi

Ettaiyapuram
Tirunelveli
Tiruchchendur
Suchindram

Trivandrum

Tiruvannamalai

Appendix: Dancers, Teachers, Critics and Others Included in the Book

COMMUNITY

Abbreviations

IS	:	*Isai Vellala*
ND	:	Naidu (this community can be both hereditary dancers/ musicians and non-hereditary). Hereditary is indicated: IS/ ND
MU	:	Mudaliar (this community can be both hereditary and non-hereditary, hereditary is indicated IS/MU
BR	:	Brahmin
NB	:	Non Brahmin
MU	:	Mudaliar
CH	:	Christian
T	:	Teacher
A	:	Teacher who teaches mainly *abhinaya*
HE	:	Hereditary
NH	:	Non-Hereditary

Aritistic Activities

*	:	Dancer who no longer performs
+	:	Dancer who also teaches dance

Gender

M	:	Male, only indicated in the case of dancers.
F	:	Female only indicated in the case of teachers
( )	:	Brackets indicate that the person has died

DANCERS

Dancers	Caste	Division	Teacher
+Alarmel Valli(T)	NB/	I	P.C. Subbarayan
	MU		Kalanidhi Narayanan
+Ambika Buch (T)	NB	IV	Kalakshetra
+Anandi*(T)	BR	IV	Kalakshetra
Anjali Krishna Rao	BR	I	U.S. Krishna Rao
Avanti Meduri	BR	II	
(+Balasaraswati T. (T))	IS	I	(T.N. Kandappa)
Bhashini Herambanathan*	IS	III	Revati
Bhaksar (M)*	NB	III	(K. Ellappa)
Bhanumati K.N.*	IS	I	(P. Vadivel)
+Bharati Shivaji (T)	BR	IV	(Lalita Shastri)
+Bragha Guruswamy (T)	BR	II	(C. Kunchitapadam)
		IV	Adyar Lakshmanan
Brinda Guruswamy	BR	II	(C. Kunchitapadam)
+Chamundeswari(T)	IS	II	(K.N. Dandayudapani)
		III	(M.D. Gauri)
+Chandrabhagadevi* (T)	BR	I	(P.S. Minakshisundaram)
+Chandralekha (T)	'BR	III	(K. Ellappa)
+Chandrashekar V. (M)(T)	BR	IV	Kalakshetra
Chitra Sundaram	BR	II	T.K.Kalyanasundaram
+Chitra Visweswaran	BR	II	T.A. Rajalakshmi
		II	(V. Ramaiya)
+Dhananjayan V.P. (M)	NB	IV	Kalakshetra
+Gautam Rajsri	NB	II	(S.K. Rajaratnam)
		I	K.P. Kittappa
		III	T. Balasaraswati
+Gayatri Venkataraman	BR	IV	Kalakshetra
Girija Pakkirirswami *	IS	II	(P. Vadivelu)
			(Shanmugamsundaram)
Gita Ramakrishna	BR	III	(Swarnasaraswati)
		II	(V. Sadasivan)
+Indra Rajan *	IS	II	(K. Ganeshan)
+Indrani Rehman *	NB	I	(A.P. Chokkalingam)
		II	(S. Ramaswamy)
+Jamuna Krishnan(A)	BR	I	(K.S. Govindarajan)
			Kalanidhi Narayanan
+Jayalakshmi Arunachalam *	IS	I	(T. Picchaiya)
+Jayalakshmi Chandrashekhar	BR	IV	(Lalita Shastri)
		IV	Kalakshetra
+Jayalakshmi Eshwar	BR	IV	Kalakshetra

DANCERS

Dancers	Caste	Division	Teacher
+Jayalakshmi (Teacher)	BR	IV	Kalakshetra
+Jayashree Venugopal	BR	II	Parvati Kumar
+Kalanidhi Narayanan(A)*	BR	II	(Kannappa)
		III	(M.D. Gauri)
+Kalaivani Govindarajan	IS	I	(K.S. Govindarajan)
+Kanaka Srinivasan	BR	II	V. Ramaiya
		I	(V. Sadasivan)
		I	Nana Kasar
+Keshavamurthy H.R. (M)	BR	II	(Gundappa)
+Kiran Saigal	NB	I	(V. Sadasivan)
		I	(K. S. Govindarajan)
+Komala Varadan	BR	II	(S. Thiruvengadam)
+Krishna Rao U.S.* (M)	BR	I	(P.S. Minakshisundaram)
+Krishnakumari Narendran	NB	II	(T. Chandrashekar)
+Krishnaveni Lakshmanan	BR	IV	Kalakshetra
+Krishnamurthy V. (M)	BR	IV	Kalakshetra
+Kubernath Tanjorkar * (M)	IS	II	(Appasamy)
+Lakshmanan (Adyar)* (M)	BR	IV	Kalakshetra
+Lakshminarayanan U.*(M)	BR	III	(K. Ellappa)
+Lakshmi Viswanathan (A)	BR	III	(K. Ellappa)
Lakshmi Rajan*	NB	I	(P.S. Minakshisundaram)
+Lakshmi Shanmugam-Knight	IS	III	T. Balasaraswati
+Lalita K. *	BR	II	(K. Muthukumar)
+Leela Ramanathan	BR	I	(P.S. Minakshisundaram)
+Leela Samson	NB	IV	Kalakshetra
+Malati Dominic	IS/NB	II	V. Ramaiya
		I	K.P. Kittappa
+Malati Srinivasan*	BR	IV	Kalakshetra
		II	(K.N. Dandayudapani)
Malavika Hemnath	IS	II	(K. Ganeshan)
Malavika Sarukkai	BR	II	T.K. Kalyanasundaram
		II	(S.K. Rajaratnam)
		IV	Bhagavatalu Sitarama Sharma
Mallika Sarabhai	BR	I	Mrinalini Sarabhai
Mangalam *	BR	II	(V. Minakshisundaram)
+Minakshi Pakkiriswami	IS	I	(A.P. Chokkalingam)
Minakshi Sabhanayagam	NB/MU	II	P.C. Subbarayan
Mahalakshmi Kameswaran	BR	II	S.K. Kameswaran
+Mrinalini Sarabhai	BR	I	(P.S. Minakshisundaram)
+Muthulakshmi T. *	IS	II	(K. Ganeshan)

DANCERS

Dancers	Caste	Division	Teacher
+Muthuswami V.S.* (M)	IS	II	(K. Muthukumar)
+Mythili Kalyanasundaram *	IS	I	(Kamalambal)
Mythili Sivakumar	BR	II	Saroja Vaidyanathan
+Nagamani *	BR	IV	Kalakshetra
+Naganandini Ramachandran	BR	II	(K.N. Dandayudapani)
		II	Malati Srinivasan
		II	Uma Dandayudapani
+Nala Najan (M)	NB	II	(K. Muthukumara)
+Nana Kasar* (M)	NB	II	Parvati Kumar
		I	(A.P. Chokkalingam)
+Nandini Raghavan	BR	III	(T. Balasaraswati)
+Narasimachari (M)	BR	IV	Kalakshetra
+Nirmala Ramachandran (A)	BR	I	(A.P. Chokkalingam)
		III	(M.D. Gauri)
(+Natarajan T.J.* (M))	IS	I	Kamalamabal
+Padma Subrahmanyam	BR	II	(V. Ramaiya)
		IV	P. Subrahmanyam
+Parvati Kumar*(M)	NB	II	(B. Chandrashekar)
		III	(M.D. Gauri)
+Pushkala Gopal	BR	II	Malati Srinivasan
		II	K.N. Dakshinamurthy
		IV	V.P. Dhananjayan
Radha Annamalai*	IS/ND	I	(T. N. Kandappa)
+Radha Jayaraman	BR	II	(V. Ramaiya)
		II	Kamala Lakshman
+Radhakrishnan*	IS	II	(Gundappa)
+Radha Srinivasan	BR	I	(T. Swaminathan)
+Radhika Natarajan	BR	IV	V.P. Dhananjayan
Rajalakshmi Kalanidhi	NB	II	(K. Ganeshan)
+(Rajendran R.S.*)	IS	I	Kamalambal
+Ramarao* (M)	BR	IV	Kalakshetra
Ramgopal* (M)	NB	I	(P.S. Minakshisundaram)
		III	(K. Ellappa)
+Rajalakshmi T.N.	IS	II	(T.P. Kuppaiya)
+Rajamani V.(M)	BR	IV	Kalakshetra
+P.S. Ramaswamy (M)	BR	II	(S. Manikkam)
+Ranganayaki L.	BR	II	(K. Lalita)
Rani Venkataraman	BR		T.V. Venkataraman
Rasika Khanna	NB	IV	(Lalita Shastri)
+Revati Ramachandran	BR	IV	(M. Durairaj Iyer)
+Ritha Devi(T)	BR	I	(A.P. Chokkalingam)

DANCERS

Dancers	Caste	Division	Teacher
+(Rukmini Devi* (T))	BR	III	(M.D. Gauri)
		I	(P.S. Minakshisundaram)
		II	(K. Muthukumar)
Sai*	IS	II	(V.S. Muthuswamy)
Samantha Kamani *	IS	III	Ranganayaki
		II	(Thiruvengadum)
		II	(V. Minakshisundaram)
Sarala	IS	II	K.J. Sarasa
		IV	Padma Subrahmanyam
+Sarasa K.J.*	IS	II	(V. Ramaiya)
+Saraswati Sundaresan	BR	II	(T.P. Marudappa)
			T.S. Shanmugansundaram
Saroja E.V. *	IS	II	(V. Ramaiya)
+Saroja Kameswaran *	BR	II	S.K. Kameswaran
+Saroja Khokar	NB/MU	II	(K. Muthukumar)
Saroja Vanchi	BR	II	(K.N. Dandayudapani)
			Malati Srinivasan
+Saroja Vaidyanathan	BR	II	K. Lalita
+Sasikala Natarajan*	IS	I	Kamalambal
			(T.K. Natarajan)
Savitri Balasubrahmaniam	BR	II	(K.N. Dandayudapani)
+Savitri Jagannatharao *	BR	IV	Kalakshetra
Savitri Mahadevan	BR	II	K.N. Dakshinamurthy
+Shanta Dhananjayan	NB	IV	Kalakshetra
+Shanta Rao *	BR	I	(P.S. Minakshisundaram)
+Sharada Hoffman(T)	BR	IV	Kalakshetra
Shoba Natarajan	BR	II	Kamala Lakshman
+Shymala	NB	III	(T. Balasaraswati)
			K. Ramaiya
+Sonal Mansingh	NB	I	U.S. Krishna Rao
Srinidhi Rangarajan	BR	II	Kamala Lakshman
		II	(V. Ramaiya)
		II	(S.K. Rajaratnam)
Subhadra Natarajan	BR	I	(A.P. Chokkalingam)
Subharaj (M)	NB	II	Uma Dandayudapani
Subhalakshmi *	IS	II	(V.S. Muthuswamy)
+Suchita Bhide (Chapekar)	BR	IV	Parvati Kumar
		I	T.P. Kittappa
+Sudharani Raghupathy	BR	I	U.S. Krishna Rao

DANCERS

Dancers	Caste	Division	Teacher
+Sujata Srinivasan	BR	II	Chitra Visweswaran
		II	(S.K. Rajaratnam)
+Sundari Sundaresan	BR	IV	Padma Subrahmanyam
Sumati Kumar *	BR	II	Parvati Kumar
		III	(M.D. Gauri)
+Swapnasundari	BR	II	(K. J. Govindarajan)
		II	K.N. Dakshinamurthy
		I	(V. Sadasivan)
+(Swarnasaraswati)	IS	II	(K. Thiruvengadam)
+Swarnamukhi *	IS/ND	IV	(Sampati Bhoopal)
+Tara Ramaswamy *	BR	III	(K. Ellappa)
Tarveen Mehra	NB	II	Girija Pakkiriswami
		II	K.N. Dakshinamurthy
+Thilagam P.R. *	IS	II	(K. Ganeshan)
+Thomas C.S (T) (M)	NB/CH	IV	Kalakshetra
+Uma Dandayudapani*	IS	II	(K.N. Dandayudapani)
Uma Kumar	BR	IV	(Lalita Shastri)
		II	M. Nagarajan
+Umamaheshwari	IS	I	(T. Arunachalam)
		II	(S.K. Rajaratnam)
			Kalanidhi Narayanan
+Uma Sriram	BR	IV	Padma Subrahmanyam
+Usha Srinivasan	BR	II	(K.N. Dandayudapani)
+Usha Narayanan	BR	I	(K.J. Govindarajan)
Vasanta T.V.S. *	BR	II	(T.S. Govindarajan)
+Vasantalakshmi	BR	IV	(Sampati Bhoopal)
Narasimhachari	(T)	IV	Narasimhachari
Veenu Dakshinamurthy	IS	II	K.N. Dakshinamurthy
+Vasantakumari Sikkil	BR	II	(S. Ramaswamy)
Vasundhara Thomas	BR	IV	Kalakshetra
+Venugopal J. *(M)	IS	IV	Parvati Kumar
+Vyjayanthimala Bali	BR	II	(V. Ramaiya)
		II	(K.N. Dandayudapani)
		I	K.P Kittappa
+Vijayalakshmi Prakash	BR	II	T.K. Kalyansundaram
+Yamini Krishnamurti	BR	IV	Kalakshetra
		III	(K. Ellappa)
		II	K.N. Dandayudapani
Yogam *	BR	II	(V. Minakshisundaram)

LIST II
TEACHERS

Teachers	Caste	Division	Teacher
@(Arunachalam)	IS	I	S. Kannuswamy (father of K. Tanjorkar)
@(Arunachalam) father of Hemnath	IS	I	(T. Picchaiya)
@(T. Bhavu)	IS	I	(T. Kandaswamy?)
@(Chokkalingam A.P)	IS	I	P.S. Minakshisundaram
@(Dandayudapani K.N.)	IS	IV	Kalakshetra
		II	(K. Nateshan)
Dakshinamurthy K.N.	IS	II	K.N. Dandayuadapani
(Devanathan T.R.)	IS	IV	Kalakshetra
@(Durairaj M. Iyer)	BR	IV	M. Natesha Shastri
@(Ellappa K.)	IS	II	(K. Thiruvengadam)
		III	(T. Balasaraswati)
(Ganeshan T.K).	IS	III	(T. Balasaraswati)
Gopalkrishnan P. M.	IS	I	(P. Muthaiya)
		I	(P.S. Minakshisundaram)
@(Govindarajan A.T.)1	IS	II	(T.P. Kuppaiya)
(Govindarajan K.)	IS	I	(Narayanaswami?)
Hemnath A.	IS	I	(Arunachalam)
Herambanathan T.B.	IS	I	(T. Bhavu)
Kalyanasundaram T.P.	IS	II	T.P. Kuppaiya
Kameswaran S.K.	BR	II	V. Ramaiya
Karunambal Govindarajan(F)	IS	II	(T.P. Kuppaiya)
Kittappa K.P.	IS	I.	(P.S. Minakshisundaram)
(Kunchitapadam C.)	NB	II	(K. Muthukumara)
(Kuppaiya T.P.)	IS	II	(Panchapakesa?)
		I	(P.S. Minakshisundaram)
Mahalingam T.K.	IS	II	(T.P. Kuppaiya)
(Minakshisundaram P.S.)	IS	I	(T. Kumaraswami) (T.S. Mahadevan)
Mohanraj	NB	II	(S.S. Manikkam)
(Muthaiya P.M.)	IS	I	(P.S. Minakshisundaram)
Nadanam K.R.	IS	II	(K.N. Dandayudapani)
Nagarajan P.M.	IS	II	(K.N. Dandayudapani) K.N. Dakshinamurthy
(Pakkiriswami K.N.)	IS	II	K.N. Dandayudapani
Ramaiya K.	IS	III	(T. Balasaraswati)
		III	(T.K. Ganeshan)
(Ramaiya V.)	IS	II	(K. Muthukumar)
(Rajaratnam S.K.)	IS	II	V. Ramaiya

TEACHERS

Teachers	Caste	Division	Teacher
(Sadasivan V.)	BR	I	(T. Swaminathan)
Samraj R.	IS	II	V. Ramaiya
Savitri Bhavu (F)	IS	I	(T. Bhavu)
Sitarama Sharma	BR	IV	Kalakshetra
Subbarayan P.C.	IS	I	(A.P. Chokkalingam)
			(P.S. Minakshisundaram)
Swaminathan P.S.	IS	I	(P.S. Minakshisundaram)
(Swaminathan T.)	IS	I	(P.S. Minkashisundaram)
Vanaja Narayanan	BR	II	K.N. Dandayudapani
(Vasudevan T.M.)	IS	I	(Picchaiya)
		I	(P.C. Subbarayan)
Venkataraman T.V	BR	III	(M.D. Gauri)
		IV	(Vitthal Iyer)
Venkataraman P.	BR	II	(K.N. Dandayudapani)

There are a total of 42 included in this sample; ( ) indicates that they are deceased.
@ = information received from family member or other source (e.g. student)

CRITICS AND OTHERS (27)

Name	Caste	Background
Arudra	BR	dance critic, scholar
Bhuvarahan	BR	former dance critic
Chandran Rajiv	BR	dance critic
Devika V.R.	BR	dance critic
Gopi	BR	*mridangam* player and brother of Adyar Lakshmanan and K. Ramarao.
Janaki S.S.	BR	Sanskrit scholar
Khokhar Ashish	NB	dance critic
Khokhar Mohan	NB	dance critic, scholar
Kothari Sunil	NB	dance critic, Professor
Krishnan Akhila	BR	vocalist for many Bharata Natyam recitals
Nagaswamy R.	BR	organizer of Chidambaram festival, Archaeologist, scholar
Parthasarathy T.S.	BR	Secretary Music Academy, critic Indian Express, Madras, scholar
Pattabhi Raman N.	BR	editor-in-chief Sruti Magazine
(Prasad V.V.)	BR	dance critic
Rajalakshmi,	BR	vocalist for many Bharata Natyam recitals
Rajan	BR	former dance critic

Name	Caste	Background
Ranga Rao V.A.K.	BR	dance critic
Sankaran T.	IS	cousin of T. Balasaraswati, musicologist, writer
Sarada S.	BR	Sanskritist, Musician
Singh Shanta Serbajeet	NB	dance critic Hindustan Times, Delhi
Sivanandam Sarada	BR	professional *vina* player and the wife of K.P. Sivanandam a descendant of the Tanjore Quartet.
Srinivasan K.S.	BR	dance critic, scholar, musicologist
Subbudu	BR	dance critic, musicologist
Subramaniam V.	BR	composer of Bharata Natyam dance dramas, sociologist of the arts
Sundaram B.M.	IS	musicologist, scholar, critic
Vajifdar Shireen	NB	critic, Indian Express, Bombay
Vatsyayan Kapila	BR	scholar, Head of National Centre for Performing Arts, former dancer
Venkataraman Leela	BR	dance critic

ANALYSIS OF APPENDIX

ANALYSIS OF LIST I: DANCERS

DANCERS (INCLUDING DANCERS WHO ALSO TEACH DANCE)

Total sample of dancers = 145

ACTIVITIES

97 of them combined teaching dance with performing
16 have left the field
32 are just dancers

GENDER RATIO

Female	Male
128	17

Analysis by Community		Analysis by Community and Gender	
		Female	Male
Brahmin	87	81	6
Isai Vellala	36	35	1
Non Brahmin	22	14	8

ANALYSIS OF LIST II: TEACHERS

Total sample	42	
Deceased	18	(11 of them died after 1985: T.M. Vasudevan, T.K. Ganeshan, K.N. Pakkiriswami, V. Ramaiya, K.J. Govinda-rajan, V. Sadasivan, V.S. Muthuswamy, C. Kunchitapadam, Shanmugamsun-daram, Lalitha Shastri, S.K. Rajaratnam.)

SEX RATIO

Female	Male
1	41

Analysis by Community		Analysis by Community and Gender	
		Women	Men
Brahmin	7	1	6
Isai Vellala	33	1	32
Non Brahmin	2		

ANALYSIS BY *BANI*: DANCERS

DIVISION	NUMBER
DIVISION I	
Tanjore Quartet (*isai vellala*)	41
DIVISION II	
Traditions taught by hereditary teachers (*isai vellala*) with *devadasis* in their lineage	79
DIVISION III	
Devadasi banis	18
DIVISION IV	
Recent *banis*	33

(Some of my sample of both teachers and dancers have been trained in several *banis*.)

ANALYSIS BY *BANI*: TEACHERS

DIVISION	NUMBER
DIVISION I	
Tanjore Quartet (*isai vellala*) *bani*	19
DIVISION II	
Traditions initially taught by hereditary teachers (*isai vellala*) with *devadasis* in their family tree	18
DIVISION III	
Devadasi bani	3
DIVISION IV	
Recent *banis*	3

(Some of my sample of teachers have been trained in several *banis*.)

Amongst the dancers almost twice the number had trained in Division II over Division I; amongst the teachers it was evenly divided between Division I and Division II. In Divisions (III, IV), there were no more than three teachers represented however a significant number of dancers had been trained in these groups.

Glossary

abhinaya	the expressive aspect of the dance; mime expressing the meaning of a song.
Abhinayadarpana (AD)	a thirteenth century Sanskrit text on dance.
adarsha	ideal.
adavus	basic dance steps in Bharata Natyam.
alap	development of the melodic line where the rhythm is apparently free.
alapadma hasta	a hand position.
alarippu	a dance in the Bharata Natyam repertoire.
anandatandava	a vigorous (*tandava*) dance pose of Shiva which expresses bliss (*ananda*).
anjali	a double hand position.
archana	temple ritual.
arangetram	debut recital The first public recital given by a dancer. Traditionally *devadasis* presented their first recital before the God of the temple and later in a secular setting. It has now become the term for a first recital for any dance style as well as music. Originally regarded as a *devadasi* custom, at the beginning of the revival of the dance, high caste girls did not present an *arangetram*. Today it has become a necessary part of a dance career. It is the custom for the student to give gifts to the teacher at this time.
Arati	"light", waving of lights before the deity.
Ayyappan	a Hindu deity.
bani	a term used to describe different ways of dancing Bharata Natyam.
Bhagavata Mela	a dance drama from southern India traditionally

	performed by men.
bhajan(a)	devotional song.
bhakti	devotion.
Bharata Natyam	A classical dance style that evolved from the earlier concert repertoire of the style of dance known as *sadir/dasi-attam* from southern India. The name Bharata Natyam was adopted in about 1933.
bhava	feeling.
brahmin	The highest status group and the one which is believed to have the highest ritual purity.
bullok	a piece of jewellery worn by *devadasis* and dancers; nose ring worn in the centre of the nose.
chamara	flywhisk.
chatura hasta	a hand position.
chauk	a square
Chidambaram Mahatmya	a fourteenth century (A.D. 1313) Tamil text which relates the most important myth surrounding Siva as Nataraja.
choli	a blouse, usually short which is worn with a *sari*.
cinna melam	"small band"; the group of musicians who accompanied both the ritual and secular component of dance prior to 1947; the instruments were *mridangam*, *talam*, *mukhavina* and later the clarinet.
dakshina	literally a gift. Specifically the gift that is given in lieu of payment for knowledge.
darshan/darsan	"seeing"; especially something sacred or special, a time when the deity is present to be seen.
devadasi	literally a female servant of god. In practice it is the name for hereditary temple dancers. Often used interchangeably in Tamil Nadu with another caste name, *isai vellala*.
Devi Mahatmya	a portion of one of the *puranas* which describes the various heroic feats of the goddess.
dharma	duty.
dhoti	piece of cloth tied at the waist and used to

	cover the lower part of the body.
Duo	two dancers sharing a programme and performing simultaneously in some pieces and solo in others.
gandharva	celestial musician, also the name of a community of musicians.
gejjai-puja	"anklet (bell) worship"; the ritual performed when a girl is first given her anklets of bells and initiated into Bharata Natyam. The anklets are tied by the teacher. Often used to refer to the name of a dance recital prior to which the dancer is given her bells for the first time.
ghatam	A clay pot that is turned upside down and played like a musical instrument.
Guru	A name for all teachers of traditional arts. Originally the term was only used for spiritual teachers. Now, however, most male dance teachers, particularly in Delhi will be addressed as "Guruji". The term is now found in the south where "Masterji and Sir" is being replaced by "Guruji".
Gita Govinda	Sanskrit poem written by Jaya Deva in the twelfth century; each of the twenty-four songs is known as an *ashtapadi* and concerns the relationship of Krishna with his mistress-consort, Radha.
guru-kula	guru's household.
guru-shishya parampara	master-disciple succession.
gurukulavasa	a traditional method of exchanging work for knowledge, either spiritual or artistic. The student would live at the teacher's home be fed, clothed and taught in return for helping with menial tasks and obediently following the wishes of the guru.
hasta/mudra	hand gesture.
Hindi	an Indo-European language spoken mainly in north India. Hindi and English are India's official languages.
isai vellala	caste name given to hereditary musicians and dancers, in particular in Tamil Nadu.

ishtadevata	a deity one chooses to worship.
jatisvaram	a dance in the Bharata Natyam repertoire.
javali	a poem set to music and danced in Bharata Natyam.
Kalakshetra	a dance Academy founded in 1936 in Madras by Rukmini Devi, a brahmin dancer.
kalyanam	wedding, rite of passage for *devadasi*, a ritual marriage.
Kama	the Hindu god of love.
Kannada/Kanarese	a Dravidian language spoken in the state of Karnataka.
kapittha hasta	a hand position.
karana	the combined movements of hands and feet in dance as described in the *Natyashastra*.
Karnatic Music	system of music followed in the southern part of India distinct from the northern or Hindustani style; indigenous to the region where Dravidian languages are spoken.
Kathak	a dance style from North India.
Kathakali	a southern dance drama which originated in the state of Kerala.
kautuvam/kauttuvam	a piece of blank verse set to dance.
kolam	decorative patterns drawn on the ground with rice paste.
kolattam	a folk dance from the state of Tamil Nadu.
korvai	several basic steps (*adavus*) performed together.
Krishna	Hindu deity.
kriti	a musical composition in Karnatic music, came into existence in the 18th century, known earlier as *kirtana*.
Kshetrayya/Kshetrajna	seventeenth century south Indian composer; his compositions centre around *sringara rasa*; his signature was Muvvagopala.
Kuchipudi	a classical dance style that originated in the state of Andhra Pradesh. Originally only performed by men who took female roles; it is now also performed by women.
Kuladevata	the family deity. This deity is usually from one's ancestral place.

kumbharati	"pot light".
Kurati/Kuravanji	a gypsy girl. An important character in a *Kuravanji* dance drama. Also a single solo dance performed by a Kurati and included in a Bharata Natyam concert.
laya	rhythm, tempo, speed (in music).
Malayalam	a Dravidian language spoken in Kerala State.
mallari	a piece of *nagasvaram* music originally used exclusively in temple ritual; has been choreographed for Bharata Natyam.
mangalam	"auspicious", the last song sung at the end of a music or Bharata Natyam recital.
manodharma	artistic imagination.
svaras	solfege syllables.
margam	"path" the full Bharata Natyam repertoire of dances presented in the correct order *alarippu, jatisvaram, sabdam, varnam, padams, javalis* (optional) , *tillana, sloka.*
madi	a ritually pure state of a person.
matras	combinations of *aksharas*; used interchangeably with *akshara.*
mela	gathering.
melakkaran	a group of hereditary musicians from South India.
Mridangam	a two-headed drum played to accompany Karnatic music; instrumental, vocal as well as those dance styles that are performed to Karnatic Music; Bharata Natyam and Kuchipudi.
mudra/hasta	hand gestures used in dance.
mukhavina	a reed instrument played in the band of the *cinna melam.* In some temples it is still played for some *pujas.* It has eight finger holes and four extra ones. It is accompanied by a bagpipe called a *sruti upanga* which is used as a drone accompaniment.
Murugan	Hindu deity, also known as Skanda, Subrahmanyam, Subramaniam, Subrahmaniam, or Kumara.
Naganrittam	"snake dance", one of the dances

	choreographed for Bharata Natyam.
nagasvaram	reed instrument with a wooden conical bore. It is two to two and one half feet and enlarges downwards. There are seven finger holes at the bottom and five other holes that serve as controllers. A reed is introduced into the metal staple at the top. *Nagasvaram* is played in temple music and processions; it is one of the instruments of the *periya melam*; the music is auspicious and is important at weddings and other life cycle events; Hindu *nagasvaram* players generally belong to the *isai vellala* community.
Naidu	a caste name for certain persons from Andhra Pradesh. In this study some traditional musicians and dancers belong to this caste.
namaskaram/namaskar	reverential greeting.
nara-stuti	"man praise" , used to describe the lyrics of a song addressed to a human being, either male or female, rather than god.
Nataraja	"Lord of the dance", an aspect of the Hindu deity Siva in a dancing posture.
nattuvanar	person who conducts a Bharata Natyam orchestra.
nattuvangam	beating cymbals and speaking rhythmic syllables while conducting a Bharata Natyam orchestra.
natya	the mimetic portion of the dance.
Natya sastra (NS)	fourth-fifth century Sanskrit text which records the theory of drama, music, poetics, dance and general aesthetics.
nautch	dance, North Indian term.
nava sandhi kautuvam	nine poems to the nine guardians of the quarters (*dikpalas*).
nayaka	idealized hero.
nayika	idealized heroine.
nayika-nayaka-bhava	the emotions exchanged between a hero and heroine in love.
nityasumangali	ever (nitya) auspicious (sumangali), a name for *devadasis*

nritta	abstract or pure dance; decorative dance without a particular story.
Nrittaratnavali	a Sanskrit text written by Jaya Senapati in the thirteenth century.
nritya	mime that includes an emphasized rhythmic component.
Odissi	a dance style that originated from the eastern part of India, Orissa. It is a modern reconstruction of two traditions the *mahari* or temple tradition and the *gotipua* tradition, danced by boys in itinerant drama groups.
Oduvar	class of temple-singers who sing the Tevaram/Devaram in Saivite temples in southern India.
ottu	a double reed wind instrument; drone played in the *periya melam* orchestra.
padam	a poem set to music and enacted in Bharata Natyam.
pada/chauka varnam	the main dance in a modern Bharata Natyam recital with alternating rhythmic sections (*jatis*) and descriptive sections (*abhinaya*).
parampara	succession.
periya melam	"big band"; processional music in south Indian temples; traditionally the instru-ments are: *nagasvaram, tavil, talam, ottu*.
prasad	sanctified food.
pushpanjali	the name of a dance piece, offering of flowers; a double hand gesture.
puja	ritual worship of a deity, usually performed by decorating images or pictures of deities with flowers and other ritual acts.
Purana	books containing extensive sources of Hindu mythology, most have a strong sectarian bias.
Purandaradasa	composer of religious songs in the Dravidian language, Kannada; died 1564.
pushpaputa	hand gesture used for holding flowers.
raga	a pattern of notes arranged in a specific way; the *raga* system of music is unique to both north and south Indian music; musical mode; the basis of melody in Indian music.

rasa	"juice, flavour"; mood; the essence of an artistic experience, aesthetic tenor, aesthetics.
rasika	connoisseur
revival	a term applied by many writers to describe what happened to Bharata Natyam in the 1930s when persons from outside the hereditary tradition began studying and performing ("revivalists").
revivalists	the name of persons who wished to "revive" an older purer style of dance, later known as Bharata Natyam.
rudraksha	beads worn by renouncers; generally by Saivites.
sadhana	penance, dedication, practice.
sadir	the old name for the concert repertoire of dance performed by *devadasis*.
sahitya	text, libretto.
sampradaya	tradition; an orally transmitted artistic or religious tradition.
Telugu	a Dravidian language spoken in Andhra Pradesh. Many songs in Bharata Natyam and Kuchipudi are in this language.
sanchari bhava (*vyabhichari bhava*)	transitory states that carry or express sentiments.
Sangitratnakara	a thirteenth century Sanskrit text with details about music and dance attributed to Sarngadeva.
seva	service.
sabdam/shabdam	a dance in the Bharata Natyam repertoire.
Saivite	worshipper of Siva.
sarukal	"sliding"; name of one group of *adavus*.
sastra/shastra	doctrine or treatise.
sisya/shishya	disciple, pupil, student.
Siva/Shiva	one of the Hindu deities.
sloka/shloka	a Sanskrit verse form; the name of a type of dance in Bharata Natyam that has been choreographed to verses of this kind.
solkattu/sholkattu	mnemonic syllables that accompany basic dance steps (*adavus*); generic term for syllables that name drum syllables.

sringara/shringara/ *shringar/sringara*	erotic love.
sruti (box)	a bellows box which serves as a drone.
suchi hasta	a hand position used in the dance.
tala	time-cycle.
talaisaman	jewellery worn on the head by dancers.
talam/tattu-kal	a block of wood beaten with a stick of wood or two metal cymbals that are beaten. The former is beaten during a dance class, the latter in performance. The metal *talam* are of different sizes depending upon where they are used; *talam* are played during a Bharata Natyam dance recital by a *nattuvanar*. *Talam* is the Tamil equivalent for *tala* and can also refers to the tempo.
Tamil	a Dravidian language spoken in Tamil Nadu. Many of the songs in Bharata Natyam are in Tamil, particularly the newer compositions. It is also the name of a people who trace their origins to Tamil Nadu.
tana varnam	*varnam* composed primarily as a piece of music.
tandava	"vigorous wild dance"; Siva performs this dance.
Tanjore Quartet	four brothers who received the patronage of the Tanjore Court at beginning of the nineteenth century; attributed to have composed most of the repertoire regarded as traditional.
tanpura	a stringed instrument used as a drone.
tattu	strike, pat.
tattu-kal	the block of wood and stick that are beaten during a Bharata Natyam dance class.
Telugu	Dravidian language spoken in Andhra Pradesh; songs in Bharata Natyam and Kuchipudi are in this language; the name of people who trace their origins to Andhra Pradesh.
tavil	barrel-shaped wooden drum used to accompany *nagasvaram* and temple processional music.
Tevaram/Devaram	collection of Tamil poetry written from the seventh to the tenth century; the songs are

	addressed to both Siva and Vishnu. Collective name given to the sacred hymns of three great saints Tirujnanasambandar, Apparsvamikal and Sundaramurti Nayanar.
tillana	a dance in the Bharata Natyam repertoire.
tirmanam	a rhythmic structure repeated three times. In practice *jati* and *tirmanam* are used interchangeably.
Tiruppuhul	Tamil songs written in the fifteenth century by Arunagiri, a devotee of one of the Hindu deities known by many names Subrahmnayam/ Subramnya/Skanda/ Murugan.
Tiruttani	a temple town in South India.
tradition	a term used to describe different ways of dancing Bharata Natyam.
tutti	a small bag-pipe like instrument used to produce a continuous drone; played in the *cinna melam*.
upacharas	prescribed ways of worship in a Hindu temple.
Vaishnavite	worshipper of Vishnu.
varnam	a dance in the Bharata Natyam repertoire.
vina	plucked lute-type of stringed instrument with frets set in wax
viraha	a state of anxiety generally induced by separation from one's beloved.
Vishnu	one of the Hindu deities.
Vrata	a religious observance that takes place as a result of a vow.
zamindar	member of land-owning gentry.

Bibliography

Abhinayadarpana, 1957, trans M. Ghosh, Calcutta: Firma K.L. Mukhopadhyay.

Anon, 1821, "A Visit to Madras Being a Sketch of the Local and Characteristic Peculiarities of the Presidency in the year 1811", in *Voyages and Travels*, Vol. V, pp. 23-35, London.

Aiya, Nagam, 1906, *The Travancore State Manual*, Vol II, Travancore.

Altekar, A.S., 1962, *The Position of Women in Hindu Civilization*, New Delhi: Motilal Banarsidas.

Ambrose, Kay, 1957, *Classical Dances and Costumes of India,* London: Adam and Charles Black.

Anand, Mulk Raj, 1977, "Coomaraswamy's Holistic View of Art", *Marg,* Bombay.

Appadurai, Arjun, 1981, *Worship and Conflict Under Colonial Rule, A South Indian Case*, Cambridge: Cambridge University Press.

Appaswamy, Jaya, 1980, *Tanjore Paintings of the Maratha Period*, New Delhi: Abhinav.

Archaeological Survey of India, 1919, Annual Progress Report for the Archaeological Survey of India for the Year Ending March 31, 1919.

Arudra, 1985a, "Chandralekha's Angika, Striking a Blow for Innovation", *Sruti* 20-20S: 51-54, Madras.

————1985b, "Suddha Nrittam: A Mangudi Specialty", *Sruti* 1985,16: 10-11, Madras.

———— ——1986, "Jewels of the Dance Repertoire II, Salvaging After the Decline", in *Sruti*: 25, Madras.

Atre, Prabha, 1986, "Teaching Music at Institutions", *Sangeet Natak* 79: 58-64, New Delhi.

Ayyangar, R. Rangaramanuja, 1972, *History of South Indian (Carnatic) Music*, Madras.

Ayyar, Jagadisa, P.V., 1920, *South Indian Shrines*, Madras; 1922, *South Indian Shrines*, revised edition, Madras.

Ayyar, Ramakrishna, 1946, *Economy of a South Indian Temple*, Annamalainagar.

Babb, Lawrence A., 1975, *The Divine Hierarchy: Popular Hinduism in Central India*, New York: Columbia University Press.

Balamurli, Krishna, 1984, "Tradition Is What Survives", *Sruti*, Jan-Feb, pp. 34-35.

Balasaraswati, T., 1980, "Bharata Natyam", *The Sacred and The Secular*, V. Subramaniam (Ed), New Delhi: Ashish, pp. 98-108.

—————1982 "Reflections", *National Centre for Performing Arts Quarterly*, Bombay, pp. 6-14.

—————1984, "On Bharatanatyam", *Sangeet Natak* 72-73: 8-14, New Delhi.

Banerji, Projesh, 1982, *Uday Shankar and His Art*, Delhi: B.R. Publishing Corporation.

Barboza, Francis, 1985, "Christian Themes in Bharatanatyam", *Bharatanatyam, Yesterday, Today, Tomorrow*, ed. L. Ramanathan, Delhi: Golden Heritage, pp. 29-32.

Basham, A.L., 1967, *The Wonder that Was India*, Delhi: Fontana Books.

Baskaran, S. Theodore, 1981, *The Message Bearers: Nationalist Politics and the Entertainment Media in South India, 1880-1945,* Madras: Cre-A.

Basu, Aparna, 1986, *The Pathfinder: Dr Muthulakshmi Reddy*, New Delhi: All India Women's Conference.

Bazaz, P.N., 1959, *Daughters of the Vitasta*, New Delhi.

Bhandarkar, D.R., 1911-12, "The Chahamanas of Marwar", *Epigraphica Indica*, Vol. XI: 26-30.

Bhandarkar, Sir R.G., 1965, *Vaishnavism, Saivism and Minor Religious Systems*, Varanasi.

Bhavnani, Enakshi, 1965, *The Dance in India*, Bombay: D.B. Taraporevala.

Bhushan, V.N., 1939, "Nritya Niranjan", *Roopa-Lekha*, Vol. I, Serial I (July), Bombay, pp. 47-64.

Boner, Alice, 1972, *New Light on the Sun Temple at Konarak*, Varanasi.

Bor, Joep , 1975, "Raga, Species and Evolution", *Sangeet Natak*, No. 35, January-March, New Delhi, pp. 17-48.

Bose, Mandakranta, 1970, *Classical Indian Dancing, A Glossary*, Calcutta: General Printers and Publishers.

—————1989, *The Evolution of Classical Indian Dance Literature: A Study of the Sanskrit Tradition*, D.Phil. thesis, Oxford University.

Bowers, Faubion, 1956, *Theatre in the East, A Survey of Asian Dance and Drama*, London: Thomas Nelson.

Brown, R., 1965, *The Mrdanga: A Study of Drumming In South India*, Doctoral thesis, Wesleyan University: Middletown, Conn.

Bruner, Helene, 1990, Book Review of "*Nityasumangali, Devadasi Tradition in South India*", Delhi: Motilal Banarsidas (1987), *Indo-Iranian Journal*, 33, No 2: 121-42.

Brown, Percy, 1965, *Indian Architecture* (Buddhist and Hindu Periods) Bombay: D.B. Taraporevala.

———1975, *Indian Architecture, Islamic Period*, Bombay: D.B. Taraporevala.

Buchanan-Hamilton Dr. Francis, 1807, *Journey from Madras Through Mysore, Kanara and Malabar*, 3 vols. London.

Bundle, 1846, *Tanjore Palace Records*, Saraswati Mahal Libråry, Tanjore.

Carmichael, Amy-Wilson, 1904, *Things as they Are*, London.

———1910 *Lotus Buds*, London.

Census of India, 1901, Vol. XIII, Madras Report, 1891, Vol XV, Madras Report, Part 1, 1901.

Chandra, Moti, 1973, *The World of Courtesans*, Delhi.

Chaitanya, Krishna, 1987, "Naive Longings for Winds of Change", *Sangeet Natak* (January-March), pp. 5-13, New Delhi.

Chari, V.K., 1980, "The Rasa Theory: Theology or Aesthetics", *The Sacred and the Secular in India's Performing Arts*, ed. V. Subramaniam, Delhi: Ashish, pp. 47-61.

———1990, *Sanskrit Criticism*, Honolulu, University of Hawaii Press.

Chatterjee, Ashok, 1979, *Dances of the Golden Hall*, New Delhi, Indian Council for Cultural Relations.

Chatterjee, Margaret, 1984, *The Religious Spectrum, Studies in an Indian Context*, New Delhi: Allied.

Chatterjee, Santosh, K., 1945, *Devadasi*, Calcutta.

Chattopadhyay, Aparna, 1967, "The Institution of *Devadasi* According to the Kathasaritsagara", *Journal of the Oriental Institute Baroda*, XVI, No. 3: pp. 216-22, Baroda.

Chaudhuri, Buddhadeb, 1981, *The Bakreshwar Temple: A Study on Continuity and Change*, Delhi: Inter-India.

Coomaraswamy, Ananda K. 1917, 1970, *The Mirror of Gesture, Being the Abhinaya Darpana of Nandikesvara*, New Delhi: Munshiram Manoharlal.

——— 1947, "Renaissance of Indian Culture", *Journal of the India*

Society of Oriental Art, Calcutta, pp. 7-17.

———— 1968, *The Dance of Siva*, New Delhi: Sagar.

Cornish, W.R., 1871, *Report on the Census of the Madras Presidency*, Vol. 1: 167-8, Madras.

Cornish, Henry Dauncey, 1937, *A Short Manual of Hindu Law*, London.

Dandayudapani, K.N. 1974, *Aadalisai Amutham*, Madras: Natyakalalayam.

Das, K.R., 1964, *Temples of Tamilnad*, Bombay: Bharatiya Vidya Bhavan.

Dasarupa: A Treatise on Hindu Dramaturgy, by Dhananjaya trans. by George C.O. Haas, New York, 1912.

Dasgupta, S.N., 1959, *Hindu Mysticism*, New York: Frederick Ungar.

Das Gupta, H.C., 1946, *History of the Indian Stage*, Vols. I and II, Calcutta.

Dass, R.M., 1961, *The Women in Manu and his Seven Commentators*, Varanasi.

De Zoete, Beryl, 1953, *The Other Mind, A Study of Dance in South India*, London: Camelot Press.

Dehejea, Vidya, 1988, *Slaves of the Lord: The Path of the Tamil Saints*, Delhi: Munshiram Manoharlal.

Desai, Neera, 1957, *Women in Modern India*, Bombay.

Deva, Chaitanya, 1973, *An Introduction to Indian Music*, New Delhi: Publications Division, Ministry of Information and Broadcasting.

————1974, *Indian Music*, New Delhi: Indian Council for Cultural Relations.

————1978, *Musical Instruments of India: Their History and Development*, Calcutta: Firma KLM.

————1987, *Musical Instruments of India, Their History and Development*, New Delhi: Munshiram Manoharlal.

Devdas, Nalini, 1980, "Sri Aurobindo's Views on the Creation and Enjoyment of Arts", *The Sacred and the Secular in India's Performing Arts*, V. Subramaniam (ed.), New Delhi: Ashish, pp. 163-78.

Devi, Ragini, 1962, *Dances of India, with an appendix on Indian Music*, Calcutta: Sushil Gupta Pvt. Ltd.,

————1972, 89, *Dance Dialects of India*, New Delhi: Vikas.

Devi, Rukmini, 1963, "The Spiritual Background of Bharata Natyam" in *Marg*, Bombay, pp. 5-6.

————1985, "Bharata Natyam Sastra in Practice" *Bharata Natyam Yesterday, Today and Tomorrow*, ed. by Leela Ramanathan, New Delhi: Sujata Dinesh, pp. 17-28.

Dhananjayan, V.P., 1984, *A Dancer on Dance*, Madras: Bharata Kalanaji.

Dhar, Somnath., 1956, *Kalhana, Poet Historian of Kashmir*, Bangalore.

Dikshitar, Raja Somasekhara, 1969, *The History of Chidambaram, Sri*

Nataraja's Temple, Tanjore: Panditha Raja.

Dubois, Abbe J.A., 1897, 1972, *Hindu Manners, Customs and Ceremonies*, New Delhi: (1972) Oxford University Press.

Dumont, Louis, 1956, *Homo Hierarchicus*, London: Granada.

Encyclopedia of Tamil Studies, 1990 "Aham", Vol I: 149-59, Institute of Asian Studies, Thiruvanmiyur, Madras.

Enthovin, R.E., 1920, *Tribes and Castes of Bombay*, Vol. I, Bombay.

Erdman, J.L., 1984, "Who Should Speak For the Performing Arts? The Case of the Delhi Dancers", *Cultural Policy in India*, ed. Lloyd Rudolph, Delhi: Chanakya.

————1985, *Patrons and Performers in Rajasthan, The Subtle Tradition*, Delhi: Chanakya.

Fawcett, F., 1891, "On Basavis; Women, who through Dedication to a Deity Assume Masculine Privileges", *Journal of the Anthropological Society of Bombay*, Vol. II, No. 6: 322-45, Bombay.

————1900-01, Bulletin, Madras Government House, Vol. III. No. 1: 1-85 and Vol III. No. 3:193-318.

Fleet, J.F., "Sanskrit and Old Canarese Inscriptions", *Indian Antiquary*, 1874: III; 1876: V; 1877: VI;1878: VII; 1879: VIII; 1880: IX; 1881: X; 1882: XI.

Francis, W. *Census of India* 1901, Madras.

Fuller, C.J., 1984, *Servants of the Goddess; The Priests of a South Indian Temple*, Cambridge: Cambridge University Press.

Gaston, Anne-Marie, 1980, "The Place of Indian Classical Dance in Traditional Indian Culture", *The Sacred and the Secular in Indian Performing Arts*, V. Subramaniam (ed.), New Delhi: Ashish, pp. 62-85.

————1982, *Siva in Dance, Myth, and Iconography*, New Delhi, 1985, 90, Oxford University Press.,

————1983, "The Effect of Changing Patronage on Indian Performing Arts", *Proceedings of the 10th International Congress of Sociology*, *Mexico City, 1982*. Institute of Culture: Sophia, Bulgaria, pp. 297-308.

————1988, "East Indian Classical Dance in Canada: The Potential for Touring and Performing", Report prepared for the Touring Office of the Canada Council, Ottawa.

————1990, "Dance Recitals at the Madras Music Academy, 1931-1988", *Journal of the Madras Music Academy*, Madras, pp. 116-145.

————1991a, "Dance and the Hindu Woman, Bharatanatyam Re-

Ritualized", *Roles and Rituals for Hindu Women*, Julia Leslie (ed.), London: Pinter.

—————1991b, "Bharata Natyam, A Classical East Indian Dance Style in Transition", *South Asian Studies Journal*, Cambridge.

—————1991c, *Continuity and Re-Creation in the Performing Arts of India; A Study of Two Artistic Traditions*, D.Phil. thesis, Oxford University.

—————1991d, "Development of the Repertoire in Bharata Natyam", *Journal of the Madras Music Academy*, Madras, pp. 95-134.

—————1994, "Secularization and De-Secularization of Indian Classical Dance", *South Asian Horizons: Enriched by South Asia*, ed. E. Tepper and J. Wood, Carleton University Press, pp. 15-34.

Gombrich, Richard, 1971, *Precept and Practice*, Oxford: Clarendon Press.

Gnoli, Raniero, 1956, *The Aesthetic Experience According to Abhinavagupta*, Rome.

Gonda, Jan, 1973, *A History of Indian Literature, Vedic Literature*, Wiesbaden.

Gopal, Ram. and Dadachanji., 1951, *Indian Dancing*, London: Phoenix.

————— 1957, *Rhythm in the Heavens*, London: Secker and Warburg.

Government of Madras, 1948, *The Madras Devadasis (Prevention) Act, 1947*, Published Madras Act XXXI of 1947.

Government of Madras (Law) Legislative Department GO. No. 23, January 26, 1948: Acts.

Govindarajan, Hema, 1985, "Nattuvangam", *Bharata Natyam, Yesterday, Today and Tomorrow*, Leela Ramanathan (ed.), Delhi: Sujata Dinesh, pp. 21-22.

Griffin R.T.H., 1853, trans. of Kalidasa's *The Birth of the War God* (*Kumarasambhava*), London.

Hanna, Judith Lynne, 1983, *The Performer Audience Connection, Emotion to Metaphor in Dance and Society*, Austin: University of Texas.

Hardy, Friedhelm, 1978, "Ideology and Cultural Contexts of the Srivaisnava temple" in *South Indian Temples*, ed. by Burton Stein, Delhi, Vikas

————— 1983, *Viraha-Bhakti;The Early History of Krsna Devotion in South India*, New Delhi: Oxford University Press.

Hardgrave, Robert L. and Stephen M. Slawek, 1988/89, "Instruments and Music Culture in 18th Century India, The Solvyns Portraits", *Asian Music*, XX #1: 1-92, New York.

Harle, J.C., 1963, *Temple Gateways in South India*, Delhi: Oxford University Press.

Hemingway, F.R., 1906, *Madras District Gazetteer, Tanjore*, Vol. I, Madras.

――――――1907, *Gazetteer of the Godavari District*, Madras.

Higgins, Jon Borthwick, 1973, *The Music of Bharata Natyam*, Ph. D. Wesleyan University.

――――――1976, "From Prince to Populace, Patronage as a Determinant of Change in South India (Karnatic Music)", *Asian Music*, Vol. Vll-2: 20-6.

――――――1983, "Balasaraswati's 'Tisram Alarippu', the Musical Content", *Performing Arts in India*, Bonnie C. Wade (ed.), Berkeley: Centre For South and South East Asian Studies.

Hobsbawm E. and Ranger T., 1989, *The Invention of Tradition*, Cambridge: Cambridge University Press.

Horner, I.B., 1930, *Women Under Primitive Buddhism*, London.

Huizinga, Johan, 1955, *A Study of the Play Element in Culture,* Boston: Beacon.

India Today, New Delhi

Iyengar, Srinivasa C.R., 1948, *Indian Dance (Natya and Nritya)*, Madras: Blaze.

Iyer, E. Krishna, 1933, *Personalities in Present Day Music*, Madras: Rochouse and Sons.

―――――― 1935, *Bharata Natyam*, Madras.

―――――― 1963a, "A Brief Historical Survey of Bharata Natyam", *Marg*, Bombay, pp. 7-9.

―――――― 1963b, "Genealogies of Gurus", *Marg*, Bombay, pp. 37-40.

―――――― 1963c "A Note on the Repertory from *Alarippu* to *Tillana*", *Marg*, Bombay, pp. 41-58.

―――――― 1969, "Bhagavata Mela Dance Drama of Bharata Natyam", *Sangeet Natak,*, No. 13: 46-7.

Iyer, K. Bharatha, 1963, *Kathakali: The Sacred Dance-Drama of Malabar*, New Delhi: Oriental Books Reprint Corp.

Jeanes, Rosemary, 1982, *Tradition and Learning in Odissi Dance of India*, Master of Fine Arts Thesis, York University, Toronto.

Jha, Akhileshwar, 1980, *The Imprisoned Mind, Guru Sisya Tradition in Indian Culture*, New Delhi: Ambika.

Jhabvala, Ruth Prawer, 1966, "Introduction, Myself in India", *How I Became the Holy Mother and Other Stories*, Harmondsworth, Middlesex: Penguin.

Journal of the Madras Music Academy, 1932, Debate held on the sixth day of the annual Conference, December 28, 1932 on "The

Encouragement of Bharata Natyam", pp. 113-23.

Joshi, O.P., 1985, *Sociology of Indian Art*, Jaipur: Rawat.

Kamaliah, K.C., 1987, *Vision of the Sacred Dance*, Madras: Kamaliah.

Kaemmer, John E., 1980, "Between the Event and the Tradition: A New Look at Music in the Socio-Cultural Systems", *Ethnomusicology*, XXIV (January), No. 1: 61-74.

Kalhana, 1900, *Rajatarangini, a Chronicle of the Kings of Kashmir*, trans. M.S. Stein, 2 Vols. Westminster.

Kalidasa, 1966, *Malavikagnimitra*, ed. and trans. C.R. Devadhar, Delhi.,
————1853, *The Birth of the War God (Kumarasambhava)*, trans. R.T.H. Griffith, London.

Kane, P.V., 1941, *History of Dharma Sastra*, Vol. II, Part I. Government Oriental Series, Class B, No. 6, Poona.

Kautilya, 1961, *Arthasastra*, trans. K.P. Kangle, Bombay.

Kersenboom, Saskia C., 1984, *Nityasumangali, Towards the Semiosis of the Devadasi Tradition of South India*, Doctoral Thesis, University of Utrecht, Holland.
———— 1987, *Nityasumangali, Devadasi Tradition in South India*, Delhi: Motilal Banarsidas.
———— 1990, "Devadasi Murai", *Sangeet Natak* 96: 44-54.

Khokar, Mohan, 1963a, "The Tradition: A Brief Historical Survey", *Marg*, Bombay, pp. 7-11.
———— 1963b, "The 108 *Karanas* at Chidambaram", *Marg*, Bombay, pp. 13-15.
———— 1963c, "*Adavus*, the Basic Dance Units of Bharata Natyam", *Marg*, Bombay, pp. 16-26.
———— 1963d, "Natya, Bhagavata Mela and Kuchipudi", *Marg*, Bombay, pp. 27-36.
————1964, *Bharata Natyam Vidwan, Muthukumarapillai,* New Delhi: Sangeet Natak Akademi.
———— 1980, *Traditions of Indian Classical Dance*, London: Peter Owen.
————1983, *His Dance, His Life, A Portrait of Uday Shankar*, New Delhi: Himalayan Books.
———— 1987, "A Momentous Transition", *Sangeet Natak* (April-June) pp. 41-47, New Delhi.

Kippen, J., 1988, *The Tabla of Lucknow: A Cultural Analysis of a Musical Tradition*, Cambridge: Cambridge University Press.

Kothari, Sunil, 1979, *Bharata Natyam, Indian Classical Dance Art*, Bombay: Marg Publications.

——————1988, "East-West Dance Encounters", *Sangeet Natak*, 89-90: 30-47, New Delhi.

Kramrisch, S., 1924, "The Vishnudharmottaram", *Journal of the Department of Letters*, Vol. IX, University of Calcutta, pp. 1-56.

Krishnamurti, Yamini, 1996, *A Passion for Dance, An Autobiography*, New Delhi: Viking.

Krishnamoorthy, K., 1985, "The Evolution of *Rasas* in Indian Literature", *Sangeet Natak* 75: 14-27, New Delhi.

Kuppuswamy, Gowri and M. Hariharan, 1979, *Readings on Music and Dance*, Delhi: B.R. Publishing Corporation.

——————1984, *Royal Patronage of Indian Music*, Delhi: Sundeep Prakashan.

——————1981, *Indian Dance and Music Literature, a Select Bibliography*, New Delhi: Biblia.

——————1982, *Glimpses of Indian Music*, Delhi: Sundeep Prakashan.

Lakhia, Kumudini, 1987, "Classical Dance Technique in Dance-Drama", *Sangeet Natak*, No. 85-86, New Delhi.

Lannoy, Richard, 1971 *The Speaking Tree—A Study of Indian Culture and Society*, Oxford: Oxford University Press.

L'Armand, Kathleen, and L'Armand, Adrien, 1978, "The Urbanization of a Cultural Tradition" in *Eight Urban Musical Cultures, Tradition and Change*, Bruno Nettl (ed.), Urbana Illinois: University of Illinois, pp. 115-45.

——————1983, "One Hundred Years of Music in Madras: A Case Study in Secondary Urbanization", *Ethnomusicology*, 27: 411-38, Michigan: Ann Arbor.

Lath, Mukund, 1989, "The 'Modern', the 'Traditional', and Criticism in the Indian Musical Tradition", *Sangeet Natak* 89-90: 5-15, Delhi.

Laws of Manu, trans. G. Buhler, *Sacred Books of the East*, Vol. 25, Delhi, 2nd reprint, 1967.

Legislative Assembly Debates of India,, 1922, 2nd session, "Resolution Re Prohibition of Traffic in Minor Girls", 27 February 1922: 2599-615.

Leiderer P.F. Beatrix, Lutze Lothan, 1985, *The Hindi Film, Agent and ReAgent of Cultural Change*. Delhi: Manohar.

Lele, Jayant, 1981, *Tradition and Modernity in Bhakti Movements*, International Studies in Sociology and Anthropology, Leiden: Brill.

Leslie, I. Julia, 1989, *The Perfect Wife The Orthodox Hindu Woman* Delhi: Oxford University Press.

Lipsey, Roger, 1977, *Coomaraswamy, Traditional Art and Symbolism*, Princeton: Princeton University Press.

Luther, Narendra, 1980, "Urban Culture in the Performing Arts", *Sangeet Natak*, No. 58, New Delhi, pp. 47-51.

Mandelbaum, David, G., 1984, *Society In India: Continuity and Change,* Vol II, Bombay: Popular Prakashan.

Manikam, V.T., 1968. "Harlots in Ancient Tamil Literature", *International Conference Seminar of Tamil Studies*, Kuala Lumpur.

Marg Magazine, 1963, *Indian Classical Dance*: Bombay, J.J. Bhabha.

————1968, *Chhau Dances of India*, Vol. XXII.

————1973, *Mohiniattam*, Vol XXVI, No. 2,

————1979, 1982, *Bharata Natyam, Indian Classical Dance Art*.

————1982, *Sivaji and the Facets of Maratha Culture*.

————1984, *Symbols and Manifestations in Indian Art*.

Marglin, Frederique, Appefel, 1985, *Wives of the God King*, New Delhi, Oxford.

Menon, Narayan, 1952, "About Indian Music", *Times of India Annual*: Bombay, pp. 59-75.

————1963, 70, *Balasaraswati*, New Delhi: International Cultural Centre.

————1984, "Bala's Repertoire", *Sangeet Natak*, No.72-73: 69-75.

————1988, "Tradition and Modernity", *Sangeet Natak*, No. 89-90: 48-52, New Delhi.

Miles Arthur, 1933, *The Land of the Lingam*, London: Hurst and Blackett.

Misra, Susheela, 1981, *Great Masters of Hindustani Music*, New Delhi: Hem Publishers.

————1985, *Music Makers of the Bhatkande College of Hindustani Music*, Calcutta: Sangeet Research Academy.

Mitter, Partha, 1977, *Much Maligned Monsters*, Oxford: Oxford University Press.

————1983-84, "The Doctrine of Swadeshi Art: Art and Nationalism in Bengal", *Visva-Bharati Quarterly*, Vol. 49, No. 1-4, May 1983-April 1984, Santiniketan, pp. 82-95.

Morinis, Alan E., 1984, *Pilgrimage in the Hindu Tradition, A Case study of Bengal*, Delhi: Oxford University Press.

Nagaswamy, R., 1965, "The South Indian Temple—as an Employer", *The Indian Economic and Social History Review*, Vol II, No 4: 367-372.

————1984, "Rajaraja Chola and the Dance", *Sruti*, 13: 7.

Nannithamby, Lokanayaky, 1969, "The Fine Arts and Recreation during the Cola Period", *Journal of Tamil Studies,* Vol. I, No. I: 59-71.

Narasimhan, Jassy, 1986, "Portrait of a Pathfinder", *Dr Muthulakshmi Reddy, The Pathfinder*, New Delhi: All India Women's Conference, pp. 13-16.

Narayan, Rajayee, 1989, "Role of Music in Dance", *Shanmukha*, XV, No. 2: 31-33, Bombay.

Narayan, Kalanidhi, 1989, "*Sthayi Bhava*-Its significance in Abhinaya Choreography and Scope For Variations", *Shanmukha*, XV, No. 2: 21-2, Bombay.

Natya Sastra, 1967, by Bharata, Vol I, Vol II, trans. and text ed. M. Ghosh.

Nettl, Bruno (ed), 1978, *Eight Urban Musical Cultures, Tradition and Change*, Chicago: University of Illinois.

——————— 1985, *The Western Impact on World Music, Change, Adaptation and Survival*, New York: Schimer.

Neuman, Daniel, 1976, "Towards an Ethnomusicology of Cultural Change in Asia", *Asian Music*, Vll-2: 1-5.

———————1977, "The Social Organization of a Music Tradition, Hereditary Specialists in North India", *Ethnomusicology*, XX1, No.2: 233-245.

———————1978, "*Gharanas*: The Rise of Musical 'Houses' in Delhi and Neighbouring Cities", *Eight Urban Musical Cultures, Tradition and Change*, Bruno Nettl (ed.), Urbana Illinois: University of Illinois, pp. 186-222.

———————1980, *The Life of Music in North India; The Organization of an Artistic Tradition*, Delhi: Manohar.

New Grove Dictionary of Music and Musicians, 1980 ed. Stanley Sadie, Macmillan: London, pp. 69-166.

O'Connell, Joseph T., 1985, *Bengal Vaisnavism, Orientalism, Society and the Arts*, Michigan: Asian Studies Centre.

O'Flaherty, Wendy, 1973, *Asceticism and Eroticism in the Mythology of Siva*, London.

———————1975, *Hindu Myths*, Harmondsworth.

Parthasarathy, T.S., 1983, "Kshetregna, and Other *Pada* Composers", *Sangeet Natak*, 69: 5-8.

———————1985, "*Padams* and Short Lyrics in Dance", *Sangeet Natak*, 75: 39-45.

———————1989, "*Suddha Nrittam*", *Shanmukha*, XV, 2: 23-24.

Parvati Kumar, Acharya, 1989, "Contributions of the Maratha Rulers— Their Influence on the Contemporary Bharata Natyam Scene", *Shanmukha*, XV, 2: 25-9.

Patnaik, D.N., 1971, *Odissi Dance*, Bhubaneshwar: Orissa Sangeet Natak Akademi.

Penzer, N.M., 1924, "Sacred Prostitution", Appendix IV in Somadeva's

Kathasaritsagara, trans. C.H. Tawney, London, pp. 231-80.

Pillai J.M. Somasundaram, 1958, *The Great Temple at Tanjore*, Tanjore: Tanjore Palace Devastanams.

Pillay, K.K., 1953, *The Sucindram Temple*, Kalakshetra: Madras.

————1963, "The Temple as a Cultural Centre", *Journal of Oriental Research, Madras*, XXIX, Part I-IV: 83-94.

Ponnuswamy, S., 1972, *Sri Thyagaraja Temple Thiruvarur*, Madras: State Dept of Archaeology.

Popley, H.A., 1986, *The Music of India*, Delhi: Award Publishing House.

Powers, Harold S., 1979, "Classical Music, Cultural Roots and Colonial Rule: An Indic Musicologist Looks at the Muslim World", *Asian Music*, XII: 5-39.

————1980, "Language Models and Musical Analysis", *Ethnomusicology*, 1: 1-60.

Prajnanananda, Swami, 1981, *A Historical Study of Indian Music*, Delhi: Munshiram Manoharlal.

Pran, Neville, 1990, "The Nautch Girls and the Sahib", in *The India Magazine*, 10, New Delhi, January, pp. 42-53.

Preston, James J., 1980, *Cult of the Goddess; Social and Religious Change in a Hindu Temple*, Delhi: Vikas.

Pudukkottai State Inscriptions, 1929, Chronological List of Inscriptions of the Pudukkottai State.

Punekar, S.D. and Rao, K., 1962, *A Study of Prostitutes in Bombay*, Bombay.

Quinn, Jennifer, 1982, *Marathi and Konkani Speaking Women in Hindustani Music 1880-1940*, Doctoral thesis: University of Minnesota.

Raghavan, V. and C. Ramanujachari, 1966, *Spiritual Heritage of Thyagaraja*, Mylapore: Sri Ramakrishnamath.

Raghavan, V., 1949, "Merattur Kasinatha—A Composer of Sabdas of the 18th Century", *Journal of the Madras Music Academy*, XIV: 130-34.

————1951, *Sringara Manjari of Saint Akbar Shah*, Hyderbad.

————1963, "Her Infinite Variety", *Journal of the Madras Music Academy*, XXXIV, Parts I-IV: 124-31.

————1964, *The Great Integrators: The Saint-Singers of India*, New Delhi: Publications Division.

————1967a, "Uparupakas and Nrtya Prabandhas", *Samskrita-Ranga Annual*, 5: 31-54,, Madras.

————1967b, *The Number of Rasas*, Adyar Library Series, Vol. 23, Madras.

————1973, "Bharata Natya", in *Journal of the Madras Music Academy*, XLV.

————1978, *Bhoja's Sringara Prakasa*, Madras: Ministry of Education and Social Welfare.

Raikar, Y.A., 1963, "Prostitution during the Yadava Period", *Journal of The Oriental Institute Baroda*, XIII, No. 2.

Rakesagupta, 1967, *Studies in Nayaka, Nayika Bheda*, Aligarh: Granthayan.

Ramachandran, Anandi, 1984, "Interview with Vempati Chinna Satyam, Tradition and Change in Kuchipudi", *Sruti*, 13: 32-3.

Ramachandran, Nirmala, 1969, "Classical Dance of the Ancient Tamils", *Proceedings of the First International Conference of Tamil Studies in 1966*, Vol II: 379-88.

Raman, Pattabhi and Anandi Ramachandran, 1984, "The Whole World in Her Hands", *Sangeet Natak*, No. 72-73, New Delhi, pp. 15-54.

Ramanathan Leela, 1985, *Bharata Natyam Yesterday, Today and Tomorrow*, Delhi: Sujata Dinesh.

Ramnarayan, Gauri, 1984-85, "The Vazhuvur Dance Tradition: Two Perspectives", *Sruti*, 14: 4-45.

Ranade, Ashok D. 1987, "Devotional Music In India", *Sangeet Natak*, 85-86.

———— 1988, "Music and its non-Music Uses", *Sangeet Natak*, 89-90: 24-29.

Rangacharya, Adya, 1966, *Introduction to Bharata's Natya Sastra*, Bombay: Popular Prakashan.

Redfield, James, and Milton Singer, 1956, "The Cultural Role of Cities", *Man in India*, 36, No. 3: 161-94.

Regunathan, Sudha, 1985, "*Abhinaya*, the Path to *Rasa*", *Sangeet Natak*, 75: 46-8.

Rele, Kanak, 1988, "Indian Classical Dance and the Challenge of its Preservation", *Sangeet Natak*, 89-90: 63-70.

Rg Veda, 1963, trans. R T.H. Griffith, 4th ed., Chowkamba Sanskrit Series, 35. 2 Vols., Varanasi.

Richmond, Farley, P. Swann, L. Darius L. Phipip Zarrilli, 1990, *Indian Theatre: Traditions of Performance*, Honolulu: University of Hawaii Press.

Rosenthal, Ethel, 1980, *The Story of India Music and Its Instruments*, New Delhi: Oriental Books.

Rudolph, Lloyd I., 1984, *Cultural Policy in India*, Delhi: Chanakya.

Sachau, Edward, C., 1879, *The Chronology of Ancient Nations*, London: William Allen and Co.

——————1887, *Alberuni*, Vol. I, London.

Sadagopala, V.V., 1970, "An Introduction to *Raga*", *Indian Music Journal*, VI, No. 11-12.

Sadasivan, K., 1990, "Art of Painting and Devadasis in Tamilnadu", *History, Archaeology, Art and Religion*, G. Kuppuram and K. Kumudramani (ed.), Delhi: Sundeep Prakashan, pp. 113-21.

Saletore, B.A., 1934, *The Social and Political Life in the Vijayanagara Empire*, Vol. II, Madras.

Sambamurthy, P. , 1971, *A Dictionary of South Indian Music and Musicians*, 3 Vols., Madras: Indian Music Publishing House.

Sangeet Natak, 1968, *Who's Who of Indian Musicians*, New Delhi: Sangeet Natak.

Sangita Ratnakara, of Sarngadeva, 1978, Text and Translation, Vol. 1. R.K. Shringy and Prem Lata Sharma.

Sankaran, T., 1983, "Papa K.S. Venkataramiah", *Sangeet Natak*, No. 67.

——————1984, "Kandappa *Nattuvanar*", *Sangeet Natak*, No. 72-73.

——————1984, "Bala's Musicians", *Sangeet Natak*, 72-73: 61-5.

Sarabhai, Mrinalini, 1965, *Understanding Bharata Natyam*, Baroda: Maharaja Sayajirao University of Baroda.

——————1976, *Longing for the Beloved, Songs to Siva-Nataraja in Bharata Natyam*, Ahmedabad: Darpana.

——————1977, *This Alone Is True*, Delhi: Hind Pocket Books.

Sarada, S., 1985, *Kalakshetra—Rukmini Devi*, Madras: Kala Mandir Trust.

Sarkar, S.C., 1928, *Some Aspects of the Earliest Social History of India*, London.

Sastri, Krishna H., 1920, "Miscellaneous Inscriptions from the Tamil Country", *South Indian Inscriptions*, Vol. III, Part III, Madras.

Sastri, Nilakanta, 1966, *A History of South India*, London: Oxford. University Press.

Sathyanarayana, R., 1969, *Bharata Natya—A Critical Study*, Mysore: Sri Varalakshmi Academies of Fine Arts.

——————1970, *Studies in India Dance*, Mysore: Sri Varalakshmi Academy of Fine Arts.

——————1988, "A Study in Tradition, Modernity and Innovation in Indian Music", *Sangeet Natak*, 89-90: 48-52.

Satyanarayan, Y., 1966, "Pushpanjali", *Journal of the Madras Music Academy*, XXXVII, I-IV: 98-105.

Seetha, S., 1981, *Tanjore as a Seat of Learning*, Madras: Madras University.

Sen, R.K., 1966, *Aesthetic Enjoyment, Its Background in Philosophy and*

Medicine, Calcutta: University of Calcutta.

Sewell, Robert, 1900, *A Forgotten Empire—Vijayanagar*, London.

Sharma, Dasharatha, 1959, *Early Chauhan Dynasties*, Delhi.

Sharma, Krishna, 1987, *Bhakti and the Bhakti Movement*, Delhi: Munshiram Manoharlal.

Shivaji, Bharati, 1986, *The Art of Mohiniattam*, New Delhi: Lancer.

Siegel, Lee, 1978, *Sacred and Profane Dimensions of Love in Indian Traditions as Exemplified in The Gitagovinda of Jayadeva*, Delhi: Oxford University Press.

Singer, Milton, 1959, "The Great Traditions in a Metropolitan Centre, Madras", *Traditional India, Structure and Change*, Milton Singer (ed.), American Folklore Society, Philadelphia.

——————1972, *When a Great Tradition Modernizes*, New York: Praeger.

Singh, Yogendra, 1986, *Modernization of Indian Tradition*, Jaipur: Rawat.

Sinha, Rinha and Reginald Massey, 1967, *Indian Dances, Their History and Growth*, London: Faber.

Sircar, D.C., 1963, "Devadasis in Buddhist Temples", *Epigraphia Indica*, XXXV, No. 12: 97-9.

Sivanandam, K.P., 1961, *The Dance Compositions of the Tanjore Quartet*, Madras: Ganesh.

Sivaramamurti, C., 1955, *Royal Conquests and Cultural Migrations in South India and the Deccan*, Calcutta: Indian Museum.

——————1969, *Some Aspects of Indian Culture*, New Delhi: National Museum of India.

——————1970, *Sanskrit Literature and Art—Mirrors of Indian Culture*, Memoirs of the Archaeological Survey of India, New Delhi: Sagar.

Somadeva, *Kathasaritsagara*, trans. C.H. Tawney, Vol I and V, 1924, London.

South Indian Epigraphy, 1924, Annual Report for the Year.

South Indian Inscriptions, 1890-1924, Archaeological Survey of India, New Imperial Series, Vols. I-IV.

——————1948, Archaeological Survey of India, Vol. X.

Shortt, D. John, 1870, "The Bayadere or Dancing Girls of Southern India", *Memoirs*, 1867—8-9, Vol. III:182-94.

Srinivas, M.N., 1966, *Social Change in Modern India*: Berkeley: University of California Press.

——————1965, *Religion and Society among the Coorgs of South India*, Bombay: Media.

——————1976, *The Remembered Village*, Berkeley: University of California Press

Srinivasan, Amrit, 1983, "The Hindu Temple-Dancer: Prostitute or Nun", in *Cambridge Anthropology*, Art and Society, Vol. 8, No. 1: 73-99.

———————1984, *Temple 'Prostitution' and Community Reform An Examination of the Ethnographic, Historical and Textual Context of the Devadasi of Tamil Nadu, South India*, D.Phil. Cambridge University.

———————1985, "Reform and Revival: The *Devadasi* and Her Dance", in *Economic and Political Weekly*, XX. (Nov. 2) No. 44: 1869-76.

Srinivasan, K.S., 1983 "The Mystique of Classical Dance", *Sangeet Natak*, 70: 19-22.

———————1985a, "The *Nayikas* of Indian Classics, Their Genesis and Rise to Glory" *Sangeet Natak*, 75: 7-13.

———————1985b, "Kavya and Nritya" *Sangeet Natak*, 75: 5-6.

Srinivasan, P.K., 1990, "National Seminar on Bharatanatyam Dance Traditions', *Shanmukha* , pp. 32-35.

Sruti, Indian Classical Music and Dance Magazine, Madras.

Stein, Burton, 1978, *South Indian Temples: An Analytical Reconsideration*, New Delhi: Vikas.

Stein, M.A., 1900, *Kalhana's Rajatarangini, Chronicle of the Kings of Kashmir*, Westminster: Archibald Constable.

Subrahmanyam, Padma, 1979, *Bharata's Art, Then and Now*, Bombay and Madras: Bhulabhai Memorial Institute, Nrthyodaya.

Subramaniam, V., 1980, "The Sacred and the Secular: Symbiosis and Synthesis", *The Sacred and the Secular in India's Performing Arts*, ed. V. Subramaniam, New Delhi, Ashish, pp. 1-10.

——————— 1980, "Religion as a Bridge between Classical and Folk Art", *The Sacred and the Secular in India's Performing Arts*, ed. V. Subramaniam, New Delhi: Ashish, pp. 11-8.

———————1980, "The God-King Concept and the Arts", *The Sacred and the Secular in India's Performing Arts*, ed. V. Subramaniam, New Delhi: Ashish, pp.19-46.

———————1980, "Editor's Postscript", *The Sacred and the Secular in India's Performing Arts*, ed. V. Subramaniam, New Delhi: Ashish, pp. 181-85.

———————1983, *Glimpses of Buddhist Culture In India: Including Four Dance Dramas*: New Delhi: Ashish.

———————1985, "The *Varnam* in Bharata Natyam, a Socio-historical Analysis of its Origins and Development", *Sangeet Natak*, 75: 28-38.

——————— 1993a, "The Historical Dialectic between Classical Music and Dance in India", *Sangeet Natak*, 110: 22-30.

————————1993b, Caste, Socio-Economic Class and the Performing Arts in India over the Centuries", *South Asian Horizons*, Elliot L. Tepper (ed.), Ottawa: Carleton University, pp. 35-50.

Tavernier, Jean Baptiste, *Travels in India*, trans. V. Ball, Vol I.1925, London.

Tawney, C.H., 1924, trans. *Kathasaritsagara*, by Somadeva, London.

Te Nijenhuis, Emmie, 1974, *Indian Music, History and Structure*, Leiden: Brill.

Thomas, P. , 1964 ,*Indian Women Through the Ages*, Bombay.

————————1971, *Hindu Religion, Customs and Manners*, Bombay: D.B. Taraporevala.

Thurston, E., 1909, *Castes and Tribes of Southern India*, Vol. II, Madras: Government Press.

Travancore State Manual, 1906, Trivandrum.

Vamana Purana, 1968 trans. a board of scholars, Varanasi, All India Kashiraj Trust.

Van Zile, Judy, 1983, "Balasaraswati's '*Tisram Alarippu*': A Choreographic Analysis"; *Performing Arts in India: Essays on Music, Dance and Drama*, Bonnie C. Wade (ed.), Berkeley: Centre for South and Southeast Asia Studies, pp. 45-103.

Van der Meer, Wim, 1975, "Cultural Evolution, A Case Study of Indian Music", *Sangeet Natak*, 35: 49-65.,

————————1986, "Teaching Indian Music, Coping with a Changing Environment", *Sangeet Natak*, 79: 53-8.

Vatsyayan, 1961, *Kamasutra*, trans. S.C. Upadhyaya, Bombay.

Vatsyayan, Kapila, 1966, "The 108 *Karanas*", *Sangeet Natak* 3:51-62.

————————1968, *Classical Indian Dance in Literature and the Arts*, New Delhi: Sangeet Natak.

————————1972, "Common Errors in Dance", *Sangeet Natak* 24: 24-38.

————————1974, *Indian Classical Dance*, New Delhi: Publications Division, Ministry of Information.

————————1978, "On Re-Creating a Tradition", *Sangeet Natak*, 48: 5-9.

————————1981, *A Study of Some Traditions of Performing Arts in Eastern India*, Gauhati: University of Gauhati.

Venkatachalam, G., 1946, "Bharata Natyam" *Roop Lekha*, III, serial No. I: 8-18, New Delhi: All India Fine Arts and Crafts Society.

Venu, G. and Nirmala Panikkar, 1983, *Mohiniattam*, Trivandrum: G. Venu.

Vijayaraghavan, Sujatha, 1985, "Learning Dance Theory: Modest

Beginnings Made", *Sruti*, 10: 8.

Vishnudharmottara Purana, 1961 (third *khanda*), Vol II, trans. Priyabala Shah, Gaekwad's Oriental Series, No. 137, Baroda.

Vishwanathan, Lakshmi, 1984, *Bharatanatyam; The Tamil Heritage*, Madras: Sri Kala Chakra Trust.

Visweswaran, Chitra, 1985, "Kavuthvams", *National Centre for the Performing Arts Quarterly Journal*, XIV, Bombay.

Wade, Bonnie C., 1979, *Music in India, The Classical Traditions*, New Jersey: Prentice-Hall.

—————1983, *Performing Arts in India: Essays on Music, Dance and Drama*, Berkeley: Centre for South and Southeast Asia Studies.

Welbon, Guy R. and Yocum Glenn E., 1982, *Religious Festivals in South India and Sri Lanka*, New Delhi: Manohar.

Waghorne, Joanne Punzo and Norman Cutler, 1985, *Gods of Flesh, Gods of Stone, The Embodiment of Divinity in India*, Chambersburg, Penn: Anima.

Winternitz, Maurice, 1972, *A History of Indian Literature*, New Delhi: Oriental Books.

Yule, Colonel Henry, 1875, *The Book of Ser Marco Polo The Venetian*, London.

Zvelebil, Kamil, 1973, *The Smile of Murugan,On Tamil Literature of South India*, Leiden: Brill.

—————1974, *Tamil Literature, History of Indian Literature Series*, Vol. X, fasc. I, Weisbaden.

—————1985, *Ananda-tandava of Siva Sadanrttamurti*, Madras: Institute of Indian Studies.

Index